ADAPTIVE
CONTROL OF
ILL-DEFINED SYSTEMS

NATO CONFERENCE SERIES

I   Ecology
II   Systems Science
III   Human Factors
IV   Marine Sciences
V   Air–Sea Interactions
VI   Materials Science

II SYSTEMS SCIENCE

ADAPTIVE CONTROL OF ILL-DEFINED SYSTEMS

Edited by

Oliver G. Selfridge
Edwina L. Rissland
and
Michael A. Arbib

University of Massachusetts
Amherst, Massachusetts

Published in cooperation with NATO Scientific Affairs Division

PLENUM PRESS · NEW YORK AND LONDON

Library of Congress Cataloging in Publication Data

NATO Advanced Research Institute on Adaptive Control of Ill-defined Systems (1981:
    Moretonhampstead, Devon) Adaptive control of ill-defined systems.

    (NATO conference series. II, Systems science; v. 16)
    "Proceedings of the NATO Advanced Research Institute on Adaptive Control of Ill-
defined Systems, held June 21–26, 1981 in Moretonhampstead, Devon, England"—
T.p. verso.
    Bibliography: p.
    Includes index.
    1. System theory—Congresses. 2. Adaptive control systems—Congresses. I.
Selfridge, Oliver G. II. Rissland, Edwina L. III. Arbib, Michael A. IV. Title. V. Title: Ill-
defined systems. VI. Series.
Q295.N37 1981   003   83-17699
ISBN 978-1-4684-8943-9   ISBN 978-1-4684-8941-5 (eBook)
DOI 10.1007/978-1-4684-8941-5

Proceedings of the NATO Advanced Research Institute on Adaptive Control of
Ill Defined Systems, held June 21–26, 1981, in Moretonhampstead, Devon, England

© 1984 Plenum Press, New York
Softcover reprint of the hardcover 1st edition 1984
A Division of Plenum Publishing Corporation
233 Spring Street, New York, N.Y. 10013

PREFACE

    There are some types of complex systems that are built like
clockwork, with well-defined parts that interact in well-defined
ways, so that the action of the whole can be precisely analyzed and
anticipated with accuracy and precision. Some systems are not
themselves so well-defined, but they can be modeled in ways that are
-- like trained pilots in well-built planes, or electrolyte balance
in healthy humans.

    But there are many systems for which that is not true; and
among them are many whose understanding and control we would value.
For example, the model for the trained pilot above fails exactly
where the pilot is being most human; that is, where he is
exercising the highest levels of judgment, or where he is learning
and adapting to new conditions. Again, sometimes the kinds of
complexity do not lead to easily analyzable models at all; here we
might include most economic systems, in all forms of societies.

    There are several factors that seem to contribute to systems
being hard to model, understand, or control. The human participants
may act in ways that are so variable or so rich or so interactive
that the only adequate model of the system would be the entire
system itself, so to speak. This is probably the case in true long
term systems involving people learning and growing up in a changing
society.

    Some kinds of true complexity arise when simple systems are put
together into numerous and complex assemblies; one might hope that
thermodynamics showed the way. But, alas!, the simple truths that
thermodynamcis seizes from simply behaving molecules may well be
unique in science; most other examples -- from schooling of fishes
to economic models of simple consumers -- are just too intractable
when they are built on any basis that corresponds roughly to
reality.

    One kind of difficulty seems to arise inevitably from
considering purposive behavior, whether directly by people or
imputedly by complex mechanisms: that is the interaction of
different purposes and goals. Sometimes the goals are in immediate

conflict, so to speak, sometimes they are cooperative, but in real
systems they are always embedded in hierarchical structures of goals
subsumed under the values of the designers and operators.

Nevertheless, although we cannot attain with some systems a
degree of understanding and control that we might with others, that
does not mean that we cannot strive to find out what controls are
possible. The notion of control here does not necessarily mean just
the dimensions of decision and manipulation; rather it also
includes the concepts of improving understanding, gathering data,
and making inferences about the feasible structures of affectors and
effectors. That is, we are interested also in the science, as well
as in the technology.

The techniques of adaptive control are well enough in hand for
the large class of dynamic systems where the plant and its dynamics
can be analyzed a priori using the mathematical techniques of modern
control theory. The purpose of this volume is to evaluate the
control techniques that may be applicable when the system is not
well defined, or may even be frankly unknown; such systems would
include, inter alia:

    human control systems where the person is learning
    complex communication networks, such as those involving people
    biological systems
    economic systems
    man-machine systems

No general rules are offered that will enable control in all,
or even most, such systems. Rather, we analyze the state of the
art, propose new approaches, and discuss possible applications and
implications.

Most of the papers were presented at a NATO Advanced Research
Institute held in Moretonhampstead, Devon, England, from June 21 to
June 26 of 1981 to analyze the current technology and the current
problems, and to assess the possiblities and to formulate a program.
For the purpose of this volume, the papers have been grouped into
six sections. Section 1 offers a variety of "Perspectives": a
dialogue constructed by the Editors to dramatize a number of the
issues addressed throughout the book; perspectives from the point
of view of man-machine system, adaptive algorithms, and economics;
as well as a historical view of adaptation in biology. Section 2
looks at adaptation and control using the well-defined mathematical
techniques of control theory and nonlinear analysis, in contrast to
Section 3 in which the planning techniques of Artificial
Intelligence and the power of the computer take over from the closed
forms of the mathematician. The final 3 sections look at different
application areas in which issues of adaptation are raised with
respect to ill-defined systems; "Motor skills" in Section 4,

"Language Acquisition and Adaptation" in Section 5, and "Development and Evolution" in Section 6.

We thank Dr. Bayraktar of the NATO committee for making the Advanced Research Institute possible, Devon for being so beautiful in June of 1981, and our authors for all they contributed to the Institute and this volume. We also thank Barbara Nestingen for her invaluable editorial assistance.

Massachusetts, March 1983   Oliver G. Selfridge
                                             Edwina L. Rissland
                                             Michael A. Arbib

CONTENTS

A DIALOGUE ON ILL-DEFINED CONTROL

Michael A. Arbib, Oliver G. Selfridge and
Edwina L. Rissland

Department of Computer and Information Science
University of Massachusetts
Amherst, MA 01003 USA

To give an introduction to the concepts addressed in the
present volume, the Editors have contrived a dialogue between two
scholars, imaginatively named A and B, which reflects the current
state of our inter-discipline. It captures many of the views
expressed in general discussions throughout the meeting.

A. When we speak as technicians seeking to understand control
strategies, a system is a "them," as distinct from the controllers
who are an "us"—dividing the universe into "us" and "them." The
task of control theory is to provide an algorithm for how "us" is to
control "them," and such an algorithm must be based on criteria of
optimality or satisfiability, but the appropriate criteria are often
unclear in an ill-defined situation. For example, in writing a
technical paper we have the conflicting criteria of "keep it short"
and "provide the reader with background material." Very often we do
not have a single criterion for our control strategy. The different
criteria may even be mutually inconsistent. Of course, if we had a
well-defined criterion for trading off amongst these criteria, then
we could optimize on that weighted criterion function. But, in
general, we do not.

Thus, one aspect of our concern with ill-definedness is not
adaptive control of ill-defined systems, but ill-defined criteria
for control of systems.

B. My most horrifying example is based on the fantasy that
finally we have incredible computers which control the economy and
production and the weapons system and everything else, and we

finally determine our ultimate criterion and issue the command: "Ensure that there is no more human unhappiness." The response—nuclear war: all human life is destroyed; and there is no more human unhappiness.

But the fact that multiple criteria pose problems doesn't mean that they are ill-defined. Isn't it a paradox to define what you mean by "ill-defined"?

A. That's like saying you can say nothing true about falsity. To speak of a system is to believe that we can limit that portion of the world (spatially or informationally or whatever) that is relevant to our interaction with respect to some stated problem. Given that, we try to come up with enough information about that portion to enable us to make some decisions about how to select or influence our interactions. The "ill-defined" results from the inevitable mismatch in how much we choose to consider of the world around us; and how we choose to describe and represent it. One might almost say that a system is ill-defined if adaptive control doesn't work very well. If adaptive control of an ill-defined system "works" then the system is sufficiently well defined.

B. But you can make a model well-defined by including more and more variables to get closer and closer to the essential interactions of the chunk of the world involved.

A. Hardly. You don't model a gas in terms of atomic interactions. You have to find the right thermodynamic variables. You have to find the appropriate generalizations. In the same way, an economic model with thousands of variables would be better defined if you knew how to pick just a few and monitor their interactions.

B. It's not practical to limit an economic model to just a few variables. There will be many variables that the Treasury and consumer groups will want to monitor even if they do not help explain part of the economy. If you counted all the outputs, you might have many more outputs than you are actively controlling. Also, because there is so much noise in the system, we need to keep track of a host of variables to take advantage of unexpected significances in their correlated trends.

A. Perhaps variables are even the wrong "atoms". Maybe our descriptive building blocks ought to be procedures and little chunks of knowledge.

B. But how can you describe what you can't define?

A.   You and I do that all the time but with different vocabularies.

Furthermore, it is not clear that we can define functional interactions between so many variables in a fashion relevant to the adaptations we are searching for. Anyway, I pose as our fundamental paradox that, by definition, adaptive control of ill-defined systems is unsuccessful control of a system—because a system is only defined with respect to a task, and if we succeed in a task, then the system is sufficiently well defined.

B.   You seem to be saying that a system is well-defined only if adaptive control works for it, but there seem to be logical systems in which you have a good understanding of what is going on, and yet adaptive control isn't even relevant. First order predicate calculus is well defined, but what is to control there? You don't want to say, I think, that well-defined means control at all by this technique.

A.   The last part of your comment suggests a fundamental misunderstanding, namely, that one can take something like the predicate calculus and call it a system. The notion of system that I had thought we were using was the notion of some chunk of the universe changing over time, while the control problem was to influence the trajectory of that system. Therefore, although people may formally use a phrase like "logical system" and say predicate calculus is a logical system, it is not the form of system we are concerned with here.

B.   But take my example seriously. Let's assume that we've got this definition of the predicate calculus, but our criterion, following your earlier comment, is ill-defined—namely, that we should prove interesting theorems. And so we try to build a system that is to prove interesting theorems in the predicate calculus. That seems to be ill-defined, but it does also seem to me that I could use an adaptive technique to gradually do better at proving interesting theorems.

A.   But that is precisely the difference: The system is the theorem prover, constrained by the rules of the predicate calculus. The system is not the formal structure of the predicate calculus itself. It is the theorem prover that will change state over time. The only source of ill-definedness in your example is then how to measure "interestingness". In other words, an ill-defined criterion on a well-defined system. Also our standards of "interestingness" may change (in ill-defined ways) and thus we have layers of ill- and well-definedness.

B.   Returning to your first remarks--why do you want that
dichotomy between "us" and "them"? The task of the economic
decision-maker is not to control a physical system that knows
nothing, but to control a system that is in turn modelling the
controllers! And, of course, the economists are part of the economy
that is to be controlled. The world, which is the ill-defined
system that we are trying to control, is a world full of people.
And they are each trying to control certain aspects of a world full
of people. And the problem is: How do we coordinate all these
different control systems to achieve some sort of overall goal when
each control system is changing the environment of other control
systems which in turn adapt and evolve. There is no more important
problem than that.

A.   I don't think it's the same kind of problem at all. Who
should define the "overall goal"? Some great social engineer in the
sky?

B.   No, all of us. The control is distributed. There are
indeed systems whose components have different goals, but which can
agree on a higher level goal for some kind of overall satisfaction.
Perhaps a good marriage is like that. Or a long-lasting peace
treaty among nations. So we are all embedded in our own control
systems.

A.   I may be physically part of the system to be controlled,
yet there is logically a separation. Consider my control of my
exploratory limb movements. I might analyze this in terms of
brain-as-controller sending a command to my limb-as-control-system
to move; sensors of the limb then send in signals, and my brain is
in a state now to integrate those signals into some building
representation of the world. Alternatively, I might just say: I
give an order to myself to know more about something--I am
controlling myself. The "us" and "them" is a logical separation,
but need not necessarily be a physical separation.

B.   I would have thought it was still a dangerous separation to
make. The word "control" has a certain connotation of brute force
about it, which is put in better perspective if we speak of
"self-control" or "control of interactions." If you're walking
across a street, and there is a fast car racing towards you, one
control strategy is to take a machine-gun and try to shoot out the
tires so that the car will roll over and avoid you! An alternative
strategy is to get out of the way. This suggests the usefulness of
studying relationships of reciprocal interaction, like the river
bank and the river, rather than of control.

Can we not develop another image of adaptive control which
replaces a "brute force" image? Imagine that you have a person

sitting down with a very elaborate computer system, of whose limits
and total properties he is not sure, and that man and machine are
actually trying to work together on a problem. Now, there the idea
of making an "us" and "them" distinction looks totally wrong, yet
the situation is certainly ill-defined in the sense that the human
is not sure what he and the computer are going to do. It seems
useful to speak of the cooperative control of a collective of
systems, rather than control of one system by another.

A. I gladly renounce any necessity of "brute force" in my
analysis. But I would still like to distinguish "us" and "them" in
analyzing adaptive interactive control by ill-defined systems.
Often, as scientists, we are not trying to control something
ourselves but rather are looking at how a collection of systems
interacts, and trying to see to what extent they are achieving some
global good, as it were. I agree with you that we should not limit
analysis to the situation where the "us" is forcing "them" to do
something. I accept your idea that we can speak of controlling our
interactions—self-control, as well as control of others.

Let me again stress that I think the notion of "ill-defined"
only makes sense with respect to some overall task: whether we are
stressing an interactive situation, or the task of the scientist as
outside observer, or if we do have a task (e.g. spaceship
navigation) in which it is appropriate to speak of a dominant
controller. I am saying that the systems involved are ill-defined
if, in fact, we can't describe them well enough to allow us to meet
our control criteria.

B. Surely you're on the wrong track. If a system is
deterministic, it is well defined—no matter what the task at hand.

A. I think that the distinction between deterministic and
stochastic is totally irrelevant to the question of whether or not a
system is ill-defined. Statisticians often feel they have solved a
problem when they can use the central limit theorem, yet the central
limit theorem is not very interesting for deterministic systems!

B. I can't agree with you. It seems to me that if a system
has noise, then you have to say it's ill-defined. Remember, too,
that we use the word "system" ambiguously. There is the system as
some relevant chunk of the "reality" out there, that we might hope
to have some control over; and there is the simplified model or
description that will enter into our calculations. If you don't
know how the "chunk of reality" works, it may be a deterministic
system but you don't know how it works. Your system-model is an
ill-defined system until you discover how the "reality" works, and
then your system stops being ill-defined.

A.   Well, I concede your point to the extent that all we can
ever talk about are aspects or models of reality. But I still think
determinism is not the essential point here. Consider the coin toss
as the classic example. If one is playing a game which involves
tossing coins from time to time, one uses a compact description of
the coin as a system which on each trial has a .5 probability of
coming up heads, or tails. With this system description, one can
often develop an excellent strategy for playing the game. Again,
treating a well-shuffled deck as non-deterministically described,
one can work out winning strategies at, for example, blackjack
(twenty-one). One can, I think, say that the system of the dealer
and the deck at blackjack is a well-defined system, and one can come
up with excellent strategies for winning.

B.   Perhaps the mistake is to try to divide the world into two
classes. Perhaps the term "ill-defined" system is fine in a
conference name, but not as a subject in itself.

A.   Groucho Marx said there are two kinds of people--those who
divide the world into two kinds of people and those who don't.

B.   What I'm getting at harks back to an ancient problem in
physics. Suppose I ask the question: "Do you believe that the laws
of physics are causal and deterministic?" Nagel answers that: "All
the laws of physics are deterministic and causal with respect to the
variables they nominate as state variables." But what are those
variables? They are the variables that are causal in the equation.
So, if you pick your context correctly, physics is entirely causal,
including quantum mechanics. It's just that the variables there are
probability amplitudes.

A.   Yes. In fact, every stochastic system is causal when we
describe its state as a probability vector. But, of course, such
probabilities can only be measured over an ensemble (unless we can
assume an ergodic hypothesis to exploit trajectory averages).
Non-determinism is relative to what we can estimate of the state for
a given system for a given time. I assume causality whenever I
speak of a system, whether deterministic or stochastic--but I say
it's well defined when the description is adequate to the task at
hand.

B.   Ah, I see a different point to be made here. The trouble
is that when you specify a task, it is in the language of human
intentionality. There is a belief that arises out of too much
contact with computers that the world runs by information. But the
universe does not run by information; it runs by dynamics that are
constrained. And so systems have their lawfulness, and you can't
impose human intentionality on them, regardless. That's the trouble
here. You can do it inside computers, which are about the worst
artefacts to use as images of the real world that I can think of,

because switching networks have totally arbitrary dynamics as symbol manipulators. But they are a very poor sample of the real world. And that's the difficulty.

What I'm suggesting is that the problem we're having with economic systems and ill-defined systems is that they are more limiting than we think. It is difficult to control these ill-defined systems because we can't understand the dynamics and the constraints on the dynamics.

A. What you're saying is you can't control it if you don't understand it. Does understanding help?

B. It seems to me that understanding helps because you can play with the boundary conditions on the dynamics. That's the point at which they're sensitive. The paradox here is that the richness of the systems comes precisely out of constraints--a system gets more interesting as it is more constrained. Only up to a point, of course!

However, I don't think "understanding" is equivalent to successful control--which gets me back to my disagreement with your definition of a system as ill-defined if you couldn't control it. In fact, I would argue that a system can be well-defined, but it may well be that you have a model of immense complexity. I have to concede you a point here--I'm prepared now to accept that a model can include stochastic things in it, without being any less well-defined. But if the algorithms required to compute optimal control are too slow relative to the dynamics of the system, then the fact that it's well-defined will not make it possible to control it.

A. Well, we seem to agree, then, that the issues here are complexity issues rather than deterministic vs. stochastic issues. If one has a very large system, one may define it very well by ten aggregated variables and yet know full well that, in fact, there will be random fluctuations about the mean of each of those variables that one couldn't have without disaggregating to millions of variables. But if, in fact, one can show that the variation is small enough that knowing that window of values for the state variables gives one enough information to implement a good control strategy, then the system is sufficiently well-defined for the purpose in hand.

Though we seem to agree on this, I shouldn't let you get away with your slur on computer science. Nonlinear mechanics is fine to describe units in a complex system, but surely the overall structure of such systems--and, even more surely, the appropriate control strategies--must be expressed in some sort of programming-like or procedure-like language. It will probably need concurrency, and

knowledge structures of the kind AI is developing, to do it right.
It is one thing to "tune" the parameters in a dynamic system to
improve performance marginally; it is quite another thing to
combine existing structures into wholly new combinations to improve
performance by great leaps.

Control theory studies feedback, state estimation, and
identification algorithms which can "tune" the parameters of a
system description when the system is of a given class of the kind
you are talking about. But what if no setting of parameters will do
the job? To turn on a slide-projector and to drink from a glass of
water requires two entirely different schemas. More generally,
interacting with a complex environment will require me to mobilize
my knowledge (schemas) about a whole host of objects. To plan our
behavior, we need to recognize the world in terms of things with
which we can interact, and those things have to be recognized in
relationship. Each of those things has to be recognized as a system
with certain general properties; and our recognition of it has then
to set certain parameters which will allow us to interact with it in
the appropriate way. With such an "assemblage," we're leaving the
domain of continuum mathematics. Of course, certain aspects of my
interaction will depend on mechanics--the way I hold the glass will
use things to do with center of gravity and mass. We have the
notion of very complex interweaving of computational structures to
get access to appropriate control systems to master the complexities
of the world around us.

B. Well, be that as it may, I do want to remind you of the
point that was illustrated in the discussion of economics: the
notion of the other systems themselves having models of you, so that
what you do is not, necessarily, simply changing the state of those
systems as in physical systems--the state per se as it were (though
these are dangerous distinctions!)--but the state of their models.
Here the notion of cooperative control becomes very interesting.
Oh, I see your point about going beyond physical systems--I suppose
you would insist on calling it cooperative computation. Borrowing
the notion of a contract from law, one interesting idea is that if
two interacting systems within this overall control problem will
accept mutual constraints, then one may be able to implement a
control strategy. Whereas, if those constraints aren't accepted,
one may be unable to implement a control strategy simply because one
system is going to do what they can to circumvent the other. This
whole situation of interaction of actors modelling each other is
going to be central to our study of adaptive control, even if we
stop using this word "ill-defined." One application on the horizon
is air traffic control. The idea is that tactical air traffic
control can be distributed into the cockpits, with the ground
control stations simply setting the flight patterns.

A. Yes, and it does seem to me that the "contract" is a computer, rather than a control, notion. Anyway, one more remark about the complexity issue. It is extremely hard to conduct useful experiments on large-scale systems, particularly when they involve multitudes of people. How do you even get reasonable data to define those systems or to see whether you are, in fact, accomplishing the objectives of your control algorithms and so on? That's a very, very serious problem that's not faced very often, but is one that will continue to plague those people who are interested in large "somewhat ill-defined" systems.

Another vast point that adds to the complexity of everything is that the evaluation criteria we use often change just as we begin to understand them well enough to use them. Just as I thought I understood that the only important goals were chocolate and sodas, I became a teenager. Similarly, large complex information systems are nearly always used for many purposes not dreamt of by their designers.

B. But surely that is just plain bad design. A good top-down design ought to be flexible enough to allow other usages.

I admit that history is against me. Perhaps that is your point about chocolate: evolution and growth do occur not only in organisms and systems, but also in the tasks assigned to them, and in the purposes and criteria they hold.

A. In that sense, then, if a system is defined with respect to our evolving or changing criterion or set of criteria, it will inevitably become ill-defined it if continues to be useful.

[This "dialogue" sets the stage for what follows. Readers are invited to add their own views to the above—settling some questions, raising others—as they read the chapters that follow. The Editors.]

HUMANS AND THEIR RELATION TO ILL-DEFINED SYSTEMS

Neville Moray

Department of Industrial Engineering
University of Toronto
Toronto, Ontario, Canada

ABSTRACT

Using a taxonomy of systems proposed by Ashby this paper examines the various species of ill-defined systems which may occur in man-machine interaction. A distinction is made between objectively ill-defined systems and effectively ill-defined systems. Various properties of humans as information processors are examined, and it is claimed that humans turn almost all systems, whether initially well-defined or objectively ill-defined into effectively ill-defined systems. It is suggested that while conscious decision making is particularly ill-suited to controlling ill-defined systems, sheer practice frequently enables humans to control them through skills which are not understood even by their owner.

INTRODUCTION

My definition of an ill-defined system is one whose state-transition matrix cannot be known, either because some states are inaccessible, or because some of the transition probabilities are inaccessible, or because the matrix is not time-invariant. Any such system is objectively ill-defined (OID). Although many industrial processes and man-machine systems in general can be to a good approximation regarded as well-defined (WDS), at least as far as the "machine" is concerned, it will be a major contention of this paper that the properties of the human operator are such as to render the man-machine combination of an effectively ill-defined system (EIDS). What is surprising is that nonetheless humans often control EIDS rather effectively.

A NATURAL HISTORY OF ILL-DEFINED SYSTEMS

What features of a system call for it to be classified as an ill-defined system? Following a classification proposed by Ashby (1956) we can divide all systems into three broad phyla, some of whose species are well-, others ill-defined.

State-Determined Systems (SDS)

State-determined systems are not generally thought of as being in any sense ill-defined. They are normally both completely and exactly predictable. All the state variables are known, and the transition matrix is completely deterministic. If the present state vector is known, then all the future of the system is determined and precisely predictable.

Not merely is it difficult to see how such a system could be an OID, it is even difficult to see at first glance what sense can be given to the concept of "control" when applied to an SDS, since all its future is completely determined. However, we may divide the state vector into two sets of elements, one of which is the "machine" and the other the "controller." Let there be two possible trajectories through state space which the system can take, which do not overlap. If the "control" variables are in one state, trajectory A is followed; if they are in the other state, trajectory B is followed. Although the outcome is completely deterministic, the "control" subset of variables has a right to be called a controller. (The question of why the controller takes one state rather than the other is a separate question, and may result in the entire system being non-deterministic. But within the system as defined the concept of control is applicable.) If then a human is controlling an SDS, then providing that the actions of the human are completely determined, the entire man-machine system is still an SDS. In theory at least an operator following exact rules of action laid down by the manufacturer would be such a controller, and a well-defined man-machine SDS should be possible.

Leaving aside for the moment the question of limitations on the determinacy of human actions, is there any sense in which an SDS could ever be ill-defined? One at least suggests itself. In all realizable systems communication takes a finite time. If a system were sufficiently large that the time taken for information to reach the controller (or, more precisely, the observer of the system) were to be long compared with the time scale of state transitions, then it would never be possible to establish the value of the system state vector, and the system would be inherently an OIDS. The controller could never choose the appropriate control state without uncertainty, even though the entire system is an SDS.

Markov Systems (MS)

Ashby's second class of systems are Markov systems. They are characterized by the fact that it is possible to know for certain the identity of the state variables and the transition matrix, but the transitions are now probabilities, not completely determined. We need not be concerned with the order of the Markov process, since as is well known we can in principle reduce any higher order Markov process to a first order Markov process by expanding the state vector, so as to have a transition matrix which allows the prediction of the next state only from the current state. (For convenience I include the values of inputs in the system state vector.) Such systems are completely, but not exactly, predictable, in the sense that we know that if the system is in state A, then it will at the next transition go either to state B, state C or state D and to no other; but which of the three is only known probabilistically. From the point of view of understanding and control, such a system is clearly an OIDS. Most non-living systems in the universe seem to be of this kind.

The discovery of suitable control strategies involves a knowledge of the probability distributions that govern the transition matrix, and the best that control strategy can do is to minimize some figure related to the parameters of such distributions (such as the minimizing of mean square error in Optimal Control). From the point of view of someone observing the system, any system having a poor signal-to-noise ratio is an MS, providing that the statistics of the noise are constant. Similarly there may be probabilistic uncertainty in the effect of exercizing control if there is noise in the control vector.

MS are the first inherently ill-defined systems. Appropriate measures of their ill-definedness would include a signal/noise ratio, bandwidth of disturbances, and span of probability. ("Span" here is used in Simon's sense of the number of elements affected. Thus an element which affects two other elements has a smaller span than one which affects three. In the present sense, a variable from which two paths diverge probabilistically has a smaller span than one from which three paths diverge, etc. (Simon, 1962).) In view of the close relation between probability, information flow, entropy, and structural complexity (Conant, 1976), it would seem desirable also to take note of the degree to which the probabilities in the transition matrix are not equal. In physical systems phenomena such as hysteresis and backlash, which introduce uncertainty into control but where the range of uncertainty is well bounded, should also be included in MS, as should some kinds of instability. The particular requirement is that the statistics of the uncertainty should remain constant over time, as should the list of state variables.

Self-Organizing Systems (SOS)

By contrast, Ashby's third phylum, that of self-organizing systems, is neither completely nor exactly predictable. The list of
variables in the state vector may not be constant, new variables may
appear, old ones disappear, and the transition probabilities may alter
from time to time. The species within the phylum are distinguished
by the several ways in which the lack of invariance of the system over
time is caused. For example, the elements of a physical system might
arbitrarily reconnect themselves in different ways from time to time,
causing some transition probabilities to fall to zero, and others to
become non-zero, but with no change in the list of elements in the
state vector. Certain kinds of instability could cause the system
to enter completely new regions of state space hitherto inaccessible,
adding or deleting elements from the state vector, but leaving almost
all of the remaining transitions unchanged. If the system contains
an "uncertainty principle" this will cause it to be ill-defined to
an observer; paradoxically, an ultrastable system (Ashby, 1954) could
also be regarded as ill-defined, at least from a controller's standpoint, since nothing the controller does makes any change to the
system beyond a transient, so that no knowledge of its structure can
be gained by operating on it. Finally, it should not be overlooked
that the ill-definedness of an observed system may be the result not
of chance but of intelligent hostility, although whether this should
be defined as OIDness or EIDness is not immediately clear. (Examples
are the random behaviour of a noctuid moth when approached closely by
a bat, and the behaviour of counter-intelligence systems attempting
to conceal the structure in agents' behaviour. The first would seem
to be an OID, the latter an EID.)

We have then two phyla of systems which are OID: MS and SOS.
Within them there seem to be at least eight species of OID:

1. High noise-to-signal ratio
2. Unstable (including random reorganization)
3. Inherently probabilistic
4. Ultrastable
5. Prone to gaining and losing states
6. Intelligent and hostile
7. Uncertainty Principle
8. Failure of intercommunication on the timescale of transitions

(this last reason for the presence of ill-definedness being the only
one which could also apply to the phylum of State Determined Systems.)

It should be noted that although all SOSs are, strictly speaking,
also OIDs, they may contain locally organized subsystems which are
quite predictable and controllable over a limited time. Indeed, as

Simon (1962) suggests, were this not the case, and were the structure of an SOS completely homogeneous, we would probably not regard it as a system at all. And just as the temporary appearance of stability should not lead us to conclude that we are dealing with an SDS, the appearance of apparently random change need not be taken, without further evidence, that we are dealing with an SOS. This is because if we have imperfect knowledge of the dimensionality of an SDS, we will view as unpredictable a system which is highly orderly in higher dimensional space. Thus unpredictability is sufficient to establish the presence of an EID, but not of an OID.

BRIEF COMMENTS ON HILL CLIMBING IN ILL-DEFINED LANDSCAPES

    It is common experience that many systems that cannot be controlled initially can be brought under control with practice. Classically this has been related to problem solving by "hill climbing," (see Selfridge and Minsky, this volume) and more recently to the idea of the acquisition of "internal models" of the system to be controlled (Conant and Ashby, 1970; Kelley, 1968). What kinds of landscapes must a problem solver traverse when hill climbing in the three different phyla described above?

    Hill climbing in a state determined landscape is straightforward. Gelologically the country is dead. What hills there are retain their topography indefinitely, and the only problem is the classical one of avoiding becoming trapped on a subsidiary peak. Markovian landscapes are more complex, but should still be reasonably safe for the traveller. Minor changes in topography occur, and what appears at one time to be a satisfactorily high peak may later seem less satisfactory. One is reminded of the changes associated with seasonal fluctuations. Water tables rise and fall, lakes temporarily dry up and snow melts, so that the relative heights of features in the landscape do change. But the changes are governed by reasonably well-defined distributions, and a statistically satisfactory choice of summit can be defined.

    The hill climber in a self-organizing landscape on the other hand will often be in serious trouble. The world is geologically active. Hills appear and disappear, volcanoes appear in valleys, and the rough ways are made smooth. The climber may well complete an ascent only to find that the entire mountain has slid down while he climbed. Providing that the dynamics of "geological time" are long with respect to the time it takes him to solve his problem, some sort of solution may be found which for a time will be satisfactory. But in more turbulent times no control, not even adaptive control, is in principle possible.

HUMANS AS A SOURCE OF EFFECTIVELY ILL-DEFINED SYSTEMS

Much of the literature on the psychology of problem solving, learning, control and the acquisition of skill deals with well-defined systems, and the vast majority of it with static rather than dynamic systems. Moreover, the study of control by humans has almost always concentrated on performance at asymptote, when the skill has reached a high level of efficiency, and not on the process of adaptation of acquisition per se. (Two interesting exceptions are papers by Young, 1969, and McRuer et al., 1968.) I shall therefore concentrate on a short review of those characteristics of the human as information processor which seem particularly relevant to understanding why he has such a problem in analyzing even well-defined SDSs when they are of more than about 10 degrees of freedom. Some of the claims made here will seem at variance with much literature published in standard psychological journals. That is because I have often drawn on applied studies, and while great subtleties of behaviour can be found under ideal laboratory conditions, humans interacting with realtime systems in real life show somewhat coarser properties!

We are concerned here with the way in which a human operator, confronted with a many-degrees-of-freedom system, tries to monitor it, to extract information from it, and so to come to predict its behaviour and to control it. Much of the data is therefore concerned with human decision making under uncertainty, and reviews of the laboratory studies in this area can be found in Schrenk, 1969; Dale, 1968; Petersen and Beach, 1964; and Moray, 1980a. Humans are reasonably good at estimating the mean of a time series, but usually underestimate its variance. They are conservative when combining probabilities, often grossly so. They delay decisions longer than they optimally should, and ask for more evidence than, strictly speaking, they need. They are heavily biassed by events early in a series, adopt hypotheses early on, and are subsequently unwilling to change them. They try to confirm, rather than to test, hypotheses. Where several hypotheses could account for the data, they consider too few. On the other hand, they are good at assessing which sources of information are the more reliable.

All the above remarks are commonly true of a human examining a single source of data. When several or many sources must be examined the problem is much harder. Because of the nature of the visual system, little or no information is read in from the periphery of vision, and none while the eyes are in motion. Consequently each source of information must be examined in turn, and man is effectively a single channel information processor with a sampling rate of less than four (usually less than two) samples per second. Moreover, while experiments on the memorizing of static information can under certain situations show remarkably stable memory, there is good evidence that when trying to hold in memory data which are rapidly changing, so that old data have to be rejected and replaced by new data, humans have

an effective memory span of only about three items. This is also
suggested by the fact that when examining the successive values of
a time series, they use only the last one or two items when predicting
what the next will be. They also appear to be subject to what Tversky
and Kahneman (1974) and Kahneman and Tversky (1973) have called "The
Law of Small Numbers," the belief that a small sample is strongly
representative of population statistics. Similar conclusions have
been reported recently in "real life" situations by Hopf-Weichel et
al., (1979), who studied the ways in which air crew deal with in-
flight emergencies. Finally, in addition to the above handicaps, the
human as an observer is subject to noise in the perceptual and other
parts of the nervous system, which inherently make decisions uncertain. The group at Bolt, Beranek and Newman (Kleinman et al.,
1970) suggest that under optimal conditions the noise/signal ratio
is about -24 dB, but poor data presentation will frequently increase
this in practice. Furthermore, the subjective expectations and the
subjectively perceived payoffs of decision outcomes can introduce
severe bias into the judgements of the human observer.

Confronted, then, even with a well-defined system of high dimensionality the human operator will not do very well. In fact, as
claimed earlier, he may be expected, usually, to convert even a well-
defined system to an EID, and make an OID even less well-defined. He
will underestimate variance, consider only a limited amount of data,
refuse to change his hypotheses, and so on. In hill-climbing terms,
he will sit on the first molehill he happens across and effectively
refuse to budge. If the mountain does not come to Mahomet, the latter
will certainly not go to the mountain.

Three examples seem to reflect these properties. Gaines (1976)
found that humans who were asked to predict sequences which were
(unbeknownst to them) random, formed hypotheses to which they stuck
with great determination, and none suggested that the series was
random. At Three Mile Island, as in many industrial accident sequences, operators stuck to a hypothesis with great determination,
and meanwhile disregarded, or did not even examine, other evidence
that would have shown that they must be wrong (see IEEE Spectrum,
November 1979). And at the time of writing, Her Majesty's government
shows all the signs of similarly being unable to abandon hypotheses
when trying (one has to assume) to control the economy for the good
of the nation!

It is interesting that this "cognitive tunnel vision" is so
strong a feature of human problem solving. As was mentioned earlier,
large OID systems usually have the property that they are nearly
decomposable into smaller subsystems, which locally may be quite well
controlled. Humans seem to behave as if this was a desirable tactic
in a strong sense. To quote again from Simon (1962), they behave as
if only "molecular" forces defined the systems they examine, and that
no long range forces existed to couple the local subsystems (within

which coupling is tight) to one another. It is as if in the human
conceptual universe only nuclear forces existed, but no gravitational
forces.   Indeed, a measure of ill-definedness might be drawn from
such considerations. The system is ill-defined to the extent that
strong coupling exists between elements which are "separated" by great
"distances."

     Yet despite all this, it is also clear that humans do, given
enough practice, frequently manage rather well to control systems
which all the evidence suggests they should not be able to. People
may not control completely optimally, but they are near enough to it
for Sheridan and Rouse to speak of their being "suboptimal," or
showing "constrained optimality," (Rouse, 1980). How can this be?

     The limits which I have emphasized are those seen when a human
tries to handle information consciously. But humans have a second
mode of information processing which seems in many respects more
powerful, and particularly effective in dealing with what, to consciousness, are EIDs. Few of us know how we ride a bicycle or even
whistle, let alone have in our conscious knowledge the equations of
motion of a helicopter. Yet many of us ride bicycles, more whistle,
and a few even fly helicopters. In some way the requisite control
equations have become embodied in the nervous system, and it is in
this sense that we speak of "internal models" in the control of
skilled behaviour (Kelley, 1968; Conant and Ashby, 1970; Wonham, this
volume). This difference has been described, in a reference I have
been unable to trace, as the difference between a description of facts
and a recipe for action. Thus a circle can be described as the locus
of all points which are equidistant from a given point. But also it
can be described as what you get if you fix one of the points of a
compass and rotate the other until it reaches the place where it
started. The former description is the one which the limitations of
man as an information processor would prevent him acquiring when
confronted by an EID. The latter is a procedure which might enable
him to control at least suboptimally even an OID. For humans, action
generates skill.

     Unfortunately, although psychology can point to this as an
empirical generalization, it can give little guidance as to how it
happens. Learning theory has concentrated almost entirely on learning
the asymptote of single responses to well-defined static stimuli.
This is almost completely irrelevant to the kind of problem with
which this conference is concerned. Rather, we need to understand
how, by interacting with an EID a human is able (to adopt the language of Optimal Control Theory for an example) not merely to adjust
his gain matrix, but actually to identify the state variables, construct the gain matrix, construct the predictor, and even construct
the appropriate estimator -- and to change them all when the EID
changes its properties. It is not merely a matter of trimming parameter values, but of choosing the appropriate parameters in the first

place, of "system identification" in the very strongest sense of that
phrase. It is as if each of the "boxes" in an Optimal Control Loop
is itself regarded as the plant to be controlled by some other loop,
which in turn has boxes which .... How deep the nesting should go
to understand the process is unclear; research is extremely difficult,
and it is no use asking humans because they are not conscious of what
they do.

We saw earlier that Simon (1962) claimed that building on early
successes could be, for humans, dangerously conservative. But if in
fact the world is "nearly decomposable," then the strategy is not bad,
since it encourages the human to concentrate on subsystems of a size
which are manageable, given his imperfections as a processor of high
dimensional dynamic information. His discovery of the laws which
control a subsystem effectively allow a recoding of the problem into
a space of smaller dimensionality, so that a hierarchical control
system is gradually generated. The subsystems come to be controlled
as individual entities; coupling between the subsystems can then be
discovered without considering action within the subsystems (control
of which is now handled by automatic, habitual information processing
routines), and so on. Mathematical proposals for this kind of partitioning of initially ill-defined structures have been discussed, for
example, by Conant (1976, 1980), and applied in practice by him to
the analysis of weather, and by Moray (1980b) to the analysis of movements of a seven-degree-of-freedom tele-operator.

As far as I am able to judge, such an "evolutionary" approach
to gaining control of an EID or OID would suffice for most of the
eight types of IDS discussed in the first part of this paper. The
exceptions seem to be an incorrect estimate of dimensionality, and
spontaneous reconnection or loss or gain of elements when the time
scale of the latter is short. Fortunately the latter two are comparatively rare in well constructed technolgoical systems.

None of the species are however completely unknown in the world
of man-machine systems. And it may be as well for me to finish by
emphasizing that not only is the study of ill-defined systems fascinating as as an intellectual enterprise, but it also has relevance to
practical problems of very great importance. The role of the human
operator in high technology systems is increasingly to watch the
system taking care of itself until it goes wrong. As soon as it
ceases to be well-defined, he is expected to supplement the automatic
safety systems. In short, he is required only to act at those times
when the problem with which he is faced is of a nature with which he
is singularly ill-equipped to cope. At Three Mile Island it is quite
clear that the operators for a long period of time were searching a
problem space which was of incorrect dimensionality, with an inadequate list of elements in the state vector defining the problem.
Variables did appear and disappear from the system for various reasons. And the system came perilously near to organizing itself into

a large number of completely decomposed subsystems!

Our relations with ill-defined systems are, in the modern world of high technology and unstable economics and politics, too important to be left to chance.

REFERENCES

Ashby, R., 1956, "Introduction to cybernetics," Chapman and Hall, London.

Conant, R., 1976, The laws of information which govern systems, IEEE Trans. Sys., Man & Cyb., SMC-6:240.

Conant, R., 1980, Set-theoretic structure modelling, Int. J. General Systems, 6:1.

Conant, R., and Ashby, R., 1970, Every good regulator of a system must be a model of that system, Int. J. Syst. Science, 1:89.

Dale, H., 1968, Weighing evidence: an attempt to assess the efficiency of the human operator, Ergonomics, 11:215.

Gaines, B., 1976, On the complexity of causal models, IEEE Trans. Sys., Man & Cyb., SMC-6:56.

Hopf-Weichel, R., Lucciani, L., Saleh, J., and Freedy, A., 1979, Aircraft emergency decisions: cognitive and situational variables, Perceptronics PATR 1065-79-7.

Kahneman, D., and Tversky, A., 1973, Belief in the law of small numbers, Psychol. Bull., 76:105.

Kelley, C., 1968, "Manual and Automatic Control," Wiley, N.Y.

Kleinman, D.L., Baron, S., and Levison, W.H., 1970, An optimal control model of human response, part I: theory and validation, Automatica, 6:357.

McRuer, D., Hoffman, L., Jex, H., Moore, G., Phatak, A., Weir, D., and Wolkovitch, J., 1968, New approaches to human-pilot/vehicle dynamic analysis, AFFDL-TR-67-150, Wright-Patterson A.F.B.

Moray, N., 1980a, Human information processing and supervisory control, M.I.T. Man-Machine System Laboratory Report.

Moray, N., 1980b, The use of information transmission as nonparametric correlation in the analysis of complex behaviour, M.I.T. Man-Machine System Laboratory Report.

Petersen, C., and Beach, L., 1964, Man as an intuitive statistician, Psychol. Bull., 68:29.

Rouse, W., 1980, "Systems Engineering Models of Human-Machine Interaction," North-Holland-Elsevier, New York.

Schrenck, L., 1969, Aiding the decision maker: a decision process model, Ergonomics, 12:543.

Simon, H., 1962, The structure of complexity Proc. Amer. Philos. Soc., 106:467.

Tversky, A., and Kahneman, D., 1974, Judgement under uncertainty, Science, 185:1124.

Young, L., 1969, On adaptive manual control, Ergonomics, 12:635.

SOME THEMES AND PRIMITIVES IN ILL-DEFINED SYSTEMS*

Oliver G. Selfridge

45 Percy Road Lexington, MA 02173

To say that something is ill-defined is more to describe us than it. That is, for some system we are dealing with, we are more or less ignorant of its working, and that means that we have special problems in trying to control it. Nevertheless, of course, most of the real systems we deal with are ill-defined in that sense -- like other people. But we do find ways to exercise some degree of control.

The main theme here is that -- regardless of exactly what control means -- it is feasible to do better by a succcession of quite small improvements in a strategy. Indeed, some of the examples I give suggest to me that evolution has improved the behavior of the organisms in this way just as much as it has improved their somatic organization. Indeed, a long enough sequence of small improvements can lead to enormous changes of effectiveness of control.

Even without a mathematical theory or a complete description of a system, without comprehending how it works, or knowing how to model its interactions, we can examine a system or a situation and choose some forms of control and behavior on our part that will do better than others. As our experience proceeds, we may redefine what "doing better" means, but we will continue to learn from successes and failures.

The word adaptation brings to mind some kind of adjustment to conditions. That it seems to depend on one's point of view may

---

* Many of the themes in this paper are developed at greater length in O.G. Selfridge: Tracking and Trailing. Bradford Books, Cambridge, MA (1983).

perhaps be illustrated whether the flow of water in a stream can
usefully be considered to be adapting to the sinuosities and
roughnesses of its banks; or are the banks adapting to the flowing
water? For me, terming that adaptation and making it analogous to
the governor on a steam engine doesn't seem to be very helpful.

Later I will argue that the apparent presence of adaptation
depends on whether our view of behavior lets us usefully describe it
in terms of purpose and purposes. For example, over twenty years
ago, there was widespread hope that useful complexity of systems
could arise merely from "self-organization." The most well know of
the efforts concerned a set of machines called perceptrons."* But
the changes in their behavior seemed not to be related to any
purposes, and in fact they failed in what was claimed for them.

Here I should like to start by considering some elementary
paradigms of adaptation, concerned with adjusting simple controls of
movement of a simple organism. The organism is a very elementary
one-celled creature called Escherichia Coli. E. Coli is only a
couple of microns long, and it moves by twirling a flagellum at one
end. The flagellum twirls in one direction like a propellor, and
drives the creature in a straight line, more or less, for distances
of, say, 10 or 20 microns. Then for some reason it decides to
rotate its flagellum in the other direction; but the structure of
the flagellum is such that it then separates into separate strands,
and E. Coli merely jerks around or "twiddles" in one spot. When the
flagellum next reverses, E. Coli takes off again in a straight line
in another direction. To some degree, the sucessive directions are
unrelated.

Such a procedure is in mathematics called a random walk, and if
that were all that E. Coli did, we should find it duller than it is.
The interesting thing is that when things are getting better for
E. Coli -- say when the concentration of some edible amino acid in
its environment rises -- then E. Coli stops reversing the direction
of its flagellum. That is, it keeps swimming much longer in the
same direction. Soon after things stop getting better, the
flagellum reverses, and twiddling is resumed. The effect is that
E. Coli can climb gradients of attractiveness, and find high
concentrations of nourishment.

The visual effect is quite startling under a microscope. Take
a Petri dish full of E. Coli swimming around uniformly; put a small
drop of, say, lysine in the middle of the dish. After it has
diffused out slowly across the dish, the germs will be seen
clustering closely around it.

------

* The work was run by the late Dr. Frank Rosenblatt at Cornell
Aeronautical Laboratory.

I call such behavior "run and twiddle" or RT for short, and I
suggest that it is an adaptive behavioral "primitive," and an
elementary fundamental mechanism or strategy of all movement.

It is a very simple mechanism. There is only one sensor,
presumably the outside membrane (there is no evidence of spatial
discrimination, and the difference in concentration at the two ends
must be very small, and beset by Brownian variations.) Such behavior
can be moderately well simulated by computer. We can make the
behavior probably simpler than it really is by representing it with
just two numbers, the probabilities P1 and P2. The former is the
probablility of twiddling when things are ordinary, the latter when
things are getting better. By adjusting P1 and P2 we can produce
tracks in a simulation which look quite like real tracks in a
microphotograph.

In fact, we can put the principle very simply — if things are
getting better, don't change what you're doing.

Let us consider a slightly more complicated expression in a
more complicated beast, Euglena. Euglena is also much bigger than
E. Coli, and it swims with cilia. It has a certain degree of
asymmetry, which results in its moving along a helical path as its
own axis rotates. As it moves, then, its axis points in changing
directions.

Euglena has chloroplasts, which derive energy from light, and
so it wants to get to where the light is, usually near the surface
of the points it inhabits. It has a light sensitive spot, and also,
at the front end, a black spot. Now this black spot casts a shadow;
and, because the beast rotates while it swims, this shadow rotates
around the eye, just so long as it swims directly towards the light.
If Euglena deviates from this optimum course, than the shadow covers
the light spot when it is pointing far enough off course. This
causes suppression of the movement of the inside cilia, just enough
to provide a correction.

Again, there is but a single sensor, and a single mode of
behavior, which we have called RT. In general, of course, a single
sensor cannot determine direction with a single measurement, and the
behavior then must depend on the history of the sensor's
measurements. With two sensors, much more complex behavior is
possible.

An example of two parallel sensors is the ant with its two
antennae. One of the behaviors commonly seen in ants is to follow a
pheromone trail; a pheromone is a chemical that can be sensitively
smelled, and ants lay trails of phermomone that can last for some
minutes. Other ants can follow such trails. If one antennae senses
more pheromone, then that antenna causes the legs on that side to

take smaller steps, pulling the ant back on to the trail.

Can such trail-following be accomplished with a single sensor? Indeed it can, but not just by the simple hill-climbing RT of E. Coli. Let us consider the silk moth. By comparison with E. Coli it is a very sophisticated creature, and in fact it takes advantages of several different mechanisms of behavior -- but each is basically a simple RT.

The male silk moth finds its mate at night, when the wind is light but not absent. The female sits on a tree at about 5 feet above the ground and emits a powerful pheromone. This is naturally enormously diffused as it drfts downwind in a spume, spreading out sideways and vertically. Some kilometers away, the male silk moth is waiting, in some tree, with extraordinarily sensitive antennae which can detect a pheromone density on the order of 1 molecule per second. As soon as this happens for a few seconds, he leaves the tree and flies upwind, zigzagging as he goes. The point of the zigzagging is to provide an integration factor for the very small densities involved. He changes direction when he detects that the concentration is falling off on one side of the trail.

A creature as complicated as a moth has, as I said, other forms of behavior. Supposing he loses the trail? Then he flies across the wind, not nearly upwind, in a succession of several attempts to recover the trail.

We can describe this trail following as consisting of several modes. First there is search for an unknown trail, which for the silk moth consists in sitting still and waiting for the trail to come to him. Second, there is following the trail towards the source; third is recovery if the trail is lost; and finally, there must be recognition that the source has been reached.

I hope that the reader will have asked how the silk moth knows which way is upwind, because he can only tell that from the pressure when he is not flying. After a fair amount of discussion in the scientific literature, the following mechanism has been shown: as soon as he smells something, he flies, starting towards the direction the wind is coming. Then he uses his very sensitive eyes (although they fly at night, even the light from stars alone give enough light) to see which way the ground underneath him is going.

And how does the silk moth tell when he has reached his goal, the female? It seems that the trigger for that decision is the mere density of the pheromone, some 10 times large than when he started. At that point, the silk moth merely lands on the nearest tree and walks in circles until he finds the female.

So the individual mechanisms are really pretty simple, but they add up to what certainly looks like purposive behavior of some power and subtlety. The individual mechanisms are the simplest form of adaptation, which I have called RT. Their combining into complex purpose structures, as in the silk moth, is what does the trick.

Now the elementary RT, as a control mechanism, is not easily susceptible to the kinds of analysis we are comfortable with. RT is not linear, it's not inherently continuous or discrete -- and of course it doesn't always work. It requires that the running and twiddling be somehow relevant to the environment.* For people the easiest way to assure that is to deal with some model of the environment, which they can understand and analyze. But of course the organisms we have discussed are not intellectually rich or powerful enough for that; and yet they survive and adapt and improve. In some sense, when we deal with systems that we do not understand -- which we can say then are ill-defined -- we have to deal with them as those organisms deal with their environments.

I hope it is clear, even from the examples above, that the elementary adaptive mechanisms are usually embedded into hierarchies of them, especially in higher animals. What are the ways that one adaptive mechanism can control another? Let us examine the RT control of E. Coli a little more closely. First, there are two probabilities of the model, P1 and P2. Then there is a factor that I did not mention: how long does it take the membrane to react; alternatively, what is its integration time for output?

The elementary unit of classical control theory is usually considered to be the servomechanism. In the control of the servomechanism, there are interesting parallels between it and the RT mechanisms here. The two probabilities are some measure of the gain of the system. That is to say, how much difference in behavior does a small change in control signal make? The integration time of each is analogous, having to do with total loop delays and impulse responses.

It was Wiener who emphasized thirty-five years ago in "Cybernetics" that control of muscles is not effected by direct impulses coming from the motor cortex straight down to the muscle fibers. Rather the cortical impulses are directed at a spinal control loop, changing its gain, as it were.

---

* This is analogous to the assertion in artificial intelligence that a very important aspect of a problem is to find the right form of representation.

But the most powerful method of control for both mechanisms is one that is in effect their purpose: what is the evaluation function for the RT? -- and what is the set point for ther servo, that is, where is the error signal zero?

For example, one form of resetting the evaluation function is to use different sensors. If a membrane is initially sensitive to chemical concentrations in the surrounding fluid, then it might not take a great change in that membrane to make it sensitive to light instead. And in some cases, that would turn out to be profitable for the organism, as with Euglena.

My picture is that evolution has built more complex behavior into organisms by building hierarchies and combinations of simple pieces of behavior; control loops controlling other loops in great structures, with little overall understanding in the human sense, and certainly with no overall sets of purposes.

Evolutionary progress has been slow indeed, I think because of that lack of a set of purposes. When we try to find out how to deal with systems that we do not understand, that are ill-defined, we start out with a fair understanding of our own complex purposes and a fair set of intellectual tools for modeling and analzying parts of the behavior of those systems. We can use these tools to put together some approximation of a strategy for controlling the system.

At that point, however, we must resort to something very like the RT strategies. It is clear, for example, that we have very little profound understanding of how economic systems work. In dealing with them, are we much better than E. Coli? Are our models of learning in children so accurate and reliable that we can derive educational strategies?

But as we try simple adaptive techniques, we learn more about the systems; every time we narrow something down, we can apply more sophisticated and powerful analytic tools, because the system we are examining becomes less ill-defined for us.

I have argued that simple adaptive techniques, applied in a reponsive environment, and put together in hierarchichal control structures, can improve control without necessarily requiring an accurate definition of the system. In that sense, finding out how to do that efficiently, and how to evaluate how well it works, can help to show us how to control systems we do not understand, even ones we are part of ourselves.

THE USE OF OPTIMAL CONTROL IN ECONOMICS

Penelope A. Rowlatt

H.M. Treasury
Parliament Street
London, SW1P 3AG

Introduction

Optimal control theory provides a powerful and efficient method of deriving rules which will enable a dynamic system to be held to a preferred path. This makes it appear at first sight eminently suitable to be used as a tool to assist economic policymakers in their task of improving the performance of the economy. Developments within the field of economics suggest, however, that there are reasons why this may not be the case. My object in this paper is to describe two reasons why economists are dubious about the efficacy of optimal control for deriving economic policy.

I shall first sketch very briefly the circumstances in which different forms of control are appropriate. It is immediately clear that for an economy, adaptive control is the appropriate form. This will allow two developments, each of which has had considerable influence on economic thinking and on the design of economic policy, to be set in context vis-a-vis developments in control theory.

Control theory applied to an economy

The appropriate rule for optimal control depends on the properties of the system which is being controlled (see Aoki, 1976 or Chow, 1975). In a purely deterministic, mechanical system, - fixed, known coefficients and no stochastic element to the laws of motion - deterministic control rules, that is, open-loop control can be used.

As soon as a stochastic element is introduced into the laws of motion, as it must be if the system we wish to control is an economy, then a different rule is needed after the first period. Information

27

from the performance in earlier periods must be fed back into the
system in order that the optimal path is followed. That is, feedback control must be used.

   More complications arise if the coefficients are not known with
certainty (as is generally the case in economics), if they are
stochastic, or if they are believed to move over time. (It is likely
that this last is also true for economic models as we shall see
later.) These are the circumstances in which adaptive control becomes
necessary. Two forms of adaptive control are available to the econ-
omist. They differ according to whether or not learning takes place,
that is whether or not information gained about the system during the
operation of the control is used to revise the parameters in the laws
of motion.

   The first point I want to develop in this paper, is related to
the problem of uncertainty about the values of the coefficients. In
a paper published in 1953, Milton Friedman elegantly demonstrated the
way in which uncertainty about the timing with which policy changes
affect the economy may lead to a policy designed to stabilize the
economy in fact having a destabilizing influence. In particular he
showed that a stabilization policy for which the effect of the policy
is uncorrelated with the economic cycle will be destabilizing.

   The rest of this paper will be devoted to the most recent
important contribution to control in economics. It began with a
paper by Lucas published in 1976. In this he explains that in an
economic system, partly as a result of problems concerning the
modelling of any effects of expectations, one would expect the
parameters of the model to depend on the policy followed by the
Government. It follows from this that a model estimated over the
past cannot be used to simulate the effects of alternative future
policies. For each future policy would require different, in
general unknown, adjustments to be made to the parameters in the
model.

   Further work by Kydland and Prescott in 1977 has demonstrated
that in this case, even if the dependence of the model parameters on
the policy chosen were perfectly known, a sequence of policy decisions each one optimal given the information available at the time
would not result in the economy following an optimal path.

Optimal rules may cause instability

   In the 1953 paper cited above, Milton Friedman pointed out some
of the problems which can arise if control is attempted of a system
in which the precise timing of effects is unknown. He presented a
very neat formal analysis which is applicable to the attempt to
dampen fluctuations in any system subject to uncertainty about
timing. The result is well known to economists but may not be

familiar to those of other disciplines.

In the days of Keynes' influence, fiscal policy and fine tuning were accepted as policies which were suitable for reducing fluctuations in economic activity. The question Milton Friedman posed concerned the conditions under which such counter cyclical policy would succeed in reducing economic instability. He concluded that a policy as likely to be wrong as to be right would be destabilizing rather than neutral. There can be little doubt that this has had a significant influence on economists' advice concerning appropriate policy actions.

The Government can affect economic activity in many ways, for example by varying its own expenditure or by varying the level of taxation. Counter cyclical policy consists of offsetting fluctuations in autonomous activity by changes in Government induced activity in such a way as to reduce the variation of output (income) about its trend path and so to dampen the consequential fluctuations in employment.

The approach taken compares the results of alternative paths for Government policy. In one, explicit action is taken with the objective of reducing the fluctuations in output. In the other no such action is taken. It is not suggested that in the second case the Government takes no actions which affect activity; rather, these actions are taken for granted and attention is focussed on those actions which the Government takes solely for the purpose of maintaining full employment.

The formal analysis represents output (or income) Z at time t as the sum of two parts,

$$Z(t) = X(t) + Y(t) \qquad\qquad\qquad (1)$$

with $X(t)$ representing income at time t in the situation in which there is and has been no counter cyclical policy while $Y(t)$ represents the entire effect at time t of counter cyclical policy whenever taken. It does not measure the effect of counter cyclical action taken at time t. No generality is lost by extracting the trend elements from both series and defining X, Y and Z as deviations from trends.

The magnitude of the fluctuations is measured by the variance – the mean square deviation of the series from its mean. For X or Z the variance (eg $\sigma_X^2 = E\,[(X - \overline{X})^2]$ where E stands for expected value and $\overline{X}$ is the expected value of X) measures the amplitude of fluctuations in income in the absence or presence of the policy. For Y the variance measures the magnitude of the effect of the counter cyclical policy taken. If no action is taken $\sigma_Y^2 = 0$.

Equation (1) leads to a simple statistical result:*

$$\sigma_Z^2 = \sigma_X^2 + \sigma_Y^2 + 2r_{xy}\sigma_x\sigma_y \tag{2}$$

The correlation coefficient of X and Y is $r_{xy} = E[(X - \bar{X})(Y - \bar{Y})]/\sigma_x\sigma_y$ and measures the timing of the counter cyclical policy. If the counter cyclical policy were always perfectly timed and of correct magnitude its effects would always be precisely opposite to those of the deviation of X from its mean and r_{xy} would equal −1. On the other hand if the counter cyclical policy were totally random, as likely to be in the same direction as the deviation of X from its mean as in the opposite direction, then r_{xy} would equal zero.

The important result in Friedman's paper is the following. A counter cyclical policy for which $r_{xy} = 0$, one which is as likely to have effects in the wrong as in the right direction, is not neutral in impact. It is destabilizing. For if $r_{xy} = 0$ the variance of the 'actual' output Z exceeds the variance of the 'policy-free' output X by the variance of Y. A noisy disturbance is being added and increases the total noise in the system.

If counter cyclical policy is to succeed in its objective, its effects must be in the right direction more often than in the wrong. The extent to which this must be so is given by equation (2). If σ_Z^2 is to be less than σ_X^2 the correlation r_{xy} between X and Y must be more negative than $\sigma_Y^2/2\sigma_x\sigma_y$ is positive. If this is not so the control policy will be destabilizing.

It is clear that if the need for action could be recognised instantaneously and translated into immediate action which was effective immediately then r_{xy} could be close to −1. But there is a lag between the need for action and the effect of action. This lag can be decomposed into three parts:

(1)   the lag between the need for action and the recognition of this need;

(2)   the lag between the recognition of the need and the taking of the action;

(3)   the lag between the action and its effects.

---

*This follows because

$$E[(Z - \bar{Z})^2] = E[(X - \bar{X} + Y - \bar{Y})^2]$$
$$= E[(X - \bar{X})^2] + E[(Y - \bar{Y})^2] + 2E[(X - \bar{X})(Y - \bar{Y})]$$

with $\quad r_{xy} = E[(X - \bar{X})(Y - \bar{Y})] // \sqrt{E[(X - \bar{X})^2]E[(Y - \bar{Y})^2]}$

and writing σ_x for $\sqrt{E[(X - \bar{X})^2]}$

For the achievement of a negative value of r_{xy} near to -1 it is
necessary that the behaviour of the system both in the presence and
in the absence of policy action can be forecast with some precision.

It seems likely that for an economic system in which parameters
are unknown and may be changing over time it will be particularly
unlikely that a high negative value of r_{xy} can be achieved. If this
is so, policies based on optimal control would lead to a worse outcome than that which would follow the adoption of a fixed (zero
variance) rule to determine the path of the main policy variables.
This result has had an important influence in the debate between
Keynesians, who support demand management or fine tuning, and
monetarists, who prefer to commit themselves to a monetary rule and
then make no attempt to iron out the fluctuations in economic activity. At present the confidence intervals around the estimated
parameters in our econometric models are such as to make precision
of forecasting of the timing of effects seem unlikely. Furthermore,
new developments suggest that the parameter values appropriate to one
policy action may be inappropriate if that policy action is changed.

The Theory of Economic Policy

The remainder of this paper will be devoted to discussing the
possibility of policy dependent parameters and the problems that
arise. These developments are best described within the framework
laid out by Tinbergen (1956). This framework is likely to be
familiar to anyone who has worked with control theory. Nevertheless,
it is probably best to lay out an explicit version of it here.

The state of the economy in time period t is described by (1) a
vector y_t of variables, which are known as "state" variables, (2) a
vector x_t of exogenous variables some of which are "instruments"
controlled by the Government, and (3) a vector ε_t of serially independent identically distributed random shocks with zero mean and
covariance matrix V. The motion of the economy from one period (eg
year or quarter) to the next is described by dynamic equations of
motion which can be written

$$y_{t+1} = f(y_t, \ x_t, \varepsilon_t), \tag{3}$$

by the distribution of the ε_t and by the behaviour of the exogenous
variables x_t.

The function f is taken to be fixed but is not known. The form
of this function is specified by economic theory, often based on
micro-economic analysis of individuals' behaviour, and can be the
subject of considerable controversy. Although interesting and
relevant to the use of control theory, these controversies will not
concern us here. It then remains to find values θ for the parameters
involved. Applied econometricians will use regression analysis to

estimate a fixed parameter vector so that we may write the equations
of motion as

$$f(y, x, \varepsilon) \equiv F(y, x, \theta, \varepsilon). \tag{4}$$

The resulting set of equations

$$y_{t+1} = F(y_t, x_t, \theta, \varepsilon_t) \tag{5}$$

will be a model of the economy which is not deterministic (in the
sense that the equation for each state variable has a stochastic
element) and in which the parameters are subject to confidence
intervals, that is, are not known with certainty. Given this model
and a social objective function it seems at first sight that,
stability apart, there should be no problems (except technical and
mathematical ones) in applying optimal control theory to derive an
optimal path. However since the parameters of the system are not
known with certainty it will, of course, be necessary to use adaptive control techniques.

The possibility of policy-dependent parameters in the equations of motion

Faith in the applicability of this framework to the analysis
of economic policy has been badly shaken by the 1976 paper of
Robert E Lucas Jr. First he pointed out that there is a discrepancy
between the Tinbergen framework and current practice of macro-
economic modellers and forecasters who construct these models and
use them for forecasting and for policy evaluation. Three common
practices among econometricians suggest that they find the above
characterisation inappropriate.

(i) Econometric forecasters rarely use data series prior to
1947 to assist in the estimation of the parameter vector. But given
the assumptions inherent in the Tinbergen theory of economic policy
more observations will always sharpen parameter estimates.

(ii) As new recent data become available econometric relationships are continually refitted and parameter estimates are revised.

(iii) It is common practice among econometric forecasters to use
patterns observed in recent residuals to revise the estimates of the
intercept (the constant term) in the relationships of F for forecasting purposes. For example, a recent series of positive residuals
on an equation (discrepancies between the predicted and the actual
value of a variable) may lead a forecaster to revise the estimated
value of the intercept downwards.

These practices imply that econometric forecasters do not
expect the relationships in F to remain constant over long periods

of time. It appears that experience suggests to them that the
parameters θ in the model may be moving. By itself this presents
no insurmountable problem. It merely restates the point made earlier:
if control theory is to be used to improve the performance of an
economy it will have to be adaptive control theory, for in addition
to uncertainty about the values of the coefficients it is likely
that they are moving over time. Lucas goes on, however, to formulate
a hypothesis about the cause of this movement in the parameters.

   The form of the function F and the parameter vector $\boldsymbol{\theta}$ are based
on economic theory. The usual procedure followed in constructing an
econometric model F is to derive the individual relationships from
the assumptions used in micro-economics to describe decisions taken
by individual agents. These decision rules usually follow from some
optimising assumption. A typical decision problem takes the form of
finding the optimum decision with respect to some individual objective function given the paths of certain exogenous aspects of the
individual's environment. In general some aspects of the future
course of the economy are relevant to the individual's decision.
His expectations concerning these will be embodied in his decision
and will affect its relationship to observed data series. <u>To assume</u>
<u>stability of $(F, \boldsymbol{\theta})$ under alternative policy rules is to assume that</u>
<u>agents disregard the effect of policy on the future path of the</u>
<u>economy</u>.

   So long as agents believe that policy measures can be effective,
they will revise their expectations concerning the future in the
light of changes in policy. To the extent that expectations are not
observed they cannot be included explicitly in the state vector y.
A change in expectations in these circumstances will change the
relationship between sets of observed series; that is, it will
change the parameter vector $\boldsymbol{\theta}$.

   The formalisation of the theory of economic policy can be re-
specified to take account of this possibility. A parameter vector
$\boldsymbol{\lambda}_t$ describes the policy shocks at time t. The controllable exogenous policy variables (or instruments) in the vector x can be
viewed as stochastic functions of this vector and of the state of
the system:

$$x_t = G(y_t, \boldsymbol{\lambda}_t, \boldsymbol{\eta}_t) \qquad\qquad (6)$$

where G is known, and $\boldsymbol{\eta}_t$ is a vector of stochastic errors. The
remainder of the economy can then be characterised by the equation:

$$y_{t+1} = F(y_t, x_t, \theta(\lambda), \varepsilon_t) \qquad\qquad (7)$$

   The behavioural parameters θ now depend explicitly on the
parameters $\boldsymbol{\lambda}$ governing policy. They depend not only on the current
values taken by the $\boldsymbol{\lambda}$'s, $\boldsymbol{\lambda}_t$, but also on expected future values of

the λ's. The econometric problem with this characterisation of the theory of economic policy is the estimation of the function $\theta(\lambda)$.

In this framework a policy change is viewed as a change in the parameter vector λ. Such a change affects the system in two ways. First it changes the time series properties of the series x_t. Second, it modifies the behavioural parameters $\theta(\lambda)$ which govern the behaviour of the rest of the system. The way in which this second modification comes about clearly depends on the way in which the policy change is carried out. A policy change which takes place with no public announcement or discussion will become known to individual economic agents only gradually. The movement to the new θ will be unsystematic and econometrically unpredictable. On the other hand if a policy change is fully discussed beforehand and understood then there is a possibility that the movement in θ may be forecast on the basis of past estimates of $\theta(\lambda)$.

So far we have seen that, in Lucas' words, ".... given that the structure of an econometric model consists of optimal decision rules of economic agents, and that optimal decision rules vary systematically with changes in the structure of series relevant to the decision maker, it follows that any change in policy will systematically alter the structure of econometric models". Lucas then goes on to say that this ".... implies that comparisons of the effects of alternative policy rules using current macro-economic models are invalid regardless of the performance of these models over the sample period or in ex ante short term forecasting". But given that changes in the relevant parameters can often be estimated either on the basis of theoretical considerations or given their observed movements in the past under similar policy changes this conclusion would appear overpessimistic. Policy simulations performed at the Treasury in the United Kingdom are typically accompanied by a large number of minor modifications of the equations which go to make up the model. These are designed to pick up just those effects which are of the type that Lucas suggests may be relevant. External users of the Treasury model for policy simulations (it is available for use by the general public) are always advised that the operation of the model for policy simulations is a highly specialist activity involving considerable experience, expertise and judgement. Indeed this behaviour by econometric modellers and forecasters, like the behaviour cited above by Lucas himself, itself lends support to Lucas' contention that the parameter vector should be considered to vary with the policy followed. But it also goes some way towards negating his pessimistic conclusions.

Optimal control of a system with policy-dependent parameters

Even if policy simulation can, after all, be performed with validity on a system which has policy-dependent parameters, it does not follow that a sequence of optimal decisions can be used to determine a policy which will hold the economy on an optimal path. Kydland and Prescott have shown that, using Lucas' revised version of the theory of economic policy and following Gordon (1976) in assuming that changes in policy do change the parameters θ in a predictable way, a sequence of optimal decisions based on information currently available will not lead to the economy following an optimal path. To illustrate this point the stochastic elements in the equations can be dropped and the coefficients can be assumed to be known with certainty as these elements of the theory of economic policy do not affect the result.

Let $\lambda = (\lambda_1, \lambda_2, ..., \lambda_T)$ be a sequence of policies for periods 1 to T (which may be infinite) and let $y = (y_1, y_2, ..., y_T)$ be the corresponding sequence of state vectors resulting from economic agents' decisions. Using the notation of Lucas' revised theory of economic policy with the stochastic terms omitted the state vector is given by

$$y_{t+1} = F(y_t, x_t, \theta(\lambda)) = g(y_t, \lambda)$$ (8)

while the path of the instruments is described by

$$x_t = G(y_t, \lambda_t).$$ (9)

A social objective function

$$U = \sum_{t=o}^{\infty} \beta_t \ u(y_t, \lambda)$$ (10)

is assumed.

The policy sequence λ is optimal if it maximises (10) subject to (8). But a policy λ_t is optimal for time t if it maximises (10) subject to all future constraints (8) given the past decisions λ_{t-i}, y_{t-i} and given that all future policy decisions will be similarly selected*. It is easy to show that a policy sequence derived as a series of policies optimal for each point in time will not be an optimal policy sequence. Before doing so we describe a simple example. The following two period example will serve to illustrate the point and to lend flesh to the mathematical bones of the proof. Consider the possibility of a Government taking costly flood-protection measures so that houses may safely be built on a plain which is liable to flooding. It is considered sub-optimal to have houses on the plain without such protection. The optimal first-period policy, when no houses have been built on the plain, is that flood-protection measures should not be undertaken. But the

---

* Kydland the Prescott call such a policy "consistent". It is the policy sequence which would result from dynamic programming.

agents know that if in the first period houses are built there then the optimal second period policy for the Government will be to take these measures. The agents build the houses and the measures are duly undertaken in the second period. This sequence of optimal policy decisions is not an optimal policy sequence because in the first period there are houses on the plain and no flood protection.

If the agents had not taken account of expected future policy when taking their decision they would not have built the houses on the plain. The Tinbergen framework for economic policy would then have been valid and the sequence of optimal policy decisions would have become an optimal sequence. But, as this example demonstrates, once it is accepted that agents' decisions are affected by their expectations concerning future policy it is no longer the case that a sequence of optimal policy decisions will be an optimal policy sequence.

The mathematical proof runs as follows. For the two-period problem equations (10) and (8) can be written

$$U = U(y_1, y_2, \lambda_1, \lambda_2) \tag{11}$$

$$y_1 = g_1(\bar{y}_0, \lambda_1, \lambda_2) \tag{12}$$

$$y_2 = g_2(y_1, \lambda_1, \lambda_2) \tag{13}$$

where $\bar{y}_0$ is the state vector at the start. If the parameters in the model were independent of the sequence of policies equations (12) and (13) would reduce to

$$y_1 = g_1(\bar{y}_0, \lambda_1) \tag{14}$$

$$y_2 = g_2(y_1, \lambda_2) \tag{15}$$

Assuming differentiability and an interior solution the condition for a sequence of policies to be an optimal sequence is given by setting the total differential of U with respect to each variable equal to zero subject to the constraints. Thus

$$\frac{dU}{d\lambda_i} = 0 \qquad i = 1, 2 \tag{16}$$

or

$$\frac{\partial U}{\partial y_1}\frac{\partial g_1}{\partial \lambda_1} + \frac{\partial U}{\partial y_2}\left(\frac{\partial g_2}{\partial y_1}\frac{\partial g_1}{\partial \lambda_1} + \frac{\partial g_2}{\partial \lambda_i}\right) + \frac{\partial U}{\partial \lambda_1} = 0 \tag{17a}$$

and

$$\frac{\partial U}{\partial y_1}\frac{\partial g_1}{\partial \lambda_2} + \frac{\partial U}{\partial y_2}\left(\frac{\partial g_2}{\partial y_1}\frac{\partial g_1}{\partial \lambda_2} + \frac{\partial g_2}{\partial \lambda_2}\right) + \frac{\partial U}{\partial \lambda_2} = 0. \tag{17b}$$

The optimal policy in period 1 is obtained by choosing λ_1, to maximise U subject to (12) and (13):

$$\frac{\partial U}{\partial y_1}\frac{\partial g_1}{\partial \lambda_1} + \frac{\partial U}{\partial y_2}\left(\frac{\partial g_2}{\partial y_1}\frac{\partial g_1}{\partial \lambda_1} + \frac{\partial g_2}{\partial \lambda_1}\right) + \frac{\partial U}{\partial \lambda_1} = 0. \qquad (18a)$$

Similarly the optimal policy in period 2 is obtained by choosing λ_2 to maximise U subject to (13) taking y as given:

$$\frac{\partial U}{\partial y_2}\frac{\partial g_2}{\partial \lambda_2} + \frac{\partial U}{\partial \lambda_L} = 0. \qquad (18b)$$

The first period equations are the same in each case. The equations for the second period would be the same if the term $\partial g_1/\partial \lambda_2$ were zero and this would be the case if the parameters in the model were independent of policy as is evident from examination of equations (14) and (15). (This result can easily be generalised to T-period problems.)

This analysis (which has been discussed, criticised and augmented by Prescott (1977) and by Modigliani (1977)) demonstrates the point made at the start, namely that if the parameters of a model are dependent on the policy followed by the Government then a sequence of optimal policy decisions will not in general result in an optimal path being followed by the system. But this is not necessarily the end of this particular story. If there were indeed no stochastic elements to the laws of motion the entire policy sequence could be solved for all time at the start. The effect of the agents taking account of expected future policy would then be built into the optimal policy decision for the first period. If this were done in the flood control example the optimal first period policy would be different; flood protection measures would be taken from the start (or laws against building houses in the flood-plain would be made more stringent). It therefore appears that by developing a backward induction method of solution, in which an optimal policy for all time is solved backwards to the present in each period, the problems described by Kydland tne Prescott may be surmounted.

Conclusion

This paper has described two serious problems concerning the use of control methods to assist policymakers in choosing optimal policies to control the path of an economy given an agreed upon social objective function. It should not be concluded however that economists have conclusively rejected the use of control methods to assist in the choice between alternative policies. Research is currently proceeding in two directions. First, experiments are being undertaken in which control methods are applied to various of the macro-econometric models in order to discover the implications of the structure of these models for policy. One interesting experiment in this category involves the derivation of an optimal policy rule for one model and its application to a second model (see Chow (1976)). The deviation of the path for the economy predicted by the second model from that predicted on the basis of the first can be fed back to the control of the first model (closed-loop or feed-back control) to generate a revised rule for the later periods*. Second, research into the problem of controlling systems in which the laws of motion depend on the policy chosen is still continuing.

REFERENCES

Aoki, M., 1976, "Optimal Control and System Theory in Dynamic Economic Analysis," North Holland, Amsterdam.

Chow, G.C., 1975, "Analysis and Control of Dynamic Economic Systems," John Wiley and Sons, New York.

Chow, G.C., 1976, Usefulness of Imperfect Models for the Formulating of Stabilisation Policies, Department of Economics, Princeton University, mimeographed.

Friedman, M., 1953, The Effect of a Full Employment Policy on Economic Stability: A Formal Analysis, in: "Essays in Positive Economics," University of Chicago Press, Chicago.

Gordon, R. J., 1976, Can Econometric Policy Evaluation be Salvaged?: A Comment, in: "The Phillips Curve and Labor Markets," K. Brunner and A.H. Meltzer, eds., North Holland, Amsterdam.

Kydland, F.E. and Prescott, E.C., 1977, Rules Rather Than Discretion: The Inconsistency of Optimal Plans, J. Pol. Econ., 85: 473

Lucas, R.E. Jr., 1976, Econometric Policy Evaluation: A critique, in: "The Phillips Curve and Labor Markets," K. Brunner and A.H. Meltzer, eds., North Holland, Amsterdam.

Modigliani, F., 1977, Should Control Theory be used for Economic Stabilisation?: A Comment, in: "Optimal Policies, Control Theory and Technology Exports," K. Brunner and A.H. Meltzer, eds., North Holland, Amsterdam.

Prescott, E.C., 1977, Should Control Theory be used for Economic Stabilisation? in: "Optimal Policies, Control Theory and Technology Exports," K. Brunner and A.H. Meltzer, eds., North Holland, Amsterdam.

Tinbergen, J. 1956, "Economic Policy: Principles and Design," North Holland, Amsterdam.

---

* This research was being done by Michael Athans, Edwin Kuh and Robert Pindyck at the Massachusetts Institute of Technology, see Modigliani (1977).

BIOLOGICAL VIEWS OF ADAPTATION - SOME HISTORICAL ACCOUNTS

F. Eugene Yates

Crump Institute for Medical Engineering
6417 Boelter Hall
University of California
Los Angeles, California 90024

Simple, inanimate systems can give a false impression of adaptability and intentionality. For example, consider a candle flame in the bottom of a tall, cylindrical chimney, but without a port for air at the bottom. It will "seek to stay alive" by leaning steadily to one side, as a baffle is lowered down the center of the chimney. By so doing the flame spontaneously (and to us cleverly) organizes the airflow into a downdraft of fresh air, and an updraft of exhaust. It seems to adapt its behavior to its circumstances, in order to persist. Failing to do this, it would gutter and die. This "adaptation" invokes the illusion of intentionality, but it gains us little, and risks unnecessary confusions, to apply the terms "adaptation" and "intention" to the candle in this circumstance. These terms should be reserved for truly complex system behavior (see the discussion of intentionality by O. Selfridge, in this volume).

Here I present selections from the classical uses of the concept of "adaptation" by those in the life sciences. Although this is mostly old material, it still serves as a solid point of departure for any attempt to grasp the adaptive behavior of complex, living systems.

Darwin on Adaptation (Darwin, 1902)

The term "adaptation" does not appear in the index of the 1902 (6th) edition of the "Origin of Species." However, Chapter V deals with acclimatization:

(pp. 199-200)

It is notorious that each species is adapted to the
climate of its own home: species from an arctic or even
from a temperate region cannot endure a tropical climate,
or conversely. But the degree of adaptation of species to
the climates under which they live is often overrated. We
may infer this from our frequent inability to predict
whether or not an imported plant will endure our climate,
and from the number of plants and animals brought from
different countries which are here perfectly healthy. We
have reason to believe that species in a state of nature
are closely limited in their ranges by the competition of
other organic beings quite as much as, or more than, by
adaptation to particular climates.

(pp. 200-201)

Hence adaptation to any special climate may be looked
at as a quality readily grafted on an innate wide
flexibility of constitution, common to most animals. On
this view, the capacity of enduring the most different
climates by man himself and by his domestic animals, and
the fact of the extinct elephant and rhinoceros having
formerly endured a glacial climate, whereas the living
species are now all tropical or sub-tropical in their
habits, ought not to be looked on as anomalies but as
examples of a very common flexibility of constitution,
brought, under peculiar circumstances, into action.

How much of the acclimatization of species to any
peculiar climate is due to mere habit, and how much to the
natural selection of varieties having different innate
constitutions, and how much to both means combined, is an
obscure question.

The adaptation being addressed by Darwin, above, mixes two
ideas probably best kept distinct: 1) adaptation as a time-and-
input-dependent adjustment of parameter values (or system structure)
that permits continuing stability in the face of environmental
changes consisting of previously-challenging inputs; 2) the
possession of forms or functions that seem to "explain" (in an
anthropomorphic, technological sense) how well an organism does what
it does in a steady environment, e.g., the tubular construction of
the bones of bird wings, or of insect legs, expresses the advantage
of the hollow cylinder as an I-girder solid of revolution, in
creating stiffness to resist bending, while minimizing weight.

D'Arcy Thompson on Adaptation (Thompson, 1961)

(pp. 237-238)

In the biological aspect of the case, we must always

remember that our bone is not only a living, but highly plastic structure; the little trabeculae are constantly being formed and deformed, demolished and formed anew. Here, for once, it is safe to say that "heredity" need not and cannot be invoked to account for the configuration and arrangement of the trabeculae: for we can see them at any time of life in the making, under the direct action and control of the forces to which the system is exposed. If a bone be broken and so repaired that its parts lie somewhat out of their former place, so that the pressure- and tension-lines have now a new distribution, before many weeks are over the trabecular system will be found to have been entirely remodeled, so as to fall into line with the new system of forces....

Herein then lies, so far as we can discern it, a great part at least of the physical causation of what at first sight strikes us as a purely functional adaptation: as a phenomenon, in other words, whose physical cause is as obscure as its final cause or end is apparently manifest.

(pp. 262-264)
It has been remarked over and over again how harmoniously the whole organism hangs together, and how throughout its fabric one part is related and fitted to another in strictly functional correlation. But this conception, though never denied, is sometimes apt to be forgotten in the course of that process of more and more minute analysis by which, for simplicity's sake, we seek to unravel the intricacies of a complex organism.

As we analyse a thing into its parts or into its properties, we tend to magnify these, to exaggerate their apparent independence, and to hide from ourselves (at least for a time) the essential integrity and individuality of the composite whole.... So it is precisely with the skeleton. In it is reflected a field of force: and keeping pace, as it were, in action and interaction with this field of force, the whole skeleton and every part thereof, down to the minute intrinsic stucture of the bones themselves, is related in form and in position to the lines of force, to the resistances it has to encounter; for by one of the mysteries of biology, resistance begets resistance, and where pressure falls there growth springs up in strength to meet it. And, pursuing the same train of thought, we see that all this is true not of the skeleton alone but of the whole fabric of the body....

Waddington's View (Waddington, 1969)

(pp. 93-94)

A population of wild type Drosophila was grown on a normal medium to which sufficient sodium chloride had been added to cause the death of the majority of the larvae. As generation succeeded generation under this stringent natural selection, the percentage of survivors gradually increased but the concentration of salt was then also raised so as to maintain the pressure. The osmotic regulation of the Drosophila larvae is known to involve a pair of papillae on either side of the anus. After twenty generations, flies from three strains which had been submitted to this section were grown in various concentrations of salt, and the size of their anal papillae compared with that of the initial strains, on which no selection had been exerted.... the selection... increased the capacity of the individuals to respond to the stress of the salt. The curve relating the size of the anal organ to the salt content of the medium is steeper in the selected strains than in the unselected. We may say that the selection has improved the adaptability. Secondly, at any particular concentration of salt the size of the anal organ is larger in the selected strain than in the corresponding unselected one. Although under selection the development has become more flexible it still is not flexible enough to allow the selected strains to regress completely to the unselected level when the environmental stress is removed.

We have here a good example of the limitations of a phraseology which attempts to call a character either an acquired one or an inherited one. In reality all characters are both acquired and inherited. But we see also how after selection the genetic system in a population may determine a phenotypic appearance which previously could only be obtained under the combined influence of the initial genotype and a specific environmental stress. This is the process which I have spoken of as the genetic assimilation of an acquired character. Although its mechanism is quite different from the Lamarckian inheritance of acquired characters, being entirely based on the concepts of orthodox Mendelian genetics, it can in fact play in evolutionary theory the very role for which Lamarckian hypotheses have often been invoked.

From Dobzhansky, Ayala, Stebbins and Valentine (1977)

(pp. 65-66)

Mutations are accidental, undirected, random, or
chance events.... very important for evolution; namely,
in the sense that they are unoriented with respect to
adaptation. Mutations occur independently of whether or
not they are adaptive in the environments in which the
organisms live. Microbiologists have known for a long
time that confronted with adverse environmental conditions, bacterial cultures give rise to new genetically
stable strains able to cope with the unusual environment.
The regularity of this result inclined some
bacteriologists to believe that the environment could
induce specific mutations favorable in that environment.
Ample evidence now exists showing that mutations arise
with certain probabilities independently of whether or not
they are favorable in the environment where they arise....
Occasionally, however, a newly arisen mutation may
increase the adaptation of the organism. The probability
of such an event is greater when organisms colonize a new
habitat, or when environmental changes present a population with new challenges. In these cases the adaptation
of the population is less than optimal and there is
greater opportunity for new mutations to be adaptive.
Needless to say, there are mutations that destroy
essential functions and thus are harmful in any
environment. This brings about the important point that
mutations are not beneficial or harmful in the abstract,
but rather with respect to some environment. The same
mutation may be harmful in some environments while
adaptive in others.

And Gould (1977)

(pp. 94-95)
Organisms evolve different life history strategies to
fit different types of environments. Among theories that
correlate strategy with environment, the theory of r- and
k- selection, developed by R. H. MacArthur and E. O.
Wilson in the mid 1960s, has surely been the most
successful.

Evolution, as usually depicted in textbooks and
reported in the popular press, is a process of inexorable
improvement in form: animals are delicately "fine tuned"
to their environment through constant selection of better-
adapted shapes. But several kinds of environments do not
call forth such an evolutionary response. Suppose that a
species lives in an environment that imposes irregular,
catastrophic mortality upon it (ponds that dry up, for
example, or shallow seas ripped up by severe storms). Or
suppose that food sources are ephemeral and hard to find,

but superabundant once located. Organisms cannot fine
tune themselves to such environments for there is nothing
sufficiently stable to adjust to. Better in such a
situation to invest as much energy as possible into
reproduction -- make as many offspring as you can, as
quickly as possible, so that some will survive the
catastrophe. Reproduce like hell while you have the
ephemeral resource, for it will not last long and some of
your progeny must survive to find the next one.

We refer to evolutionary pressures for the
maximization of reproductive effort at the expense of
delicate morphological adjustment as r- selection;
organisms so adapted are r- strategists (r is the
traditional measure of "intrinsic rate of increase in
population size" in a set of basic, ecological equations).
Species that live in stable environments, near the maximum
population size that the environment can support, will
gain nothing by producing hordes of poorly adjusted
progeny. Better to raise a few, finely tuned offspring.
Such species are k- strategists (k is the measure of
environmental "carrying capacity" in the same set of
equations).

HOMEOSTASIS AND FEEDBACK

Both from an engineering and from a biological viewpoint,
living systems look adapted to their regular environments. The
epitome of that impression is surely found in L.J. Henderson's book
"The Fitness of the Environment" (1913).

(pp. 1-6)
With a suddenness which to many seemed catastrophic
Darwin's hypothesis of natural selection changed the whole
aspect of the problem (of purpose). Law appeared as the
basis of purpose just as it had appeared as the basis of
order, and adaptations become, in the judgement of most
men, the necessary results of an automatic process.
Today,.... there is no longer room for doubt that the
fitness of organic beings for their life in the world has
been won in whole or in part by an almost infinite series
of adaptations of life to its environment, whereby,
through a corresponding series of transformations, present
complexity has grown out of former simplicity.

The great and fruitful ideas which Darwin brought to
the attention of the whole world have long since been
incorporated in human thought. Not the least important
among them is the new scientific concept of fitness, as it

emerges from the discussion of natural selection. Before
Darwin, this concept possessed all the vagueness of an
idea which, though in part founded an observation, was not
to be explained with the help of existing scientific
theories. But although Darwin's fitness involves that
which fits and that which is fitted, or more correctly a
reciprocal relationship, it has been the habit of
biologists since Darwin to consider only the adaptations
of the living organism to the environment. For them, in
fact, the environment, in its past, present, and future,
has been an independent variable....

Unfortunately, contrary to Henderson, Darwin's work did <u>not</u>
solve the problem of "fitness," but intensified our concern about
it.

An attempt to create a theory of fitness or of adaptation, as
it might be seen from the vantage point of the <u>single organism</u>, was
launched by Claude Bernard (1878):

   The stability of the internal medium is a primary
   condition for the freedom and independence of certain
   living bodies in relation to the environment surrounding
   them. Physiological mechanisms have to function therein
   assuring the maintenance of conditions necessary for the
   existence of the cell elements composing them. For we
   know that there is neither liberty nor independence in the
   case of the simplest organisms in direct contact with
   immediate universal circumstances. The possibility of
   arranging their own internal medium is an exclusive
   faculty of organisms which have reached a higher stage of
   complexity and organic differentiation.

   Such stability in the internal medium applies to an
   extremely perfect organism, able continuously to balance
   outside variations. The greater the freedom of the
   creature with regard to its external environment, the
   closer will be, on the other hand, the connection of its
   cells with such internal medium, which will necessarily
   have to maintain perfect regularity in its qualities,
   possible only if it has regulatory processes in operation
   as precise as the most sensitive chemical balances.

Sechenov, in Russia, had similar ideas at about the same time
(about 1875; see the 1952, 1956 English translation):

   Generally speaking, the combined action of all the
   vegetative processes leads in the adult to a definite
   quantitative and qualitative status quo of all parts of
   the organism; in the child, it leads to an increase in the

mass of the body the quality of which remains invariable,
and in old people -- to a decrease of the mass of the body
with the same invariability of its physiological
properties.... What, then, is the essence of the
vegetative acts of the organism? It can be described as a
continuous, life-long chemical metamorphosis of the
external substances absorbed by the organism -- a
metamorphosis in which the organism itself is one of the
links.

Any organism is inconceivable without an external
environment for its existence; hence, a scientific definition of the organism should include also the environment
by which it is influenced. Since the organism cannot
exist without the external environment, all the talk about
what is more important for life -- the environment, or the
organism itself -- is absolutely senseless.

Finally, Walter Cannon supplied the name "homeostasis" to the
regulatory accomplishments of living systems (Cannon, 1929), and in
so doing attracted the attention of biologists to feedback.
"Homeostasis" is usually thought of as a settling down to fixity.
Although Cannon admitted the possibility of steady motion, this
caveat didn't stick in the memory of the scientific community.

As von Bertalanffy correctly noted (1968):

(pp. 160-161)
        ... the concept of feedback regulation... is basic in
cybernetics and was biologically formulated in Cannon's
concept of homeostasis.... As is generally known, the
basic model is a circular process where part of the output
is monitored back, as information on the preliminary outcome of the response, into the input.... thus making the
system self-regulating; be it in the sense of maintenance
of certain variables or of steering toward a desired
goal.... Phenomena of regulation following the feedback
scheme are of widest distribution in all fields of
physiology. Furthermore, the concept appeals to a time
when control engineering and automation are flourishing,
computers, servomechanisms, etc., are in the center of
interest, and the model of the "organism as
servomechanism" appeals to the Zeitgeist of a mechanical
society. Thus the feedback concept sometimes has assumed
a monopoly suppressing other equally necessary and
fruitful viewpoints: The feedback model is equated with
"systems theory" in general.... or "biophysics" is nearly
identified with "computer design and information
theory".... It is therefore important to emphasize that
feedback systems and "homeostatic" control are a

significant but special class of self-regulating systems
and phenomena of adaptation.

However inadequate his own General System Theory later proved
to be (see Berlinski, 1976), von Bertalanffy grasped well the
limitations of feedback control as an account of the regularities
and adaptability of biological systems. There is no general systems
theory based on concepts of feedback or optimal control capable of
accounting for intentional, biological systems. The limitations of
conventional feedback theory are many, and chief among them are the
requirements that goals and costs be <u>stated</u> <u>in</u> <u>advance</u>; that only
one controller be present; that reference values be provided as set
points; that high gain, high quality feedback loops be maintained;
and that some signals be compared (algebraically subtracted) to
generate "error" signals. There are negative feedback loops within
biological systems, but these are not the main basis of the
stability regime of the system, and they do not meet the requirements for formal feedback analysis. Very often there are multiple
controllers addressing the same system (e.g., the thermoregulatory
system), with the different controllers having only partially over-
lapping information. Under such circumstances, so-called modern,
optimal control theory produces equations that are intractable.
Worse than that, feedback control theory does not provide any fundamental insights into how biochemical, reaction-diffusion-convection
systems become self-organizing, and self-sustaining (autonomous).
Therefore, a different sort of theory is required.

Equivalent network modeling and computer simulation of
selected, limited physiological systems, and biochemical systems
will always help interpret data. Nevertheless, so far these are
very largely models <u>of</u> <u>data</u>, and not models <u>on</u> <u>theory</u>.

ORGANISMAL ADAPTATION AS MARGINAL STABILITY

Ontogenetic adaptation has to occur, if at all, within a time-
span less than the lifetime of the individual; in contrast,
adaptation of breeding populations occurs over generations. The
mechanisms of these two kinds of adaptation are different, and they
should not be treated together. The quotations from Darwin mixed
the two types. D'Arcy Thompson addressed organismal adaptation;
Dobzhansky, et al., addressed population adaptation (which
ultimately, of course, produces adapted or adaptable individuals);
Gould also considered population (breeding) effects, as did
Henderson. Bernard, Sechenov and Cannon focused on organismal
adaptations and so did von Bertalanffy. It can be seen that it is
essential, for clarity, to keep track of which of the two kinds of
adaptation is being discussed, even though organismal adaptive
competence may arise out of past population adaptations. (It can
also arise from unpredictable interactions between previously

neutral mutations, chromosome rearrangements, etc.) A proper treatment of adaptation in biological systems would have to deal with
individuals, breeding groups, and ecological niches. Adaptation,
then, is an hierarchical concept.

Readers with leanings toward informational rather than
dynamical views of complex systems will recognize, perhaps, adumbra-
tions of von Neumann's complexity threshold (von Neumann, 1963) in
some of the comments on adaptability. For, surely, there must also
be some **reliability** involved, for persistence. Von Neumann showed
that the synthesis of reliable automata from unreliable components
required a threshold of reliability for the components, and of
complexity for the system.

Ashby's Homeostat (Ashby, 1963)

A complicated, but not complex, system (it fails to maintain
itself with continuous, cyclic transformations of energy and is not
autonomous), was developed by W. R. Ashby to illustrate adaptation
and stability. One model of it (called a "homeostat") was
constructed from a few multi-pole, ten-position switches out of an
old telephone exchange; from two ammeter assemblies which had
current also running down the indicator arms (running in a wire
which ended in an uninsulated loop, which in turn dipped into a
circular-arc trough filled with slightly conductive salt water; at
the ends of each trough were contacts which moved one multi-pole
switch, if the wire went that far); and from a few other
miscellaneous electrical components -- wires, resistors, lamps, dry
cells, etc.

These were haphazardly connected together. When the dry cells
were switched in, the ammeter arms swept back and forth a few times,
the multi-pole switches clacked to new positions a few times; but
then the whole complicated haphazard device settled down, and as
Grey Walter said disappointedly, "did nothing." However, this
result was precisely what pleased Ashby about the device. He
pointed out that it was behaving homeostatically -- because, if you
were to push on one ammeter arm, or put more salt in one trough, all
parts of the system would adapt slightly; but they would come back
to their original positions if you stopped pushing, or replaced the
too-conductive salt water with more of the original solution.

An important additional property of Ashby's device could be
seen after the homeostat had settled down into its first stable
state. Ashby would then cut a haphazardly chosen wire, or add a
resistor in a whimsically chosen location. He noted that sometimes
very little changed, but that even when a larger state change
occurred (such as stepping of one of the switches), the homeostat
would settle down in some new state, and would reinstitute its
policy of "doing nothing." But it was not "dead," because pushing

an arm would still result in smooth adaptation of other parameters, and in return of that arm (and of the whole state) to its latest preceding stable position, if he again stopped pushing. And he could add connections, or cut them, several more times, before the homeostat would become sufficiently disabled to "die."

This unplanned, but typical occurrence of several steps or stages of stable states Ashby called "ultrastability," meaning that the haphazardly-assembled device not only found an initial stable state, but also usually showed series of stable (but not "dead") states, after random breakages (or additions) of one or another components. The stability in each state was static, i.e., the homeostat did not depend upon changing energy conversions for persistence of state.

In living systems, which are truly complex and ill-defined, states are maintained dynamically. Each state is only marginally stable. The challenge is to produce a physical theory that explains their marginal, dynamic stability, and their seemingly goal-directed behavior, without the use of a _deus ex machina_, or borrowed intelligence. Furthermore, we want a _quantification_ of "viability," or "homeostatic competence" or "adaptive capacity," based upon dynamic testing.

CONCLUSION

The selected, historical accounts of adaptation, presented above, give the biologists' views of one of the most fascinating properties of living things. These descriptions and reflections retain their freshness to this day, because we have not yet produced a satisfactory dynamical or informational account of self-organization, or adaptation. This book now attempts to show how modern scientists of different specialties frame the same, time-honored questions. Perhaps they also show the shape of the answers to come.

ACKNOWLEDGMENTS

I am indebted to my colleague Donald O. Walter for providing the description of Ashby's "homeostat", and Harry Soodak for the image of the "intentional" candle flame.

REFERENCES

Ashby, W. R., 1963, "An Introduction to Cybernetics," Wiley
    (Science editions), New York.
Berlinski, D., 1976, "On Systems Analysis: An Essay Concerning the

Limitations of Some Mathematical Methods in the Social, Political, and Biological Sciences," MIT Press, Cambridge, Massachusetts.

Bernard, C., 1878. "Lecons sur les Phenomenes de la Vie, Communs aux Animaux et aux Vegetaux," Balliere, Paris.

Bertalanffy, L. von, 1968, "General System Theory: Foundations, Development, Applications," Braziller, New York.

Cannon, W. B., 1929, Organization for physiological homeostasis. Physiological Reviews, 9: 397-429.

Darwin, C., 1902, "Origin of Species," (Sixth edition) American Home Library Company, New York.

Dobzhansky, T., Ayala, F. J., Stebbins, G. L., and Valentine, J. W., 1977, "Evolution," W. H. Freeman and Company, San Francisco.

Gould, S. J., 1977, "Ever Since Darwin: Reflections in Natural History," W. W. Norton and Company, New York.

Henderson, L. J., 1913, "The Fitness of the Environment: An Inquiry Into the Biological Significance of the Properties of Matter," (Beacon paperback, 1958) Beacon Press, Boston.

Neumann, J. von, 1966, Theory of self-reproducing automata. Part 1, Fourth Lecture: "The Role of High and of Extremely High Complication," edited and completed by A. W. Burks, University of Illinois Press, Urbana, pp. 64-73.

Sechenov, I., 1952, 1956, "Selected Physiological and Psychological Works," (edited by K. Koshtoyants: translated from Russian by S. Belsky) Foreign Languages Publshing House, Moscow.

Thompson, D'Arcy, 1961, "On Growth and Form," (Abridged edition edited by J. T. Bonner) Cambridge University Press, London.

Waddington, C. H., 1960, "The Ethical Animal," Midway Reprint (1975), University of Chicago Press, Chicago.

ADAPTIVE BEHAVIOR IN MANUAL CONTROL AND THE

OPTIMAL CONTROL MODEL

Sheldon Baron

Bolt Beranek and Newman, Inc.
10 Moulton Street
Cambridge, MA 02238

INTRODUCTION

Adaptive control is epitomized by skilled humans performing
manual control tasks. The well-trained, motivated human
controller is capable of adapting his control strategies and
responses to an extensive degree, in response to variations in
task variables, such as controlled element dynamics and input
characteristics, or to compensate for the controller's own
inherent limitations. In this paper, we examine some of the
human controller's remarkable adaptability in performing manual
control tasks and show that much of this behavior can be
explained and unified in terms of an appropriate model, namely,
the Optimal Control Model (OCM) of the human operator (Baron and
Kleinman, 1968; Kleinman, Baron and Levison, 1970; Baron, 1976).

Before proceeding to a discussion of several aspects of the
adaptive nature of the human controller and of the OCM's ability
to reflect it, it is useful to make a distinction between
controller adaptation and learning. If an automobile operator
owns both a stick-shift and an automatic-shift vehicle, he/she is
equally capable of operating either one and we say the operator
adapts his/her behavior to the vehicle currently being operated.
However, if the operator owns only an automatic shift vehicle and
rents a manual shift vehicle, a period of learning is required to
modify the preexisting behaviors to meet the requirements of
shift and clutch operation. Following this period of learning,
the operator can call up the relevant behaviors on demand. Thus,
in the present context, we will define adaptation as the calling

up of previously-learned behaviors suitable to the circumstances
and context of concern. Learning, on the other hand, will refer
to the acquisition of these desirable behaviors on the basis of
practice or repeated experience.

       In most practical cases of consequence this distinction
becomes blurred. Consider the transfer of experience from one
aircraft control to another for the first time. Certain features
of the behavior appropriate to one are also appropriate to the
other. Upon first exercise of the new vehicle the pilot utilizes
the multidimensional feedback available to discover those old
behaviors that remain appropriate to the new context, while other
features require new learning to incorporate them into his/her
repertoire. Still others fall in between where the pilot must
learn to modify old behaviors, but there will be considerable
savings in acquiring them based on the old habits. Finally,
although rare, a few situations are encountered in which negative
transfer is experienced in skill training. That is, more
practice is required to master new behaviors because of the
interference from the old habits.

       The above definition implies that, for the most part, this
paper will examine human control when the system is well-defined.
It is felt that it is essential that this type of adaptation be
understood thoroughly before control of ill-defined systems can
be considered.

       In the remainder of the paper, the OCM is described first.
Then various types of human adaptive control behavior are
examined. It is shown how disparate types of adaptation are
reproduced by the OCM and, therefore, how they are a consequence
of fundamental assumptions about the performance of skilled
operators.

THE OPTIMAL CONTROL MODEL

       In this section, a conceptual and verbal discussion of the
OCM is presented. The reader is referred to Kleinman, Baron and
Levison, 1970, and Baron, Kleinman, et.al., 1970, for
mathematical details.

       The human controller, if motivated and given information
about his performance, will attempt to change characteristics so
as to perform better. On the other hand, human performance is
limited by certain inherent constraints or limitations and by the
extent to which the human understands the objectives of the task.
These observations serve as the basis for the fundamental
assumption underlying the OCM, namely, that the well-motivated,
well trained human operator will act in a near optimal manner
subject to the operator's internal limitations and understanding
of the task. This assumption is not new in manual control (e.g.,
Roig, (1962)) or in traditional human engineering (e.g., Simon

(1957) calls it the Principle of Bounded Rationality). It is also consistent with the information processing view of skilled performance, which asserts that humans bring to any skilled task a collection of both capabilities and limitations, and the process of becoming proficient at the task involves utilizing and enhancing the capabilities to an extent that is sufficient to overcome or compensate for the debilitating effects of the limitations. What is novel in the OCM are the methods used to represent human limitations, the inclusion in the model of elements that compensate optimally for these limitations and the extensive use of state-space concepts and the techniques of modern control theory.

Clearly, if the basic optimality assumption is to yield good results, it is necessary to have reliable, accurate and meaningful models for human limitations. Insofar as possible, these models (or their parameters) should reflect intrinsic human limitations or should depend primarily on the interaction of the operator with the environment and not on the specifics of the control task. It is also desirable that the description of human limitations involve as few parameters as possible and that it be commensurate with the modern control system framework that is being employed for the analysis. These principles have guided the development of the models for human limitations that will be described below.

There were several reasons for employing a modern control approach to analyzing manual control tasks, even though methods based on classical control techniques had been fairly successful. Initially, the principal motivation was provided by the basic logic of the optimality assumption and by the belief that state-space techniques provided a systematic approach to multi-input, multi- output systems that avoided some of the difficulties associated with the application of multi-loop analysis to man-in-the-loop problems. The powerful computational schemes associated with these techniques also were attractive in light of the complex monitoring and control problems that were becoming of interest. The basic approach to human limitations and the optimality assumption appeared to suggest a model that might adapt to task specifications and requirements "automatically", and not through a subsidiary set of adjustment rules. Finally, it was expected that the use of a normative model[*] and time-domain analysis would facilitate "modular" and "graceful" development of the model as new facets of human behavior were considered and understood. These hopes and

---

[*] The model is normative in that it predicts what the human should do, given his limitations and the task. Thus, for a new situation one need only determine the operative limitations and what should be done. The fact that this assumption works well is testimony to the adaptability and capability of the trained operator.

expectations have been substantially fulfilled in the past decade of development, application and extension of the OCM (see Baron, 1976, or Baron and Levison, 1981, for overview of this progress).

In order to apply the OCM, the following features of the environment must be given: 1) a linearized state variable representation or model of the system being controlled; 2) a stochastic or deterministic representation of the driving function or environmental disturbances over which the operator must exert control; 3) a linearized "display vector" summarizing the sensory information utilized by the operator (including visual, vestibular and other sources, as appropriate); and 4) a quantitative statement of the criterion or performance index for assessing operator/machine performance (criteria such as minimizing rms tracking error and control effort are typical). The specific assumptions concerning this description that are necessary to apply the theory are given in Kleinman, Baron and Levison (1970).

Given this environmental description, the model of the operator's behavior incorporates the elements shown in the lower

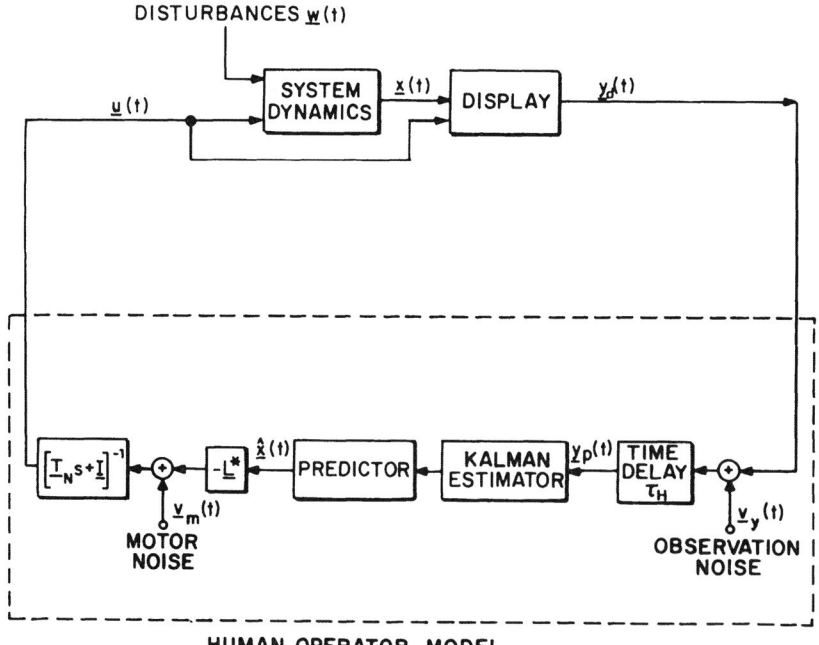

Figure 1. Structure of optimal control model.

half of Figure 1 (the upper half represents the system). The figure illustrates only a single dimensional control task but the variables illustrated should be regarded as multi-dimensional vectors. First, the displayed variables are assumed to be

corrupted by "observational noise" introduced by the human
operator.* This noise is analogous to the internal noise level
postulated in signal detection theory, and provides one means by
which the model can mimic human limitations in processing and
attentional capacity. Different noise levels may be assumed for
different displayed variables, and, if several visual displays
are providing useful information, the noise level associated with
each may be adjusted to account for the distribution of attention
assigned by the operator. Alternatively, a model of attentional
scanning (Levison, Elkind and Ward, (1971)), may be introduced to
predict the noise level and associated with each variable in
order to produce optimal performance with respect to the
criterion variable. This attention sharing model, which is
discussed in more detail later, is crucial for predicting
performance in complex, multivariable tasks. It can also serve
as a basis for developing a variety of operator monitoring models
(Kleinman and Curry, 1977).

At this point the model is dealing with a noisy
representation of the displayed quantities. That representation
is then delayed by an amount τ, representing internal human
processing delays. It is possible to assume differential delays
for different sensory channels, but this additional complication
has not been found necessary in past model applications to manual
control data.

The central elements of the model are represented in the
blocks described as the Kalman estimator and predictor.** Their
purpose is to generate the best estimate of the current state of
the system, based on the noisy, delayed perceptual information
available. These blocks compute the estimate of this state so as
to minimize the residual estimation uncertainty. What is being
captured is a representation of the operator's ability to
construct from his understanding of the system and his incomplete
knowledge of the moment-by-moment state of the system, a set of
expectancies concerning the system behavior at the next moment in
time. It is in these blocks that it is assumed that the operator
has both an internal model of the dynamics of the system being
controlled, and a representation of the statistics of the
disturbances driving the system. This representation is

---

* If visual or indifference thresholds are important, such as with
non-ideal displays or external visual cues, these can be
introduced in the model at this point (Kleinman and Baron,
(1971)). The method employed involves a statistical threshold
that results in a rapid increase in observation noise when the
signal is below the assumed threshold value. This is directly
analogous to the threshold notions of signal detection theory.

** See, for example, Meditch (1969) or the original paper by Kalman
and Bucy (1961).

analogous to the schema of current human performance theories, and it is interesting to note that, in this formulation, the schema must incorporate knowledge of both the expected signals and the system dynamics being controlled.

Given the best estimate of the current system state, the next block (labelled L*) assigns a set of control gains or weighting factors to the elements of the estimated state, in order to produce control actions that will minimize the defined performance criterion. As might be expected, the particular choice of the performance criterion determines the weighting factors, and thus the effective control law gains.

Just as an observation noise is postulated to account for input processing inadequacies, a motor noise is introduced to account for an inability to generate noise-free output control actions. In many applications this noise level is insignificant in comparison to the observation noise, but where very precise control is important to the conditions being analyzed motor noise can assume greater significance in the model. Finally, the noisy output is assumed to be filtered or smoothed by a filter that accounts for an operator bandwidth constraint. In the model, this constraint arises directly as a result of a penalty on excessive control rates introduced into the performance criterion. The constraint may mimic actual physiological constraints of the neuromotor system or it may reflect subjective limitations imposed by the operator.

As the previous discussion shows, control strategy and motor response are separated from information processing in the OCM. This structure allows the OCM to be modified so as to treat decision-making problems. The estimator/predictor portion of the model generates all the statistical information necessary for optimal decision-making, giving the assumptions that have been made concerning the system. Thus, by simply replacing the control law with an appropriate decision rule, one has a theoretical model for human decision making. For a normative model, the decision rule must be determined from optimization of an appropriate decision criterion (such as expected utility).

This, then, provides a conceptual description of the elements of the optimal control model of the human operator. It should be emphasized that the parameter values that must be provided by the investigator correspond to the human limitations that constraint behavior. With these limitations as constraints, the OCM predicts the optimal strategy and performance of the human operator. A large backlog of empirical research provides the data necessary to make realistic estimates of the appropriate parameter settings in the manual control context. This research has shown that these parameters are relatively invariant with respect to changes in task environment, thus enhancing the model's predictive capacity.

CONTROLLER ADAPTATION

The skilled human controller will adapt his/her response to the particulars of the control task, i.e., to the system dynamics, the disturbances, the displays or the criteria. Here, data and OCM model results are presented illustrating various instances of this adaptation. It is worth emphasizing that the adaptation exhibited by the OCM is a consequence of the fundamental assumptions underlying the model and is not the result of phenomenological changes introduced to "match" the data.

Adaptation to System Dynamics

Controller adaptation to changes in system dynamics is most readily seen and understood in relatively simple single-input, single-output systems. Consider a disturbance regulation task in which the controller attempts to minimize errors arising from random disturbances that enter the system. The correct strategy for the controller will depend on the system dynamics and the disturbance characteristics. Table 1 lists three systems, and a corresponding control law for each, that will yield "good"

Table 1. Simple System Dynamics and Corresponding Control Laws and Approximate Human Operator Describing Functions

System Type	Dynamics	"Good" Control Law	Approximate Human Operator Describing Function
Position Control	$\dot{e}(t) = K_s u(t)$	$\dot{u}(t) = Ke(t)$	$\dfrac{u(j\omega)}{e(j\omega)} = \dfrac{K_h e^{-j\omega\tau_e}}{j\omega}$
Rate Control	$\dot{e}(t) = K_s u(t)$	$u(t) = Ke(t)$	$\dfrac{u(j\omega)}{e(j\omega)} = K_h e^{-j\omega\tau_e}$
Acceleration Control	$\ddot{e}(t) = K_s u(t)$	$u(t) = K\dot{e}(t)$	$\dfrac{u(j\omega)}{e(j\omega)} = K_h (j\omega) e^{-j\omega\tau_e}$

performance, as predicted by classical control theory. In this table, e and u denote error and control, respectively, and a dot over a quantity indicates its time derivative. Note that the three different systems require substantially different control strategies. For example, for a system in which the error is proportional to the control, the rate of change of control input should be proportional to the error (or the control should be proportional to the integral of the error); on the other hand, for one in which rate of change of the error is proportional to

control, a strategy of making the control directly proportional
to the error is required.

These adjustments in control strategy, necessary to achieve
good performance for different system dynamics, are exhibited by
human controllers and are embodied in the well-known "crossover
model" of manual control theory (McRuer, et.al., 1965). The
crossover model predicts that human operator describing functions
will approximate the "good" control laws (in the frequency
domain) as shown in Table 1.* The describing functions account
for the portion of the controller's output that is linearly
correlated with the input; those given in the table are valid in
the neighborhood of the system's crossover frequency. (The
crossover frequency is that frequency at which the magnitude of
the open-loop describing function is unity).

Figures 2-5 (from Kleinman, Baron and Levison, 1970), show
both the measured describing functions and those predicted by the
OCM for the three systems in Table 1. The two curves in each
figure give the gain, $|h_e|$, and phase, angle respectively, of the
h_e controller describing function as a function of frequency.
System crossover frequency for these cases is in the neighborhood
of four rad/sec and it can be seen that the controller describing
functions do, in fact, approximate the desired responses in this
region. The OCM yields the desired behavior as well, which is to
be expected inasmuch as the notion of "optimizing" performance is
intrinsic to the model. These figures also show that the OCM
reproduces, with remarkable fidelity, the characteristics of the
human controllers over the entire measurement band. Though not
shown here, the model also matches the portion of the
controller's response that is not linearly correlated with the
input (the remnant). Moreover, this level of agreement is
achieved with hardly any variation in the parameters that model
the human's limitations.

Adaptation to Input Characteristics

The operator will also adapt to the nature of the
disturbance input; in particular, to the input bandwidth, ω_i. It
has been observed that as input bandwidth approaches and
increases beyond the crossover frequency that would be obtained
with low bandwidth disturbances, the controller will lower
his/her gain and, consequently, the system crossover will
"regress" to lower frequencies (McRuer et.al., 1965). This
strategy results in a reduction of error. In Figure 5, the
describing function gain predicted by the OCM is shown for
different input bandwidths (ω_i=.5,1,2,4,8). The system dynamics

---

* The crossover frequency, ω_c, and the "effective" time delay, τ_e,
  are parameters of the crossover model that depend on both task
  variables and human limitations.

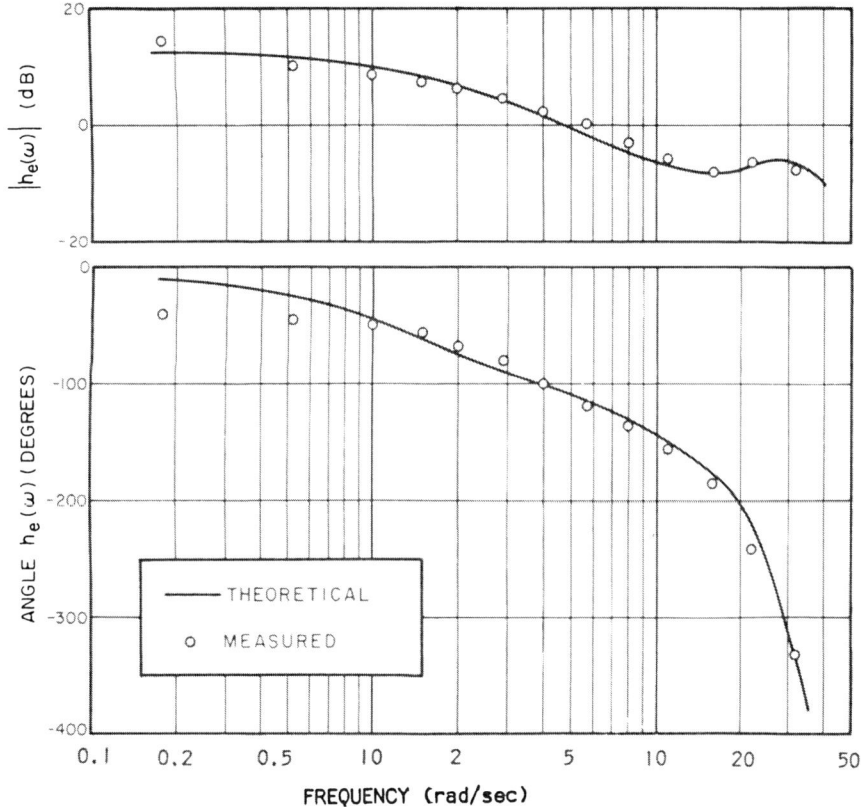

Figure 2. Measured and predicted frequency domain measures,
           k dynamics.

correspond to the rate control system of Table 1. The system
crossover frequency, as a function of ω_i, is given by the
intersection of the line AA'$=\omega^2$ with $|h_e(\omega)|$. For low input
bandwidth, crossover is relatively invariant at $\omega_c \approx 4.8$ rad/sec.
However, as ω_i nears this value, the OCM predicts that optimizing
performance results in a regression of crossover frequency to
lower values.

Adaptaton to Cue Presentaton

Skilled controllers can make use of a variety of stimuli
(cues) to perform their control tasks. Aircraft pilots make
particular use of the vestibular and tactile cues provided by
aircraft motion. An important question in the design of flight
simulators concerns the need for providing such cues in training
or research simulators. This has been a difficult issue to
resolve because pilots can adapt their behavior in response to
the presence/absence or fidelity of such cues.

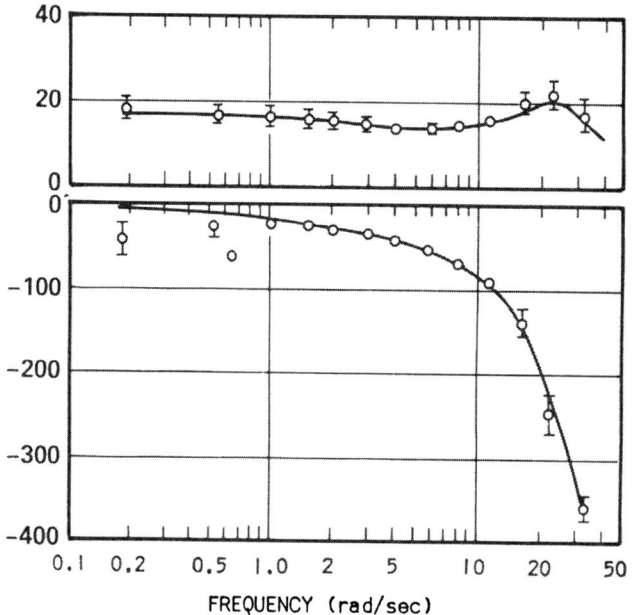

Figure 3. Measured and predicted, K/s dynamics.

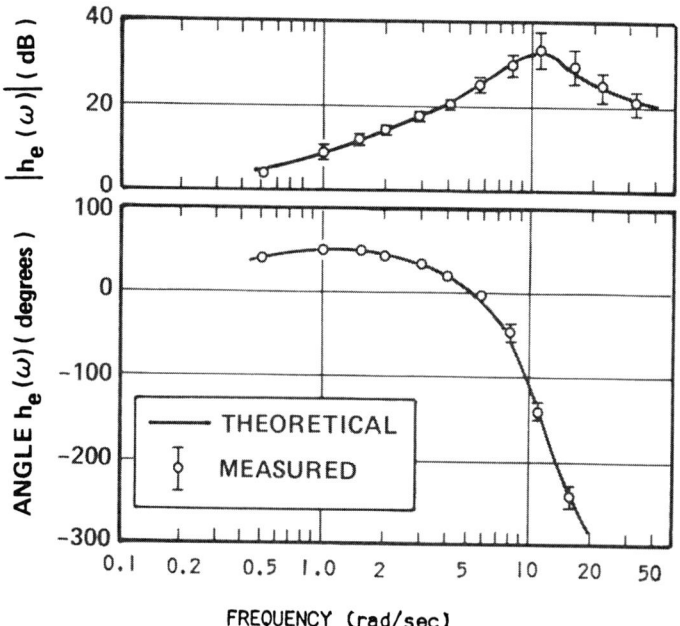

Figure 4. Measured and predicted, K/s^2 dynamics.

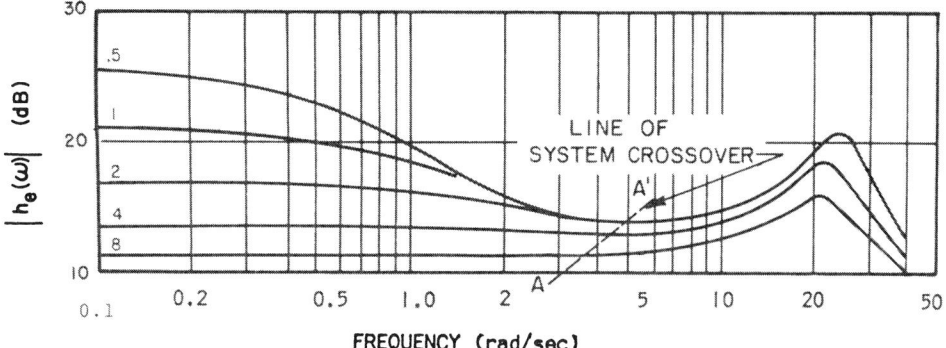

Figure 5. Effects of input forcing function bandwidth on model describing function gain, k/s dynamics.

The adaptation to cue environment was clearly demonstrated in a study of the effects of motion cues on roll-axis tracking conducted by Levison and Junker (1977). Subjects controlled a simulated high-performance aircraft and performed both disturbance-regulation and target-following tasks, under two conditions: one when only visual cues were available and the other when these cues were augmented with confirming motion cues. The two different tasks and the two cue conditions resulted in four distinctly different control strategies, as is evident in the describing functions shown in Figure 6. There we see that for target tracking, the only significant change is that motion allows the pilot to introduce some lead (positive phase angle) at low frequencies. On the other hand, for the disturbance input, the addition of motion cues results in an increase in low frequency gain and in high frequency lead. Though not shown here, the effects of motion cues on rms errors were also significantly different for the two different tasks: the addition of motion had no effect on rms error for the target input case but resulted in a substantial reduction in error for the disturbance input.

These tasks were analyzed with the OCM in an attempt to provide a unifying framework for understanding the four distinct behavioral patterns. The availability of motion cues was modelled by augmenting the set of perceptual variables to include position, rate, acceleration and acceleration-rate of the motion simulator. It was also hypothesized that the pilot would share attention between visual and motion modalities (see below). This straightforward informational model allowed accurate model predictions of the effects of motion cues for both the target-following and disturbance regulation tasks, as can be seen in Figure 6.

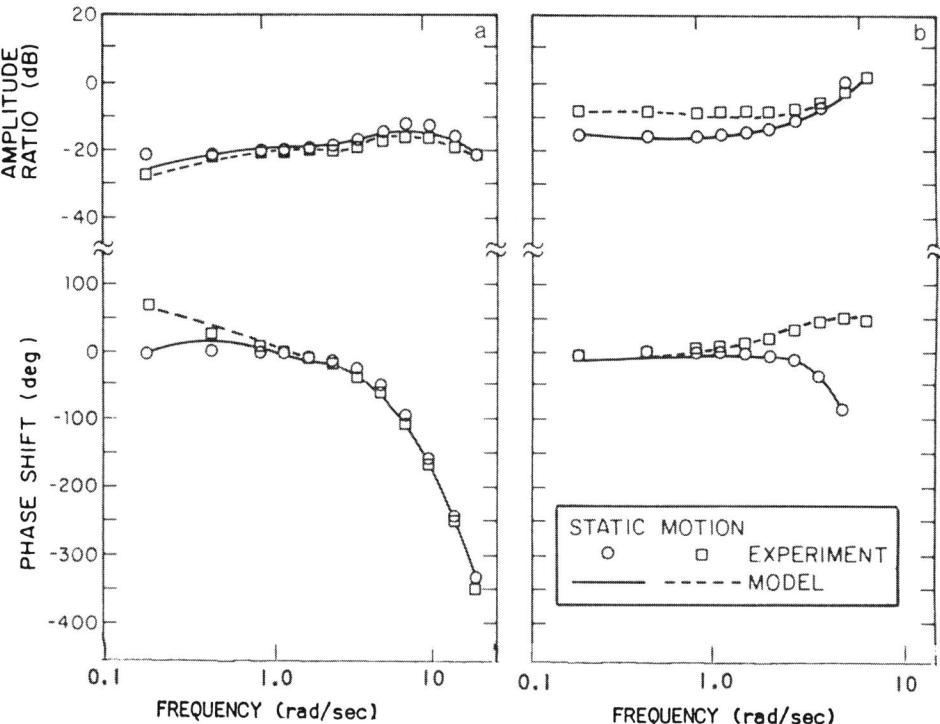

Figure 6. Comparison of model and experimental frequency response
average of 6 subjects; (a) target input and (b) disturbance input.

Attentional Allocation

When faced with multiple tasks to perform, or multiple
information sources for performing a single task, a controller
must devise, either consciously or unconsciously, some strategy
for allocating attention to the multiple tasks and/or information
sources. The development and implementation of an efficacious
attentional allocation strategy are recognized as important
components of expertise in tasks requiring such division of
attention.

The effects of multiple tasks on manual control behavior
were studied by Levison, Elkind and Ward (1971). They performed
an experiment in which subjects had to control four independent
rate-control systems with the errors in each system presented on
separate displays. The subjects were required to fixate one
display and use peripheral vision for tracking the other axes
throughout the experiment (i.e., visual scanning was not

allowed). The reader is referred to the source for further detail.

Figure 7 shows the effect of attention-sharing on controller remnant spectra and describing functions. The results are presented for the foveally-fixated display, but the other tasks (displays) show the same effects. From a phenomenological standpoint, the effect of adding tasks is to increase controller remnant (i.e., "noise") and high frequency phase lag (delay) and to reduce controller gain. Table 2 presents the error scores for each display condition when the corresponding task was performed in isolation and when all four tasks were performed together. As expected, the performance deteriorates on each of the tasks with the addition of other tasks, thus showing the interference effect directly.

A model for attentional allocation is an integral part of the OCM. Given a set of attentional factors, the model transforms them into equivalent observation noises, based on the assumption that reducing attention on a particular task variable can be represented by a corresponding increase in the base observation noise associated with single axis, full attention tracking. Thus, we are led to the following model for central attention-sharing:

$$P_i = \frac{P_o}{f_i} \cdot \frac{1}{f_t} \qquad (1)$$

where f_t is the portion of the "total" attention that is devoted to the control task as a whole, f_i is the fraction of that attention devoted to display variable i, P_i is the noise/signal ratio associated with perception of display i, and P_o is a baseline noise/signal ratio associated with a high workload, single-variable tracking task.

Typically, a value of .01(-20 dB) is associated with P_o, as it is representative of values obtained in a variety of single-variable laboratory tracking tasks in which subjects have been highly trained and motivated to perform to their limits. The effort involved in these tasks is substantial and a requirement to sustain such a level of attention to the manual control task over other than short or moderate periods of time would probably be undesirable in other than laboratory situations. However, $P_o = -20dB$ is not an absolute limit on human performance; control tasks that are extremely demanding have yielded substantially lower noise/signal ratios (Levison, Elkind, and Ward, 1971) (see below). Because of this, in workload sensitivity studies, f_t is allowed to take on values greater than one to compensate for the arbitrary choice of -20dB for P_o. The fractional attentions, f_i, are required to add to unity, i.e.,

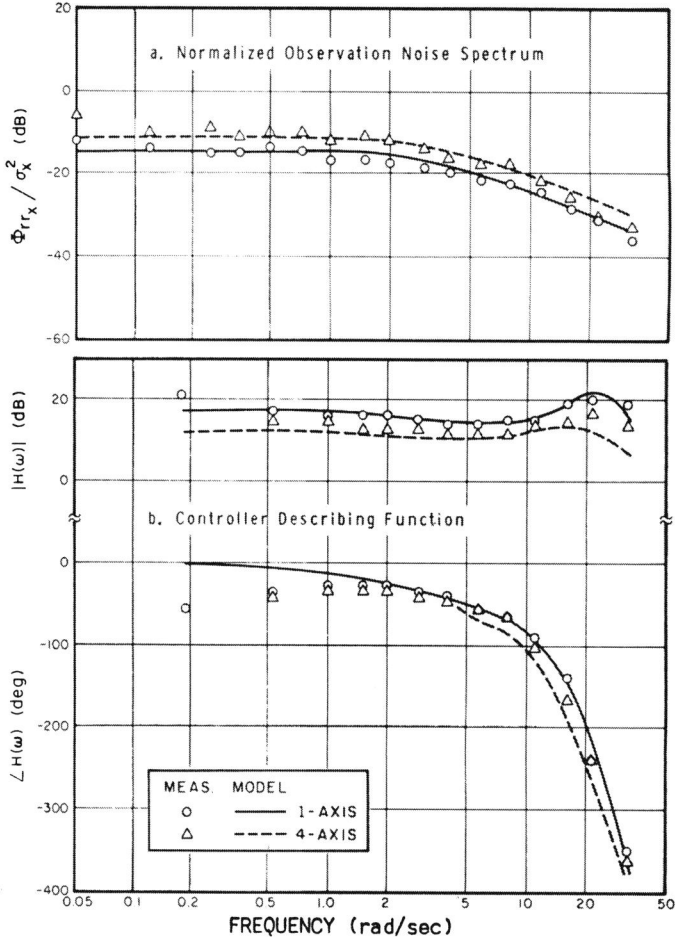

Figure 7. Effect of number of axes tracked on frequency domain measures; foveal viewing (average of 4 subjects, 2 trials/subject).

Table 2. Comparison of Measured and Predicted Error Variance Scores for 4-Axis Experiment

	Measurement	Foveal	Viewing Condition 16° Periph Ref Ext.	16° Periph No Ref Ext	22° Periph No Ref Ext	Total Score
(a) Measured	1-axis	.11	.25	.42	.96	1.7
	4-axis	.27	.94	1.3	1.6	4.1
(b) Predicted: Optimal Behavior	1-axis	.11	.25	.39	.98	1.7
	4-axis	.49	.82	1.1	1.8	4.2

$$\Sigma_i \ f_i = 1 \qquad\qquad (2)$$

When using the OCM to predict performance, the fractions f_i that result in optimal performance, subject to the constraint (2), are computed (Kleinman, 1976). These yield noise ratios P_i, via (1), that are used to determine operator and system performance. This was done for the task interference experiment described above, and model results are presented and compared with data in Figure 6 and Table 2. Apart from the overall agreement between the model results and the data, two points are especially noteworthy. The model results suggest that the limited capacity of the human controller causes an increase in controller noise (remnant). To optimize performance in the face of this increased noise, the controller adapts by lowering the control gain and performing additional filtering (hence, the increase in the phase lag). It should be emphasized that the OCM predicts that these adaptive responses arise to compensate for the attention-sharing limitation of the human controller. The second point is reflected in the results in Table 2. It is seen that the OCM predicts the effect of interference on total score much better than it predicts the individual scores.[*] This is apparently due to the fact that there is a relatively broad minimum for total score. In other words, in the neighborhood of the minimum, the total score is not very sensitive to tradeoffs in performance among sub-tasks. When this is the case, the system is forgiving and idiosyncratic behavior on the part of the controllers is tolerated. (This can be a desirable situation). Note that in Table 2 the subjects obtain a lower score for the foveal task than is predicted by the OCM. This suggests that more attention was paid to this task than predicted by the computed optimal strategy. This is not surprising in view of the minimal effect on total score and what probably is a strong psychological set in favor of concentrating on the foveal task.

Performance vs. Workload Tradeoff

Human controllers have the capability of trading performance and workload, adaptively. Thus, they can work harder to achieve better performance in the light of an unfavorable set of conditions. Or, if not sufficiently motivated, they may not choose to work as hard in one circumstance as another. Because the human controller may eventually "fail" when stressed by a high workload, it is important to be able to identify high workload conditions independently of performance. We will not examine this issue in depth here, but will focus instead on illustrating controller adaptation in terms of a performance-workload tradeoff.

---

[*] Subjects were instructed to optimize total score.

The parameter f_t in equation (1) representing attention to the control task as a whole may serve as a metric for task workload (see, for example, Baron and Levison, 1975).[*] It can be thought of as reflecting the intensive aspects of attention, as contrasted with the f_i which reflect the selective aspects. Thus, Wewerinke (1974) suggested that this parameter (actually, a related one) was indicative of level of arousal and was dictated largely by the properties of the stimuli. He employed this notion to develop a workload index which yielded good agreement with subjective workload assessments obtained in a series of single axis tracking tasks.

Early experimental evidence of the adaptability of the attention level with task variables was found by Levison, Elkind and Ward (1971). They studied a tracking task in which the vehicle dynamics were an unstable version of the acceleration control task shown in Table 1, namely

$$\ddot{e}(t) - \dot{e}(t) = ku(t) \tag{3}$$

For this task, matching the experimental data required an observation noise/signal ratio, P_i of -26 dB, as compared with -20 dB for all cases in Table 1; this corresponds to $f_t=4$.

The reduction in P_i (increase in f_t) for the unstable control task was explained by examining the sensitivity of performance (mean-squared error) to changes in P_i. In particular, the payoff for reducing the noise level to -26 dB was more than three times as great for the unstable case (Equation 3) than for the previously studied acceleration control task. Thus, the increased sensitivity of performance to workload (f_t) motivated (or allowed, through better feedback) the controller to achieve more precise control through reductions in his/her own noise levels.

The above notions have proven to be quite important in utilizing the OCM for system evaluation. For example, Baron and Levison (1973) incorporated the performance-workload tradeoff analysis in a display evaluation methodology which has since been used in several studies. The basic idea has also been employed by Levison (1979) in developing a scheme for predicting pilot opinion ratings of vehicle handling qualities.

Adaptation Within a Task

The above examples all involved human controller adaptation to conditions that remained fixed during the performance of a

---

[*] Alternatively, we may set $f_t=1$ and let P_o, in equation (1), vary and be the metric.

task. Thus, once the controller learned the appropriate
strategy, further change was unnecessary. Another form of
adaptation involves changing response behavior to adjust to
time-varying conditions, i.e., within task (rather than across
task) adaptation.

     Basic time-varying changes in controller strategies may
arise as a consequence of variations with time in the system
dynamics, the information base, the input or the criterion, i.e.,
in any of the relevant task variables. Each of these situations
has been examined in the literature and treated with the OCM (see
Baron (1976) and Baron and Levison (1980) for a brief review).
Here, we examine one situation, adaptation to an "apparently"
time-varying input because the example illustrates an interesting
aspect of adaptation and other important modelling concepts.

     The problem of interest involves the visual tracking by an
anti-aircraft artillery (AAA) operator of an aircraft executing a
straight-and-level fly-by. For this type of trajectory, the
target moves with constant velocity in Cartesian coordinates.
However, in terms of sight angle, that is in visual coordinates,
the motion is nonlinear, being described by inverse tangent
functions. As seen by the human tracker, then, the target
velocity, and hence the task difficulty, changes with time during
the course of a single fly-by. This can be seen in the target
velocity profiles in Figure 8. The point of maximum azimuth
velocity (zero azimuth angle) is called target crossover.

     Many attempts have been made to model the AAA operator, both
with and without the OCM. Much of the modelling with the OCM has
focused on choosing an "internal" model for the target
trajectory. Early work by Kleinman and Perkins (1974) and by
Baron and Levison (1974) assumed an internal model consisting of
a piecewise constant angular velocity (or acceleration).
Furthermore, it was postulated that the human did not know the
value of the incremental step changes in the target's angular
velocity (or acceleration). This approach assumes, effectively,
that the AAA operator does short term linear prediction of target
angular position (velocity) based on his/her current estimate of
target velocity (acceleration). The assumption allows the
overall model for the operator to remain linear which, of course,
is a very useful simplification. Moreover, model results
obtained with this construct predict the mean and variance of the
data with good fidelity up to target crossover and particularly
in the region where most hits are likely. On the other hand,
model results do not reproduce operator behavior subsequent to
crossover, regardless of adjustments in basic model parameters.
A comparison of model results and the data is given in Figure 9.
It can be seen that the operators were able to avoid the large
overshoot after crossover that was characteristic of the model

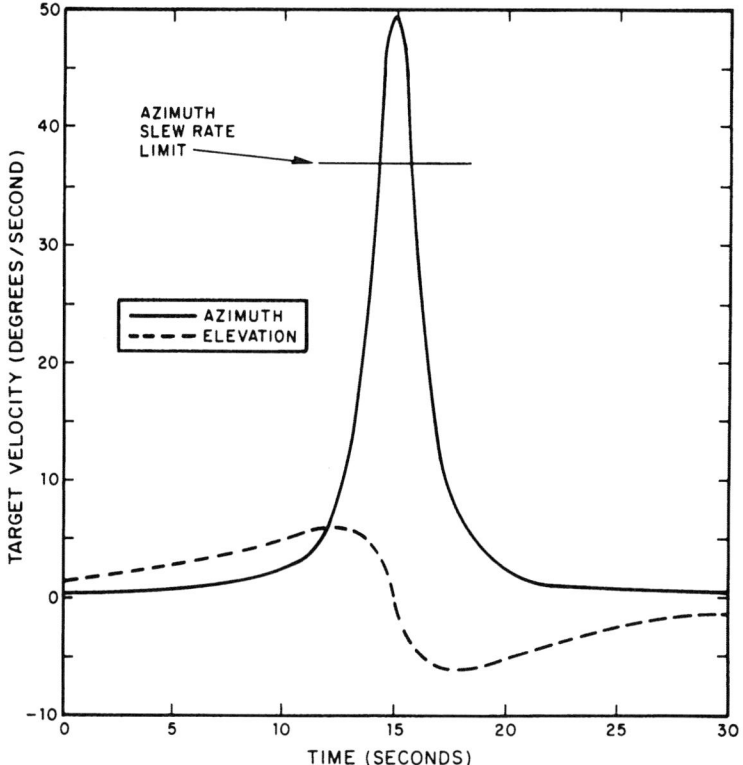

Figure 8. Velocity profile for target trajectory.

results. It seems clear that experienced operators can
anticipate that a target flying with constant linear velocity
will appear to slow down, in angular velocity, after crossover
and they can use this knowledge to adapt their response and avoid
large errors.

      Recently, we have attempted to capture the AAA operator's
conception of the task more directly to see if we could reproduce
the behavior after crossover (Caglayan and Baron, 1981).
Specifically, we assumed the internal model for the target was a
constant (but unknown) velocity fly-by in Cartesian coordinates.
In addition, target range was assumed to be unknown by the
operator. The visual observations were then related to the
internal states by the appropriate nonlinear, spherical
transformation equations. Thus, the OCM was given the correct
model structure for the fly-by, but with unknown parameters. The
difficulty with this conceptually appealing approach is
theoretical in that it leads to a nonlinear estimation problem.
To treat this problem, an extended Kalman filter was implemented

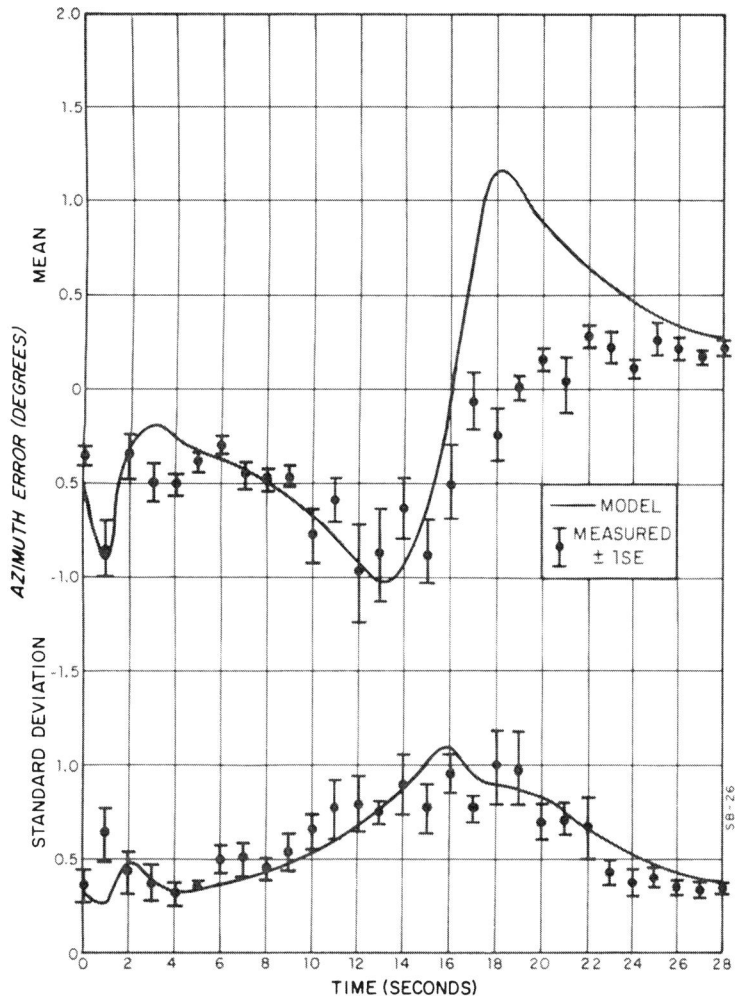

Figure 9. Comparison of model and measured AAA tracking performance.

reproduces the qualitative nature of the data in terms of the asymmetry of the error trajectory about crossover.* The results in the estimator portion of the OCM.*

Figure 10 presents the tracking error for this model. It can be seen by comparison with Figure 9, that the revised model

---

* The extended Kalman filter employs local linearization about the latest estimate of the state to compute filter gains. It retains the basic filtering logic of the Kalman filter.

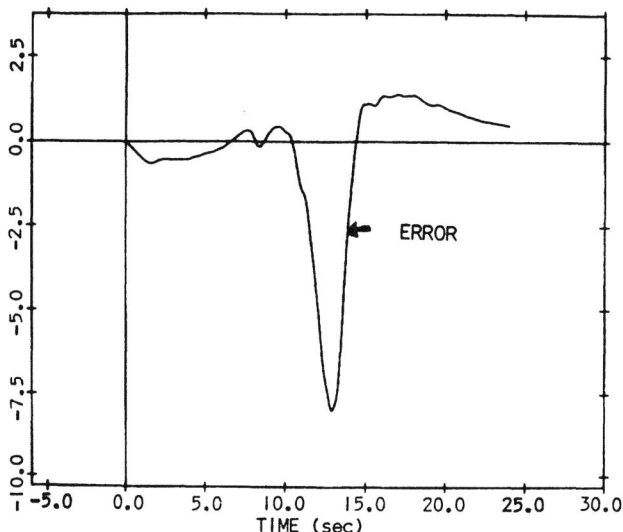

Figure 10. Ensemble mean of tracking error (N=15).

can be explained by reference to Figures 11 and 12 which show the model's estimates of target position (θ_T) and velocity ($\omega_c=v/r_o$). The estimates improve dramatically as crossover is neared which, along with the correct internal model, allows better prediction of target behavior after crossover and, therefore, reduced overshoot. Inasmuch as no other changes are necessary to make the OCM produce the desired qualitative response, we infer that the adaptive response of the AAA operator is based solely on learning or identifying the target's parameters (linear velocity and range at crossover) on the basis of observing its trajectory. It is of fundamental interest, as well, that formulating the internal model so as to correspond to the actual situation (and not for mathematical tractability) results in the appropriate behavior.

CONCLUSION

    In this paper, the adaptive control behavior of skilled human controllers has been examined. It has been shown that a wide range of adaptive responses exist and that they are predicted by a model that assumes the operator optimizes performance subject to a detailed knowledge of the task and the operator's own inherent limitations. Thus, for the (OCM) controller the system is completely defined, at least in a

---

* Quantitative comparison with Figure 9 is inappropriate because target velocity was different in the two cases.

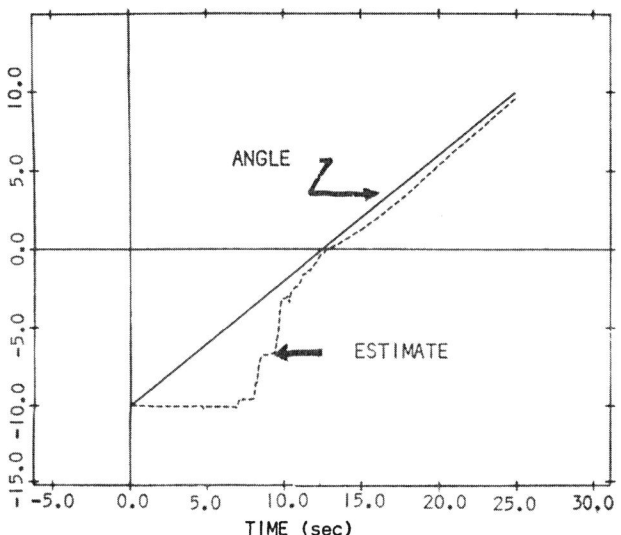

Figure 11.   Estimation of target azimuth angle (θ_T).

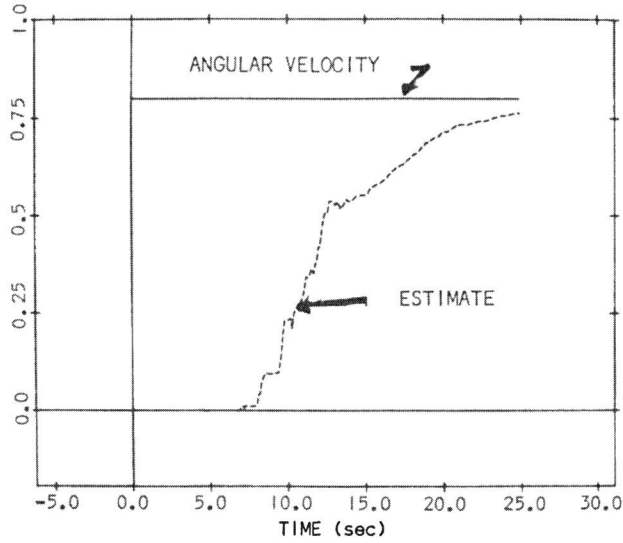

Figure 12.   Estimation of target crossover angular velocity (ω_c).

statistical sense (the input is random). Inasmuch as the OCM replicates the experimental data examined herein with substantial fidelity, it would appear that the assumption is well-founded for highly proficient controllers of moderately simple systems. A question remains about the validity of the assumption when the human is less proficient or the system is more complex; i.e., the system is less well-defined or is ill-defined for the human controller. Such situations have received only limited attention (e.g., Baron and Berliner, 1977) and, clearly, will require much more research before an adequate understanding of them is achieved.

REFERENCES

Baron, S., "A Model for Human Control and Monitoring Based on Modern Control Theory", J. of Cybernetics and Information Sciences, Vol. 4, No. 1, Spring 1976, pp. 3-18.

Baron, S. and J. Berliner, "The Effects of Deviate Internal Representations in the Optimal Model of the Human Operator", US Army Missile Research and Development Command Tech Rept. TD-CR-77-3, July 1977.

Baron, S. and D.L. Kleinman, "The Human as an Optimal Controller and Information Processor", NASA CR-1151, Sept. 1968 (Also IEEE Trans. Man-Machine Systems, Vol. MMS-10, No. 1, March 1969, pp. 9-16.)

Baron, S., D.L. Kleinman, D.C. Miller, W.H. Levison, and Elkind, J.I., "Application of Optimal Control Theory to the Prediction of Human Performance in a Complex Task", Wright-Patterson Air Force Base, AFFDL-TR-69-81, March 1970.

Baron, S. and W.H. Levison, "Analysis and Modelling Human Performance in AAA Tracking", BBN Report No. 2557, Bolt Beranek and Newman, Inc., Cambridge, MA, March 1974.

Baron, S. and W.H. Levison, "An Optimal Control Methodology for Analyzing the Effects of Display Parameters on Performance and Workload in Manual Flight Control", IEEE Trans. on Systems, Man and Cybernetics, Vol. SMC-5, No. 4, July 1975.

Baron, S. and W.H. Levison, "The Optimal Control Model: Status and Future Directions", Proc. of Conf. on Cybernetics and Society, Boston, MA, Oct. 1980.

Caglayan, A. and S. Baron, "On the Internal Target Model in a Tracking Task", Proc. of Seventeenth Annual Conf. on Manual Control, Pasadena, CA, 1981.

Kalman, R.E., and R.S. Bucy, "New Results in Linear Filtering and Prediction Theory", J. Basic Eng. (ASME Trans.), Vol. 83, 1961, pp. 95-108.

Kleinman, D.L., "Solving the Optimal Attention Allocation Problem in Manual Control", IEEE Trans. on Auto. Control, Vol. AC-21, No. 6, Dec. 1976.

Kleinman, D.L. and S. Baron, "Analytic Evaluation of Display Requirements for Approach to Landing", NASA CR-1952, Nov. 1971.

Kleinman, D.L., S. Baron, and W.H. Levison, "An Optimal-Control Model of Human Response, Part 1: Theory and Validation", Automatica, No. 6, 1970, pp. 357-369.

Kleinman, D.L. and R.E. Curry, "Some New Control Theoretic Models for Human Operator Display Monitoring", IEEE Trans. on Systems, Man and Cybernetics, Vol. SMc-7, No. 11, Nov. 1977, pp. 778-784.

Kleinman, D.L. and T. Perkins, "Modelling the Human in a Time-Varying Anti-Aircraft Tracking Loop", IEEE Trans. on Auto. Control, AC-19, 1974, pp. 297-306.

Levison, W.H., "A Model-Based Technique for Predicting Pilot Opinion Ratings for Large Commercial Transports", Rept. No. 4153, Bolt Beranek and Newman Inc., Cambridge, MA, July 1979.

Levison, W.H., J.I. Elkind, and J.L. Ward, "Studies of Multi-Variable Manual Control Systems: A Model for Task Interference", NASA-Ames Research Center, NASA CR-1746, May 1971.

Levison, W.H. and A. Junker, "A Model for the Pilot's Use of Motion Cues in Roll-Axis Tracking Tasks", Proc. of Thirteenth Annual Conf. on Manual Control, MIT, June 1977, pp. 377-388.

McRuer, D.T., D. Graham, E.S. Krendel, and W. Reisner, "Human Pilot Dynamics in Compensator Systems", AFFDL TR-65-15, July 1965.

Meditch, J.S., "Stochastic Optimal Linear Estimation and Control", McGraw-Hill Book Co., New York, 1969.

Roig, R.W., "A Comparison Between Human Operator and Optimum Linear Controller RMS-Error Performance", IRE Trans. on Human Factors in Electronics, HFE-3, 1962, pp. 18-22.

Simon, H.A., Models of Man, John Wiley ' Sons, New York, 1957.

Wewerinke, P.H., "Human Operator Workload for Various Control Situations", Tenth Annual Conf. on Manual Control, Wright Patterson Air Force Base, Ohio, 1974.

REGULATION, FEEDBACK AND INTERNAL MODELS

W.M. Wonham

Systems Control Group
Dept. of Electrical Engineering
University of Toronto
Toronto, Canada M5S 1A4

INTRODUCTION

In this paper we describe some recent developments in control theory, with emphasis on the problem of regulation and tracking. Our objective is to survey the key ideas in an intuitive fashion; for a rigorous treatment of the technical issues, the reader may consult the bibliography.

The broad concept of regulation and tracking will of course be familiar. As shown in Fig. 1, the basic ingredients are the following: (1) A plant (or main process or object to be controlled) which admits as inputs, control signals and, possibly, disturbance signals; certain plant responses are designated as outputs to be controlled. (2) The control signal inputs are supplied by a controller, on the basis of information obtained (via suitable sensors) about the specific plant response to the control and disturbance signals currently being processed; this information is conveyed by outputs that are directly measured. (3) In some form or another, a reference signal defines for the controller what it is that the controlled plant is supposed to do: the controller's task is to generate suitable control signals so that the plant's controlled outputs behave with respect to the reference signal in a prescribed way.

In so far as the information utilized by the controller in computing the current control signal represents current plant response (or nearly so), the controller is said to employ feedback; and to

W. M. WONHAM

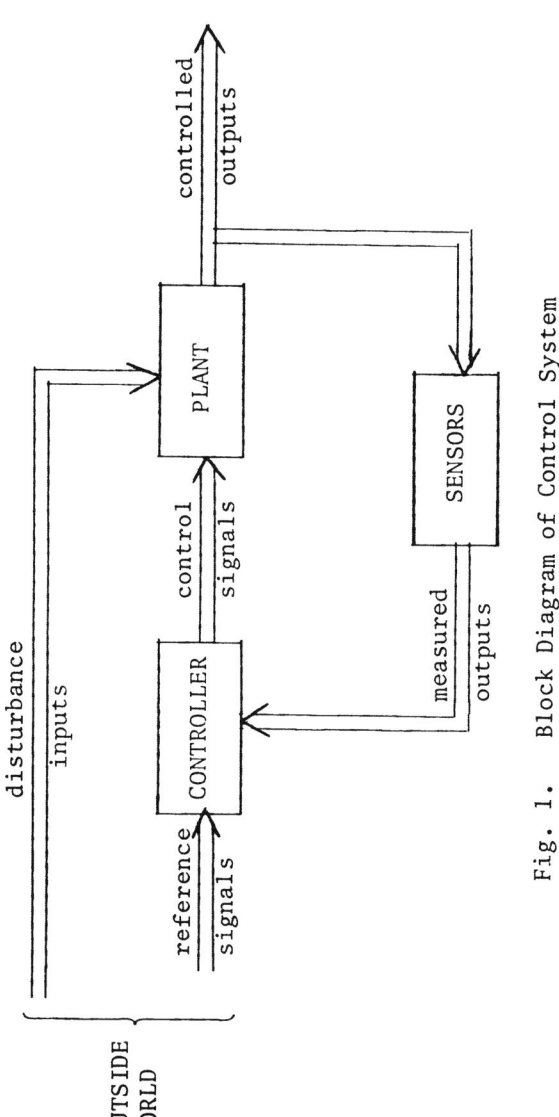

Fig. 1.   Block Diagram of Control System

the extent that the control computation utilizes future disturbance or reference values, the controller employs feedforward. In many cases the controller functions in both these ways at once.

All this will appear familiar, even trite, to the nonspecialist, if he considers some everyday example: take the plant to be an automobile, for instance, and the controller as the motorist in situ. Feedback information is the current plant response, which includes vehicle position and velocity relative to adjacent traffic; feedforward information might include the location of a traffic light or a bend in the road ahead.

Actually, the foregoing illustration can be made a lot more complicated in various interesting ways. For instance, a skilled motorist may succeed in manipulating gearshift, brake and accelerator so as to minimize fuel consumption plus wear-and-tear, subject to constraints imposed by his schedule, the highway code, and acceptable levels of risk; namely the control problem is formalized by means of a cost or objective function that is optimized.

In addition our illustration admits a multilevel or hierarchical version if we imagine the motorist as driver-owner, who controls his vehicle not only on the "fast" time scale (seconds) of dynamic control on the road, but also on the successively slower time scales pertinent to completing his journey (minutes - hours), regulating fuel level and maintenance parameters (hours - days - weeks), and operating his car as an economic unit subject to periodic replacement (months - years). These various "levels" actually incorporate distinct control processes in their own right, each with its own objective function and descriptive language, exploiting (say) differential equations embodying Newton's laws on the fast time scale, through to discrete renewal processes within some economic model on the slowest time scale.

If the control process at each level is modeled as a feedback loop, then our hierarchy of levels is perhaps best pictured as a nesting of the corresponding loops, with the fastest loop at the center. The controlled output of each loop, together with its reference input, generate (via a comparator and the loop controller) the reference signal or operating point (setpoint) for the next innermost loop, without which the latter's objective would fail to be defined; conversely an inner loop supplies the "infrastructure", or subprocess implementation for the next outermost, without which the latter's objective could not be physically realized. In general, stability and efficiency of the overall system seem to require the ratio of time scales from one loop to the next to be something on the order of two to ten (Allwright and Wonham, 1980).

Next, we mention the possibility of decentralized control whereby any of the foregoing levels may be split horizontally into

semi-autonomous components, that must be <u>coordinated</u> by the next
higher level (or next outermost loop), which now plays the additional role of <u>supervisor</u>. It is clear that decentralization may
well be needed to achieve the desired overall performance capability; in our metaphor replace the single car by a fleet of radio
taxis supervised by a dispatcher.

Finally we remark that our setup may be further complicated
by the presence of uncertainty at all levels about system parameter
values or even broader features of system structure.

What is our state of knowledge in respect to the questions that
have been implicitly raised? Quickly summarized, it is that control
and optimization of first-level linear multivariable systems are
fairly well in hand (e.g. Rosenbrock, 1974; Postlethwaite and
MacFarlane, 1979; Wonham, 1979). Nonlinear dynamics of low order
can usually also be dealt with, at least numerically, and structural results are available here for specific classes of nonlinear
systems, as for example the differential geometric theory of smooth
systems (Isidori et al., 1981) or (at the other extreme) the theory
of sliding-mode regulators (Utkin, 1978). Multilevel systems have
been treated mainly from the viewpoint of optimization, using ideas
of problem decomposition originating in mathematical programming
(Findeison and Bailey et al., 1980). By contrast, the logic or
synchronization problems of supervisory control that underlie the
software engineering of real time programs for concurrent control
processes have scarcely received any attention from a theoretical
viewpoint, such techniques as currently exist being drawn from
practice in the design of computer operating systems (Per Brinch
Hansen, 1973). Finally, current methods to reckon with uncertainty
embrace a range of mainly statistical techniques for on-line identification (estimation) followed by adaptive adjustment (tuning) of
controller parameters. In this connection, we may note the success
of self-tuning regulators in the adaptive control of first-level
linear dynamics with initially uncertain parameters (Åström et al.,
1977). Again, however, higher-level adaptive techniques in a
logico-linguistic framework (inspired perhaps by artificial intelligence) have not yet made much progress as a domain of systems
control. It seems likely that the present decade will witness
systems control, as a discipline, borrowing from and contributing
to the theoretical foundations of computer science (i.e. logic
and language conceived procedurally), just as in the past, control
science has been supported technically by Fourier analysis (1948-57),
differential equations and functional analysis (1958-69), or abstract
algebra (1968-80). However, at this time (1981) the paradigms of
control in logic and language have still to be formally articulated.

In the remainder of the paper we shall examine just one specialized but important group of problems: the regulation theory of
first-level, centralized, dynamic systems with known, time-invariant

parameters; but we shall relate the results to the general theme of "control of ill-defined systems".

REGULATION OF LINEAR MULTIVARIABLE SYSTEMS

Control theory is still largely devoted to linear systems (Rosenbrock, 1974; Postlethwaite and MacFarlane, 1979; Wonham, 1979; Byrnes and Martin, 1980). This section displays one particular formalization of the linear regulation problem in mathematical terms. To the reader unfamiliar with matrices and differential equations, the details of the technical discussion later on will be of no particular interest and may be glossed over. The gist, however, can be paraphrased as follows.

The behavior of the controlled system is described as a trajectory or path of its state x in an abstract, many-dimensional space, the state space X. The evolution of the state $x = x(t)$, i.e. where the path goes as time runs on, depends on the controlling input signal. The designer's objective is to arrange that this control signal be determined by the state itself ("state feedback control"), in such a way that two fundamental conditions are satisfied. The first of these, "internal stability", says that in the absence of any reference signal to be tracked or disturbance to be rejected, the system state path returns to a fixed equilibrium position (the "origin" or "zero state" of state space), where it happily resides until further notice. Now suppose that a reference signal or a disturbance (or both at once) appears on the scene. The effect is that the system state is suddenly displaced from the origin to some nonzero "initial state", and begins to move along a path determined by the feedback control. Where does it go? As time runs on, our path approaches arbitrarily close to a certain hyperplane in the state space. This hyperplane passes through the origin; it is determined by the detailed structure of the plant, the feedback, and the reference/disturbance signals; in our formalism we denote it by X_a. The situation is roughly as shown in Fig. 2, where X is pictured as 2-dimensional and X_a as 1-dimensional.

So eventually, for large values of the time t, our path x(t) will be driven into the hyperplane X_a. X_a is the smallest subset in X with this property; and for this reason X_a is called a "global attractor" (hence the subscript 'a') for the motion in state space. Different choices of feedback control will result in different orientations of X_a in X.

In order to state our second requirement, that of "output regulation", we must bring in one more geometric object. This is the set of states corresponding to zero tracking error, namely zero deviation from ideal system behavior. This state set is also, in the linear theory, a hyperplane in state space; it is denoted

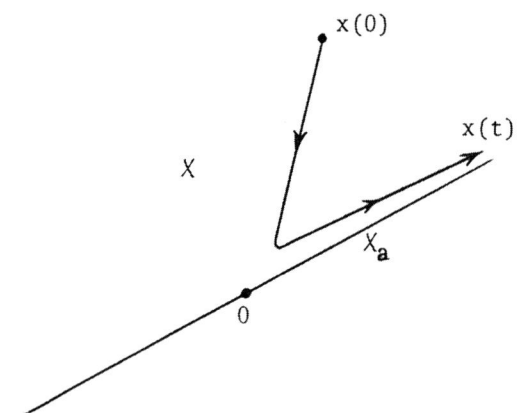

Fig. 2.   Asymptotic Behavior of x(t) as t → ∞

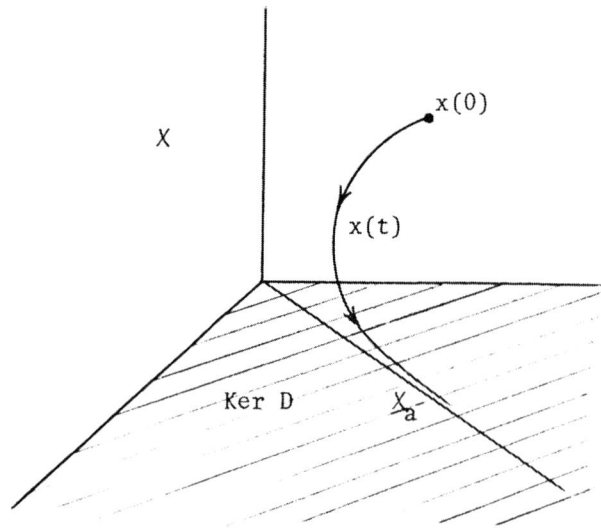

Fig. 3.   Regulation: x(t) → Ker D   as   t → ∞

by Ker D, for notational reasons that will be made clear below. Finally, output regulation requires simply that the state path be driven eventually into Ker D; but since we know it is driven to X_a, and X_a is minimal, our requirement takes the nice geometric form that "the hyperplane X_a must lie in the hyperplane Ker D" (formally, $X_a \subset$ Ker D). The picture is sketched in Fig. 3, in a case where the dimensions of X_a, Ker D and X are respectively 1, 2 and 3.

We now provide a few of the technical details, for the reader who has some background in control theory. In state space terms the plant (with state vector x_1) is described by a linear differential equation

$$\dot{x}_1 = A_1 x_1 + A_3 x_2 + B_1 u \tag{2.1}$$

One could alternatively treat a discrete-time version by the corresponding difference equation. Here A_1, A_3, B_1 are linear operators defined on appropriate real linear spaces; but we shall just suppose that the latter are finite-dimensional, so our operators are represented by matrices whose entries are real numbers. The vector u represents the control (u = u(t)) and x_2 the vector of reference signals and/or disturbance signals. To make the description explicit we suppose that x_2 is also determined by an equation

$$\dot{x}_2 = A_2 x_2 \tag{2.2}$$

Here no control variable appears inasmuch as (2.2) represents an outside world or exosystem which is inaccessible to influence by the controller. As a metaphor: x_1 represents the angular position and velocity of an antenna that is disturbed by wind pressure ($x_2^{(1)}$) and is to be controlled (by u) to track a satellite trajectory specified by $x_2^{(2)}$; here $x_2 = (x_2^{(1)}, x_2^{(2)})$. We also need to define the tracking error, say

$$z = D_1 x_1 + D_2 x_2 \tag{2.3}$$

as well as the variables that can be directly measured, say

$$y = C_1 x_1 + C_2 x_2 \tag{2.4}$$

As for the controls, assume (however idealistically) that

$$u = F_1 x_1 + F_2 x_2 \tag{2.5}$$

(i.e. $u(t) = F_1 x_1(t) + F_2 x_2(t)$) for some F_1, F_2. On setting $x = (x_1, x_2)$ and combining the matrices into block form we can write (2.1)-(2.5) as

$$\dot{x} = Ax + Bu, \qquad y = Cx, \qquad z = Dx, \qquad u = Fx$$

The problem requires that $F = (F_1,F_2)$ be selected to satisfy three conditions. The first is that the control respect the constraint that only $y = Cx$ can be directly processed by the controller, namely

$$u = Fx = \hat{F}Cx = \hat{F}y$$

for some $\hat{F}$; algebraically this means that F must factor through C, or (by a standard result in linear algebra) that

$$\text{Ker } F \supset \text{Ker } C \qquad\qquad (2.6)$$

Here Ker F is the set of states x where $Fx = 0$; and similarly for Ker C. Thus the set Ker D, already introduced, is indeed just the set of states x where the tracking error $z = Dx$ is zero. For technical reasons it is necessary to assume that C be rather special, in that Ker C is A-invariant. This means that if x is any state such that $Cx = 0$ then also $CAx = 0$; by some algebra, it follows that any free motion $x(t)$ (corresponding to setting the control $u \equiv 0$) that starts at a state x_0 with $Cx_0 = 0$ continues to satisfy the condition $Cx(t) = 0$ as time t runs on. Such a motion is said to be unobservable via the output y; and the condition that Ker C be A-invariant can be arranged (in effect) by use of a device called an observer.

The second condition we require is internal stability, namely $A_1+B_1F_1$ has all its eigenvalues in the left half complex plane $\mathbb{C}^-$, or some specified 'good' subset $\mathbb{C}_g \subset \mathbb{C}^-$, namely[*]

$$\sigma(A_1+B_1F_1) \subset \mathbb{C}_g \qquad\qquad (2.7)$$

Finally, the output regulation condition itself amounts to saying that, for all initial states $x(0) = x_0$, $z(t) \to 0$ as $t \to \infty$ with exponents in $\mathbb{C}_g$ as well. Since $\dot{x} = Ax+Bu = (A+BF)x$, we have

$$z(t) = Dx(t) = De^{t(A+BF)}x_0 .$$

Our regulation condition is therefore

$$De^{t(A+BF)} \to 0 \quad \text{as} \quad t \to \infty , \qquad\qquad (2.8)$$

exponentially as just described. We are now in a position formally to define the Regulator Problem with Internal Stability (RPIS): Given (A,B,C,D), find F to satisfy (2.6)-(2.8).

---

[*] For simplicity in this brief exposition, we gloss over issues of plant observability and controllability in writing (2.7).

Our problem can be made much more appealing by bringing in the state space X as a geometric object, together with the subspace of unstable or attractive modes $X_a(A+BF) \subset X$. This is obtained by factoring the characteristic polynomial $\alpha_F(\lambda)$ of A+BF as

$$\alpha_F(\lambda) = \alpha_{aF}(\lambda)\alpha_{gF}(\lambda) \tag{2.9}$$

where α_{aF} (resp. α_{gF}) has all its zeros in $\mathbb{C}_a := \mathbb{C}-\mathbb{C}_g$ (resp. $\mathbb{C}_g$). Then

$$X_a(A+BF) := \text{Ker } \alpha_{aF}(A+BF)$$

and (2.8) can be written

$$X_a(A+BF) \subset \text{Ker } D \tag{2.10}$$

Nex let $B \subset X$ denote the image of B, i.e. the set of all vectors b = Bu which are images of control vectors u. Let $<A|B> \subset X$ be the subspace

$$<A|B> := B + AB + \ldots + A^{n-1}B$$

where $n = \dim(X)$. The subspace $<A|B>$ is precisely the set of all states that can be reached from the zero state by applying arbitrary control inputs u to the system $\dot{x} = Ax+Bu$. It is then natural to identify $<A|B>$ with the state space X_1 of the plant. On this assumption, it can be shown that (2.7) can be written

$$X_a(A+BF) \cap (<A|B> + \text{Ker } C) \subset \text{Ker } C \tag{2.11}$$

Namely, any state that is both attractive, and can be expressed as the vector sum of a plant state and an unobservable state, must be unobservable. Finally our official version (Wonham, 1979) of the Regulator Problem with Internal Stability, is: Given (A,B,C,D) with Ker C A-invariant, find F to satisfy the three geometric conditions (2.6), (2.10) and (2.11) on $X_a(A+BF)$, representing respectively the requirements of realizability, output regulation and internal stability.

Despite its possible obscurity to the novice, the compact algebraic notation in which RPIS has now been expressed lends itself admirably (for the specialist) to an intuitive yet rigorous approach to a solution of the problem. This notational power is analogous to that of a high-level computer language, in that it allows the economical manipulation of the relevant concepts while suppressing irrelevant details of implementation or (in the present case) of coordinatization.

As stated, RPIS is purely qualitative. In practice a designer

will also be concerned with transient response, or how pleasantly
the limit (2.8) is approached; but this just amounts to seeking an
optimal F within the class of F's for which RPIS is solvable.

The basic issue is to determine when this class is nonempty.
The full answer is rather complicated, reflecting the possibility
of a subtle incompatibility between output regulation (2.10) and
internal stability (2.11). Here is a simple instance of how solva-
bility may fail. In the signal flow graph shown in Fig. 4, s is
the Laplace transform variable, and the branches 1/s represent pure
integrators.

One is allowed any control of form

$$u = f_{11}x_{11} + f_{12}x_{12} + f_2 x_2$$

where the f's are scalars. The objective is to stabilize the plant
while arranging that $z(t) \rightarrow 0$ for any initial value of $x = (x_{11} x_{12} x_2)$.

The reader is invited to check for himself that stabilization requires that $f_{12} \neq 0$, namely a signal path is created from x_{12} to u;
but this path, unfortunately, inserts an integration from x_2 to u
whose effect on z cannot be cancelled in a stable fashion by any
link f_2 from x_2 to u. Otherwise expressed, plant stabilization produces a signal flow of form shown below.

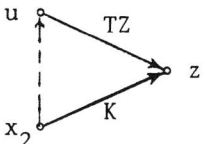

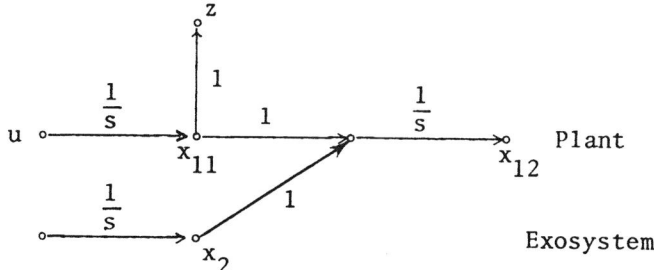

Figure 4. Signal Flow Graph of a Simple Regulator.

Here the branch labelled TZ incorporates a transmission zero at precisely the complex frequency (s = 0) of x_2. This "zero" blocks the error corrective signal (shown dotted) needed to compensate for the direct coupling K from x_2 to z. Furthermore, K cannot be reduced to zero by any "splitting" process involving merely a change in coordinatization.

We sum up by crudely paraphrasing the general result as follows: RPIS is solvable if and only if the plant's unstable transmission modes split the unstable transmission modes of the total system comprising plant and exosystem.

Of course in the rigorous theory these terms are given a precise, coordinate-invariant meaning; and the criterion just stated admits constructive verification (Wonham, 1979).

In the remainder of this paper we shall have to skip technical details and appeal very largely to the reader's intuition. Let us focus on the issue of structural stability. For regulation theory to be of practical use, account must be taken at least of small variations of plant parameters (but not exosystem parameters) away from their nominal values. We say that RPIS is well-posed at some parameter list p (in Euclidean N-space R^N, say) if it is solvable throughout some neighborhood of p. It turns out that RPIS is well-posed just when the mode-splitting property above is present by virtue of spectral disjointness between the plant transmission modes and the modes of the exosystem: this means that the plant, as a signal processor, is right-invertible for signals of the type generated by the exosystem; say the plant is quasi-invertible. When this is true, it is even true, remarkably, that a fixed-parameter nonadaptive controller exists that preserves the property of output regulation throughout a neighborhood of p. Such a controller (a strong synthesis) must be of error-feedback type (that is, driven by z), and must incorporate in the feedback loop a suitably reduplicated model of the (fixed) exosystem. These structural features, which generalize the well-known engineering technique of integral control, constitute what we call the Internal Model Principle. To summarize, our two major results (Wonham, 1979) are the following.

1.   RPIS well-posed $\Longleftrightarrow$ Plant is quasi-invertible

     $\Longleftrightarrow$ A strong synthesis exists

2.   Synthesis is strong $\Longleftrightarrow$ Control loop incorporates feedback and an internal model.

We conclude with a paraphrase of these results in terms of the picture sketched at the beginning of this section. With reference to Fig. 3, the orientation of the global attractor X_a in X will depend on the values of our parameters $\underline{p}$. In general, if $\underline{p}$ varies slightly to a nearby list of values, say $\underline{p}'$, the attractor X_a may very well "rotate out" of the containing hyperplane Ker D, and this means that the output regulation property will break down. Structural stability implies that any rotation of X_a under the influence of a variation $\underline{p} \rightarrow \underline{p}'$ must take place in Ker D. Very roughly, a strong synthesis works as follows: error feedback pins down X_a into Ker D, while the internal model provides sufficient (dimensions of) space in Ker D for X_a to rotate under parameter variations while remaining imbedded in Ker D.

REGULATION OF NONLINEAR MULTIVARIABLE SYSTEMS

      To what extent are the facts just described for linear systems capable of generalization? While this is still very much an open question, we can report a few preliminary results. The basic geometric object in the linear theory was X_a(A+BF), the subspace of attractive (unstable) modes induced in X by the action of the exosystem. If F solves RPIS, then the plant dynamics are rendered stable, and X_a(A+BF) is indeed a global attractor for the system trajectories $x = x(t)$. Because, again, F solves RPIS, this attractor lies in the subspace Ker D, and thus $z(t) \rightarrow 0$ $(t \rightarrow \infty)$ as required. So the essence of the regulation property is the existence of a global attractor induced by the exosystem and lying in a suitable, predefined subset of the state space.

      For smooth nonlinear systems this geometric picture has been partially recovered (Hepburn, 1981; Hepburn and Wonham, 1981). The state space will now be a differential manifold X, and X_a becomes a submanifold (the "center-unstable manifold") that we shall call the endomorph $X_a \subset X$. The subspace Ker D becomes a submanifold $K \subset X$. Internal stability will imply that X_a is well defined and is a global attractor, while the regulation condition amounts to saying that $X_a \subset K$. The situation may be visualized, in general, as in Fig. 3, but with Ker D and X_a replaced by a curved surface K, and imbedded curved line X_a, respectively.

      This setup may well prove to be a useful guide in design work. On the other hand, nonlinear design will invariably exploit a good deal of structure that is special to the application, and it would be naive to expect a general theory of regulator synthesis, even if one were possible in some nontrivial sense, to provide instant recipes for practical use.

      What can be said about structural stability, and the necessity of feedback and an internal model? In the simplest case, where the reference and disturbance signals are constant in time (i.e. constant over long periods demarcated by stepwise jumps), the linear results go through essentially unchanged. That is, nonlinear regulation against step inputs can be preserved under quite general plant variations (a Whitney neighborhood in the space of vector fields) by means of feedback of the regulated variable and by 'integral control' in each error channel. Furthermore, this structure can be shown to be logically necessary. Step inputs do not, of course, take one beyond the most rudimentary regulation systems. To achieve richer tracking behavior in a structurally stable way it is very plausibly conjectured that (under broad assumptions) <u>the plant itself must play the role of internal model of the exosystem.</u> In other words, for complex task performance the plant must be structurally specialized <u>ab initio</u> and cannot be regarded simply as a passive transmitter of control signals as it is possible (in principle) to do in the linear situation. As before, the feedback controller itself will serve to synchronize the internal model (now the plant) dynamics with the dynamics of the exosystem. Furthermore, this controller can admit a rich class of structural perturbations without affecting stability or regulation, provided it never blocks error corrective signals (the transmission zero behavior of linear systems already discussed) and provided such corrective signals are effectively transmitted by the comparator precisely when tracking error is nonzero.

In this sense the Internal Model Principle can be understood as a necessary, universal, underlying concept of high performance tracking and regulation. Stated baldly, its essential thesis is that "the more complex the task a system has to perform, the better matched to the task structure the system has to be". While this thesis may astonish no one, the job of the theorist nevertheless remains to confirm it with precision.

REFERENCES

Allwright, D.J. and W.M. Wonham, 1980. Time scales in stably nested hierarchical control systems. Large Scale Systems 1 (4), pp. 229-244.

Åström, K.J., U. Borisson, L. Ljung, and B. Wittenmark, 1977. Theory and applications of self-tuning regulators. Automatica 13, pp. 457-476.

Byrnes, C.I. and C.F. Martin (Eds.), 1980. Geometrical Methods for the Theory of Linear Systems. Reidel, Dordrecht.

Findeison, W., F.N. Bailey, et al., 1980. Control and Coordination in Hierarchical Systems. Wiley, New York.

Hepburn, J.S.A., 1981. The Internal Model Principle of Regulator Theory on Differentiable Manifolds. Ph.D. Thesis, Dept. of Electrical Engineering, University of Toronto.

Hepburn, J.S.A. and W.M. Wonham, 1981. The internal model principle of regulator theory on differentiable manifolds. Preprints, IFAC/81, Kyoto.

Isidori, A., A.J. Krener, C. Gori-Giorgi, and S. Monaco, 1981.   Non-
    linear decoupling via feedback: A differential geometric
    approach. IEEE Trans. Aut. Control, AC-26 (2), pp. 331-345.
Per Brinch Hansen, 1973. Operating System Principles. Prentice-
    Hall, Englewood Cliffs.
Postlethwaite, I. and A.G.J. MacFarlane, 1979. A Complex Variable
    Approach to the Analysis of Linear Multivariable Feedback
    Systems. Lecture Notes in Control and Information Sciences,
    No. 12, Springer-Verlag, New York.
Rosenbrock, H.H., 1974. Computer-Aided Control System Design.
    Academic Press, New York.
Utkin, V.I., 1978. Sliding Modes and Their Application in Variable
    Structure Systems. Mir, Moscow.
Wonham, W.M., 1979. Linear Multivariable Control: A Geometric
    Approach. Second edition, Springer-Verlag, New York.

THE DYNAMICS OF ADAPTATION IN LIVING SYSTEMS

F. Eugene Yates

Crump Institute for Medical Engineering
6417 Boelter Hall
University of California
Los Angeles, California 90024

The topic of this essay is adaptation of a mature, adult
organism to a challenging, sustained change in its environment. I
do not consider here the evolutionary aspects of adaptation at the
species level of organization. (As I pointed out in my companion
Chapter - "Biological Views of Adaptation - Some Historical
Accounts" - the ontogenetic adaptive capabilities of individuals
need to be distinguished from the phylogenetic adaptations of
species.) The approach I shall use is that of the branch of
nonlinear mechanics coming to be known as general bifurcation
theory, a splendid introductory account of which can be found in
Abraham and Shaw (1982). It is an extended stability theory that
claims to apply to the dynamics of complex, nonlinear systems. To
general bifurcation theory, I shall add ideas from the physics of
complex systems, that has been called "homeokinetics" (Soodak and
Iberall, 1978).

Complex Systems

For the purposes of this discussion, a complex system is any
system with substantial delays in the equipartitioning of energy
internally. The delays arise out of hydrodynamic processes in
chemically-reactive fields. Because of the delays, complex systems
appear to an observer to be "soft-coupled" - that is, the causal
connections between recent inputs and ongoing outputs is often
difficult, or even impossible, to establish. An extreme form of
internal delay is seen in systems that we say have "memory". If
memory is present, a complex system may even appear to us to be
acausal, in that we can observe changes in output (arising from

remembered traces of past inputs and internal states, and current
internal fluctuations) without any seemingly appropriate variation
in current or recent inputs.

A system does not have to be large, with respect to numbers of
components or levels, to be complex, though complexity tends to
increase with large number, but it does need to be highly inter-
connected. A network of 30 neurons is sufficient for cooperativity,
hysteresis, memory and reliability (Shaw et al., 1982), and a three-
dimensional array of 3^3 atomistic particles is sufficient to model
all three hydrodynamic transport modes: diffusion, wave propagation
and convection (see Iberall and Soodak, 1983). A hydrodynamic field
becomes complex when the atomistic entities that comprise it have
internal energy-transforming processes that can be affected by their
external interactions. Such fields are not momentum-dominated, but
rather are action-dominated. (Action is given by energy x time
product or the energy-time integral.) The bulk/shear viscosity
ratio has been proposed as a measure of hydrodynamic complexity - as
the ratio increases, the field processes begin to reveal complex,
nonlinear behavior such as hysteresis, thixotropy and memory
(Iberall and Soodak, 1983).

In tight or hard-coupled systems, which are simple systems with
immediate, deterministic or stochastic-deterministic correlations
between inputs and outputs, the causal linkages can usually be
successfully revealed by the study of lesions (e.g., if a motor
nerve is cut, its attached muscle won't contract appropriately).
However, the delaying internal processes of complex systems (soft-
coupled systems) make analysis through the study of lesions very
unsatisfactory, both practically and logically. A lesion of an
essential part may produce no short-term effect, or conversely, a
lesion of a part may produce a strong effect that is not related to
a normal cause in the intact system. "The Cartesian reductionist
view confuses the nature of the perturbation itself with the 'cause'
of the system's normal functioning" (Lewontin, 1983). Thus we see
why neurophysiologists know well what motor nerves do (tight
coupling) in the motor control of behavior, but not what the basal
ganglia (soft coupling) do.

Because of their internal delays, complex systems are
dynamically ill-defined, and that is the basis of their fascination
to scientists, who are usually brought up intellectually through the
study of fictitious, non-dissipative, tight-coupled systems
following conservative mechanics, preferably linear. Such systems
have only limited trajectories to rest or equilibrium states. To
analyze the properties of living organisms, including their capacity
for adaptation, we require a more generalized dynamical approach. I
plan to introduce an unconventional view of the physics of complex
systems to accomplish this task. For more background concerning
this physical construct, the reader may consult the following

references (Iberall, 1975, 1977, 1978; Iberall and Soodak, 1978; Soodak and Iberall, 1978; Iberall and Soodak, 1983; Yates, 1982a,b; Yates and Iberall, 1983). Table 1 lists typical attributes of complex systems.

Information and Dynamics

In this paper I shall take a dynamical view of adaptive control of living systems, because dynamics (motion and change governed by physical laws, and initial or boundary conditions) dominate the character of inanimate natural systems. However, in the case of biological systems the dynamical analysis must ultimately be complemented with some kind of "informational" analysis. For example, in the extreme case of computers (biological artifacts -- see Table 2) dynamics matter not at all from the point of view of the operator, because switching networks performing logical operations have absolutely arbitrary, non-physical dynamics. The laws of logic and the laws of physics are not derivable each from the other. Much as we may wish for a unitary world-view (one science for all) it may not be possible to account for all that seems interesting to us about biological systems without using a pluralistic approach. This issue is still unsettled, because information is only weakly a physical variable. It is not conserved; it is manipulated by arbitrary rules rather than by physical laws. It is time- or rate-independent.

In order to store or represent information, physical degrees of freedom must be used, and there are ultimate physical limits on computation (Landauer, 1976). But there also may be a limitation on dynamical analysis: it has been claimed that no adaptive or planning system can be based upon dynamics alone (Rosen, 1974), and that such systems have an absolute requirement for a time-independent, informational, internal representation of aspects of themselves and/or their external environments (see also the chapter by Wonham, this volume). Rosen claims that without these static representations, a dynamical infinite-regress would be encountered in such systems.

For a readable account of the view that an information theoretic must be added to physical science, see Campbell (1982) who believes that:

> Evidently nature can no longer be seen as matter and energy alone. Nor can all her secrets be unlocked with the keys of chemistry and physics, brilliantly successful as these two branches of science have been in our century. A third component is needed for any explanation of the world that claims to be complete. To the powerful theories of chemistry and physics must be added a late arrival: a theory of information. Nature must be interpreted as matter, energy, and information.

From a different persepective, Pattee (1977) claims that complex
systems have both linguistic (informational) modes and dynamical
modes, and that these are complementary in the technical, physical
sense. In contrast to both Campbell and Pattee, I have hope that
the physical dynamics of complex systems will prove adequate to
account for both their dynamic and their linguistic modes. I am not
convinced that information science necessarily lies outside of
physics, nor that it is complementary to dynamics, though admittedly
it has not yet been reduced to physics epistemologically.

Shannon information theory entropy (H) (or its associated
selective information) and statistical mechanical (Boltzmann)
entropy (S) are formally related (see Brillouin, 1962). (Therefore,
both are related to classical thermodynamic macroscopic entropy
too.)

$$S = k \ln W \tag{1a}$$

where k is Boltzmann's constant, and W specifies the number of
microstates representing possible, equilibrium arrangements of
the parts of the system

$$H = -\sum p_i \log_2 p_i \tag{1b}$$

where H is the entropy of a selection, i is one kind of
representation from a long sequence (or large set) of representations, p_i is the prior probability of the occurrence of i and
hence its average frequency of occurrence. (The p_i's do not
all have to be equal.) H is also called the average amount of
selective information per representation.

The identity of H and S does not, however, accomplish a physical
account of the context-dependent signalling and "interpretations"
(changed dynamic contingencies) observed universally in biological
systems. Even the blowfly, which appears to be absolutely incapable
of learning, changes its response to osmic stimuli when its gut
becomes empty and contracts vigorously (C. Gallistel, personal
communication). The state of the gut establishes the context for
the interpretation of smells. This fact is not an example of
Fisher-Shannon-Weaver-Hartley-Nyquist-Szilard-von Neumann-Pearson
information in transmission lines or channels, but is something
beyond.

DYNAMICS AND STABILITY

Dynamics is the physical science of lawful motion and change.
Deterministic dynamical behavior can be represented either in

continuous system form or in discrete-time form. In the continuous
system view, dynamic behavior is usually abstracted in a broad
vector equation:

$$\dot{X} = f(X,\ Z,\ P_1\ \ldots\ P_n, U, t) \qquad X = X_0 \text{ at } t = 0 \qquad (2)$$

where: X is the state vector

Z is the (usually additive) noise vector

$P_1 \ldots P_n$ are parameters in the dynamical and auxiliary
equations

U is the vector input to the system, possibly from
controllers, but also from the environment

t is time

$f(\cdot)$ specifies the dynamical laws of the system.

Including t as an argument emphasizes that most real systems
have parameters that change in time (albeit slowly, compared to the
time constants or frequencies of the dynamics inherent in the
function $f(\cdot)$, the equation of motion). These nonautonomous aspects
of the system, expressible through its P(t)'s, are of at least two
kinds: 1) decay -- the aging or senescence or wearing-out of the
system, so that it becomes less competent to perform its functions,
and less likely to endure; 2) adaptation -- the stabilizing
adjustment of parameter values (and even of system structure --
which is presumably an expression of changes in parameter values at
a lower level), to any repeated or continuous inputs of the system
that initially tend to drive it toward instability at an extreme of
one or another of its characteristic behaviors. A "characteristic
behavior" is a behavior consistent with the persistence of the
system while its originally paramount forms and functions remain
intact. A model of state and change for any (non-symbol-dominated!)
macroscopic system may involve parameters, noise, dynamical laws,
boundary conditions, control laws and other auxiliary statements.
In some cases initial conditions matter, but not always.

As mentioned above, an informational view may be needed to
complete or extend the dynamical view. The estimate of that need is
a deep unsolved problem. In physics, dissipation, entropy,
information and probability are related, but each is only poorly
understood, described or defined.

Stability

For abstracted linear systems (i.e., linear models) the eigenvalues of their equations express the stability properties. The

presence of:

    a)   all negative real parts implies asymptotic stability,
    b)   some positive real parts implies conditional stability,
    c)   all positive real parts implies instability, and
    d)   all zero real parts implies neutral stability.

    For nonlinear systems with one degree of freedom, the Poincaré-
Bendixson theorem specifies that any physical stability regime or
locus (attractor) is either a limit point or a limit cycle in a
phase plane representation. But the proofs draw heavily on the ·
assumption of two-dimensionality of the phase portrait. Dynamical
systems can be pictured for convenience by a "phase space" of twice
as many dimensions as the system has total degrees of freedom. In
the phase space each degree of freedom is specified by two numbers -
a "spatial" magnitude coordinate and a tangent, velocity vector.
The instantaneous state is a point in phase space, and the motion as
time passes is a trajectory in the space. The trajectories can
originate from all possible initial conditions, and are governed by
a set of n first-order differential equations, where n is the number
of degrees of freedom of the system, $P_1, P_2, \ldots P_m$ are the parameters
and x_i is a state variable. In general,

$$\frac{dx_i}{dt} = f_i(x_1, x_2, \ldots x_n; P_1, P_2, \ldots P_m) \qquad i = 1, 2, \ldots n \qquad (3)$$

Conservations act as constraints that reduce the dimensionality by
binding some of the state variables to each other, thereby
diminishing the degrees of freedom. Nonholonomic (non-integrable)
constraints further reduce the dimensionality, because they limit
the possible trajectories available to the system when it is in
motion. Any system that has fewer degrees of freedom in motion than
it has at rest is under a nonholonomic constraint. Biological
systems are such systems, and exhibit numerous many-to-few mappings
(e.g., genotype-phenotype).

    The above, classical approach to dynamics is inadequate to
describe the stability and adaptive capability of a living organism.
We need a nonlinear mechanics for systems of high dimensionality and
of marginal stability. In dimensions higher than two, the compact
regions of topological state space to which nonlinear systems tend,
from their initial conditions, can be "strange" or "chaotic"
attractors (the Roessler or Lorenz attractors are examples for
physical systems of rather low dimensionality -- see the volume
edited by R. H. G. Helleman, 1980, for numerous accounts of such
nonlinear dynamics). Chaotic attractors represent a new class of
mathematical objects. They arise from systems describable by
deterministic, continuous differential equations, or by
deterministic difference equations. Chaotic dynamics are
characterized by flows in phase space in which orbits converge to an

attractor which is neither a fixed point, nor a limit cycle. The "equilibrium" behavior is motional, but aperiodic; it may look very stochastic, but under other parameter values it may generate lines in its power spectrum. Thus the spectral properties of the dynamics are varied: the lines in the spectrum may suggest colored noise, or there may be a broad band like that resembling the spectrum of an aperiodic system.

Chaotic dynamics are usually very sensitive to initial conditions, and a slight change in the initial conditions may lead to very divergent pathways to different attractors in phase space, at which the "memory" of the initial conditions is lost. The classical Lyapunov stability criterion may not apply. This is a qualitative test that asks to what extent small perturbations may affect nearby trajectories: if the nearby, perturbed trajectories converge to a small neighborhood of the original equilibrium point or cycle in phase space, the system has Lyapunov stability. But none of the above topological objects describes the stability regimes of biological systems. Empirically we find that biological systems express their stability in the form of a trajectory through a closed loop of only marginally stable behaviorial modes. In the case of the human being, the total number of behavioral modes is about 20, of which half to three quarters are in the global stability loop (Yates et al., 1972). A cyclic trajectory through about 10-15 modes represents the global stability of the system, i.e., the global stability is itself a dynamic, nonlinear stability of the asymptotic, orbital, near-periodic type. This unusual stability regime requires mathematical description not yet available. Roessler has proposed a new, generalized, high-dimensional, limit cycle stability regime that he calls "hyperchaos" (Roessler, 1979) that may be pertinent. As I have pointed out elsewhere (Yates, 1982b), any physical theory of an organism that would be useful in biology would have to describe and predict the peculiar stability characteristics we see in multi-cellular forms of life, for example in mammals. Mammals don't buzz about with the randomness of Brownian movement, nor do they dance with the stately, clockwork rhythms of the planets, stars, and galaxies.

The problem, as I see it, is to find relatively low-dimensional, near-periodic attractors for high-dimensional nonlinear, nonconservative systems. At any given time, such systems will be able to find only one attractor region out of the set of possible attractors, and will manifest only one behavioral mode for a while. We need to map high-dimensional dynamics onto lower dimensional basins of attraction.

Behavioral Modes

In music a mode is either a fixed scheme of intervals of the

eight diatonic tones of an octave, or a rhythmical scheme. It is
the latter sense that is analogous to the technical use of "mode" in
mechanics. Specifically, for example, in conservative, linear,
mechanical systems with two (or more) degrees of freedom, the
equation of motion can be transformed into a set of separated
equations, each describing the motion of one variable (i.e., the
response matrix is diagonalized).

Each variable, x_1, may have an independent oscillatory
behavior, so that in the complete system we find a composite motion.
Normal modes are rhythmic patterns that emerge from the composite
behavior. A double pendulum (one hanging below and attached to the
other) is a simple example. It possesses two normal modes for one
parameter set:

1) the low frequency mode in which the two pendula swing in
   the same direction, and

2) a high frequency mode in which they go in opposite
   directions.

Whatever way the pendula are started up, the system will pass
through these two modes repeatedly.

In the case of nonconservative, nonlinear systems, which is the
case of actual interest here, pure normal modes do not exist. The
system cannot always be analyzed into a set of separate, explicit
equations for each variable, and even when that is possible, the
system usually possesses only one "behavioral mode" for a given
parameter set. As a proposal based on experimental observation, we
have introduced the notion that nonlinear, nonconservative systems
also have normal modes (Yates and Iberall, 1973), characterized by
cyclic behaviors (as described in the next section). The proposal
claims that a behavioral mode of a complex, nonlinear, nonconservative biological system is a distinctive performance in which
some particular group of limit-cycling subsystems are mutually
entrained so as to produce a marginally-stable condition. Each
marginally-stable condition (behavioral mode) defines a particular
kind of action for the whole system. Each mode is characterized by
a (broad) line spectrum.

A "mode," generalized to include nonlinearity, is the behavior
in a compact region of phase space in which a system may reside
(marginally stable) for only a limited period of time. Nonlinear
modes differ from each other on either of two structural bases: 1)
the membership in a group of mutually-entrained oscillators differs,
or 2) the parameters of the same oscillators in the group are
changed from mode to mode. These possibilities are not mutually
exclusive. Transitions from one mode to another are not difficult,
because there are no high energy barriers between them. The various

modes are nearly equienergetic. Transitions are provoked by cues
(switching signals) that may arise internally or externally, and may
be either aperiodic or periodic. In living systems a closed
trajectory among the behavioral modes is initiated and assured by
internal "information" transports (see later section: Physical
Basis of Language). In my view, this high level, closed trajectory
manifests the properties of a Markov chain, in which past states
influence the transitional probabilities among the various modes.

Physical Stability of Complex, Autonomous Systems

For any system that is thermodynamically open to mass, energy
or even "information", and that can persist both in a varying
environment, or in a time-invariant environment (i.e., it has
physical autonomy), we must have a physical theory of its stability,
because persistence of an open system is never trivial. In such a
persistent system, adaptation becomes a problem in structural
stability, that is, in parameter change stability. (Such physically
autonomous systems are mathematically nonautonomous.) In all cases
of life stability (persistence with bounded performance) is an
important issue, but when stability is assured competition may then
become the dominant issue.

The Modal Near-Periodicity Hypothesis

I believe that there is a semi-formal argument that can
establish the following hypothesis:

IF a system has four characteristics -

1) if it is an open system exchanging matter and energy (and
   perhaps "information") with its environment;

2) if it is dissipative, converting energy from an order that
   can do work to an order less able to do work, while
   throwing away entropy into its environment (items (1) and
   (2) define the system as non-conservative);

3) if it is persistent, manifesting marginally stable behavior
   that constitutes a "life" epoch; and

4) if it is complex and physically autonomous (that is, not
   closely dependent on time-varying inputs for its time-
   varying behavior)--

THEN, it follows that the system must also have internal
nonlinear mechanics with modal, nearly periodic behavior, in a
close-to-equilibrium range (Yates, 1982b). (Even if the conclusion
were not true strictly as stated, I believe it is very important to
establish the conditions that would guarantee this conclusion,

because biological systems appear to behave in this manner.)

In such systems energy is equipartitioned internally very
slowly. There are internal process delays as energy moves through
fluid-like dissipative steps among the many internal degrees of
freedom. Iberall(1975) has suggested that a measure of the process
time over which thermodynamic closure is achieved is the bulk/shear
viscosity ratio. This term, according to Tisza, measures the ratio
of action involved in cycles of internal processes, to action
appearing in fluctuating translational processes. The details and
assumptions behind this argument can be found in the various
references by Iberall, Soodak and Yates.

The physical model that I think most closely resembles the
stability regimes of living systems, their cyclic thermodynamic
engines, and their adaptability, is an **ensemble of coupled, nonlinear oscillators**. Some properties of such systems have recently
been reviewed by Winfree (1980). The behavior of these systems has
a stability domain with near-periodic orbiting as an attractor in
its state space T^n, the n-torus. Ordinarily we think that high
dimensionality abolishes the "'lateral ordering' of trajectories
characteristic of two dimensions..." (Roessler, 1979), because
flows can be "elevated" into the next higher dimension, and then put
back, with a resulting entanglement, and absence of periodicities.
Yet we find periodicities at all levels of biological systems. The
stability of rest states or equilibrium systems is not applicable:
empirically we know that living systems are not at equilibrium, they
are not at rest, and they are not on a simple, relaxational course
toward equilibrium. They do, of course, die, but the point of
interest here is their persistence in their life phase, near to
equilibrium (Yates, 1982b). Bounded-input-bounded-output (bibo)
stability is not a useful description -- some bounded inputs can
kill a living system, and very high frequency fluctuating inputs can
overload its information-handling capability and disorganize it.

Again, in my opinion, the only stability regime that is
unambiguously appropriate is that of asymptotic, near-periodic,
orbital stability in a high dimensional phase space that can map
onto multiple attractors of lower dimensionality, that show limit-
cycle like orbits with different periods uncorrelated with each
other -- the whole operating close to equilibrium in a thermodynamically defined range, cycling among its various action modes.

Spectroscopy of Complex Systems

Because complex systems that meet the various criteria given
above must transform energies cyclically according to my hypothesis,
they can be described spectroscopically; that is, they show power
deployed at preferred frequencies. Because of nonlinearity, various
spectral peaks will represent processes phase-constrained to some

relationship; thus bispectra and higher spectra may be needed to give additional insights. The human spectrum ranges from oscillations with periods of approximately several milliseconds, as in the EEG, to oscillations in food intake and bodyweight with periods as long as two years, as seen in some manic-depressive patients. In between are the well-known oscillations with periods of about one day (the circadian rhythms), and with periods of about one month (the menstrual cycle). There are numerous other lines in the spectrum, but it is nevertheless only sparsely filled, compared to a continuous spectrum. Now, what does it mean for such a system to adapt?

ADAPTATION

"Adaptation" is an anthropomorphic concept, carrying with it all the logical hazards that bedevil evolutionary theory, viz, the tautological emptiness of the notions of "progress," or of "fitness." To be physically valid, these notions have to be stripped of their facility and then repaired by means of independent criteria of fitness, other than survival, which criteria do not merely reflect a design of Man. Machines, in contrast to living systems, are artifacts, and can be judged as "fit," or "optimal," or as "adapted," according to the intentions of the human designer (Table 2). Not so with living systems -- physical realism requires that their state, and their changes in state, must be describable without taking out a "loan of intelligence," i.e., without invoking intentionality, feedback with given set-points, optima, or goals. If that can be done, then we can ask how the appearances of intentions and intelligence, of messages with content, and associated teleonomic behavior and information, arise out of physical laws and their constraints. Once established, the informational system need not depend further upon laws of physics for the specific <u>content</u> of its messages.

Adaptation occurs (if it all) when an environmental change (external or internal) with some inherent regularity (i.e., a static displacement, or a near-periodic occurrence) perturbs a system over a time long compared to the internal process time constants and frequencies, and displaces the operating point of some of the internal, cyclic, energy conversions. Stability is challenged or threatened. The "fit" system response is then made up of parametric changes that result in greater stability under the new conditions; the system operates in a new region of phase space. It is this response of living systems that we need to rationalize.

Dynamical systems describable by Equations (2) or (3), above, do not exactly account for the process of adaptation, even though they do address structural stability as affected by parameter

changes. How do we get appropriate parameter changes so the system
survives the challenge? If we rule out a deus ex machina as the
basis for fine-tuning parameters so that a new stability regime is
reached after a threat to a system, we are left only with the
system's own "informational" or dynamical properties to draw upon.

According to my view of the physics of complex systems, any
dynamic regulation of internal degrees of freedom of a system
requires that the mean states of internal variables be attained by
physical action of thermodynamic engines. I propose that adaptation
occurs (abstractly) in the crossing of separatrices that partition
the phase and parameter spaces of the system into basins of
attraction. The crossing can be provoked by an environmental input,
or by an imposed controller dynamics that switches the system from
one basin to another by means of a small, catalytic perturbation of
parameters.   In either case, linguistic processes are involved, as
described later. The picture I wish to convey is that of an
organism (system) with very many latent (a priori) basins of
attraction, only a restricted number of which are available at any
given set of parameter values in the equations of motion of the
system. If a control signal or a random fluctuation perturbs one or
more of the parameters, the system can only:

a) damp out the fluctuation,

b) suddenly fall apart and die,

c) relax slowly to an equilibrium death, or

d) find a new cluster of basins of attraction among which it
    can re-establish its characteristic behavorial modes and
    continue to meet its thermodynamic requirements for
    autonomous persistence (e.g, eating, repairing).

The physical theory of such adaptive behavior is incomplete,
but its foundations have been described (Soodak and Iberall, 1978;
Iberall, 1975; Iberall, 1977-78; Yates et al., 1972; Yates, 1982a,b)
under the name "homeokinetic physics." It is a theory of dynamic
regulation by parametric modulation of the operating points of
ensembles of coupled, nonlinear oscillators. See also Abraham
(1983) and Abraham and Shaw (1982, 1983).

HOMEOKINETICS AND ADAPTATION - PERSISTENCE OF OPEN SYSTEMS

Having argued sketchily that current work arising out of
nonlinear dynamics and bifurcation theory, though topologically
fascinating as exploration of structural stability, does not account
for the physical stability of living systems, and having proposed

multiple limit-cycle-like behaviors in (phase space) dimensions higher than two as the image of biological dynamic attractors and stability regimes, I would like to summarize my case.

Consider first the following thermodynamic argument concerning persistent motion. I note three points:

1) If a system is open (i.e., if it can exchange energy and matter with its environment), and if it persists with energy-converting processes occurring, then it must have bounded interactions within. The kinds of interactions will be limited by the constraints that give the system its persistence (it doesn't evaporate or fly apart). Therefore, as energy, matter or "information" flow through, there must be <u>repetitive patterns of motion</u>: certain things must repeat over and over again, because the lifetime of the system is long compared to the relaxation times or characteristic process time constants of individual interactions within. Such conditions permit a mathematical description by harmonic functions (a spectrum).

2) The simplest example of sustained, repetitive motion is that of the ideal linear oscillator in a one-degree-of-freedom closed system (e.g., L-C electrical circuit; mass-spring mechanical system). The differential equation describing the ideal motion expresses the First Law of thermodynamics. Total energy is conserved, and there is no degradation of the order of the energy.

$$M\ddot{x} + Kx = 0 \qquad (4a)$$

or

$$\ddot{x} + \omega_o^2 x = 0 \qquad (4b)$$

where x = displacement (in mass-spring example)
      M,K are positive parameters (mass, and spring constant)
      ω_o = natural, circular frequency = $(K/M)^{1/2}$

A convenient form of the solution is:

$$x(t) = A \cos(\omega_o t - \theta) \qquad (4c)$$

where A = amplitude of the periodic motion (determined by the initial conditions)
      θ = phase of the cosine motion

Kinetic energy in the motion of the mass trades back and forth with the potential energy stored in the spring. Once started up from initial conditions, the system oscillates in perfect, simple harmonic motion forever. But this motion is fictitious because the Second Law of thermodynamics is not satisfied. We must add a dissipative term.

3)   Linear, dissipative systems do not have persistent motion. For
example, real oscillators (e.g., clocks) experience damping as a
result of dissipative processes that degrade free energy into local
heat; i.e., there are losses. Such losses represent the operation
of the Second Law. A typical dissipation term is $C\dot{x}$ (C is
positive), describing the frictional or viscous properties of
motion. The resulting equation of motion that satisfies both
mechanics and irreversible thermodynamics is the classical:

$$M\ddot{x} + C\dot{x} + Kx = 0 \qquad\qquad (5)$$

Yet Equation (5) does not ordinarily yield persistent repetitive
motion. The motion described by Equation (5) is ballistic, not self-
renewing. It is merely a fading echo of the initial conditions.   The
clock runs down.   There are some real systems, called "high Q"
systems in engineering, in which the coefficient C is very small, so
the system oscillates for a long time after a single initiating
impulse, i.e., it persists, while obeying Equation (5). Organ pipes
are designed in this fashion, as are some electrical circuits.   The
solar system is a conspicuous example. However, these are rather
special systems that have very little dissipation of energy within
them, though they always have some.   In contrast, the metabolic
system, and life itself in all forms we know, is highly dissipative.
Equation (5) does not predict the persistent, autonomous, cyclic
metabolic performance actually observed. We must therefore address
the problem of obtaining persistence of repetitive motion in a
highly dissipative system, in the face of both the mechanical and
the thermodynamic requirements.

    Persistence is accomplished by the introduction of a nonlinear
coupling, an "escapement" forcing function, that permits a pulse of
energy, ε, to be drawn from a constant or slowly changing source of
potential and injected into the system at a specific appropriate
phase, ϕ_0, (not time) during each cycle. The magnitude of $\varepsilon(\phi_0)$ is:

$$\varepsilon(\phi_0) \cong \overline{C\dot{x}} \qquad (\varepsilon \text{ not continuous}) \qquad\qquad (6)$$

where the overhead bar indicates a cycle average. The physically-
valid periodic motion is that of a nonlinear, limit cycle
oscillator. From (5) and (6) for the forced system:

$$M\ddot{x} + Kx = \varepsilon(\phi_0) - C\dot{x} \qquad\qquad (7)$$

Each cycle is separately initiated. The amplitude of the limit
cycle oscillation will be that which can have its dissipative losses
just made up by the escapement pulse. This nonlinear oscillator is
independent of its initial conditions, and the equation of motion
incorporates the laws of both mechanics and thermodynamics. A price
we must pay in analyses of such a design is loss of use of the

powerful principles of conservative mechanics, yet over each cycle the system is describable by the equation for linear, persistent, isochronous harmonic motion (Equation 4a), because the right hand term of Equation (7) averages out to zero over a cycle.

The Poincaré-Bendixson theorem established that the stability regime for such nonconservative, nonlinear systems (of two dimensions in phase space) is either asymptotic, orbital stability, i.e., a limit cycle, or else an equilibrium point. If $\epsilon(\phi_o)$ is drawn from potential sources that are part of the system, and are relatively constant, then we have a physically autonomous oscillator. Note that ϵ itself cannot be constant, continuous, or a function of time if an autonomous system is to result. In the case of life we are not interested in a deus ex machina that runs the clockworks from the outside; we are interested in autonomy. The living persistent system must serve itself.

This elementary theory of the clock in two dimensions (in phase space) is merely an example of a much broader physical principle, which I now generalize intuitively as point (4) below.

4)   The flow of energy through an open persistent dynamic system of high dimension, from a source to a sink, will be accomplished by at least one thermodynamic engine cycle within the system. Each thermodynamic engine sustains its lossy, cyclic motions by drawing pulses of energy from a constant or slowly changing potential source. The behavior is describable as nonlinear (limit-cycle-like) oscillations, and the stability regime is asymptotic orbital stability, in a near-to-equilibrium region.

5)   From the above generalization I suspect that a spectral analysis of processes in living systems should reveal a line spectrum, with at least one cyclic process being devoted to recharging on-board potential sources. Because of noise on amplitudes, and on frequencies (as warble or wow), the spectral peaks may be broad (Iberall, 1978; Yates, 1979, 1980, 1981a,b). The lines will not be harmonically related.

6)   In stable, open systems of very high number of internal degrees of freedom, multiple thermodynamic engines (cyclic energy conversions) will be present, and many of them will be weakly coupled and mutually entrained. However, the constellations of nonlinear oscillators will show neither fixed behavior, nor wild instability. The stability will be marginal in the structural sense, so that some external environmental influences, and some internal catalytic, low-power, "linguistic" fluxes can change the operating points of the ensembles by relatively minor perturbation of parameters. After the change, the system will remain organized, in both time and space, but in new domains.

PHYSICAL BASIS OF LANGUAGES

In set theoretic terms, a formal language consists of symbols
of an alphabet; a vocabulary that is an infinite list of individual
variables; quantifiers; sentential connectives and syntactical
rules; and predicate variables of various, finite ranks. Formal
languages are aspects of logic, and are not the physical languages
of dynamical systems under discussion here. In contrast, we have to
look to the catalytic features of chemical languages to account for
the modal switchings that occur in complex systems. In human
beings, for example, hormones and neural signals are invoked to
accomplish modal switching. A comparison of enzymes, which are
formally catalysts, and hormones, shows that hormones may be thought
of as being as catalytic as are enzymes. Both enzymes and hormones
have energy-requiring synthetic processes to build their structures;
both have degradation reactions that destroy them; neither an enzyme
nor a hormone is permanently altered by the processes it modulates
or evokes; both enzymes and hormones exist in concentrations that
are very small compared to the magnitude of the fluxes they affect;
enzymes catalyze the conversions of substrates to products, and
hormones similarly catalyze the "activation" step of the coupling of
a receptor in a cell to the processes it can modulate.

In chemical languages the hormonal lexical units have the same
kinds of bond energies and exchanges as do the power fluxes of
cells. There is no energetic scaling that can identify a linguistic
process from a cellular power process. A hormone has to be
synthesized, its covalent skeleton determines its shape, its shape
determines its chemical complementarity and its recognition. Weak
bonding to receptors is very much like the bonding of substrates to
enzymes. (Sometimes covalent bonding is involved in recognition, as
well as in substrate-to-enzyme connections.) But languages in
organisms are nevertheless low-power, in the sense that the
magnitudes of their fluxes and concentrations are small compared to
those of the processes they modulate. In other words, both enzymes
and hormones act as amplifiers or at amplification stages within or
among living cells. Thus chemical languages are the catalytic
linkages among nonlinear, cycling thermodynamic engines in soft-
coupled (complex) systems. At the receiver they can both provoke
and evoke changes in state. An evocation requires that the memory
structures participate. Neural signals can be thought of as special
cases of hormonal transmissions, in which the hormones (transmitters
and neuromodulators) flow through narrow, specific synaptic clefts,
instead of being broadcast through the bloodstream on a "to whom it
may concern" basis.

Chemical languages are always made up of the materials and
processes at hand. Their syntax arises from either spatial or
temporal ordering. The structures of senders and receivers are

configured in a complementary fashion so that the flow of chemical
signals conveys syntactical order at the point of departure from the
sender, and upon arrival at the receiver. Spatial order dominates
in the genetic code of DNA, or in the amino acid sequence of the
primary structure of proteins. However, cells at their surfaces
commonly integrate over time instead of space, to detect a chemical
signal.

The "meaning" or context of the message received appears as
changed dynamical contingencies in the receiving cell. The changed
dynamical contingencies are the "interpretations" of received
transmissions, and draw upon memory as well as on-going signal
reception (see Yates and Iberall, 1983). This view of the physical
basis of language has led to a new derivation of the familiar
Zipfian distribution that, empirically, characterizes almost all
written languages (Iberall, 1977-78). A Zipfian distribution is one
in which the frequency of usage of a word is inverse to its rank
ordering, i.e., the second most used word is used one half as
frequently as the first, the third most used word is used one third
as frequently as the first, etc.

The appearance of symbol-like elements in metabolic and
endocrine systems was first proposed by Tomkins (1975). I have
given an extended account of the linguistic aspects of the metabolic
system (Yates, 1982a). I concluded that article as follows:

Linguistic analysis of hormone action shows that
cells require relatively few switching signals to permit
them to function according to a limited repertoire of
action modes set by their genetic programs. The action
modes number perhaps six. The languages number perhaps
nine. Hormonal communications employ relatively simple
syntactical rules, and bear short messages.

The linguistic richness of living systems is found at
the extremes represented by the eukaryotic genome and by
the human brain and its cultural institutions.
Intermediate levels of organization seem to require only
rather primitive information fluxes, but these primitive
fluxes may lead to elaborate interpretations (as in insect
molts, or tadpole metamorphosis, or embryogenesis). The
elaborateness arises from the informational resources of
the genome and is not inherent in the simple messages that
reach it. A complex machine can elaborate on a simple
message (but a simple machine can do only simple things,
whatever the message).

The genome and the brain, using very different
methods, play the same game: they schedule, they impose
coherence on multiple processes otherwise weakly coupled,

and they work impressive and delayed elaborations on
simple inputs...

The "information" referred to in the above section is not the
coding-theory, selective information of Shannon, as I hope I have by
now made clear: it is the changed dynamical contingencies of a cell
brought about by physicochemical variations in the environment of
the cell, playing on or through its surface, and interacting with
the memory of the cell. At every stage, language, syntax and
meaning are physical in this analysis. The "information" of the
memory elements is found in the structures of the cell, including
DNA, but is not exclusively confined to DNA. (Note that structures
are dynamical processes with very long time-constants.)

THE NATURE OF ORGANISMIC ADAPTATION

In the case of threatening environmental change, or an internal
failure of a part, the ensemble of coupled, limit-cycle-like
oscillators that make up a complex organism must find a new
stability domain consistent with the new parameter values, in the
neighborhood of a new attractor that has new nearly-periodic orbits
-- or it must die out. There is no guarantee that such a new
stability region of phase space will be reachable -- but if it is
reached, an "adaptation" has occurred. Adaptation looks
"intentional" to us, but it is merely the locking-up of a dynamical
system in a basin of attraction that happens to be reachable (from
the prior states and parameter values) after a parameter change.

Conrad (1983) has just published an excellent book entitled
"Adaptability: The Significance of Variability from Molecule to
Ecosystem" that presents a thermodynamic account of adaptation in
complex systems. In contrast to my view that organismic adaptation
and the adaptation of species should be treated separately, Conrad
writes:

> ...Over the broad spectrum of biological nature, one can
> find the most diverse mechanisms of adaptability and also
> the most diverse strategies for using these mechanisms.
> This great diversity may invite a certain amount of
> pessimism as to the possibility of understanding, or even
> describing, the patterns of adaptability which actually
> exist in nature. Fortunately, however, the problem is
> simpler than it appears at first. This is because all the
> different mechanisms and modes of adaptability have one
> thing in common: they are all adaptations to the
> uncertainty of the environment. This means that we can
> expect all forms of adaptability, regardless of their
> diversity, to have some common denominator.

Conrad goes on to say (in agreement with my view) "The problem of adaptability also has a crucial conceptual connection to the problem of stability. The ability to cope with an uncertain environment is clearly a necessary condition for the maintenance of a relatively permanent form of organization, hence for stability."

Conrad further comments about adaptability:

...A number of deep and rather subtle issues...arise. Adaptability involves the use of information about the environment. So information processing and reliability of information processing must be considered. Another fundamental connection is between adaptability and the structural and functional transformability of biological systems. Transformability turns out to be a generalization of reliability. A self-contained treatment requires a close analysis of fundamental biological concepts, such as information, complexity, efficiency, and fitness. Some questions of special importance concern the legitimate ways of using information measures in biology, the connection between energy and adaptability, and the relation between adaptability and various dynamical notions of stability, such as orbital stability and structural stability. To understand the relation between stability and complexity correctly it is necessary to understand the relation between stability and adaptability. There is also an important link between the adaptability of a system and the extent to which its dynamics are predictable.

I regret that I cannot give here a fuller account of the original and thoughtful thermodynamic treatment of adaptation accomplished by Conrad. Instead, I shall summarize my own view of the issues.

SUMMARY

The dynamical approach to adaptation requires recognition that both internal and external environments of living organisms are fluctuational. The environmental fluctuations that an organism can survive are band-limited (extreme high frequencies can be lethal) and limited in amplitude as well -- intense fluctuations can destroy an organism. Therefore adaptation can occur only within a limited set of possible environmental conditions. Within that set, fluctuations can be creative -- that is, they can drive an organism through a dynamical bifurcation into a new stability regime with new dynamics (including the emergence of new forms).

In principle, transitions from one adapted state to another

adapted state in a different environment should represent either
first-order physical transitions (resembling equilibrium phase
changes) or second-order (e.g., high Reynolds number) physical
transitions. The Prigogine school represents those dynamical bifur-
cations that create complexity as being of the latter type (see the
references to and criticism of that view in the Introduction to
Section VIII in Yates, 1983). I argue that living systems operate
thermodynamically near-to-equilibrium, by the measure that their
thermodynamic potentials are defined, and their transport
coefficients in the equations of change associated with each of the
conservations are functions of those potentials, and not of time
(Yates, 1982b). A logical consequence of that view is that
adaptation is a first-order physical transition of an organism
occurring as a bifurcation under nonholonomic constraints. Those
constraints are "informational" and realized as new structures. The
new structures provide boundary conditions for, or constraining
forces on, the new dynamics. I cannot here give a full development
of this view of the dynamics of adaptation, but I wish to emphasize
that it stands in strong contrast to the far-from-equilibrium model
proposed by the Prigogine group. In my opinion, they confuse nonlinearity with "nonthermodynamic" conditions -- whereas the only
conditions to which the thermodynamics I propose could not apply
would be found in shock waves and knocking engines. But biological
systems (nonlinear) do not show shock waves, and their metabolic
engines do not knock. In all environments, surviving biological
systems operate close to equilibrium, in a thermodynamic domain. In
that domain fluctuations and dissipations combine creatively to
accomplish a marginal stability, characterized by multiple,
marginally-stable behavioral (action) modes. Catalytic, linguistic
signals switch the dynamics through the modes in a global, closed
trajectory that is a hypercycle. Adaptations (and also the ordinary
modal-switchings in an environment to which the organism is already
adapted) represent parametric modulations of ensembles (networks) of
weakly-coupled, nonlinear, limit-cycle thermodynamic engine
oscillators. That is the physical image of adaptation yet to be
mathematized.

> What we need is imagination. We have to find a new view
> of the world.   (R. P. Feynman)

ACKNOWLEDGMENT

    This work was supported by Grant GM 23732 from the U.S.
National Institutes of Health.

TABLE 1

Some Typical Properties of Complex Systems
(Expanded from Yates, 1982a)

1. Large number of parts, internal degrees of freedom, or
    interactions among parts.

2. Nonlinearity.

3. Nonintegrable (nonholonomic) constraints.

4. Nonstationarity (the parameters or transition matrices change
    in time -- mathematically nonautonomous characteristics).

5. Inherent uncertainty (e.g., Markovian transition matrices).

6. Noise (perhaps with inconstant statistical properties).

7. Constructed by either or both of two organizing forces

    a) electromagnetic (many subtypes)

    b) gravitational.

    (Weak interactions and nuclear binding forces are subatomic,
    and thus generally below the levels that generate the dynamics
    of adaptation.)

8. Three modes of transports:

Type	Properties
a) Diffusion	linear, local, incoherent
b) Wave propagation	linear, local, coherent
c) Convection	nonlinear, global, coherent

9. Multiple levels (hierarchical) -- at least one atomistic
    fluctuational level and one continuum field level.

(continued)

TABLE 1 (Continued)

---

10. Competition at various scales between different tendencies or forces in field equations of motion, leading to an apparent competition between:

    a) potential energy vs. entropy (or kinetic energy)

    b) broken symmetry vs. symmetry

    c) incoherent diffusive transport vs. coherent convective transport.

11. High bulk/shear viscosity ratio, with prolonged internal processing times (delays). "Soft" couplings.

12. Cyclic energy conversions.

13. Physical autonomy (system persists without close dependence on time-varying inputs).

14. Fluid-plastic-elastic behavior, action-dominated rather than momentum-dominated.

15. Linguistic and dynamic behavioral modes.

All of the above properties can emerge from a small set of strategic physical principles (see Iberall and Soodak, 1983).

TABLE 2

A Taxonomy of Real Systems*

I.   Natural systems

     A.   Inanimate

     B.   Biological

II. Machines (biological artifacts that operate physically --
     substantiations of Man's will)

     Inanimate systems and machines may be simple or complex (see
Table 1, and text), but biological systems at the cellular level
(the minimal structural level for life) or above, are always
complex.

---

*(See the Chapter by N. Moray for Ashby's taxonomy of systems.
Curiously, the recombinant-DNA organism is classifiable in my scheme
only as a machine, under Class II.)

REFERENCES

Abraham, R. H., 1983, Dynamics and self-organization, in: "Self-Organizing Systems: The Emergence of Order," F. E. Yates, ed., Plenum Press, New York.

Abraham, R. H., and C. D. Shaw, 1982, "Dynamics: The Geometry of Behavior, Part One - Periodic Behavior," Aerial Press, Inc., Santa Cruz, California.

Abraham, R. H., and C. D. Shaw, 1983, Dynamics - a visual introduction, in: "Self-Organizing Systems: The Emergence of Order," F. E. Yates, ed., Plenum Press, New York.

Brillouin, L., 1962, "Science and Information Theory," Academic Press, New York.

Campbell, J., 1982, "Grammatical Man: Information, Entropy, Language and Life," Simon and Schuster, New York.

Conrad, M., 1983, "Adaptability: The Significance of Variability from Molecule to Ecosystem," Plenum Press, New York.

Helleman, R. H. G. (ed.), 1980, "Nonlinear Dynamics," Ann. N. Y. Acad. Sci., Vol. 357: 1-507.

Iberall, A. S., 1975, On nature, man and society: A basis for scientific modeling, Ann. Biomed. Eng., 3: 344-385.

Iberall, A. S., 1977, 1978, A field and circuit thermodynamics for integrative physiology (in three parts), Amer. J. Physiol./ Reg., Int. Comp. Physiol., 2: R171-180, 1977; and 3: R3-R19, and R85-R97, 1978 (Part 2 with H. Soodak and F. Hassler).

Iberall, A. S., and H. Soodak, 1978, Physical basis for complex systems - some propositions relating levels of organizations, Coll. Phen., 3: 9-24.

Iberall, A. S., and H. Soodak, 1983, A physics for complex systems, in: "Self-Organizing Systems: The Emergence of Order," F. E. Yates, ed., Plenum Press, New York.

Landauer, R., 1976, Fundamental limitations in the computational process, Ber. Bunsen - Gesell. Physik. Chem. (fruher Zeit. fur Electrochemie), 80: 1048-1059.

Lewontin, R. C., 1983, The corpse in the elevator (review of two books on modern biology), N. Y. Rev. Books, XXIX (Nos. 21 and 22, January 20): 34-37.

Pattee, H. H., 1977, Dynamic and linguistic modes of complex systems, Int. J. Gen. Systems., 3: 259-266.

Rosen, R., 1974, Planning, management, policies and strategies. Four fuzzy concepts, Int. J. Gen. Systems, 1: 245-252.

Roessler, O. E., 1979, Chaotic oscillations: An example of hyperchaos, in: "Nonlinear Oscillations in Biology," Lectures in Applied Mathematics, Vol. 17. F. C. Hoppensteadt, ed. American Mathematical Society, Providence, Rhode Island, pp. 141-156.

Shaw, G. L., E. Harth, and A. B. Scheibel, 1982, Cooperativity in brain function: Assemblies of approximately 30 neurons, Exp. Neurol., 77: 324-358.

Soodak, H., and A. S. Iberall, 1978, Homeokinetics: A physical
    science for complex systems, Science, 201: 579-582.
Tomkins, G. M., 1975, The metabolic code, Science, 189: 760-763.
Winfree, A. T., 1980, "The Geometry of Biological Time," Springer-
    Verlag, New York (Series in Biomathematics, Vol. 8).
Yates, F. E., D. J. Marsh, and A. S, Iberall, 1972, Integration of
    the whole organism: A foundation for a theoretical biology,
    in: "Challenging Biological Problems: Directions Towards Their
    Solution," J. A. Behnke, ed., AIBS 25 year celebration volume,
    Oxford Press, pp. 110-132.
Yates, F. E., and A. S. Iberall, 1973, Temporal and hierarchical
    organization in biosystems, in: "Temporal Aspects of
    Therapeutics," J. Urquhart, and F. E. Yates, eds., Plenum
    Press, New York, pp. 17-34.
Yates, F. E., 1979, Physical biology: A basis for modeling living
    systems, J. Cyber. Info. Sci., 2: 57-70.
Yates, F. E., 1980, Spectroscopy of metabolic systems. Proc. 24th
    Annual Meeting of the Society for General Systems Research, San
    Francisco, January 7-11, pp. 65-74.
Yates, F. E., 1981a, Temporal organization of metabolic processes:
    A biospectroscopic approach, in: "Carbohydrate Metabolism:
    Quantitative Physiology and Mathematical Modeling," R. N.
    Bergman, and C. Cobelli, eds., John Wiley and Sons, Inc., New
    York, pp. 389-417.
Yates, F. E., 1981b, Analysis of endocrine signals: The engineering
    and physics of biochemical communication systems, Biol. Repro.,
    24: 73-94.
Yates, F. E., 1982a, Systems analysis of hormone action: Principles
    and strategies, in: "Biological Regulation and Development,
    Vol. III - Hormone Action," R. F. Goldberger, and K. R.
    Yamamoto, eds., Plenum Press, New York, pp. 25-97.
Yates, F. E., 1982b, Outline of a physical theory of physiological
    systems, Can. J. Physiol. Pharmacol., 60 (3): 217-248.
Yates, F. E., ed., 1983, "Self-Organizing Systems: The Emergence of
    Order," Plenum Press, New York.
Yates, F. E., and A. S. Iberall, 1983, A skeleton of physical ideas
    for the dynamics of complex systems, Math. Comp. Simul., Volume
    XXIV, Numbers 5 and 6 ("Special Issue on Modeling of Biomedical
    Systems") J. Eisenfeld, and V. C. Rideout, eds., (in press).

ADAPTIVE CONTROL: FROM FEEDBACK TO DEBUGGING

Marvin L. Minsky

Artificial Intelligence Laboratory
Massachusetts Institute of Technology
Cambridge, MA 02139 USA

1. The Cybernetic Origins

I'm going to talk about control systems of the sort that my
colleagues work on, in this field called Artificial Intelligence.
From this perspective, I tend to think about control in terms of
knowledge. When you talk about tuning or hill climbing, the system
is changing its state, and you can say that it knows different
things after it's got whatever it's controlling under control. If
you're trying to have adaptive control, then the knowledge of the
system keeps changing; and if you have expert control, which is the
sort of thing one looks for in humans, then as the situation changes
you learn general strategies for bringing about desired changes, so
that long-term learning certainly can be seen.

There's a long history of about 30 years of slow progress from
the first cybernetics systems to the kinds of expert systems that
Buchanan describes in his paper. In the early days of cybernetics,
Ashby designed systems that didn't do anything. What is the use of
ultra-stable systems which have the property that if you subject
them to some influence, they change to an equilibrium state but
don't even remember where they were? Warren McCulloch was a great
fan of Ashby, and so finally I asked him, "Well, why do you think
this is so important?" And he said, "Because he explains it so

---

* The Editors have prepared this talk by extensively editing the
transcript of Professor Minsky's "Closing Remarks" at the
Moretonhampstead meeting.

clearly." I went back and read <u>Design for a Brain</u> again and couldn't
but agree with McCulloch that Ashby had managed to explain something
more clearly than everyone else put together. The fact that the
systems didn't do anything was a little bit disappointing, but that
was as nothing compared to the clarity. So, if you want to explain
something, you should read <u>Design for a Brain</u> and use that as a
model for your next paper.

Anyhow, except for ultra-stable systems, the key ideas in
cybernetics were systems that could look at the present state and a
desired state and could use the difference between the two states as
feedback to do something about it. With some systems, the states
could be represented as points of a vector space, and so the system
could take the difference between the present and desired state, and
use it as the control signal. In the cybernetics systems that
people were able to analyze, one assumes that there's a nice
relation between the difference and the appropriate control signal;
and in fact, you hope that the relation is linear. And so the
numerical models and the hill-climbing models and most of the
pre-artificial-intelligence cybernetics models really depended on
the idea that you would have state variables that resembled the
state variables of physical systems and were vectors of real
numbers. Well, this is a nice paradigm and, as everybody knows, it
became one kind of model for what one means by intentional behavior
- the use of a negative feedback system to drive a system towards
some numerically specified "good state".

Now, you can look at a control system in many ways. You can
look at it as a sensory-motor knowledge system, perhaps, if you
believe that detecting the difference between actual and "intended"
state is the thing you really want to detect, which is the knowledge
to tell the system what to do. But where does the method for
converting error into control signal come from? In adaptive
systems, you might find this by an evolutionary process. Perhaps
you don't know what the right method is, so you try a method and you
see if the difference gets worse, and if it does, you try the
opposite method. That means you have to have a little knowledge
about the nature of the methods: what does it mean to reverse a
method?

People in Artificial Intelligence take this feedback theory for
granted, pretty much. In the 1950's, there was a lot of work on
trying to formalize this idea more generally so that it didn't
depend on states being numerical - we can see the celebrated GPS
system of Newell, Shaw, and Simon as a symbolic servo-mechanism. It
said: If you have a description of a state and a description of a
goal and some way of finding a description of the differences
between these, even though these are symbolic and not numerical,
then we should have methods for dealing with differences and
reducing them.

In GPS, they went up to six or eight differences and were able
to do symbolic integration and play simple games, and so forth. If
you had state variables with a hundred different possibilities, and
you wanted to get to one of a hundred kinds of goals, you might need
10,000 pieces of advice. So, goals are great things if you have a
lot of variables and continuity; and then linearity is important,
and you can get a control system that can first acquire a few points
by experience and then generalize to the rest through linearity or
whatever substitutes for it. That is, you get a machine that shows
a little sign of intelligence in the sense that it can handle things
it's never seen before. But, people get carried away by this idea
of differences too much. There is a simpler system, which is to
have a state, and a goal state, and a box which takes those pairs
directly and looks up a control action on the basis of the two
inputs, not just in terms of their difference. You can do lots of
things without this idea of an intention or a goal; but one must
ask what's the point of having intentions?

2. Frames, Scripts and Representations

Now let me jump over to a real life non-cybernetic situation.
We see the same sorts of structures in modern systems, but the
emphases are very different because now they are of the nature of
the descriptions and the nature of the knowledge rather than on the
little loops and dynamics that the people who talked about adaptive
systems talked about. One of the issues in adaptive control theory
that I'll raise is: What's the relation between this classical
micro-theory of feedback and coupled oscillators and linearity and
the different kind of knowledge-based theories that the people in
Artificial Intelligence often claim are the true route toward
understanding intelligence.

To paraphrase an old paper of McCarthy's called "The Advice
Taker," I had to solve the problem of getting to the meeting and I
couldn't walk because the Atlantic was an obstacle. It's the same
canonical example that you have in early cybernetics – to get from
Boston to Exeter, I have to overcome the difference in some way. In
fact, if we talk about a long distance, then for most of us the
first thing we think of is "to fly" and the problem goes away.
Alright, how does it go away? We have an origin and destination,
and we have to describe both of them rather than their difference,
which is the traditional way.

I go and look up in my memory for some sort of pattern that
matches that. In AI, we say that in your head there are things
called frames which are prototype situations, things that you
can--in some manner or other--retrieve from your memory, and which
are somehow automatically matched to situations. Those people in AI
who use a methodology called production systems have their frames in
two parts, a situation and an action, and a lot of modern

programming is done just in terms of these little pairs. If the
sensory situation or the internal state situation of your mind is
such and such, then your memory says, "Well, here's the thing for
dealing with that, perform the following action." In the present
case, the obstacle is a long distance or crossing an ocean, and the
action associated with that, in a little sub-frame, is a certain
method of transport such as flying. Incidentally, one can regard a
lot of English grammar-- not the recursive part, but the surface
part of a typical phrase that doesn't have any phrases within it--as
given in terms of frames which match the main phrase types. When
you dissect a sentence from the point of view of verb case frame
analysis, then you don't get a Chomskian phrase structure grammar
exactly; but a prepositional grammar. Consider "I went from Boston
to London." You have a thing called "go" and their cases, "origin,"
"destination." Typically in English the cases are designated either
by position or by prepositions. So an origin is usually represented
in terms of "from," destination is "to." There is an instrumentality
or vehicle which, for some verbs, is "with" - in the case of
transportation, it's "by," so I can say "by car," "by plane," and so
forth. I can say "I went to London from Boston by plane" or "I went
by plane from Boston to London" and so forth. The word order can be
dismissed if you have enough prepositions. One is allowed in almost
any verbal case frame to have another thing called "for," in this
example, it's "for going to this meeting." Of course, the
prepositions are adjustable. Sometimes they depend on the clause
structure, but one can make an argument that most of natural
language is formed around a rather small number of such things.

Each verb, for historical and other reasons, has its specific
choices of adverbs, but the prepositions are not quite arbitrary
designators for the slots in the frame. So, if somebody tells you a
sentence, you can figure out what it means by dissecting it into a
case frame; then, in your knowledge structure, these case frames
are associated in many cases with cybernetic loops. In his early
work, Roger Schank described a formalism which had 10 or 20
primitives, as they're called, and a lot of the primitives were of
the form "trans"-- for transport, whether physical or mental. The
beauty of Schank's so-called conceptual dependency language is that
he describes just enough fragments that, sure enough, if you take
some structure like "I went from Boston to London by plane" it turns
out that you can usually describe it. For example, I can begin to
solve my original problem if I realize that I can drop into the
"for" slot that I can overcome this obstacle of crossing the ocean
by going by airplane.

Now, understanding, whatever that means, is a very variable
thing. You understand something if you have the ability to embed it
in some networks of knowledge and elaborate any of their branches.
In philosophy there's a confusion between potential calculation and
real calculation. The reason for this confusion is that

philosophers are enamored of logic, and logic has no time in it. As
a result, philosophers can't tell the difference between having the
information available to make a deduction, and the deduction itself.
So, for example, you'll find some of these very smart people are
confused about whether, if you know that 2 and 2 is 4, and that 4
and 2 is 6, do you know that 2 and 2 and 2 is 6? You only know it
in the sense that if you follow the threads of the representations,
you can find it out. It's very unlikely that in somebody's brain,
if you put in several sentences, that somewhere else in the brain
there will instantly appear all the other sentences that could be
deduced from them. So, understanding is ill-defined in the sense
that people don't subscript the word understanding with the amount
of calculation or time or intention or whatever that has to go into
a particular act of understanding something to one degree or
another.

In the trip planning problem, the prepositional phrase "by
plane" doesn't raise any problems for any of us because the symbolic
equivalent in our heads is already connected to elaborate libraries
of situational scripts, and so forth. If you have ever taken a
plane, then you have many memories of it and the degree to which you
solve problems or understand or adapt that script is very variable.
If you have taken many planes, then you may have a whole calculus of
combining that kind of knowledge. I do not like reservations, and
so for me there is a simple script sequence. (I like Roger Schank's
use of the idea of 'scripts' which came some years after conceptual
dependency.) The typical way of thinking about dealing with a plane
is you make a reservation, or you go to the counter and buy a
ticket, and you get on the plane and then who cares what happens and
then you get off at your destination. My script for "Buy ticket."
is "give them this credit card and this ticket appears." Schank
would say, "You have a canonical script for getting something that
you want," which might be: "I will threaten the agent and if he
doesn't give me a ticket, I will choke him." And if you take the
word "threaten", it will again be explained in terms of a trajectory
notion: Take a concept with origin in the buyer's head, and
destination in the ticket-giver's head. The buyer has to put into
that person's head the idea that if he doesn't give him the ticket,
his health will suffer. Then we leave it to common knowledge that
people don't want their health to suffer." And, in fact, in Schank's
system, we tell him that his health will go from +10 to -10.
Everything works out.

The structure for "threaten" is very elegant, because what
Schank has is a duality of physical transportation: If I buy the
ticket, then I physically transport money to the person and he
physically gives me the ticket, and that's all very straightforward.
When I threaten him, I transfer an idea from my head to his head.
That doesn't have so much conservation. I can still have an idea

after giving it away, which is why we're all so generous with our
ideas, I suppose.

Rieger, a former student of Schank, analyzed mechanical
structures, and built programs that in some sense understand
complicated gadgets like the ball-cup flush toilet and various other
machines. He found that he needed 40 or 50 different concepts of
causality to do this smoothly. He had to say that, "If you have a
one thing supported by another, then there's a relation between
these which is a continuous causality. This thing causes that to
stay there as long as this one's here. If you nail it on, the act
of nailing causes it to stay there for good. From the point of view
of the nail, it's continuous causality. If you have that
microstructure, then you also know that if you move the nail, then
it will fall down, and so forth."

If you're interested in this question of how to represent the
kind of knowledge that one usually assumes that everybody knows,
look at the work of Rieger. He found that he needed a lot of
primitives to do what he wanted, although if you look at his
primitives you can reduce them as Schank did down to a smaller
number with more cumbersome structures.

Many people are so enraged by the simplicity of this idea that
they say, "No, it can't be that simple." Indeed, it can't. And they
say, "Well, I won't even start with that." So, there are lots of
people who are still rediscovering these things. That's not the
answer to all problems, of course, but one of the points I'm trying
to make is that a basic approach is to take the old cybernetic
concept of an origin and a destination and an obstacle and replace
simple feedback by use of appropriate knowledge. In the old
Newell-Simon GPS, there was nothing but origin, destination, and a
difference, and they never managed to get a GPS-type system to
handle anything like linguistic problems. But between the origin
and the destination, there are more things than one of difference.
There's the obstacle which is separate; sometimes there's the
method, which is a way of diminishing the difference; and there's a
goal, which isn't always the same as the method.

One of my complaints is that after cybernetics started to
clarify the idea of intention and goal, it made a dreadful mistake.
We all made it. We thought the problem was solved because it looked
like the difference is almost the same as the goal, and it isn't.
Schank didn't get it very clear either, and I haven't yet, but my
present theory is that the standard frame for understanding a
situation has several different things in it. The ones I've got are
pretty complicated, but the idea is to make an adaptive system that
can either create these things "on the fly", or has a huge store of
them. Some of the arguments at this Workshop had to do with some
people preferring that the system be so adaptive that it doesn't

need all this memory, but that's an impossible goal. If the system
has a lot of variables, like an air traffic control system does, you
just have to have prior knowledge or planes will crash before you've
figured out how to wiggle all the planes around to get them to avoid
each other.

3. Learning (to Learn)

Part of the development of understanding is to get
representations of new pieces of knowledge into your head. But how
do you do that? The people I like in Artificial Intelligence are
working on two things:

The first is this question of how knowledge is represented,
with little regard for control theory. I'm schizophrenic in this
regard, because I'm half mathematician, and I love the idea that
from a few axioms you can control the system; but if you don't have
the quasi-linearity of the physical system, then you don't get this
elegant structure of classical mechanics for control. Instead, you
get big tables of matrices, or big sets of productions a la
Buchanan, where you do the best you can by collecting a great set of
anecdotes and use a matching process so that when, for example, some
disease comes up which you've never seen before, you find a best
match by some other method like how many symptoms or signs it has in
common with another one. You are imposing continuity on a structure
where you are not sure of a reason for it, and as medicine makes
progress, it inevitably replaces some of the ad hoc matching by
alleged mechanisms, and sometimes those mechanisms are nice and
continuous. In the case of the nervous system, I have grave doubts
about continuity, because although neurons are like other cells in
some ways, they are not like them in more important ways.

A second is the principle concern of a group I would call
"Reflection Theorists." (That's a new word.) I would say that I
myself, Gerry Sussman, Ira Goldstein, John Doyle (and other
theorists who don't yet deserve to be heard of) are working from the
viewpoint that there might be some basic cybernetic mechanisms for
acquiring knowledge, like the old associationist method. Everything
that happens in your short-term memory, perhaps, gets stashed in
long-term memory automatically. That's Newell's theory, for
example, and on the surface it looks like a pretty good theory but
those people haven't yet made good enough learning machines for me
to feel that that's adequate. But anyway, there's one theory which
is: Every time you solve a problem, your mind is in a certain state
when you've solved it, with various things in short-term registers
and so forth. What you do is simply store that state in long-term
memory. Then, if you ever get a problem like that, you pull out of
long-term memory the analogous mental state and run it. I have a
paper in Cognitive Science called "K-Lines" which discusses that
idea very theoretically.

But I think that in order to get anything like a realistic
theory, there's another recursion, namely, at any particular point
in our development, we know how to learn things, but we have to
learn how to learn. Fodor or Chomsky would say, "Nonsense, there's
no evidence that people learn to learn. It's just there. That's
what they're born with," and they may be right to some extent. We
have no way of judging, right now, how much we are born with. In
any case, I prefer to at least try to develop the theory of how you
would make a machine that gets better at learning.

Oliver Selfridge, who did some of the first pioneering work on
adaptive learning systems, has been complaining for a very long time
that people should study learning more, and I parted company with
him a long time ago and went over to an AI which was without
learning techniques. I'm not sorry I did, because the theory of
representation of knowledge is fantastically more advanced now than
it was 20 years ago. In the course of that, though, all of us,
Newell and McCarthy and me and everyone in our field but Charlie
Rosen and Nils Nilsson said, "You shouldn't worry about learning,
because you probably won't be able to figure out how to get a
machine to learn something until you can figure out how the machine
will look before and after its learning." In other words, before you
can design a learning machine, you should have at least some shred
of a representation theory. In all modesty, we were unduly
influential. It was not entirely our fault — the people who worked
on learning machines didn't get any better ideas. Maybe this was
because they didn't have good representation theories, and maybe
because they were simply scientifically unsophisticated. Machines
like the Perceptron (which Rosenblatt announced as the great advance
in learning machines in 1958) probably sucked away 10 or 15 years of
all the smartest people in cybernetics because Rosenblatt offered
the promise that you could make a sophisticated learning machine
without having an internal representation of any quality.

So, the artificial intelligence people went their way and the
adaptive control people went theirs. Somewhere along the way the
adaptive control people had the idea of model, but in my view, their
idea of model is extremely unhealthy because it's too simple-minded.
Their idea of a model inside the machine is one that has the same
continuous physical state variables as the one outside. Well, if
you do that, then there isn't any hope of a machine learning in a
nice way. It's either got to guess the model right or fail
completely. If it has a wrong model, it can tune the parameters
just so well and fail. But unless an adaptive control system has
knowledge about making models, you lose, because the system will
never be able to adapt outside of the designer's design envelope.

So, AI went off this way in thinking about ways to make models
while adaptive control went off in the direction of trying to find
optimal control theories for models of a given structure. Those are

hard mathematical problems and I'm sure lots of progress was made.

4. Debugging Theory

The task is to bring AI sophistication in representation back into adaptive control theory. What I think is the most promising line in this highest level of adaptive control has the ugliest name, debugging theory. So far, there are hardly any results in it. What frames, what kind of knowledge, does a person have to know to acquire a skill? He has to be able to see what he's doing and say, "There's something right about it and there's something wrong about it. I see such and such a bug". In order to recognize that your behavior has a bug, you need a bunch of knowledge about differences in perceptual things. You can't learn a skill until you can see what's going wrong.

You have to know what the bug is, but that's not enough. A bug is just a difference between what a program does and what it should, but what do you do about the methods? The kind of work that Papert, Goldstein and I and other people, principally at MIT, worked on was: What are the kinds of bugs? In order to be good at acquiring skills, you have to have the knack of looking at a process and saying, "What are the kinds of things wrong with it?" Not what's specifically wrong with it, but what are the kinds of things wrong with it? For example, you might have two procedures which have conflicting goals. What you discover if you analyze a task like juggling is that the worst thing you can do is to keep your eye on the ball, because visual tracking is no use in the 200 milliseconds before you have to catch it. Your reaction time is too slow. What you should do in juggling, as you're keeping many balls going, is look at the top of the arc, and as soon as you've determined that, get your hand over to catch the ball. But keep your eye off that ball. After all, there are three balls there, so it certainly doesn't pay to keep your eye on "the ball" in that test.

What we need is a classification of types of bugs, and it would be nice if some hints about types of bugs could come out of fundamental theories, like dynamics. There are a few we know. If you overcorrect, you oscillate - an example of a classical bug from cybernetics. But there are many other kinds of bugs that are very important for sophisticated tasks that simply don't emerge from the analysis of mechanics and poles and zeroes and stability.

If you read Goldstein's and Sussman's theses, you find a catalog of bugs. Sussman proposes developing a "bug library" and describes his program for learning to debug other programs. His thesis was written in 1972, but the program was never written! Goldstein's thesis also describes a program for learning to draw things from verbal descriptions and that program was half finished. A recent thesis by John Doyle describes a program for making other

programs realize intentions and that program was never finished.
And the best learning program around (not counting the recent
ones—it looks like John Holland has finally got one that's on the
right track) was Winston's in 1970 which learned to recognize
certain structures. That program _was_ finished, I believe! But
that's 10 years ago and nobody has pushed that direction. I can't
understand this strange shortage of actual work on a fairly obvious
line of machine learning.

Debugging is an ugly word—what I really mean is the theory of
diagnosing processes and changing them to make them better, to
realize whatever intentions you have. One thing that's been holding
up the field is that there are only two ways to represent processes,
neither much good. One is by mathematics, and the other is by
computer programs in good languages. If you write a computer
program in FORTRAN or PASCAL or ALGOL, then I offer you no hope.
Those 25-year-old languages are just not able to express the kinds
of concepts we want. If you use something like Hewitt's PLANNER or
some of the fancier production programs, then you get a little
closer to a natural way to describe intentions, but not very. The
AI people who like LISP say it's the easiest and best language for
describing complicated intentional programs. But in a way they're
lying. LISP is the most flexible language around right now because
of its milieu, the environment and know-how. In fact, this is a
language that's so extensible that when anybody writes a program
they very swiftly write the language they want. By contrast, you
can't write an adaptive production language in PASCAL without a lot
of trouble. LISP is flexible for a cultural reason rather than a
technical one.

Traditional mathematics with state variables is even worse than
FORTRAN for describing processes, if possible, because mathematics
doesn't describe conditionals. You can't say, "If A, then B" in
mathematics without using the word "if". And if you look in a
mathematics paper, you see equation, equation, equation, and then
there's some English which says, "if this" "if that" and so forth,
and the whole thing deteriorates - you might as well use a
programming language. But in the programming languages that we
have, it's very hard to describe bugs. Goldstein's thesis is
probably the clearest explanation of the problem and some approaches
to it. A typical bug is that you stick two processes together, but
one process leaves the situation in a state that's not acceptable as
input for the other one. A very common bug is that you handed a
floating pointing number to a program that wanted a fixed point one.
More modern systems try to deal with data types automatically, but
data types are just the surface of the problem.

The programming languages are so clumsy that they've been
holding up the theory of their own bugs. I don't know quite what's

to be done about that. I'd almost rather see processes and bugs described in a natural language and then have a really smart computer that understands English or French; it wouldn't really be much worse. That's the present bottleneck. We know a lot about representation of knowledge, but our ways of describing processes haven't progressed much, because both mathematics and programming science have done as much harm as good in being able to describe how to put together systems in a natural way. Mathematics is really miserable at that. Much as I love it, logic isn't very good either.

I hope that out of the next generation of programming languages we'll see something that's more expressive. I think that discoveries of ways to describe things in computer science are occurring at a very high rate. It might take 25 years before somebody hits on a good way to describe control systems for computers, but I think that it will happen. The present systems aren't good enough. They're good enough to make systems; but they're not good enough to make the theories of their own bugs in a natural way. Yet it's this kind of knowledge that's central for adaptive control theory. If the machine can't describe to itself what's wrong, then it can't have a memory or even a problem solver to fix it that works much better than hill climbing. And hill climbing doesn't work when the space isn't decently smooth.

In talking about the kinds of knowledge that people need in order to learn something, I have been focusing on the debugging knowledge. There is also general knowledge about your own knowledge. If I give you a problem, it is only rarely that, out of all your memories you can get just the right ones straight away. People usually can't retrieve the right knowledge for a problem or it wouldn't take them so long to solve hard ones. So a lot of the knowledge you have is useless unless you also learn what it is for in some different structure. I bet that surface knowledge is 10% of real knowledge in a person who can use what he knows. It is only with "What's it for? Who told me it? What circumstances? What kinds of circumstances should this be retrieved in?" that you can solve this problem of getting appropriate responses out of your memory.

So, besides the debugging knowledge, this sort of positive knowledge of knowing what a certain thing is good for is vital, but no one knows much about that. I think maybe research is beginning on this with the so-called knowledge-based systems in AI where data bases are starting to get large numbers of facts -- even in parallel computers, you get in trouble if you retrieve too many associations with anything. So you have to start to classify them, and the first thing you pick up are simple retrieval cues like in management systems. But eventually you have to make a model of what you know and use that for steering your other thoughts.

THE ROLE OF THE CRITIC IN LEARNING SYSTEMS

T. G. Dietterich and B. G. Buchanan*

Stanford University
Stanford, California 94305

ABSTRACT

Buchanan, Mitchell, Smith, and Johnson (1978) described a general model of learning systems that included a component called the Critic. The task of the Critic was described as threefold: evaluation of the past actions of the performance element of the learning system, localization of credit and blame to particular portions of that performance element, and recommendation of possible improvements and modifications in the performance element. This article analyzes these three tasks in detail and surveys the methods that have been employed in existing learning systems to accomplish them. The principle method used to evaluate the performance element is to develop a global performance standard by (a) consulting an external source of knowledge, (b) consulting an internal source of knowledge, or (c) conducting deep search. Credit and blame have been localized by (a) asking an external knowledge source to do the localization, (b) factoring the global performance standard to produce a local performance standard, and (c) conducting controlled experiments on the performance element. Recommendations have been communicated to the learning element using (a) local training instances, (b) correlation coefficients, and (c) partially-instantiated schemata.

---

*This research was supported in part by the Advanced Research Projects Agency of the U.S. Department of Defense under contract MDA 903-80-C-0107 and by the Schlumberger-Doll Research Laboratory.

127

INTRODUCTION

A model of learning systems has been described (Buchanan et al., 1978) that attempts to capture the key components that must be included in any learning system. That model (shown below in Figure 1) is centered around the Performance Element--the component whose behavior the learning system is attempting to improve. The Performance Element (PE) responds to stimuli from the environment, and the purpose of learning is to make the responses better, in some sense. The Blackboard (BB) provides a common means of communication among the elements and ensures that all elements have access to changes made by the others. The Instance Selector (IS) selects suitable (sometimes random) training instances from the environment to present to the Performance Element. The Critic (CR) in this model evaluates the responses of the PE by comparing them against some standard of performance to determine how well the PE has done. In addition to this global evaluation, the Critic determines which parts of the PE are responsible for good and bad behavior. And, in this model, the Critic then recommends to the Learning Element (LE) what should be done to reinforce good behavior or improve bad behavior, but not precisely how to do it. Finally, the whole learning system operates within a conceptual framework, called the World Model (WM), that contains the vocabulary, assumptions, and methods that define the operation of the system.

The present paper attempts to extend this model by analyzing, in detail, the role of the Critic in existing learning systems. According the model, the Critic has three basic tasks: (a) to

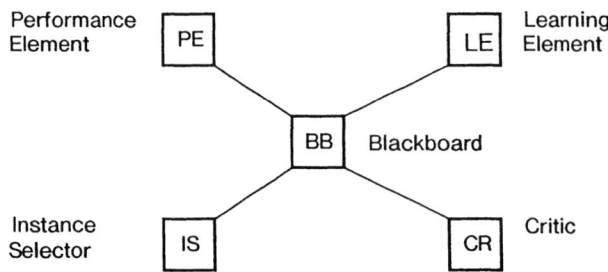

Figure 1. A model of learning systems (after Buchanan et al., 1978).

evaluate the current performance of the PE, (b) to localize
responsibility for good and bad performance to particular parts of
the PE, and (c) to make recommendations to the LE regarding desirable
changes in the PE. The Critic can be viewed as an expert system that
performs fault diagnosis and repair (similar to systems such as MYCIN
(Shortliffe, 1976) and DART (Bennett and Hollander, 1981)). These
systems evaluate the performance of some complex system (in this
case, the PE), localize the causes of detected faults, and recommend
repairs. The remainder of this paper discusses these three tasks in
detail and then surveys the methods that have been employed in
existing learning systems to accomplish them. Finally, our
observations are summarized, and the implications for the design of
future learning systems are assessed.

The reader is warned that many of the examples cited in this
paper are necessarily brief, since the purpose of the paper is not to
present existing work, but to describe and analyze the methods that
have been employed to perform the Critic's three tasks. Readers
desiring a fuller survey of the learning systems mentioned in this
paper are encouraged to consult the article "Learning and Inductive
Inference" (Chapter XIV (in Volume 3) of the Handbook of Artificial
Intelligence, Cohen and Feigenbaum, 1982).

THREE TASKS OF THE CRITIC

Evaluation

The first and most obvious function of the Critic is to evaluate
the actions of the PE. This is usually accomplished by developing a
performance standard, that is, some sort of index against which the
PE's behavior can be compared. For example, in the Meta-DENDRAL
system (Buchanan and Mitchell, 1978), the PE's task is to simulate
the operation of a mass spectrometer. The simulator accepts a
molecular structure as input and produces a simulated mass spectrum
as output. Meta-DENDRAL's Critic employs an external performance
standard in the form of an actual spectrum measured by a mass
spectrometer. The subprogram INTSUM compares the simulated spectrum
with the actual spectrum, and the differences serve to guide the
search for new simulation rules.

The Critic, in its role as an evaluator, can be viewed in broad
terms as the test portion of a generate-and-test method. The
learning element is the generator. It proposes modifications in the
PE, and the Critic tests these modifications by evaluating the
actions of the PE on particular training instances. Every learning
system can thus be viewed as learning by trial and error (usually
heuristically-guided trial and error). It is through the PE and the
Critic that the hypotheses developed by the LE are tested
empirically.

Localization of responsibility

The second task of the Critic--to localize responsibility for
good and bad behavior to particular portions of the PE--was first
pointed out by Minsky (1963), where he called it the credit-
assignment problem. The credit-assignment problem arises whenever
the PE has composite structure and only a global performance standard
is available. By composite structure, we mean that the decisions of
the PE are determined by some composite decision-making process. The
PE, for example, may evaluate a complex expression or apply a series
of rules to arrive at a decision. In order for the LE to improve
individual subexpressions or individual rules, the Critic must
localize credit and blame for overall performance to these particular
subexpressions or rules.

For example, consider the learning problem addressed by
Mitchell's LEX system (Mitchell et al., 1981). LEX solves symbolic
integration problems. This performance task has composite structure:
In order to solve an integral, LEX must apply a sequence of
integration operators. Furthermore, LEX has only a global
performance standard; it knows it has solved the problem when it has
succeeded in removing the integral sign from the expression being
integrated. Once LEX has found a sequence of operators that solves
the problem, it must apportion credit and blame among the individual
operators in that sequence and among operators in any other
unsuccessful sequences that it investigated.

The credit-assignment process can be viewed as the process of
converting a global performance standard into a local performance
standard. The local performance standard indicates what the proper
outcome of each move (or each subdecision) should have been. Once a
local standard is obtained, credit assignment is straightforward.

LEX must break its global performance standard, which indicates
how good an entire solution path is, into a local performance
standard that indicates how good each step (each application of an
integration operator) is. The exact global performance standard used
by LEX is the length of the shortest known solution path, as measured
by computation time and space. The local performance standard for
each solution step is the length of the shortest known path from the
starting state of that step to a solution state. These various
performance standards are shown in Figure 2.

Once LEX has developed the local performance standard for each
step, it can complete the credit-assignment process by evaluating
every step in its tree of solution paths and partial paths. A step
is judged to be a good decision if it leads to a solution whose path
length is less than 1.15 times the local performance standard for
that step. Otherwise, the step is judged to be a bad step. This has
the effect of crediting all steps on the best known path (and on any

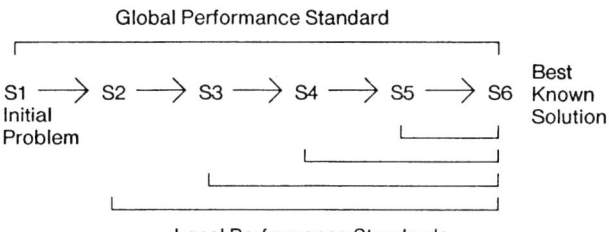

Figure 2.   Global and local performance standards in LEX.

other paths that have nearly the same length as the best known path). Blame is assigned to any step that leads from a state on the shortest path to a state not on the shortest path. All other decisions remain unevaluated (see Figure 3).

It is important to observe that the credit-assignment problem only arises when the units of knowledge being learned constitute small subcomponents of the PE. There would be no credit-assignment problem in LEX if, instead of trying to learn heuristics for individual integration operators, LEX simply memorized complete operator sequences. Exactly this kind of learning is performed by STRIPS (Fikes et al., 1972). Furthermore, one can imagine creating a learning system in which a series of credit-assignment problems must

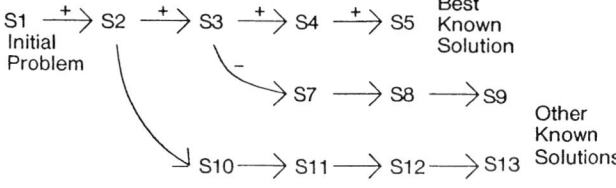

+ Good Decision
- Bad Decision

Figure 3.   Credit assignment in LEX.

be solved. Such a system could have, for example, a layered
performance element in which the overall decision was made by a set
of production rules, and each production rule depended in turn on
evaluating some complex expression. The first credit-assignment
problem would be to develop a local performance standard for each
production rule. This would be followed by a second credit-
assignment process in which a local performance standard would be
computed for each subexpression that makes up each production rule.
In summary, the difficulty of the credit-assignment problem depends
on the level of analysis carried out by the LE. As the relative size
of the "learnable unit" of knowledge becomes smaller, the credit-
assignment problem becomes more difficult.

Recommending changes in the Performance Element

Once global and local performance standards have been obtained
and, thus, the causes of poor performance have been isolated, the
Critic must recommend to the LE how the PE should be modified. These
recommendations can be thought of as verbs such as generalize,
specialize, and replace, along with some information that indicates
what should be modified.

In systems that learn from examples, the recommendation is
usually to generalize or specialize a particular rule or concept in
order to make it consistent with some new training instances. In
LEX, for example, the final output of the Critic is a set of
instances of the proper (and improper) application of integration
operators, gleaned from the trace of the problem solving process.
These training instances are supplied to the learning element along
with instructions to generalize or specialize the heuristics that
recommended the use of those integration operators.

In other learning systems, the recommendations may take the form
of fairly specific instructions for how to modify the knowledge base.
In Sussman's HACKER (1975), for example, the Critic provides a
partially filled-in schema describing a Conniver demon (or, more
correctly, an "if-added method"). The learning element must fully
instantiate this demon and install it in the knowledge base. The
schema includes instructions for how to generalize certain parts of
the demon, as well.

The dividing line between the Critic and the LE is not always
clear. In many learning systems, there is no separate recommendation
phase. Instead, the LE directly employs the local performance
standard to modify the PE. In systems that discover single concepts
from training instances (such as Winston, 1970; Mitchell, 1978;
Michalski, 1978; and Hayes-Roth and McDermott, 1978), the information
provided by the training instances and their correct classifications
suffices to guide the LE. Mitchell's version space algorithm
(Mitchell, 1978), for example, applies a matching process directly to

the training instances themselves in order to decide how the current concept description should be modified. The performance standard determines the nature of the change: Positive training instances lead to generalization, and negative instances lead to specialization, of the concept description.

METHODS FOR OBTAINING A GLOBAL PERFORMANCE STANDARD

Now that we have reviewed each of the three tasks of the critic, we turn our attention to the methods that have been used in existing systems to accomplish these tasks. Several methods have been employed for finding a global performance standard. These can be grouped into three general categories: knowledge sources external to the Critic, knowledge sources within the Critic, and search.

Knowledge sources external to the Critic

The first method of obtaining the global performance standard is to ask the outside world to provide one. We have already mentioned Meta-DENDRAL's use of an actual mass spectrum as a standard of performance for its mass spectrometer simulator. Many programs that learn concepts from examples expect the training instances to be correctly classified in the input. Winston's (1970) ARCH learning system, for example, relies on the teacher to indicate for each training instance whether that instance is an "arch" or a "near miss."

Another system that employs an external performance standard is Samuel's checkers program (1963, 1967). One configuration of the checkers program uses an outside knowledge source in the form of "book moves"--moves taken from recorded checkers matches between masters. Samuel's program attempts to learn an evaluation function that computes the worth of a given board position. The program learns by following book games, first applying its current evaluation function in order to select a move and then comparing the selected move with the global performance standard--the book move.

Davis' (1976) TEIRESIAS program provides another example of a system that turns to an expert for performance feedback. TEIRESIAS provides knowledge acquisition and debugging support for EMYCIN-based expert systems. The EMYCIN system serves as the performance element. It is presented with cases, which it processes by applying the rules in its knowledge base. When the consultation is completed, TEIRESIAS steps in and asks the expert whether the PE's conclusions are correct. At this point, the expert responds with a simple YES or NO. If the answer is NO, TEIRESIAS assists the expert in actually locating and repairing the problem (typically a missing or incorrect rule). The expert's yes/no answer serves as the global performance standard.

The technique of obtaining the global performance standard by consulting some source of knowledge external to the program is most useful in situations where the PE is attempting to model or mimic the behavior of a physical system or a human expert. In such cases, if the physical system is opaque or the human expert is unable to introspect well, the only information available to the learning system is the overall behavior of the unknown system. This global behavior can serve as the global performance standard.

Knowledge sources internal to the Critic

A second approach to obtaining a global performance standard is to employ some source of knowledge inside the Critic. Waterman's (1970) poker player, in its implicit training mode, is a good example of such a system. The performance task of the poker player is to decide what bets to make during a round of play of draw poker. This is a composite task, since a <u>sequence</u> of decisions must be made. At the end of each round of play, Waterman's Critic invokes an internal knowledge source to produce the global performance standard. The knowledge source is a rule-based system containing an axiomatization of the rules of draw poker along with rules describing how bets accumulate and how betting behavior is related to the quality of the players' hands. It contains definitions of the four basic actions available to the PE (CALL, DROP, BET HIGH, and BET LOW). The rule describing the CALL action, for example, is represented as

ACTION(CALL) & HIGHER(YOURHAND, OPPHAND) =>
          ADD(LASTBET, POT) & ADD(POT, YOURSCORE).

(I.e., if you call and your hand is superior, then you win the pot as augmented by your last bet.)

To evaluate a round of play, the Critic first determines the truth values of certain predicates such as GOOD(OPPHAND) and HIGHER(OPPHAND, YOURHAND) and then tries to prove the statement MAXIMIZE(YOURSCORE) by backward chaining through the rule base. The resulting proof indicates whether the PE could have won more money than it did.

Internal sources of knowledge are useful in domains where it is possible to encode some--but not all--of the knowledge needed to guide the performance element. For poker, it is easy to provide the basic rules of the game to the program. Unfortunately, the PE needs to know more than just the rules in order to play well. Consequently, the only use of the poker rule base in Waterman's system is to provide the Critic with a global performance standard.

An interesting characteristic of poker--and of many other task domains such as medicine, law, and politics--is that expertise consists of knowing <u>in advance</u> what actions should be taken. It is relatively easy to tell retrospectively what the performance element should have done. In these task domains, if the knowledge required for retrospective analysis can be incorporated into the learning system, then it can provide a global performance standard for the PE.

Search

In most problem solving tasks, deeper searches provide more information about the best solution. In LEX, for example, deeper and wider search leads to several alternative solutions to the integral. As we have seen above, LEX uses this fact to obtain the global performance standard. LEX chooses the path length of the shortest known solution and uses it as an upper bound on the lengths of other paths. During problem solving and credit assignment, whenever a path exceeds the upper bound, it is dropped from further consideration.

Samuel's checkers player--in an alternate configuration that does not employ "book moves"--uses deep search to obtain its global performance standard. Recall that Samuel's system is attempting to learn an evaluation function for board positions. One way to determine the quality of a board position is to search deeper into future game positions, apply the same evaluation function to the tip positions, and compute the mini-max backed-up value. Since the backed-up value based on a deep search is more accurate than the value calculated directly from the board position in question, it can serve as a global performance standard for the evaluation function.

In summary then, there are three basic approaches to finding a global performance standard. In domains where a physical system or an expert is being modeled, the external environment can provide the performance standard in the form of the actual behavior of the physical system or the expert. In domains where retrospective analysis is easy, the knowledge required for such retrospective analysis can provide the standard. Finally, in domains where deeper searches produce more information, simple search can provide a global performance standard.

METHODS FOR ASSIGNING CREDIT AND BLAME--OBTAINING A LOCAL PERFORMANCE STANDARD

Once we have an overall performance standard, how can we localize credit and blame to individual decisions? Three basic methods can be discerned. One approach is to side step the problem by consulting some knowledge source outside the program, a second approach is to factor the global performance standard into a local performance standard, and the third approach is to conduct controlled experiments by varying some subcomponent of the PE and observing the resulting changes in the global behavior of the PE.

Knowledge sources external to the Critic

Of course it is possible to finesse the credit-assignment
problem completely by simply asking the external world to provide a
move-by-move performance standard. In one configuration of
Waterman's poker learner, for example, a human expert provides
feedback after each bet decision. TEIRESIAS also relies on the human
expert to examine the performance trace and localize the point at
which the PE went wrong. This approach is useful in situations where
an expert is available who can successfully criticize particular
cases. The particular cases serve to focus the expert's attention
and trigger his or her memory. This is an important aspect of the
standard knowledge engineering methodology (See Davis, 1976).

Another situation in which the external world provides the local
performance standard is program debugging. When a programmer is
testing a program, he or she must have some idea what the proper
outputs of the program should be--that is, the programmer must know
the global performance standard. When one of the outputs is
incorrect, interactive debugging tools, such as the INTERLISP BREAK
package, enable the programmer to inspect intermediate states within
the program. However, the programmer must also have some idea what
the correct internal states should be--that is, the programmer must
figure out what the local performance standard is. Some programming
language features, such as run-time type checking and run-time
correctness assertions, allow the programmer to partially specify the
local performance standard so that the programming system can
automatically compare it with the actual behavior of the program.

Factoring the global performance standard

A second approach to solving the credit-assignment problem is to
factor the global performance standard into local standards that
correspond to the subparts or subdecisions of the PE. This approach
relies on discovering some substructure within the global performance
standard. In Meta-DENDRAL, for example, the global performance
standard--the actual mass spectrum for a molecule--is factored into
its individual lines. This factoring takes advantage of the fact
that the global performance standard has some substructure--it is
made up of spectral lines. Of course not any factorization will
work. The spectral lines must correspond somehow to the PE
subcomponents that the Critic is attempting to evaluate. In Meta-
DENDRAL, the subcomponents of interest within the PE are cleavage
rules that predict, for a given molecular bond or set of bonds,
whether those bonds will break. Each spectral line corresponds to
some combination of one to three individual cleavages.

In Meta-DENDRAL, the credit-assignment process is carried out by
the subprogram INTSUM, which is a transparent version of the PE (the

mass spectrometer simulator). When INTSUM is given a molecule, it simulates the cleavage process and produces a simulated spectrum. More importantly, however, each line in the simulated spectrum is annotated with a record of which cleavages led to the creation of that line. Thus, the correspondence between spectral lines and PE subcomponents is computed. Now credit assignment is trivial. If the simulated line matches an actual line, then the cleavages that "caused" the simulated line are credited. Otherwise, if the simulated line does not match a real line, the cleavages are blamed.

Meta-DENDRAL starts the learning process with a "half-order theory" of the mass spectrometer. This half-order theory can be thought of as a small set of very general cleavage rules that state that just about every bond in the molecule will break, with a few exceptions (e.g., double bonds, triple bonds, bonds in aromatic rings, and bonds incident to the same atom). The learning process improves the half-order theory by specializing it to predict more precisely when bonds will break.

Figure 4 provides a schematic diagram of the process of factoring the global performance standard, comparing it to the intermediate decisions of the PE, and assigning credit and blame to various subcomponents of the PE.

A second system that successfully factors the global performance standard is Sussman's (1975) HACKER system. HACKER is a blocks-world planner; given an initial blocks configuration and a desired configuration, it must develop a sequence of operations (a plan) that will achieve the given goal. HACKER employs an internal knowledge source--a blocks world simulator--as its global performance standard. Once the PE (the planner) has developed a plan, the simulator simulates it to see if the plan will in fact attain the goal.

The simulator can be factored to obtain a local performance standard. The simulation is conducted one step at a time; after each step, the state of the world can be compared with what the PE expected it to be. In fact, the simulator detects three kinds of errors: illegal actions, violated expectations, and unaesthetic actions. Illegal actions are actions, such as picking up a whole stack of blocks, that are illegal in the blocks world. Violated expectations are precisely that--steps whose intended effects were not achieved. Unaesthetic actions are actions in which the program moves the same block two times in succession with no intervening action. Once one of these errors is detected, HACKER proceeds immediately to develop a bug demon that will detect the problem and patch around it in future plans. HACKER does not conduct further credit-assignment to determine which of its planning methods was at fault. Planning methods--such as the method that states that conjunctive goals can be achieved independently--are never modified;

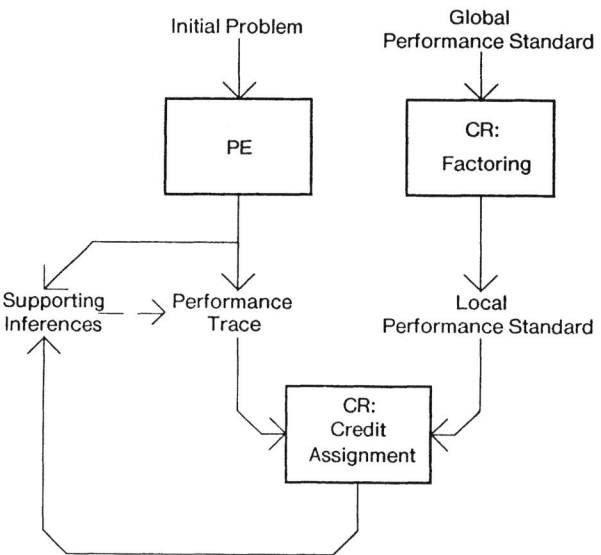

Figure 4.   Diagram of the factoring and credit-assignment process.

badly formed plans are just patched prior to execution.

In order for HACKER's credit-assignment strategy to work, it is very important that the PE provide a detailed trace of its planning process. This trace lists the subgoals that each plan step is expected to achieve. The simulator compares these expectations with the simulated execution of the plan and localizes blame accordingly.

Waterman's (1970) poker player is a third system that factors the global performance standard. Recall that the Critic attempts to prove the statement MAXIMIZE(YOURSCORE) using an axiom system that encodes the rules of poker and some knowledge about how bets accumulate. The proof provides a global performance standard; it indicates whether or not the performance element could have improved its winnings during the round of play. In addition, the proof provides a local performance standard. It discovers the sequence of bet decisions that would have led to the best score for the program.

The description of the axiom system given above is slightly
inaccurate. It gives the impression that only one proof is conducted
for each round of play. In fact, a separate proof of the
MAXIMIZE(YOURSCORE) statement is conducted for <u>each</u> bet decision in
the round. Waterman has analyzed, in advance, all of the ways in
which previous bet decisions can influence subsequent bet decisions.
His analysis is incorporated into the axiom system using a few
predicates such as LASTBETOPP(BET HIGH), which says that the
opponent's last bet was high. For each bet decision, the truth
values of such "connective" predicates are determined by examining
previous bets, and then the axiom system is invoked to see if the
current bet was appropriate. In essence, Waterman has manually
factored the performance standard so that it can be applied to
individual bet decisions.

The three systems just described--Meta-DENDRAL, HACKER, and
Waterman's poker player--all obtain their local performance standards
by factoring the global performance standard. Meta-DENDRAL factors
the spectrum into its individual lines, HACKER factors the overall
simulation of the plan's execution into the simulation of each plan
step, and Waterman factors the proof for the whole round of play into
individual proofs for each bet decision.

Conducting controlled experiments

The third approach to solving the credit-assignment problem is
to modify some subcomponent of the PE and observe how the global
performance changes. This is the technique employed by computer
engineers when they attempt to localize a fault by swapping a single
printed-circuit board and then observing the overall behavior of the
system to see if the problem goes away. It is a powerful technique,
but it only provides unambiguous information if the global
performance of the PE actually changes. If changing a subcomponent
has no effect, it is difficult to distinguish the case in which the
subcomponent is unimportant from the case in which the component is
vital, but a second problem in the PE is masking the effects of the
component change.

Three existing learning systems can be viewed as performing
controlled experiments in order to localize PE faults. One system is
Samuel's checkers player, which attempts to learn the coefficients of
a polynomial evaluation function. In order to assign credit and
blame to individual coefficients, Samuel computes the pairwise
correlation between the value of each checkers board feature and the
global performance standard. Features whose changes correlate
positively with the global performance standard are given positive
coefficients, and features that vary inversely with the global
performance standard are given negative coefficients.

This approach to solving the credit-assignment problem makes an

independence assumption: It assumes that credit and blame can be
allocated to each part of the PE independently. For the polynomial
evaluation function, this makes sense because the use of the
polynomial itself is based on the premise that the overall value of a
checkers move can be obtained by computing a weighted sum of various
board features. Samuel's research has shown, however, that the
linear polynomial fails to capture much of the knowledge employed by
checkers masters because of this independence assumption. Hence, the
pairwise correlation approach, although adequate for the polynomial
representation, may not be adequate in general.

The second system that employs controlled experiments is
Samuel's signature table checkers system. This system uses a
signature table, instead of a polynomial, to represent the evaluation
function. A signature table is an n-dimensional array of cells.
Each dimension corresponds to some numerical checkers board feature,
such as the number of kings or the number of open squares in the back
row. The features are measured and then used to index into the
signature table to obtain the corresponding cell. The cell contains
a numerical rating of that board position. Thus, in principle, the
signature table can represent a different rating for each distinct
board position, and hence, the independence assumption is not needed.
Samuel's experiments with signature tables indicated that they did
indeed perform better than simple polynomial evaluation functions for
this reason.

Unfortunately, a single signature table for Samuel's 24 checkers
board features would be prohibitively large (roughly 10^{12} cells).
Instead, Samuel employs a three-level tree of smaller tables as shown
in Figure 5. The PE first determines the values of the 24 board
features. These values are used to index into the first set of
signature tables to obtain new values. Each of these first-level
values is then used to index into the second-level tables where the
cells contain values that in turn serve as indexes for the final
third-level table. The cells in the third-level table provide the
actual evaluation of the board position.

We can think of this three-level set of tables as a three-level
production system in which the results of the first-level inferences
are tested in the condition parts of the second-level production
rules. The second-level rules produce values that serve to trigger
third-level rules. Credit assignment for signature tables is
accomplished by computing a correlation coefficient for each cell in
each table, in a fashion similar to that used for the polynomial
evaluation function. Each cell is associated with two tallies,
called A and D, which are initially zero. At each board position
during a game, the program is faced with a set of alternative moves,
one of which is indicated by the performance standard to be the best
move. Each possible move can be mapped to one cell in each signature
table. A 1 is added to the D tally of each cell whose corresponding

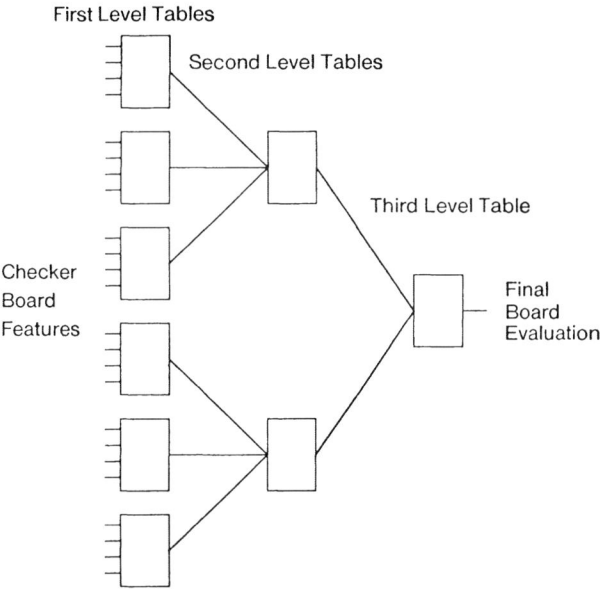

First Level Tables

Second Level Tables

Third Level Table

Checker
Board
Features

Final
Board
Evaluation

Figure 5. Samuel's three-level signature table scheme.

move is <u>not</u> the correct move, and a total of <u>n</u> (where <u>n</u> is the number
of incorrect alternatives) is added to the A total of each cell
correponding to the correct move. From the A and D totals, a
correlation coefficient C = (A - D)/(A + D) is computed and used to
update the contents of the cells in the signature tables.

This tally method effectively credits the entire inference tree
corresponding to the correct move and blames all alternative trees.
This is not a problem for the first-level cells, since it is always
clear which cells correspond to the best board position. However,
for the second- and third-level tables, the cells corresponding to
the best move are not necessarily those cells selected by the first-
level tables--especially during the early phases of learning when the
first-level tables still contain incorrect values. Samuel's system
credits them anyway and relies on a huge number of training instances

(approximately 250,000 moves) to correct eventually any errors
introduced by this procedure. Samuel also found it necessary to
apply interpolation procedures to the signature tables during the
early phases of learning, since, at that point, most cells in the
first-level tables were empty. Thus, the pairwise correlation method
of assigning credit and blame is not entirely adequate for signature
tables either, but the large number of training instances gradually
corrects any errors introduced through this credit-assignment
process.

    Finally, the third system that conducts controlled experiments
is LEX. As we have seen above, LEX evaluates alternative operator
applications by investigating the subtrees rooted at each of the
alternatives. The move that leads to the shortest subtree is
credited, and all moves leading to significantly larger subtrees are
blamed. This method works well as long as the subtrees are carefully
investigated. Unfortunately, during the early stages of learning,
the performance element is easily overwhelmed by combinatorial
explosion and, hence, cannot fully investigate these subtrees. Even
more troublesome is the behavior of the performance element when it
has learned an overly specific heuristic. Such a heuristic causes it
to ignore an operator even when that operator should be applied.
This leads the PE to overlook possible solutions and hence, resulting
in incomplete investigation of the alternative subtrees.

    We have examined three existing systems that employ some form of
controlled experimentation to localize credit and blame: Samuel's
polynomial system, Samuel's signature table system, and Mitchell's
LEX system. In general, controlled experimentation--that is,
systematic variation of a single subcomponent of the PE--is a
powerful method. There are some difficulties however. First, it is
necessary to assume some independence among the faults within the PE.
If multiple interdependent problems exist, then one fault can mask
another and varying a single component will not necessarily lead to
any change in system performance.

    A second difficulty is that, in some performance elements,
adequate controls may not be available. In order to create a
controlled experiment, it must be possible to vary some aspect of the
performance element while keeping all other parts fixed. This is not
possible in LEX, for example, where choosing a different integration
operator leads to a different search tree, which must be thoroughly
investigated in order to permit accurate comparisons. This is a kind
of factoring of the performance element into nearly independent
subcomponents. Such factoring is similar to the factoring of the
global performance standard.

    A question for future research is to try to understand exactly
when the PE or the global performance standard can be properly
factored and to develop factorization methods. This is equivalent to

the deeper question of what structures are ultimately learnable. Do
there exist systems that are so complex that they cannot be
sufficiently factored to allow learning to occur? One speculation is
that a task that cannot be factored can still be learned at a more
abstract level of analysis. Suppose, for example, that adequate
controls were not available in LEX to evaluate individual
applications of integration operators. It would still be possible to
expand the level of analysis and simply memorize entire sequences of
operators. In tightly coupled interdependent systems, there may be
no useful detailed level of analysis. The heuristics describing when
a particular operator should be applied would necessarily become
extremely complex and lengthy in order to capture all of the
interdependencies in such a system*. Thus, the credit-assignment
problem may be solvable in all cases either by successfully factoring
the global performance standard, by factoring the PE and conducting
controlled experiments, or by changing the level of analysis to learn
larger units of knowledge.

METHODS FOR DEVELOPING RECOMMENDATIONS

        Once the problems have been localized to individual decisions
within the PE, the PE must be modified so that these problems do not
recur. There are many ways that a performance element can be
repaired. In production systems, for example, the antecedents of the
production rules can be generalized or specialized, the consequents
of the rules can be altered to perform different actions, new rules
can be added, and conflict-resolution strategies can be modified. In
concept-learning systems, the definition of the concept can be
generalized, specialized, or completely changed. Sometimes a
decision must be made about whether to repair the problem directly or
create a demon to detect the problem in the future and patch around
it.

        The final task of the Critic is to figure out what <u>kind</u> of
change should be made, rather than to actually make the modifications
itself. In order to accomplish this, the Critic must have some way
of mapping kinds of faults into kinds of repair. This mapping has
been fairly straightforward in existing learning systems. In LEX,
for example, if an integration operator was applied in a situation
when it should not have been, then the solution is to specialize the
heuristic attached to that operator so that it will no longer
recommend its use in such situations. Conversely, if an integration

---

*Notice, however, that this argument does not address the possibility
 that the entire task could be reformulated to reveal a much simpler
 internal structure (e.g., as Ptolemaic astronomy was superseded by
 Copernican astronomy).

operator should have been applied, but was not, then the solution is to generalize the associated heuristic.

For HACKER, the mapping between kinds of faults and proposed fixes is more indirect. This is because the basic cause of all of HACKER's errors is its "linearity assumption"--that conjunctive goals can be pursued completely independently. Rather than modifying this assumption, HACKER's solution is to patch around it. Consequently, when a fault is detected, HACKER must decide which particular kind of patch should be applied. This is accomplished by examining the subgoal structure of the failed plan step and matching this structure against a set of subgoal interaction schemata. The matching schema has an associated skeletal demon that, when fully instantiated and installed in the knowledge base, will detect future instances of the problem and fix them prior to the execution of the plan.

In addition to indicating what kind of repair should be undertaken by the learning element, the Critic usually provides the LE with additional information to guide the modifications. In systems that learn from examples, the Critic provides local training instances to the LE. A local training instance is an instance of the use of a particular rule along with the local performance standard for that rule application. This is to be distinguished from a global training instance, which has the form of a global problem situation paired with a global performance standard. In Meta-DENDRAL, for example, a global training instance has the form of a known molecular structure and its associated actual mass spectrum. The local training instances are comprised of individual bond cleavages and the corresponding spectral lines that they produce. It is these local training instances that are generalized by the LE to develop general cleavage rules.

In LEX, the global training instance is the initial integration problem coupled with the global performance standard (i.e., the shortest known solution path length). The local training instances are the positive (or negative) examples of the correct (or incorrect) application of integration rules. These local instances are processed by the candidate-elimination algorithm (Mitchell, 1978) to develop integration heuristics.

Instead of local training instances, Samuel's checkers Critic provides a set of correlation coefficients to the LE. As we saw above, the correlation coefficients indicate how the individual features in the evaluation function are correlated with the global performance standard. These correlation coefficients are rescaled by the LE and then substituted for the previous weights in the evaluation polynomial.

Finally, as we mentioned above, HACKER's Critic provides the LE with a partially-filled-in bug demon that will detect and correct

bugs in future plans. The skeletal demon provides instructions for
how to complete the instantiation process and tells which parts of
the demon should be generalized.

In summary, the task of deciding what kind of changes should be
recommended to the LE is fairly straightforward. In existing
systems, the recommendations have been communicated to the LE using
local training instances, correlation coefficients, and skeletal
demons.

SUMMARY

In this paper, we have reviewed the three tasks of the Critic:
obtaining a global performance standard, converting it into a local
performance standard, and recommending to the learning element how
the PE should be improved. For each of these tasks, we have
attempted to list the methods that have been employed in existing
learning systems to accomplish them. Global performance standards
have been obtained by asking the external environment to supply them,
by consulting some internal source of knowledge, and by conducting
deeper searches. Local performance standards have been obtained by
asking external sources, by factoring the global performance standard
in some way, and by conducting controlled experiments. Finally,
recommended changes have been communicated to the LE in the form of
verbs such as generalize, specialize, or replace along with
information such as local training instances, correlation
coefficients, and skeletal bug demons.

One of the most interesting results of this analysis is the
conclusion that the credit-assignment problem may be solvable in most
learning situations. If a system can be factored, then controlled
experiments can be conducted to localize faults. If a system resists
factoring, then the level of analysis can, and should, be modified to
learn larger units of knowledge. A disadvantage of learning these
larger units of knowledge is that many more of them will need to be
learned. However, in complex systems it is likely that no simple
generalizations can be found at the level of individual rules, and
hence, the learning system has no choice but to learn larger units of
knowledge.

Another result of this analysis is the observation that the
Critic requires a model of the internal operation of the PE and some
understanding of the semantics of the PE's knowledge base. Credit
and blame cannot be localized to individual rules in the knowledge
base unless the Critic has access to and can understand those rules.
Similarly, recommendations for change require at least some
understanding of how the PE interprets the knowledge base.

Thirdly, the Critic must have access to a trace of the internal decision-making process of the PE. Without this additional information, it is impossible to compare the PE's internal decisions with the local performance standard.

Finally, this paper has analyzed the Critic as if it were a separate expert system with its own knowledge base. We have attempted to catalog the kinds of knowledge that such an expert system would need and the kinds of methods it would apply. However, most of this knowledge is still not well formulated. Making it explicit is a necessary part of the research needed to provide knowledge acquisition tools for expert systems.

ACKNOWLEDGMENTS

The authors wish to thank the Advanced Research Projects Agency of the U.S. Department of Defense and the Schlumberger-Doll Research Laboratory for supporting this research. Thanks also go to Charles P. Paulson and James S. Bennett for comments on early drafts of this paper.

REFERENCES

Bennett, J. S. and Hollander, C. R., 1981, DART: An expert system for computer fault diagnosis, Proceedings of IJCAI-81, Vancouver, Canada.

Buchanan, B. G., Mitchell, T. M., Smith, R. G., and Johnson, C. R. Jr., 1978, Models of learning systems, in: "Encyclopedia of Computer Science and Technology."

Buchanan, B. G. and Mitchell, T. M., 1978, Model-directed learning of production rules, in: "Pattern-Directed Inference Systems," Waterman, D. A. and Hayes-Roth F., eds., Academic Press, New York.

Cohen, P. and Feigenbaum, E. A., 1982, "The Handbook of Artificial Intelligence," Volume III, Kaufmann, Los Altos, California.

Davis, R., 1976, "Applications of meta-level knowledge to the construction, maintenance, and use of large knowledge bases," Rep. No. STAN CS-76-552, Stanford University, Stanford, California.

Fikes, R. E., Hart, P. E., and Nilsson N. J., 1972, Learning and executing generalized robot plans, Artificial Intelligence, 3:251-288.

Hayes-Roth, F. and McDermott, J., 1978, An interference matching technique for inducing abstractions, Communications of the ACM, 21(5):401-410.

Michalski, R. S., 1978, "Pattern recognition as knowledge-guided induction," Rep. No. 927, Department of Computer Science, University of Illinois at Urbana-Champaign.

Minsky, M., 1963, Steps toward artificial intelligence, in:

"Computers and Thought," Feigenbaum, E. A. and Feldman, J., eds., McGraw-Hill, New York.

Mitchell, T. M., 1978, "Version Spaces: An approach to concept learning," Rep. No. STAN-CS-78-711, Stanford University, Stanford, California.

Mitchell, T. M., Utgoff, P. E., Nudel, B., and Banerji, R. B., 1981, Learning problem-solving heuristics through practice, Proceedings of IJCAI-81, Vancouver, Canada.

Samual, A. L., 1963, Some studies in machine learning using the game of checkers, in: "Computers and Thought," Feigenbaum, E. A. and Feldman, J., eds., McGraw-Hill, New York.

Samuel, A. L., 1967, Some studies in machine learning using the game of checkers II - recent progress, IBM Journal of Research and Development, 11(6):601-617.

Shortliffe, E. G., 1976, "Computer Based Medical Consultations: MYCIN," American Elsevier, New York.

Sussman, G. J., 1975, "A Computer Model of Skill Acquisition," American Elsevier, New York.

Waterman, D. A., 1970, Generalization learning techniques for automating the learning of heuristics, Artificial Intelligence, 1(1/2):121-170.

Winston, P. H., 1970, "Learning structural descriptions from examples," Rep. No. MIT AI-TR-231, MIT, Cambridge, Massachusetts.

EXAMPLES AND LEARNING SYSTEMS*

Edwina L. Rissland

Department of Computer and Information Science
University of Massachusetts
Amherst, MA 01003, U.S.A.

INTRODUCTION

Any system that learns or adapts -- whether well- or
ill-defined, man or machine -- must have examples, experiences, and
data on which to base its learning or adaptation. Too often,
however, the examples that form the basis of learning are taken for
granted. This paper will concentrate on the examples as a study in
their own right.

BACKGROUND

The importance of examples to learning systems can be seen in
many well-known A.I. programs. For instance, Winston's program
[1975] learns the concept of "arch" from a sequence of examples: of
arches and non-arches. The initial example, and examples that fail
to be an arch in just one aspect, "near misses", are what drive this
learning system. Samuel's Checker Player is another classic AI
program that makes use of examples [1963, 1967]. Samuel gave his
program libraries of specific book moves. His work is an example of
the interplay between examples, adaptation and learning systems.

Selfridge's recent COUNT and sorting programs [Selfridge 1979,
1980], as well as his classic PANDEMONIUM [Selfridge 1958], also
depend heavily on example data and problems. COUNT would not learn

---

*The research reported in this paper was supported in part by the
National Science Foundation under grant no. IST-8017343.

its task -- how to count the number of symbols in a string -- if not
presented with a sequence of challenging but not too difficult
problems to solve. The sorting program would not be able to
adaptively tune itself -- learn the "best" choice of sorting method
to use-- if it did not have abundant experience with problems of
sorting lists.

These same observations can also be made about Soloway's
BASEBALL program [Soloway 1978], which learns the concepts and rules
of baseball by "watching" baseball games; and about Lenat's AM
program [Lenat 1977], which discovers new mathematical concepts
partly on the basis of how the concepts and control heuristics fare
on examples.

Examples also play a critical role in non-computer systems like
law, mathematics and linguistics. For instance, the law --
especially common law, which is based on the doctrine of precedent
("stare decisis") -- is a wonderful example of a system which is
hard to define (despite its superficial resemblance to a rule-based
system) and which runs entirely in response to the examples -- i.e.,
cases -- presented to it. Cases must be adjudicated; the court
expresses the results as "holdings" and "dicta" (rules and comments
of the case); these lead to the further evolution of concepts and
rules which are then modified by further cases [Levi 1949, Berman
1968]. In legal scholarship and education, the cases may be
hypothetical; in some law classes, "hypos" become as "real" and
have as much import as actually litigated cases.

Examples are central to reasoning in mathematics in the cycle
of "proofs and refutations" [Lakatos 1976]: a mathematical concept
is refined in response to how the system, that is the mathematical
theory with all of its definitions, theorems, proofs, examples,
etc., fares in the face of examples, ranging from standard examples
to unusual "monsters". Of course, a rich set of examples is needed
for the guessing and inductive inference needed to get the system
started in the first place [Polya 1968].

In linguistics, examples too are central to theory formation
and in fact, many theories are built in response to what have now
become famous examples, or counter-examples, to other theories.
(See for instance, Gazdar's [1981, 1982] response to Chomsky's
assertion that English does not have phrase-structure grammar.) In
fact, Kuhn has pointed out that this interplay between an evolving
system and examples is ubiquitous in the history of science [Kuhn
1970].

Finally, in computer programming itself there is an "inevitable
intertwining" [Swartout and Balzer 1982] of the evolving system
(e.g., a program), as expressed in code and specifications, and the
examples used to test it out. One writes code, tests it out on

example data, and then (usually) revises the program; specifications also evolve in this way. The programming and debugging process is thus completely analogous to the cycle of proofs and refutations in mathematics.

Thus, in summary, examples (by which is meant experiences, data, instances) are critical grist for the mill of learning and adaptation. Once this obvious, but key, point is recognized, one is led immediately to questions like the following:

1. How should examples be grouped into types?
2. Do examples have structure?
3. How are examples related to one another?
4. What properties should an example satisfy?
5. Where do the desired properties come from?
6. How can knowledge of examples be applied to ill-defined systems?

The rest of this paper addresses these questions.

TAXONOMIES OF EXAMPLES

When one considers the different effects and uses examples can have with respect to learning systems, one can distinguish different classes of examples. In this section, we briefly review the "epistemological" classes of examples that we have found useful in disciplines like mathematics and law [Rissland 1978, 1982].

It is important to recognize that not all examples serve the same function in learning. For instance, expert teachers and learners know that certain perspicuous ("start-up") examples provide easy access to a new topic, that some ("reference") examples are quite standard and make good illustrations, and that some examples are anomalous and don't seem to fit into one's understanding. We can develop a taxonomy of items based upon how we use them to learn, understand and teach:

(a) start-up examples: perspicuous, easily understood   and easily presented cases;
(b) reference examples: standard, ubiquitous cases;
(c) counter examples: limiting, falsifying cases;
(d) model examples: general, paradigmatic cases;
(e) anomalous examples: exceptions and pathological cases.

Start-up examples are simple, easy to understand and explain cases. They are particularly useful when one is learning or explaining a domain for the first time. Such examples can be generated with minimal reference to other examples; thus one can

say they are structurally uncomplicated. A start-up example is
often "projective" in the sense that it is indicative of the general
case and that what one learns about it can be "lifted" to more
complex examples.

Reference examples are examples that one refers to over and
over again. They are "textbook cases" which are widely applicable
throughout a domain and thus provide a common point of reference
through which many concepts, results and other items in the domain
are (indirectly) linked together.

Counter-examples are examples that refute or limit. They are
typically used to sharpen distinctions between concepts and to
refine theorems or conjectures. They are essential to the process
of "proofs and refutations" [Lakatos 1976].

Model examples are examples that are paradigmatic and generic.
They suggest and summarize expectations and default assumptions
about the general case. Thus, they are like "templates" or "frames"
[Minsky 1975].

Anomalous examples are examples that do not seem to fit into
one's knowledge of the domain, and yet they seem important. They
are "funny" cases that nag at one's understanding. Sometimes
resolving where they fit leads to a new level of understanding.

An example of applying this classification scheme for an
introductory study of continuity from the domain of real function
theory might classify: the function $f(x)=x$ as a start-up example;
$f(x)=x**2$, $f(x)=e**x$ as reference examples; $f(x)=1/x$ as a
counter-example; "$f(x)$ with no gaps or breaks" as a model example;
and $f(x)= sin(1/x)$ as an anomalous example. The first example,
$f(x)=x$, is also a reference example (the "identity" function).
Thus, such a classification need not be exclusive. The anomaly
$sin(1/x)$ will most likely become a favorite counter-example as one
understands that a function can fail to be continuous in at least
two ways, that is, by having gaps and breaks and by failing to
settle down to a limit. Thus, such a classification is not static.
Increased understanding will of course lead to qualifications on the
above model of a continuous function, although it will still serve
to summarize one's expectations.

In introductory LISP programming one deals with lists of atoms.
For the novice, the lists (A) and (A B C) are start-up examples; (A
B C) is also a reference example; NIL or ( ), a counter-example;
"left-paren atom atom atom ... right-paren", a model example.

The point here is not the particular parsing out of examples
into classes, for this depends on many considerations such as one's

level of expertise and purposes for taxonomizing; but that there
are classes of examples, and that such epistemological knowledge
about classifying examples (and other items) is an important part of
one's understanding. Such knowledge can be used to help focus one's
attention in learning and explaining, for instance by suggesting
heuristics like "Check out the conjecture on reference examples
before believing too strongly in it" or "Look for counter-examples
in the class of known counter-examples".

STRUCTURAL ASPECTS OF EXAMPLES

     In a complex domain like mathematics or law, there are several
types of structure. We can distinguish items, relations, spaces:

     (1) items are strongly bound clusters of information: for
     instance, the statement of a theorem, its name, its proof, a
     diagram, an evaluation of its importance, and remarks on its
     limitations and generality.

     (2) relations between items: for instance, the logical
     connections between results, such as predecessor results on
     which a result depends logically and successor results which
     depend on it.

     (3) spaces are sets of similar types of items related in similar
     ways: for instance, proved results and their logical
     dependencies. Such a set of items and relations constitute a
     space, in the case of results, a Results-space.

     In essence the idea is that examples (and other items) are
cohesive clusters of information which do not exist in isolation
from one another; there are relations between them. What
distinguishes a "space" from a "set" is the prominence of the
relations. The structure of a complex domain like mathematics
contains not just one but many spaces, each of which describes a
different aspect of knowledge. Examples are but one type of "item"
that comprise the knowledge in such domains; others include
concepts, results, strategies and goals [Rissland 1978, 1981b . Of
concern in this paper are examples by which we mean specific
situations, data or experiences.

     An example has many aspects or pieces of information that
comprise it: its name, taggings and annotations as to
epistemological class and importance, lists of pointers to other
examples from which it is constructed and to whose construction it
contributes, the process of how it is constructed, a schematic or
diagram, pointers to items like definitions in other spaces,

statements of what the example is good for or how it can be misleading, sources of further information about the example.

Examples can be related by constructional derivation of how one example is built from others. Examples plus this relation constitute an Examples-space. For instance, in the LISP programming example, the examples ((A) B C) and (A (B C)) can be thought of as constructionally derived from the reference example list (A B C) by the addition of parentheses.

The construction of a new example from others is a process that is found in many fields, for instance law and mathematics. In teaching the law, one frequently makes use of "hypothetical" examples ("hypos") which are often constructed by modification of a well-known reference example, e.g., a textbook case. In a Socratic discussion between a law professor and his class, the teacher may spin out a sequence of hypos to test out the class's understanding and biases on a doctrinal proposition. Such a sequence might contain increasingly more complex or extreme cases.

The following hypothetical examples are taken from a class discussion in contract law. They were used to point out the difference between the doctrines of "consideration" (which emphasizes what the promisee gives the promisor in return for the promise) and "reliance" (which emphasizes how the promisee acts in reliance on the promise). These are two different ways to approach the problem of determining which contracts are legally enforceable as opposed to which are gratuitous gifts. The base case from which the hypos are constructed through modifications is Dougherty v. Salt, a standard case in a course in contract law [Fuller and Eisenberg 1981].

Hypo1:
Facts: Aunt Tillie says, "Charlie, you are such a nice boy; I promise to give you $10,000."

Hypo2:
Facts: Same as Hypo1 with the addition that Charlie says, "Dear Aunt Tillie, I can't take something for nothing, let me give you my third-grade painting."

Hypo3:
Facts: Same as Hypo2 except that Charlie offers to mow Tillie's lawn.

Hypo4:
Facts: Same as Hypo2 except that Charlie's last name is Picasso.

Hypo5:
Facts: Same as Hypo1 with the addition that Aunt Tillie's assets
are in ruin and that keeping her promise to Nephew Charlie means her
own children starve.

Hypo6:
Facts: Same as Hypo1 with the addition that Charlie then makes an
unreturnable deposit on a new car.

Thus in summary there are internal and external structural
aspects to examples. The internal structure of an example concerns
the cluster of strongly bound information that comprises the
example, including pointers to other items like examples. The
external aspects concern the relations among examples, for instance
how one example is constructed from others.

CONSTRAINTS AND EXAMPLES

An important aspect of examples with respect to learning
systems is the obvious fact that examples possess certain
properties. For instance, the "near misses" in Winston's work are
examples that fail to be arches in exactly one of the required
properties of archness. What perhaps may not be so obvious is that
in selecting examples to give to a learning system, one does not
pick them at random: examples are generated for a purpose -- like
giving evidence for or against a conjecture -- and thus examples are
usually (carefully) chosen to possess certain desired properties,
which we call constraints.

We have called this process of generating examples that meet
prescribed constraints "Constrained Example Generation" or "CEG".
In past work, we have described, built, and experimented with a
model of the CEG process. See for instance, [Rissland 1980, 1981a,
Rissland and Soloway 1980a, 1980b]. It is based upon observations
of humans working problems in which they are asked to generate
examples satisfying certain constraints. Our model of CEG
incorporates three major phases: RETRIEVAL, MODIFICATION, and
CONSTRUCTION.

When an example is sought, one can search through one's
storehouse of examples for one that matches the properties desired.
If one is found, the example generation problem has been solved
through RETRIEVAL. In retrieval, there are many semantic and
contextual factors -- like the last generated example -- and
therefore one is not merely plunging one's hand into an unorganized
knowledge base. Thus even though retrieval sounds simple, it can be
very complex.

However, when a match is not found, how does one proceed? In
many cases, one tries to MODIFY an existing example that is judged
to be close to the desired example, or to have the potential for
being modified to meet the constraints. Often the order of examples
selected for modification is based on judgements of closeness
between properties of known examples and the desiderata, that is,
how "near" the examples are to what is sought.

If attempts at generation through modification fail,
experienced example generators, like teachers or researchers, do not
give up; rather they switch to another mode of example generation,
which we call CONSTRUCTION. Under construction, we
include processes such as combining two simple examples to form a
more complex one and instantiation of general model examples or
templates to create an instance. Construction is usually more
difficult than either retrieval or modification.

General Skeleton of the CEG Model

CEG has subprocesses for: Retrieval, Modification, Construction,
Judgement, Control

Presented with a task of generating an example that meets specified
constraints, one:

1. SEARCHES for and (possibly) RETRIEVES examples JUDGED to satisfy
    the constraints from an EXAMPLES KNOWLEDGE BASE (EKB); or

2. MODIFIES existing examples JUDGED to be close to, or having the
    potential for, fulfilling the constraints with domain-specific
    MODIFICATION OPERATORS; or

3. CONSTRUCTS an example from domain-specific knowledge, such as
    definitions, general model examples, principles and more
    elementary examples.

In examining human protocols, one sees two types of generation:
(1) retrieval plus modification; and (2) construction. That is,
one does not necessarily try first retrieval, then modification,
then construction; sometimes construction is attempted
straightaway. Clearly, this model needs many other features to
describe the CEG process in its entirety; more details can be found
in [Rissland 1981a].

To give the reader an idea of the richness and complexity of

the CEG process, we present here a synopsis of a CEG problem taken
from the domain of elementary function theory. The problem is:

> Give an example of a continuous, non-negative
> function, defined on all the real numbers such that it
> has the value 1000 at the point x=1 and that the area
> under its curve is less than 1/1000.

Most protocols for this question began with the subject
selecting a function (usually, a familiar reference example
function) and then modifying it to bring in into agreement with the
specifications of the problem. There were several clusters of
responses according to the initial function selected and the stream
of the modifications pursued. A typical protocol went as follows
[Rissland 1980]:

> "Start with the function for a "normal distribution". Move it
> to the right so that it is centered over x=1. Now make it
> "skinny" by squeezing in the sides and stretching the top so
> that it hits the point (1, 1000)."

> "I can make the area as small as I please by squeezing in the
> sides and feathering off the sides. But to demonstrate that the
> area is indeed less than 1/1000, I'll have to do an integration,
> which is going to be a bother."

> "Hmmm. My candidate function is smoother than it need be: the
> problem asked only for continuity and not differentiability. So
> let me relax my example to be a "hat" function because I know
> how to find the areas of triangles. That is, make my function
> be a function with apex at (1, 1000) and with steeply sloping
> sides down to the x-axis a little bit on either side of of x=1,
> and 0 outside to the right and left. (This is OK, because you
> only asked for non-negative.) Again by squeezing, I can make the
> area under the function (i.e., the triangle's area) be as small
> as I please, and I'm done."

Notice the important use of such modification operations as
"squeezing", "stretching" and "feathering", which are usually not
included in the mathematical kit-bag since they lack formality, and
descriptors such as "hat" and "apex". All subjects made heavy use
of curve sketches and diagrams, and some used their hands to
"kinesthetically" describe their functions. Thus the
representations and techniques used are very rich.

Another thing observed in all the protocols (of which there
were about two dozen for this problem) is that subjects make
implicit assumptions -- i.e., impose additional constraints -- about
the symmetry of the function (i.e., about the line x=1) and its
maximum (i.e., occurring at x=1 and being equal to 1000). There are
no specifications about either of these properties in the problem

statement. These are the sort of tacit assumptions that Lakatos
[1976] talks about; teasing them out is important to studying both
mathematics and cognition.

CONSTRAINT GENERATION

     Generating examples from constraints presupposes that there are
constraints. That is, that properties of examples can be expressed
in a language of constraints, and that one actually knows what one
wants in the example sought, that is, the constraints. To put it
another way, there is a prior problem of constraint generation.

     The constraints are often generated from consideration of one's
intended use for the example-to-be. For instance, if one were
testing a program known to work on simple cases, one would want
examples that are more complex or rare, for instance an anomalous or
counter-example. If one could not find a satisfying example in
one's "Examples Knowledge Base", perhaps organized as an
Examples-space, one would need to generate it. To do this one could
express the desiderata for the example in terms of constraints and
then proceed with the CEG process.

     In hypos for a Socratic discussion in law, such constraints
would include pedagogical, rhetorical, doctrinal constraints, such
as, those in our previous example, arising from the doctrine of
consideration. The constraint upon the object given by Nephew
Charlie to his Aunt Tille might be loosely described as "being
something of value"; this constraint is then varied from something
of little value (the typical third-grade painting), to something of
some value (mowing the lawn), to something of great value (a
"Picasso" third-grade painting).

     If one were giving examples of lists to a neophyte LISP
programmer, one would make use of domain-specific constraints having
to do with "length" (of the list), "order" (of atoms in the list),
"depth" (of certain atoms), and whether the list is a "LAT" (i.e., a
list of atoms) or a more complex list [Rissland and Soloway 1980b].
For instance, one might want a list such that: (1) it has length 3,
and (2) the depth of the first atom is 3. The list (((A)) B C)
satisfies both constraints and may be thought of as generated from
the reference example (A B C) by a sequence of modifications
affecting depth. The lists (((A) B) C) and (((A B C))), which are
also generated by modifications affecting depth through the addition
of parentheses, satisfy the second (depth) but not the first
(length) constraint. Thus, modifications designed to remedy one
constraint deficiency might, in the language of Sussman [1973],
"clobber a brother goal", that is, another constraint. Such
interactions can make the CEG problem quite complex.

APPLICATIONS TO ILL-DEFINED SYSTEMS

In this section we suggest how examples can be used in probing, debugging, specifying, or otherwise dealing with an ill-defined or not well-understood system.

Examples can be useful for probing a system. Consider the following scenario. We've just logged on and are trying to learn how to use or test a system, or a new feature of it. Suppose it were a program to sort letters into alphabetical order.

To probe this program, we might start off by saying, "If this program really works, it ought to do simple little things; it certainly ought to handle A, B, C. If it fails on A, B, C, we know there's a problem from the very beginning." Suppose we find it's OK on A, B, C, a standard start-up or reference example in this mini-domain.

Now we'd try something a bit more complex, like a longer list, say more of the beginning of the alphabet. This is a slight embellishment of the beginning example, arising from a length constraint. Suppose it works on such an example -- which is good since the program didn't have to do "anything" -- let's give the program an opportunity to exercise itself on some other simple cases like C, B, A or the alphabet in reverse order. Then, we might introduce a couple of letter interchanges like A, C, B or M, O, N, P, R, Q. These involve order as well as length constraints and can be generated with an "interchange" modification.

Thus we're probing the system with a sequence of increasingly complex cases derived from standard simple ones. With a minimal level of confidence in the program established, we could go on to test it on more difficult or limiting cases.

We might now check if the program can handle known troublesome examples like a singleton list, like "A", or the empty list, which are known from experience to be some of the cases that make programs cough and sputter, that is, counter-examples. The singleton list often causes problems because of the false assumption that there's (always) going to be more than one element. A LISP programmer would know of another well-known trouble maker: the empty list, NIL. It is an important case in recursive procedures. In fact, it is a favorite (i.e., reference) example with any LISP hacker. In the sorting domain, there would be some other specific things that are known to cause problems, for instance, repeated elements. Thus we are using knowledge about the examples and about the context and task in evaluating a system.

Note that we are not examining or altering the code, which can be considered a lower level representation of the program; rather we're staying on a representational level more akin to the purposes of the program, that is, what the program is supposed to do, or more realistically, what we believe it's supposed to do. We're dealing with the system at arm's length and just probing and asking if the program appears to work by our experience with it on selected, and well-chosen, examples.

Such probing of a system in this manner is similar to testing theorems. (Again, we have the analogy with mathematics, which has been discussed by De Millo et al. [1980].) One can never show that it works by just trying examples, we can only show, perhaps, that it doesn't work, just as one counter-example can refute a conjecture. However, having a variety of instances that work establishes confidence, even if it doesn't end the verification process. By selecting enough well-chosen cases, one can "span" the possibilities and obtain a sense of the program's correctness. One of the differences between a novice and an expert programmer (or mathematician) seems to be the richness of the "spanning" examples used: novices tend to forget to check the program on complicated or known counter-examples and anomalies, even simple ones like NIL. Thus part of the art of expert programming is epistemological knowledge of the type we have described in previous sections of the paper.

Also note that in this scenario the problem of evaluating the answer required little work on our part: alphabetical order is obvious by inspection. In other cases of generating test data, there's a lot more work involved to being a critic. (See [Dietterich and Buchanan] in this volume.)

These remarks also apply if we are writing or debugging a program. Using specific examples to work out a solution helps one to deal with the complexity or lack of specification of the solution. It might well be the case that the kind of examples used in probing might be different from those in design and implementation.

Since it is impossible to completely specify a program under every condition -- because, for instance, the context of the system is changing or one is not sure of what one wants -- using examples to show what the program should do in certain situations, especially those that matter to the specifier or that are too difficult to describe in symbols or words -- provides another means of describing the program. Together traditional specifications in words, logic or symbols joined with example cases provides a better specification than either alone; each mode compensates for and complements the other.

CONCLUSIONS

In this paper we have discussed examples in their relation to learning systems and in their own right. In particular, we have described the structural aspects of examples, including their internal structure as a strongly bound cluster of information and their external relations to other examples through construction. We have used constraints to approach the problem of generating examples with specific properties and have described the prior problem of constraint generation which involves interactions between the system and the examples or example user. Lastly, we have suggested that examples are central to probing, debugging and even specifying systems: they can probe a system and they can help describe it by showing how it does or should operate.

Thus, in our approach we concentrate on the role that examples (that is, experiences, instances, data) play in systems, well- or ill-defined, and find that they are a rich study in themselves. Not only are they interesting, in fact they are central. As that great polymath Oliver Wendell Holmes put it:

"The life of the law has not been logic; it has been experience"

And it is experience we are capturing with examples.

REFERENCES

Berman, H. J., "Legal Reasoning". In International Encyclopedia of the Social Sciences, MacMillan, 1968.

De Millo, R.A., Lipton, R.J., Perlis, A.J., "Social Processes and Proofs of Theorems and Programs", Communications of the ACM, Vol. 22, No. 5, May 1979. Reprinted in the Mathematical Intelligencer, Vol. 3, No. 1, 1980.

Fuller, L. L., and M. A. Eisenberg, Basic Contract Law. West Publishing Co., Minn., 1981.

Gazdar, G., "Phrase Structure Grammar". In Jacobson, P., and G.K. Pullun (Eds.) The Nature of Syntactic Representation, Reidel, 1982, pp. 131-187.

Gazdar, G., "Unbounded Dependencies annd Coordinate Structure". Linguistic Inquiry 12 (1981), 155-184.

Kuhn, T. S., The Structure of Scientific Revolutions. Second
    Edition. University of Chicago Press, 1970.

Lakatos, I., Proofs and Refutations. Cambridge University Press,
    London, 1976. Also in British Journal for the Philosophy of
    Science, Vol. 14 , No. 53, May 1963.

Lenat, D. B., "Automatic Theory Formation in Mathematics",
    Proceedings of Fifth International Joint Conference on
    Artificial Inteligence. Cambridge, MA., 1977.

Levi, E. H., An Introduction to Legal Reasoning. University of
    Chicago Press, 1949.

Minsky, M. L., "A Framework for Representing Knowledge". In The
    Pyschology of Computer Vision, Winston (ed), McGraw-Hill, 1975.

Polya, G., Mathematics and Plausible Reasoning, Volumes I and II.
    Princeton University Press, 1968.

Restatement, Second, Contracts. American Legal Institute,
    Philadelphia, 1981.

Rissland, E. L., "Examples in the Legal Domain: Hypotheticals in
    Contract Law". In Proceedings Fourth Annual Conference of the
    Cognitive Science Society. Ann Arbor, August 1982.

_____, Constrained Example Generation. COINS Technical Report
    81-24, University of Massachusetts, 1981a.

_____, The Structure of Knowledge in Complex Domains. COINS
    Technical Report 80-07, University of Massachusetts, 1981b.
    Also to appear in Proceedings NIE-LRDC Conference on Thinking
    and Learning Skills, Lawrence Erlbaum Associates.

_____, "Example Generation". In Proceedings Third National
    Conference of the Canadian Society for Computational Studies of
    Intelligence, Victoria, B. C., May 1980.

_____, The Structure of Mathematical Knowledge. A.I. Tech Report
    472, A. I. Laboratory, Massachusetts Institute of Technology,
    1978.

_____, "Understanding Understanding Mathematics". Cognitive
    Science, Vol. 2, No. 4, 1978.

Rissland, E. L., and E. M. Soloway, "Overview of an Example
    Generation System". In Proc. First National Conference on
    Artificial Intelligence. Stanford, August 1980a.

_____, "Generating Examples in LISP". Proceedings International
    Workshop on Program Construction. Bonas, France, 1980b.

Samuel, A. L., "Some Studies in Machine Learning Using the Game of
    Checkers". In Computers and Thought, Feigenbaum and Feldman
    (Eds.), McGraw-Hill, 1963.

_____, "Some Studies in Machine Learning Using the Game of Checkers.
    II--Recent Progress". In IBM J. Research and Development,
    11:601-617, 1967.

Selfridge, O. G., "Pandemonium -- A Paradigm for Learning". In
    Symposium on the Mechanization of Thought Processes.
    Teddington, England, 1958.

_____, "An Adaptive Sorting Algorithm". In Proceedings Third
    National Conference of the Canadian Society for Computational
    Studies of Intelligence, Victoria, B.C., May 1980.

_____, "COUNT — How a Computer Might Do It". Internal Report, Bolt
    Beranek and Newman Inc, 1979.

Soloway, E. M., "Learning = Interpretation + Generalization: A
    Case Study in Knowledge-Directed Learning". COINS Technical
    Report 78-13, University of Massachusetts, 1978.

Sussman, G. K., A Computational Model of Skill Acquisition. A.I.
    Tech Report 297, A. I. Laboratory, Massachusetts Institute of
    Technology, 1973. (Doctoral dissertation.)

Swartout, W. and R. Balzer, "On the Inevitable Intertwining of
    Specification and Programming". CACM Vol. 25, No. 7, July
    1982.

Winston, P. H., "Learning Structural Descriptions from Examples" in
    The Psychology of Computer Vision, Winston (ed), McGraw-Hill,
    1975.

CONCEPTUAL MODELS OF ILL-DEFINED SYSTEMS

Richard M. Young

MRC Applied Psychology Unit
Cambridge
England

I take it that an essential property of an ill-defined system is that it lends itself to no single analysis which is both correct and also adequate to answer all relevant questions. Instead of this, we have to make use of a variety of different views, hoping to find (at least) one which is appropriate for a given purpose. These alternative analyses are only partial, and to a certain extent fictional. None of them can be taken as an account of the system "as it really is".

This situation is not unique to the case of ill-defined systems. Even for determinate systems, it is a familiar argument that a variety of different perspectives, levels of analysis, and so on are needed in order to understand a complex system properly. The difference is that in the case of ill-defined systems we have no choice: the multiplicity is forced upon us. But this also means that, far from being "worse" than determinate systems, ill-defined systems have the merit of laying out the possibilities more unambiguously, and thus serve to clarify our thinking about complex systems in general.

If our intention is to create techniques for the understanding and control of complex and ill-defined systems, a useful viewpoint to consider is that of the operator (or user) of such a system. In contrast to other approaches which focus more on the formal analysis and technical properties of the system itself, this orientation places its main emphasis on an essentially psychological question, that of the structure and content of the knowledge needed to utilise the system effectively. The aim of this paper is to speculate about the possibility of applying to ill-defined systems a technique which has been developed for the analysis of users' conceptual

models of much simpler and determinate devices, such as pocket
calculators and computer command languages. In order to do this, I
will present a summary of the technique before considering its
proposed application. For more information about the technique in
its own right, the reader is referred to the account given in Young
(1981).

USERS' CONCEPTUAL MODELS OF POCKET CALCULATORS

There exists no general agreement as to what is meant by an
operator's "conceptual model" of an interactive system or device.
Instead there are as many different notions of what it might be as
there are people writing about it (Young, 1982). What they seem to
have in common is the idea that when interacting with the device,
the user will adopt some more or less definite representation or
metaphor to guide his actions and help him interpret the machine's
responses. It is agreed that the properties of the conceptual
model are an important factor in the usability of a machine, and
that the requirement for the machine to have a simple, clear, and
consistent model is a relevant consideration for the designer. One
reason pocket calculators prove to be a rewarding class of devices
to study is because the ones in common use include a range of
radically different designs, while at the same time, by comparison
with the more complicated devices such as computer operating
systems, they are small and manageable enough that it is still a
feasible project to analyse them completely.

Surrogate models

This paper presents two different suggestions as to the form
of the users' model. The first kind is referred to as a surrogate
model, and consists of a description of a simple physical mechanism
which provides an analogical account of how the real system works.
Such a model is not to be thought of as a full engineering specification of the actual device, but rather as a simplified "cover story"
which predicts the gross functional features of its behavior. This
kind of model is called a "surrogate" because it simulates certain
aspects of the real machine, and so can be used in place of the
machine itself for answering certain questions about its behavior.
The clearest illustrations of such hypothetical machines as conceptual models come from their use in the teaching of simple computer
programming languages, where they have for example been used as a
way of providing students with a picture of how the programming
language interpreter works (Mayer, 1981; du Boulay, O'Shea and Monk,
1981).

An elegant example of a surrogate model is provided by those
calculators which make use of Reverse Polish Notation (RPN). RPN
is a notation for writing arithmetical expressions without the need

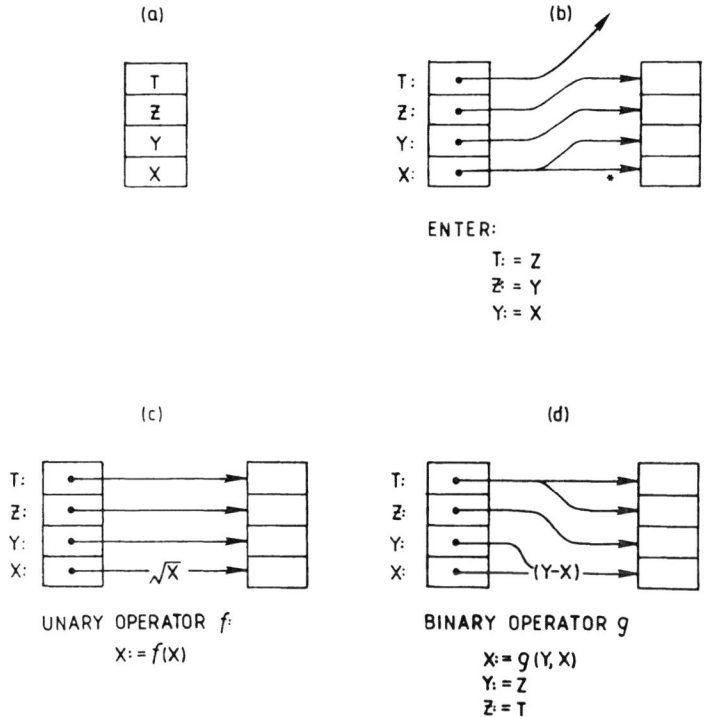

Fig. 1. Stack model for the RPN calculator

for parentheses, by placing operators after the operands they apply
to instead of between them as in ordinary algebraic notation. On
these calculators, a key marked ENTER is used to separate consecutive
numbers. Thus to add 2 and 3 on an RPN calculator, the sequence of
keys would be "2 ENTER 3 +".

    RPN calculators have the interesting property that they arrive
with explicit surrogate models presented in the manufacturer's
instruction manuals. Figure 1 is derived from such a model. It
shows that the calculator is built round an internal <u>stack</u> consisting of four registers, called X, Y, Z and T, each capable of holding
a number. It is always the number in X which appears on the calculator's display. The stack model is used to explain the effects
of the various keys. Figure 1d for example shows the action of the
binary operator "-". The operator takes as its operands the numbers
in the Y and X registers (in that order) and "consumes" them. The
result is written into X, while the prior contents of the Z regis-

ter are copied into Y and of T into Z. Similarly for the other
operator keys. Once a few points of detail have been taken care
of, it turns out (perhaps surprisingly) that the stack model can
predict the response of the calculator to any sequence of inputs.

Another class of calculators, which I will refer to as "Four
Function" (FF) machines, are "algebraic" in the sense that they
employ ordinary infix notation for binary operators, but offer no
parentheses and no relative precedence among the operators:
operations are performed in the order they are typed in. A certain
range of calculations can be done with these machines using a notation not too different from the way arithmetical expressions are
normally written. A simple binary calculation can be done by typing

$$2 + 3 = ,$$

an iterative calculation (like adding up a column of numbers) by

$$2 + 3 + 4 + 5 = ,$$

(though notice that "2 + 3 x 4 =" yields 20, not 14), and a cumulative calculation by

$$2 + 3 = + 4 = .$$

In addition to these straightforward uses, the particular calculator
I examined (Young, 1981) also retains from one calculation to the
next the operator that was used and its second operand. These can
be used again in the next calculation simply by inputting a new
(first) number and pressing the "=" key. After calculating "5 x 17
=", for example, other numbers can be multiplied by 17 just by keying "7 =", "12 =", and so on. These are referred to as constant
calculations. It is not difficult to construct for this FF calculator a model, similar in spirit to that for the RPN, which copes
with all these different calculations. Details are shown in Figure
2, which again, like the stack model for the RPN machine, is capable
of predicting correctly the response of the FF calculator to any
sequence of keystrokes.

Despite the simplicity of this machine and the fact that its
behavior is captured by the model in Figure 2, certain aspects of
its use are awkward and confusing. The machine has no key for
reciprocals (commonly labelled "1/x" on other calculators), but the
reciprocal of a number or computed result can be found by typing
 "÷ = =". Thus keying "5 ÷ = =" gives the answer 0.2, a result
most people find surprising. Similarly the expression 6/(3 + 5)
can be evaluated by the sequence "3 + 5 ÷ = 6 =". Although these
behaviors are logically necessary consequences of the way the
machine handles constant calculations, they nevertheless strike
prospective users as bizarre. Stepping momentarily into the role

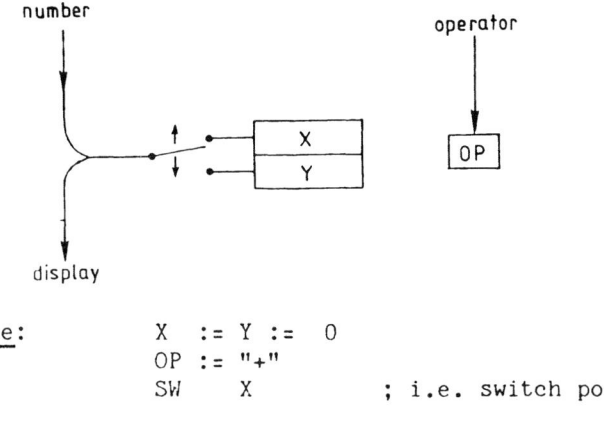

```
Initialise:              X  := Y :=  0
                         OP := "+"
                         SW  X            ; i.e. switch points to X

Input number N:    *SW := N              ; store N in register
                                         ; SW points to

Press operation f: if implied "=", do actions for "="
                         OP := f
                         Y  := X
                         SW  Y            ; set switch to Y

Press "=":               X  := OP(X,Y)
                         SW  X            ; set switch to X
```

Fig. 2. Register model for the Four-Function calculator.

of Human Factors advisors, we can predict that this area of the
calculator's use will cause trouble. People will mis-remember the
magic sequences, will feel uncomfortable with these kinds of
calculations, and will go to some lengths to avoid having to use
these facilities.

It should by now be becoming clear that as a proposal for the
form of conceptual models, surrogate models are in a number of
ways unsatisfactory. Firstly, the model of the FF calculator
shown in Figure 2 fails to exhibit certain psychologically
important properties of the calculator, such as the confusing
behaviors just discussed. It is true that the model is
"objectively" correct, so that running the model on these
sequences is as good as using the calculator itself to demonstrate
the existence of the problems. But simply examining the model
gives no hint of the difficulty. It is therefore not only
inadequate as a psychological model but also misleading as a basis

for design. Secondly, surrogate models lend themselves best to
what is a rather atypical use of the machine, that of predicting
its response to a given sequence of keys. Normally, of course,
using a calculator involves being given a task and having to
devise the necessary input steps. And thirdly, another way the
surrogate model fails to reflect the psychology of the user is
that it has no way to capture the common observation that for
simple, routine calculations the user soon builds up a learned
repertoire of steps which saves having to re-derive them each time
from basic principles. Each of these shortcomings suggests that
it would be profitable to examine more directly the relationship
between the calculation being performed and the actions the user
has to take. This is done by the kind of model discussed next.

Task/action mapping models

    The second kind of conceptual model, called a task/action
mapping model, derives from the observation that the performance
of a particular calculation, such as the addition of 2 and 3, can
be viewed from at least two different perspectives. In terms of
the task domain of arithmetic, the calculation can be described as
the numerical evaluation of an arithmetical expression consisting
of the binary operator "+" applied to the two operands 2 and 3.
In the action domain of keypresses and answers from the calculator, the same calculation can be described as the typing of the
key sequence "2 + 3 =" followed by the reading of the result from
the display. Clearly, these two descriptions are closely related.
The task/action mapping model is a way of characterising the
correspondence between them.

    The mapping analysis begins by trying to describe the structure
of the task and action domains in such a way that there is a simple
and direct mapping between their corresponding parts. The simplicity of this mapping serves as a measure of the acceptability of
the proposed model, and the possibility of constructing a satisfactory model of this kind acts as a criterion for the quality of
an existing or proposed design. Normally it will not be possible
to achieve a direct mapping over the whole of the domains, so one
or more central core tasks and their corresponding core action
sequences are chosen which can be put into close correspondence.
For the FF calculator discussed above, the description of the
domains is shown in Figure 3. The core, prototypical task is
taken to be a "basic calculation" (i.e. a binary operation applied
to two numbers), and the other tasks are cast as variants of it.
For instance an iterative task such as adding up a column of numbers is described as a repeated series of basic calculations, the
result of each step being used as the first operand for the next.
In the action domain, the possible sequences are described by a
grammar which casts them as variants of the core sequence "Number
Operator Number =", each component of which corresponds directly

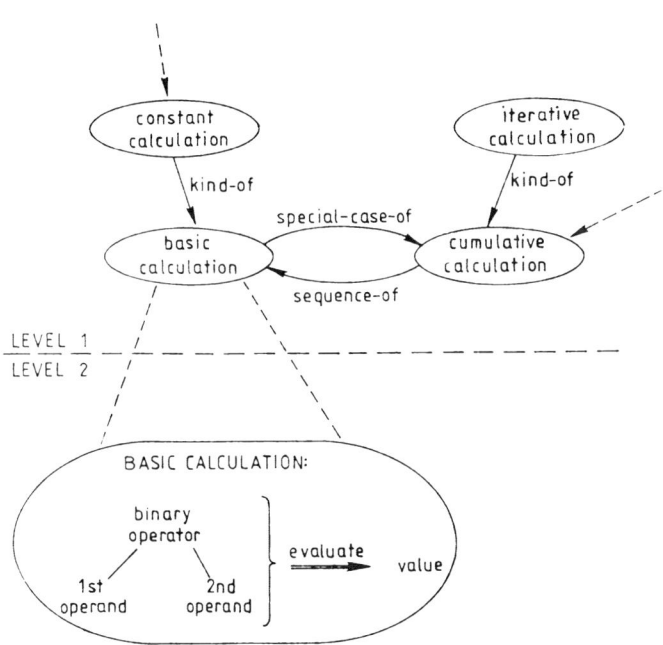

Fig. 3. Task and action domains for the Four-Function calculator.

to a part of the core task. In order to map from a given task to
its corresponding action sequence, we first express it as a
variant of the core task, then link from there to the core action
sequence, and finally from there to the appropriate variant. The
organisation of this linkage means that the direct connection
between the cores of the respective domains acts as a kind of
"communication channel" which funnels all the mappings between the
two domains.

    Since the cores are, by definition, subareas of the domains
between which there exists a simple and direct mapping, it follows
that the core entities are of closely similar internal structure,
i.e. isomorphic. They can therefore be seen as realisations in
the different domains of the same, more abstract, structure. This
higher-order commonality between the cores of the domains (referred to in Young (1981) as their "abstract prototype") provides a
coherent, integrative characterisation of the overall functioning

of the device. The FF calculator, for example, can be seen as essentially a machine for performing basic calculations. The RPN calculator can be viewed as a device for computing a different kind of calculation (called a locally structured binary (LSB) calculation--the term will be needed again below). Similarly a third type of calculator, an Algebraic machine which provides parentheses and is arranged to perform multiplications and divisions before additions and subtractions, can be characterised as being (more or less) a machine for evaluating formulae. Unlike the previously discussed surrogate models, these summary characterisations are oriented towards the normal use of the calculator, i.e. performing calculations, and concern the mapping from desired calculation to corresponding input sequence.

These mappings overcome most of the defects of the surrogate models, and because of their greater psychological fidelity lend themselves to a number of applications. First, they allow us to resolve the paradox of the FF calculator, which presents an apparently simple (surrogate) model but is still in certain respects confusing. The full analysis shows that although the mapping is straightforward in the case of basic calculations, it becomes considerably more complex, with interactions and interdependencies between its different components, for those calculations which involve the defaulting of the second argument. The actual details (Figure 4) are that, to begin with, the action grammar itself

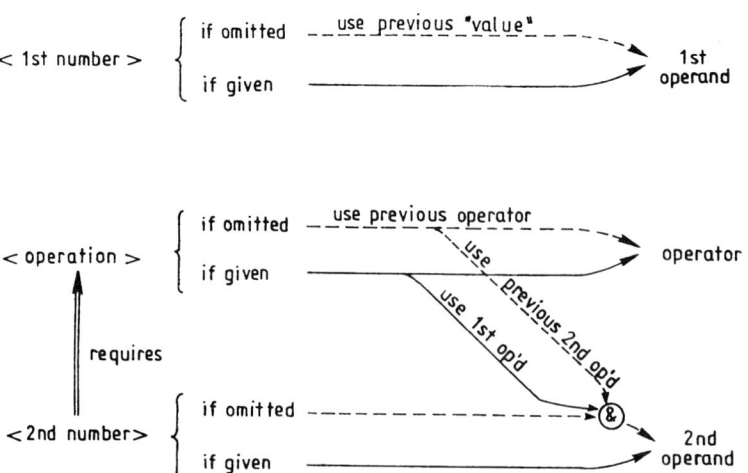

Fig. 4.   Mapping between task and action on the Four-Function
          calculator.

imposes a dependence between the second number and the operation,
so that a second number can be input only if a new operation is
also input, even if that operation is the same as the last one
given and is therefore what the default would be anyway if no new
operation were specified. Then also, keying the operation changes
the default used for the second argument from its previous value
to the value of the first argument. (An illustrative consequence
of these interactions is that, following the sequence "2 + 3 =", a
further "=" causes the calculator to display 8 whereas a "+ ="
results in 10.) This analysis not only captures the confusingness
of the FF calculator, it also correctly localises its source (i.e.
to the interaction of the defaulting arrangements for the operation and second argument). In comparison to the surrogate type
of model, the mapping model is not only more valid psychologically
but also offers a better basis for design.

A second area of application is the hotly debated question of
the rival merits of RPN and Algebraic calculators, a controversy
which has been addressed both within ergonomics (Kasprzyk, Drury &
Bialas, 1979; Card, 1979) and by the promotional literature
(Hewlett-Packard, 1979). The mapping analysis (again, for details
see Young, 1981) supports not the overall superiority of either
design, but rather the idea that there exist particular kinds of
calculational task for which each is the better suited. As
already mentioned, for evaluating arithmetical formulae the
Algebraic machines offer a fairly simple mapping between task and
action, and so are simple and satisfying to use. Similarly the
RPN machines cope elegantly with what I have called LSB calculations. But to use either calculator for the other's preferred
task requires elaborate and error-prone mental transformations, in
one case to "parse" the formula, in the other case to "linearise"
the structured calculation. Each calculator thus has its own area
of superiority.

Finally, it should be noted that since the analysis involves
identifying a core area in the task domain and describing other
tasks as its variants, the analysis imposes a particular structure
on the task domain, i.e. from a more psychological point of view,
it induces a structure in the user's representation of the task.
Furthermore, because the core chosen will vary from one design to
another, these induced structures will be different for different
calculators. An iterative calculation, for example, such as
adding up a column of numbers, is handled by the FF calculator as
a cumulative calculation where numbers are added successively to a
running sum, by the Algebraic calculator as a sum-of-series formula, and (with difficulty) by the RPN as an LSB calculation. The
psychological significance of these differences is that a user's
extensive experience of and familiarity with a particular design
of calculator will lead him to a particular view of the domain, so
that different users will carve up the space of calculations in

different ways. This variation of perceived structure provides a
concrete illustration of how a variety of perspectives can be held
on what is nominally the same domain--something which is surely
true of ill-defined systems.

APPLICATON TO ILL-DEFINED SYSTEMS

     As mentioned at the beginning of this paper, ill-defined
systems have the essential property that no single model can
suffice for answering all relevant questions. Instead there has to
be a range of models, appropriate for different purposes. However,
the fact that alternative views are possible does not mean that any
one view is as good as any other. One of the useful results of the
mapping technique in its application to ill-defined systems is a
basis for assessing the validity of a proposed model and clarifying
the role it might play.

     There are three broad classes of reasons why a particular par-
tial model may be unsuitable for a given purpose. First the model
may be too narrow, i.e. the phenomena in question may lie outside
its scope, and it may simply have nothing to say about them.
Second, it may be too shallow. In other words, it may cover the
relevant phenomena to the extent of mentioning them, but still not
provide enough detail to answer the questions of interest. Third,
the model may be inaccurate, in the sense that it may purport to
answer the question but simply be wrong in what it says. (Such a
model presumably compensates for its obvious shortcomings by coping
well in other areas).

     In its application to ill-defined systems, the technique just
outlined would be used to provide one or more partial models of the
system as seen from the viewpoint of the operator. Some of these
may take the form of "surrogate" models, particularly if a convenient representation is needed for predicting the effects on the
system of specified input sequences. But more directly useful
would be one or more "mapping" models, each of which identifies the
core of a coherent aspect of the system's behavior and describes it
in terms of the actions to be taken by the operator in order to
bring about some desired result. The system would be controlled
and understood by the operator in terms of these partial models,
each dealing with a sub-range of the system's capabilities. It
would be hoped that these partial models are not too numerous, so
that a small number of them suffice to cover the phenomena of
interest. Over the long term, the process of assimilating and
mastering a particular system would consist of a series of exercises of increasing scope, building and probing conceptual models
to cover more and more aspects of the system's behavior and
exploring the relationships between them.

Such an approach evidently falls short of being a "method" for analysing ill-defined systems, comparable to the techniques of transfer function analysis applicable to certain types of linear and quasi-linear systems (c.f. Baron, this volume; Wonham, this volume). Apart from the directive to examine the relations between task and action, it leaves the detailed realisaton of the plan to the ingenuity, skill and experience of the individual analyst. Nevertheless the technique has much to offer in the way of help with the task of understanding and controlling ill-defined systems:

1. It yields a worked-out notion of a certain kind of conceptual model known to be psychologically faithful to the standpoint of the human operator. By focussing on the mapping between desired behaviors of the system and the inputs needed to achieve them, the model bears directly on the operator's control of the system.

2. The mapping model yields an integrated view of (part of) the system's behavior, which provides a perspective on its overall use. The mapping also acts as a "channel" for the connections between tasks and actions.

3. The technique provides a basis for evaluating a proposed conceptual model of the system, by examining the properties of its mapping between task and actions.

4. The model imposes on the task domain a structure which itself reflects the properties of the system, this structure being one for which a simple and clear mapping is possible.

The approach being advocated can also predict certain places where trouble is likely to arise. Given that different partial models will be used for different purposes, and that each model has certain main areas of application as well as more marginal ones, difficulties can be expected where a particular task lies on the "edge" of a particular model's territory. Other cases can arise where a task is apparently covered by two or more different models, and this can cause problems if the actions dictated by the models are incompatible.

I was careful earlier to describe this attempt to apply conceptual models to the domain of ill-defined systems as "speculative". There is a limit to how much can be achieved by discussion and argument at this level. In the end, the only way to test the validity of these ideas and develop them further is to try them on a life-sized example of an ill-defined system, examine their strengths and weaknesses, and modify them accordingly.

REFERENCES

Card, S. K., 1979, A method for calculating performance times for
    users of interactive computing systems. In Proceedings of the
    1979 Conference on Cybernetics and Society. Denver, Colorado.

du Boulay, J. B. H., O'Shea, T. and Monk, J., 1981, The black box
    inside the glass box: presenting computing concepts to nov-
    ices. International Journal of Man-Machine Studies, 14, 237-
    249.

Hewlett-Packard, 1979, Advanced calculator logic HP RPN/Algebraic:
    A comparative analysis. Hewlett-Packard Corporation.

Kasprzyk, D. M., Drury, C. G. and Bialas, W. F., 1979, Human
    behavior and performance in calculator use with Algebraic and
    Reverse Polish Notation. Ergonomics, 22, 1011-1019.

Mayer, R. E., 1981, The psychology of how novices learn computer
    programming. Computing Surveys, 13, 121-141.

Young, R. M., 1981, The machine inside the machine: Users' models
    of pocket calculators. International Journal of Man-Machine
    Studies, 15, 51-85.

Young, R. M., 1982, Surrogates and mappings: Two kinds of
    conceptual models for interactive devices. In D. Gentner and
    A. Stevens (Eds.), Mental Models. Hillsdale, N. J.: Erlbaum
    (in press).

CREATIVITY IN SKILLED PERFORMANCE

L. Henry Shaffer

Department of Psychology
University of Exeter
Exeter, England

Boden (1981) relates the maxim given by Descartes as advice
to the young mathematician, that having solved a problem he should
check carefully through the steps of proof. This is surely similar
in intent to a heuristic given more recently by Polya (1945), that
finding a solution to a problem should mark not the end but the
beginning of a mathematical inquiry, which attempts to find simpler
solutions, other kinds of solution, and generalizations of the
problem. The problem solver is thus motivated to refine his techniques and to find a perspective for the problem that places it in
a broader domain. The implication of the advice is that a good
problem solver is also a problem seeker.

With little modification the description of a good problem
solver can serve for the exponent of a motor skill, for a variety
of skills. Skilled performance is creative in two ways: first, in
the sense intended by Chomsky (1957) for language, it is based on
a generative grammar which enables the construction of an infinite
variety of sentences (sequences, patterns) using a finite set of
rules; and second, over time the person may explore the consequences
of modifying or extending parts of the grammar. Both these ideas
have been illustrated by Gleitman (1981) in the context of the
acquisition of language and speech. The task here is to demonstrate
their relevance to other skills.

I shall make free use of the concepts of a performance grammar
and a motor program. A performance grammar is a generative grammar
that constructs a movement sequence from an intention. Liberman
(1970) described such a grammar in showing that the grammars in
linguistic theory must be supplemented by further levels of rules

in order to get from a phonological string to speech. A motor
program constructs a set of representations of output within the
grammar, and makes use of a control system that arranges their
translation, or expansion, one from another in a hierarchy of
abstraction spaces (Sacerdoti, 1974) terminating in motor output.
Note that a generative grammar is not an algorithm for constructing
sequences, but a set of rules providing the options for constructing
an output or parsing an input.

The first skill I shall discuss is copy typing. This may seem
an unpromising beginning, since the task defines a problem that
is easily solved by setting up a control structure that uses the
sequence of operations: (1) read a symbol of text, (2) find its
corresponding key on the keyboard, (3) press that key, (4) go to
the next symbol in the text and repeat the cycle. This together
with a few ancillary rules for line returns, stopping etc., constitutes a sufficient solution to the problem, and with practice a
beginner typist can get better at iterating on this cycle, increasing her speed from, say, a symbol every two seconds to about two
symbols per second as the keyboard topography becomes more familiar.
However, internal constraints on information processing prevent
her from going faster than this without altering the control
structure. This can be demonstrated in the context of a study on
highly skilled secretaries (Shaffer, 1973, 1976).

In this study the typewriter keyboard was coupled to a computer,
which generated text on a video screen and recorded the keys pressed
and their clock times. Renewal of displayed text was determined by
the typing responses, and the amount of text on display at any time
was a controllable parameter. Thus the typist was in a closed loop
situation in which, depending on the experimental condition, she
received a fixed amount of preview of what she had to type next,
which could range from only the next symbol to a whole row of text,
or she could be given postview of the part of the text she had just
typed.

If the display immediately presents just the next symbol to be
typed, this provides the optimal input condition for the control
structure described above. In this condition typing speed was about
0.6 seconds per symbol for the best typists.

We can next contrast typing with control skills such as tracking,
described by Baron (1981). In a tracking task the goal is to
control output so as to maintain a null signal as the input varies.
Optimal performance can be achieved by modelling the time series
of the input and extrapolating the series to compute the next
control response. In typing, the analogy would be to use syntactic
information in the prior text, when it is prose, to predict the
next symbol or prepare the next response. Giving postview of the
text provides an aid to memory, in case this information cannot be

stored. In fact postview conferred very little benefit and typing
became only slightly faster.

Giving preview of prose text, however, led to dramatic changes
in speed, and performance improved with every additional symbol up
to an asymptote at 8-10 symbols of preview. At this level the best
typist maintained a speed of over 100 words per minute, or about
9-10 symbols per second. Note that a preview of 8-10 symbols is
close to the eye-finger span of normal skilled typing, i.e. the
mean distance between the point of the eye fixation in the text and
the symbol currently being typed.

Another variable manipulated was text structure. A prose
text could be degraded into another by randomizing its word order,
the syllable order within words, or the letter order within words.
The first randomization had virtually no effect on performance,
but there was a progressive slowing with the other randomizations,
the speed dropping to about 3 symbols per second on randomized
letter texts.

From these results a better guess at the control structure of
skilled typing is that text is read in the largest feasible syntacti
units, up to the level of a word or short phrase, to construct a
representation of an extended letter sequence for output. A motor
system translates this representation into movements at a rate
determined by the average renewal rate of the representation.
Parsing the text in larger syntactic units enables a faster renewal
rate (Shaffer, 1973).

The errors of typing support this picture (Shaffer, 1975) and
their similarity to errors of speech (Fromkin, 1973) indicate a
commonality of control structure between these skills (Shaffer,
1976). Briefly, letters migrating from their correct position
tended to go to the corresponding position in another syllable or
word, except for transposals with an adjacent letter, which tended
to remain within a syllable. These results, obtained from an
intensive study of the fastest typist, are likely to be fairly
general, but the next result from this particular typist may be
more idiosyncratic. Nearly all the pairwise transposals involved
alternate hands in typing the two letters, and significantly often
the effect was to perpetuate a run of hand alternation, LRLRL--, or
a run on the same hand, RRRR--. A spectacular example was WNE TODNW
typed for WENT DOWN, involving four transposals, one of them including the space. The space was usually typed with the hand
alternate to the previous letter, and so the correct hand sequence
LLRLRLRLR was corrupted to LRLRLRLRL. It therefore appears that the
motor program labelled each letter in the output representation
according to hand and then passed its motor command to an output
buffer for that hand. Control of output sequencing was then
achieved by pointing in turn to the buffer containing the next

command. This aspect of control is perhaps related to the fact
that this typist had also been a pianist.

A logistic extension of the performance grammar of this
typist can be observed in the details of timing. In typing the
same word on different occasions she reproduced a definite pattern
of latencies of onset from one letter to the next, over the word.
These temporal patterns were investigated with texts in which
repeating letter sequences took changing contexts (Shaffer, 1978).
This revealed in particular that the patterns were sensitive to
right-context. For example the WHI sequence was typed with a
markedly different latency pattern in THE WHIG and THE WHIM. The
letter M was typed on the same hand as H and I, but G was typed by
the other hand (see Figure). The anticipation of this suggests
that the typist typed not one letter at a time but groups of letters
coordinated in a compound movement trajectory. The consistency of
the latency profiles on different occasions demonstrates that she
had rules for grouping letters, and since she may seldom have
typed the words WHIG and WHIM before we can suppose that the rules
formed a generative component of a performance grammar.

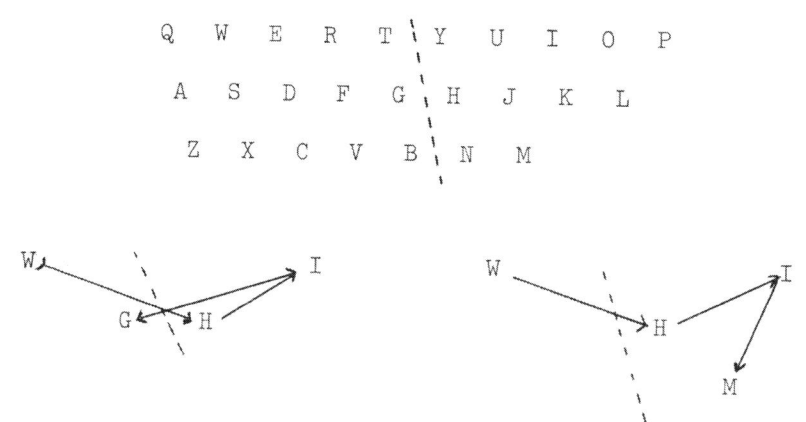

Another kind of elaboration of the control structure also
appeared in the timing of performance. I wanted to simplify the
movement transitions in typing successive letters and so constructed
texts which, on the normal conventions of finger allocation, would
involve strict hand alternation (Shaffer, 1978). The phrase
DICKENSIAN NEUROTIC could be a fragment of such a text. The fast
typist typed these texts faster than usual and with less variance
(she was not aware of this or of the distinctive character of the
texts). More interesting is that the time series of latencies
showed strong negative autocovariance, which indicates that she was
using an internal clock to pace these performances. Since the
latencies on normal text showed aperiodic patterns, this tactic

of metronomic typing seems to arise from the particularly simple
logistic structure of the 'alternation' texts.

We see that in skilled performance the control structure
developed for a task can go beyond its requirements: for some people,
at least, a task presents an open-ended challenge to go on refining
a skill. This becomes more evident in an artistic activity like
playing a piece of music, in which in any case the task is less well
defined. In typing, the text is unambiguous (except perhaps in
the vagaries of handwritten text), but a musical score underspecifies
the output. A musical score formally assigns values of note pitch
and duration, and of tempo (when it gives a metronome figure rather
than an Italian marking, like Allegretto) but the composer expects
the performer to depart expressively from these values in ways he
can only vaguely indicate. Also, the player is free to interpret
dynamic (intensity) and manner of playing (e.g. legato-staccato),
which can be only approximately indicated by the notation. One
need not put the onus on the notational system, since the composer
usually regards his piece of music as the basis for a creative
interpretation by the performer, and so provides him with only what
is essential for his musical intention.

The concert performer comes to a piece of music armed with a
grammar of its musical language and hints from an oral tradition,
passed on by teachers, on the style and intentions of the composer.
There have been recent attempts to model aspects of the grammar of
tonal music, and here I should mention Winograd (1968), Longuet-
Higgins (1976), Lerdahl and Jackendoff (1977) and, on a slightly
different tack, Steedman (1977). The grammatical knowledge serves
several purposes: it provides the starting point for constructing
an interpretation of the piece; it provides a basis for coding the
music in memory, since the concert musician usually plays without
a score; and at the beginning of practice it enables him to parse
the music and play it at sight at something like its proper tempo.

Thus the first important point about the skilled performer
is that he can usually give a competent, fluent rendering from the
score of a piece of music he has never seen or heard before. Using
a grand piano specially adapted for computer recording (Shaffer, 1981),
I have recorded a practice session of a pianist learning a Beethoven
bagatelle. After a brief glance through the score he played it
straight through and spent the rest of his time refining details of
expression. The music can be parsed while it is being played, and
the depth of parsing has been demonstrated in at least two ways in
our data on pianists.

The first arose from a performance of a Bach fugue played
from the score without preparation, and not previously played by the
pianist for several years (Shaffer, 1980, 1981). A quirk of

notation at the top of a page in the score, which temporarily changed
a stave marking, precipitated the player briefly into a chain of
errors. What is interesting is that the wrong notes played were
not those that would arise by transposing the music into the wrong
stave, but instead were notes compatible with the correct harmony
at that point in the music. They can best be understood as an
improvisation on this harmony in the interval that the player sought
to regain his place in the music.

He also gave a second performance of the fugue, and on analysis
it was found that the two performances agreed in a large number of
details that were not specified by the score, affecting accent,
rubato (tempo change) and dynamic. The least significant resemblance
is that the performances, lasting about $1\frac{1}{2}$ minutes, differed in
duration by only about 1/4 second. This shows, as one might expect,
that a musician has a well developed internal clock, and I have
shown using covariance analysis how this clock is used to create a
beat structure for the performance (Shaffer, 1981). More interesting
here is the extent to which expressive variation in timing and dynamic
was reproduced. The pianist could not memorize this amount of detail:
musicians are no better than anyone else at remembering arbitrary
analogue information and Eric Clarke, at Exeter, has demonstrated
this by asking pianists to reproduce short melodies they hear,
containing timing deformation in a single pair of notes. Almost
inevitably the pianist bends the deformation in the direction of a
notatable rhythm. Hence the pianist playing Bach could make consistent use of expressive variation across performances only by
having an expressive grammar with which to construct the variation
according to features in the music.

How to model a generative grammar of expression is still uncertain. It is one of three components of a performance grammar,
the others being syntactic and logistic. The syntactic component is
used to construct an abstract structure which includes the marking
of pragmatic features; the logistic component is used first to
construct a categorial representation of output (its motor commands)
and then to translate these into movement. The expressive component,
then, uses the pragmatic information to deform, or modulate, the
canonic (inexpressive) values of variables like timing, force and
pitch. Cutler and Isard (1980) describe some of the prosodies of
speech and discuss the problems of going from this description to a
grammar of prosody. Since the role of expressive rules is to modulate
an output, they are likely to have relational rather than metrical
predicates, of the form 'increase X in context Y'.

The attempt to analyse expression in musical performance is
very recent. An analogue of a timing phenomenon in speech (Gleitman,
1981) can also be observed in playing music (Shaffer, 1980), and this
is the lengthening of elements at the end of a syntactic unit.

Speech and music have a hierarchy of units and the terminal lengthening rule can apply recursively at each level of unit. First John Sloboda and then Eric Clarke have used the piano at Exeter to study how pianists realize the meter of simple melodies for the right hand. The meter of music is specified as a recurrent group of beats in which the notes on certain beats take stronger stress. The group boundaries are marked in the score by bar lines. The stress on a beat is a formal notion and it is at the discretion of the performer how often and in what way it is realized.

A set of melodies was constructed by taking a series of note durations, defining a temporal rhythm, and shifting the series in relation to the bar lines, sometimes adding one or two notes to the beginning or end. The pitch of notes was kept constant as much as possible across pieces, but sometimes in Clarke's study pitch was altered to make the notes on stressed beats harmonically acceptable. Pianists were given the melodies in random order to play, and over the session each melody was played a number of times. There were no expressive marks in the score and the player was not told how to play the pieces.

In Clarke's data it is clear that a pianist tended to make consistent use of stress in the repeats of a piece, but that different pianists used it differently. Also, comparing the use of stress in different pieces shows that it was a complex variable tied neither to the temporal rhythm not to the meter. What seems to happen is that the player constructs a melodic grouping which can cut across the metrical grouping indicated by the bar lines, and it is the interaction of these groups that determines stress. Melodic grouping is based upon factors of harmony, melodic contour and temporal rhythm, and this grouping can vary from one player to another. Furthermore, stress was realized in the performances by raising intensity, prolonging the note, or playing it early or late. If a melodic group cut across the meter its boundary was sometimes indicated by playing the last note staccato, thus introducing a brief pause.

Clarke later repeated the experiment using atonal rather than tonal melodies, so that changing the position of the bar lines no longer conflicted with pitch expectations. The result is that one pianist made more consistent use of stress on major beats in the meter, while another pianist regarded the freedom of atonality as an invitation to do something different on every performance of every piece.

I have said nothing about improvisation, by the continuo player in Baroque music given a figured bass, a series of numbers abstractly specifying a harmony; by the jazz musician exploring the harmonic or modal properties of a tune; or by a musician like Bach who could improvise at the keyboard a four part fugue on a given theme. These are the more obvious levels of creativity in skill and everyone can quote their own examples.

In conclusion, I have tried to show that skilled performance is creative both in the generative sense and in the sense that, over years of practice, the performer goes on elaborating a control structure for performance. Thus a typist, who may begin by reading and typing one letter at a time, learns to construct internally a hierarchic representation of output, together with procedures for translating these rapidly into movement. A pianist who has mastered the basic techniques of playing can go on refining these and, just as important, can go on developing a (personal) interpretive grammar for giving expressive soul to the music.

REFERENCES

Baron, S. Modeling pilot adaptive behavior using the optimal control model. 1981 (this volume).
Boden, M.A. Philosophical aspects: failure is not the spur. 1981 (this volume).
Chomsky, N. Syntactic Structures. The Hague, Netherlands: Mouton, 1957.
Cutler, A. and Isard, S.D. The production of prosody, In B. Butterworth (ed.), Language Production. New York: Academic Press, 1980.
Fromkin, V.A. (ed.) Speech Errors as Linguistic Evidence. The Hague, Netherlands: Mouton, 1973.
Gleitman, L. Richly specified input to language learning. 1981 (this volume).
Lerdahl, F. and Jackendoff, R. Toward a formal theory of tonal music. Journal of Music Theory, 1977, 21, 111-171.
Liberman, A.M. The grammars of speech and language. Cognitive Psychology. 1970, 1, 301-323.
Longuet-Higgins, H.C. Perception of melodies. Nature, 1976, 263, 646-653.
Polya, G. How to Solve It: A New Aspect of Mathematical Method. New York: Doubleday, 1945.
Sacerdoti, E.D. Planning in a hierarchy of abstraction spaces. Artificial Intelligence, 1974, 5, 115-135.
Shaffer, L.H. Latency mechanisms in transcription. In S. Kornblum (ed.), Attention and Performance IV. New York: Academic Press, 1973.
Shaffer, L.H. Control processes in typing. Quarterly Journal of Experimental Psychology, 1975, 27, 419-432.
Shaffer, L.H. Intention and performance. Psychological Review, 1976, 83, 375-393.

Shaffer, L.H.   Timing in the motor programming or typing.   Quarterly
    Journal of Experimental Psychology, 1978, 30, 333-345.
Shaffer, L.H.   Analysing piano performance: a study of concert
    pianists.   In G.E. Stelmach and J. Requin, Tutorials in
    Motor Behavior.   Amsterdam: North-Hooland, 1980.
Shaffer, L.H.   Performances of Chopin Bach and Bartok: studies
    in motor programming.   Cognitive Psychology, 1981, 13,
    326-376.
Steedman, M.J.   How the blues was born - a generative approach.
    Unpublished paper, University of Warwick, 1977.
Winograd, T.   Linguistics and the computer analysis of tonal
    harmony.   Journal of Music Theory, 1968, 12, 2-49.

This research was supported by grant No. HR 4676 from the
Social Science Research Council, UK.

THE CONCEPTS OF 'ADAPTATION' AND 'ATTUNEMENT' IN SKILL LEARNING

H.T.A. Whiting

Department of Psychology
Interfaculty of Human Movement Science and Education
The Free University, Amsterdam, The Netherlands

INTRODUCTION

While an ill-defined system may be difficult to delineate and while such delineation may not hold for all systems, the concept has a certain value when man is being considered as a skilled 'actor'*. As Jones (1967) points out:

> Biological modes of operation are self-organising, evolutionary, growing, decaying, differentiating and self-reproducing. In all, a system of high variety. But besides its biological nature, in which ergonomic man can be described as a 'skilled animal', the human being is capable of conscious thoughts, he has a personality and may possess other non-material qualities which characterise his performance, which defy description in system terms and which are usually left out of calculations.

The relevance of such an issue for those engaged in helping others to acquire skill is implicit in the fact that unless they can understand what the learner intended to do in carrying out a particular action, it is difficult, if not impossible to provide relevant feedback that might promote learning. In this sense, the teacher/coach is often faced with what for him is an ill-defined system. Another of his problems is that of removing uncertainty by coming to understand the system with which he is working. This 'modelling' of another human system is exemplified most prominently is social interaction situations, particularly when people are

---

* Following Fowler & Turvey (1979) the term 'actor' is used to designate anyone who performs an action.

187

meeting for the first time. Initial exchanges of information, the
use of stereotypes for classification purposes and the wrong
impressions which are often formed on 'first acquaintance' are all
indicative of ill-defined systems.

This paper addresses such an issue in the context of skills that
have a major movement component. The extent to which such an analysis
has application in other categories of skill is left open.

Adaptation or Attunement?

Goals for skilled actions are generally ill-defined! They are
ill-defined in the sense that there is a tolerance band within which
behaviour is deemed to be successful. Moreover, the methods of
reaching the criterion may, within fairly broad limits, vary a great
deal from person to person or in the same person on different
occasions. Since the system is – to use Lavorel's terms (see his
chapter in this text) – 'only approximately efficient' it is to be
expected that minor and major reorganization possibilities would be
provided for in the evolutionary course of development of the central
nervous system. Even when consistent movement patterns over occasions
are observed, such consistency – as Bernstein (1967) so cogently
remarked – cannot be explained by:

> The older naively materialistic conception of
> gradually 'beaten' tracks or synaptic barriers
> in the central nervous system.

Which interpretation, he suggested, 'may already be considered to be
relegated to the archives of science'.

The importance of Bernstein's statement relates to his
insistence on the 'non-univocality of movements', expressed as
follows:

> ...the relationship between the result – for
> example the movement of a limb or one of its
> joints – and such commands as are delivered
> to the musculature from the brain through
> the effector nerves is very complex and non-
> univocal.

That is to say, the same movement (to an external observer) may be
produced by different initial innervations, or different movements
by the same innervation. The explanation of this apparent
contradiction is, that in programming the requisite innervation, the
brain must take account of current conditions, such as the position
of the limb, its velocity and acceleration, as well as the state of
the force fields within and external to the body. This is not to deny
that the neuromuscular system of the body can produce consistent
movements, but, that it does so by a means other than the gradual
'wearing of a pathway' through specific synaptic junctions in the
nervous system.

Man, in the process of acquiring skill, can then be looked upon

as an adaptive system in that while his goal at any one time may not
change, the methods of achieving the goal may differ. Such
differences may manifest themselves in:
(a) more enduring changes of a general nature (e.g., methods of
    approach to solving the problem) or,
(b) in more immediate adjustments to ongoing movements in order to
    meet exigencies in the system. Whether the term adaptation should
    be used with respect to both extremes is a question which will be
    returned to later.

With respect to the more immediate adjustments, consider the
'simple' act of walking while carrying a bowl of water, where the
goal is 'not to spill a drop'. The pattern of internal forces
operating will differ from occasion to occasion and, dependent upon
where the walking takes place, so will the external force field.
Out of the more immediate adjustments necessary to attain the goal
will be distilled an approach to 'bowl of water carrying' as a new
class of skill. Nevertheless, even when such skill is acquired to a
high level the need for these more immediate adjustments, because
of relative unpredictability in the system, will always be present.

Glencross (1975) in his research into the effects of changes in
task conditions (e.g., resistance to cranking, handle radius,
direction of cranking) on the temporal organization of a repetitive
speed skill - hand cranking - has worked out this idea in more
detail. He proposes a two-level control system. The 'motor program
level' operating in an open-loop fashion and an executive control
system level responsible for integrating all the feedback arising
from the task and thereby controlling the motor program. It is
further proposed that one basic structure or program can be used to
effect an appropriate response even though there may be a number of
changes in the task condition. This is reminiscent of Reynolds'
(1980) distinction between what he calls the 'strategic' and the
'tactical' motor systems. Both systems show 'adaptive' characteristics
in the manner already distinguished.

What is clear from this kind of study and way of thinking is
that any analysis of skilled action must take account of both forces
within the individual to be generated, forces in the external
environment to be overcome and the way in which they are brought
into alignment. This suggestion is implicit in Hull's (1974) comments
on system adaptability:

> A system is goal-directed with respect to a goal
> G during the interval T, if and only if, during
> T any primary variation either in the system or
> in the environment, within a certain range, is
> accompanied by adaptive variations.

But, there is an additional factor. The actor is not at all
times at the mercy of his environment. Thus, methods of alignment
are influenced by personal preferences, strategies, movement tempos,
cognitive styles etc. which are difficult to incorporate into any
comprehensive skill model. That they affect the way in which

alignment is brought about is clear. This poses problems for training methods as will be apparent from later discussion. The issue is operationalized in Warburton's (1969) extended analysis of Cattell's personality structure, when at the third order level he is left with two major factors - 'Adaptation' and 'Thrust' - the balance between which gives rise to the fourth order factor or 'Integration' understood as 'overall success in dealing with the environment'. With respect to human learning and performance, this third order factor 'thrust' should not be forgotten in that it implies an attempt by the individual to impose himself on the environment.

Interpretations of skill in a manner similar to that being hinted at here, have been made by Fowler and Turvey (1979). They see a parallel between 'a species participating in the slow process of evolution' and an individual animal 'participating in the comparatively rapid process of learning'. Both, they propose, are adaptive systems. From an ecological viewpoint, they consider a species to be 'a particular biological attunement to a particular environmental niche'. By analogy, the person as a skilled 'actor' is a particular attunement to a particular task he performs skilfully. Both adaptation and attunement are considered by them to be synonymous with the fit of a species to a niche. But, in this paper it is preferred to retain the term adaptation for more long term variations - in the sense of acquiring a new skill or extending an extant movement repertoire in response to repeatedly presented problems from out the environment - and the term attunement for the adjustments which are necessary in order for the system to align itself to the more immediate exigencies of the situation.

Koestler (1964) makes a similar point in proposing that the exercise of a skill is always under the dual control of:
(a) a fixed code of rules (which may be innate or acquired)
(b) a flexible strategy guided by environmental pointers - the ' lie of the land'.

Boden (this volume) raises a similar issue when she distinguishes between 'the fine tuning of an already adapted system' and 'changing the constraints of the system itself'. Again, the distinction is not unlike that made by van Rossum (1980) between 'schema' acquisition and 'schema' alignment. That the two concepts have a mutual relationship is clear.

In an extension of their analysis, Fowler and Turvey (1979) invoke Gibson's (1979) concept of 'affordances' in relation to the special features of the environment to which the animal becomes 'attuned'. Affordances of the environment - Gibson maintains - are what it offers the animal, what it provides or furnishes, either for good or ill.

It is not intended here to dwell on the value of such an interpretation, but simply to suggest that such a cognitive/affective concept may have an important higher level control function. If such a concept is considered useful it is important to recognise that affordances are personal constructs in psychology.

An environment/niche affords something to <u>somebody</u>. While communal affordances may present themselves in particular spheres of skilled activity where possibilities for variation may be constrained by the nature of the environment or existing rule systems, they are likely to be exceptions. The relativity of the term must be recognized.

One of the criteria for successful adaptation is the ability to formulate adequate working models of the future. This is conditioned by the particular model of the skill system that the actor up to that time has built up. Affordances are part of such a model. There is no reason to suppose that within any system of affordances, the organization and structure is the same for different individuals or that they are equally elaborate.

The interesting generalization that can be made from such a construct is that people differ with respect to the skill they consider to be of the most adaptive value as well as in the way that they attune themselves to particular task requirements and to what they attune. Moreover, such attunement/adaptation is of a dynamic nature, as is the environment itself.

A related question is the extent to which such adaptation or attunement is the result of conscious decision-making on the part of the actor. It is presumably these realizations that have motivated the search amongst control engineers for 'a satisfactory description of the human operator in dynamic terms' - albeit according to Garner (1967) with limited success. As Bowen (1967) states:

> I think the lesson coming out of the kinds of
> work I have instanced is that we cannot be
> successful in utilizing the resources of man
> in a system until we accept the fact that he
> contributes a qualitatively different form of
> operation in comparison to machine elements.
> He operates adaptively and has the capability
> of managing whatever resources the system
> affords him to meet the challenges of the
> situation.

It was not for nothing that Eysenck in 1966 was led to comment that very often in perceptual-motor performance research, individual differences alone can account for more of the variability in performance than any of the other factors on which the experimenter has chosen to focus his attention.

EXPERIMENTAL ANALYSIS

The difficulty with much of the work on skill acquisition is that it focuses very often on a single dependent variable - usually an 'outcome' measure - and pays little attention to the way in which the individual brings about his attunement to the task requirements. Thus, generalizations about methods of attunement cannot be made.

The situation is somewhat like the control engineer being faced only
with the display of the changing parameter being controlled (e.g.,
a dial showing fluctuations in control performance) and having no
information about what the controller did to produce such
fluctuations.

The important question to which the remainder of this paper is
addressed is whether an alternative approach can provide that kind
of information. I was particularly cognizant of this fact when in
1967 I carried out my first operational analysis using at that time
a continuous ball throwing and catching task that I had devised.
This method of approach has since then been used extensively in
laboratory work on skill learning and performance with which I have
been involved. Such approaches, while being laboratory based, require
only slight modifications to normal task variables, and different
experimental treatments can still be introduced. In comparison with
traditional laboratory experimental approaches, its advantage is that
it allows individual subject strategies to be utilized to the full
in solving the particular motor problem confronting the subject
(Tyldesley, 1979; Tyldesley and Whiting, 1982; Whiting, 1982). The
utilization of such procedures is also based upon a particular
philosophy which has recently been reiterated in another context
by Franks (1980), namely, that the outcome of a motor task as
measured by overall achievement (some global measure) cannot stand
alone as a dependent variable in motor learning experiments:

> Since the production of a movement involves
> the interplay of several psychological and
> physiological sub-routines during a specified
> time period, the measurement used to describe
> motor performance should be both diverse and
> complete with regard to these complex processes.

Only by this kind of analysis - he suggests - can a comprehensive
description of the performance be built-up and a more integrated
view of the manner in which a subject acquires a movement sequence
be provided. Hayes and Marteniuk (1976) at the University of
Waterloo in Canada have for some time been interested in identifying
what they term 'the output-code' during motor learning, i.e., on
what parameters did the subject alter his movements to achieve
success?

In the experiment on the acquisition of a continuous ball
throwing and catching task such an analysis was attempted. It is
interesting to reconsider this experiment (Whiting, 1967). The task
of the subject was to make a continuous series of aiming and catching
movements* of a ball that was suspended on a fine chain from the
laboratory ceiling and which traced out an elliptical flight path
after having been directed at the target (Fig. 1). The objective was

---

* This in itself is a relatively new approach and is to be compared
  with the analysis of short discrete actions which are normally
  carried out in the skill laboratory.

Figure 1.   Continuous ball-throwing and catching apparatus.

to maximize the score (a combination of 'number of throws' and 'accuracy') during successive periods of one minute over a period of 10 successive days practice.

The combined results for all subjects on the 'total score' criterion – the generally used 'outcome' type measure of performance – are given in Fig. 2. It will be noted that the performance curves follow typical exponential lines and that increases in the 'total score' are contributed to by increases in both 'accuracy' and 'number of throws' achieved.

While this is a useful <u>descriptive</u> measure of improvement in performance, it has little explanatory value; it says nothing about the way in which the subjects brought about such improvement, i.e., it gives very little information which might be useful to a person wishing for example to set up a training program for this skill. What advice would he be able to give other than 'try to get in as many throws as possible' and at the same time 'try to improve your accuracy'! If however, the analysis is followed a stage further and the question is posed as to what happens to a series of selected parameters during the ten days training, it may provide some general information about the way in which the human operator attunes himself to the requirements of the task. Five parameters were selected for analysis (they are not exhaustive and it should be noted, as in all operational analyses, that the usefulness of the results obtained is dependent upon the ability to select the most

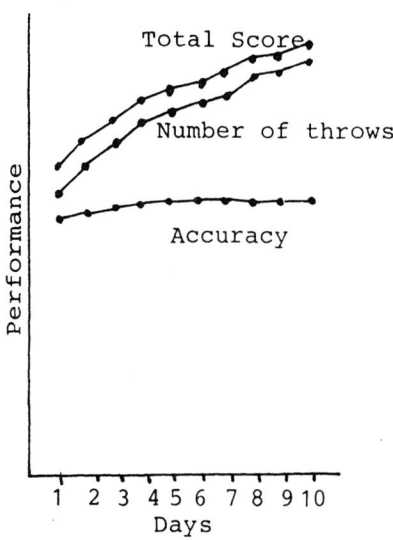

Fig. 2.   Scores on 'outcome' criterion measures over ten days
           of training.

meaningful parameters for measurement). Choosing the appropriate
parameters is a topic addressed by Moray (this volume) in the
context of man's interaction with an effectively ill-defined system).
While it is difficult to say (from the analyses made) what
contributes to increased accuracy, it is clear that the 'number of
throws' can be increased by combinations of 'reducing the time in
flight of the ball' and 'reducing the time for which the ball is
held'. Subjects did not maintain a standard strategy in this respect.
One subject for example, increased his number of throws primarily by
reducing the time in flight of the ball while another did so by
decreasing the time for which the ball was held.
     It is interesting to speculate on these so-called different
strategies, adaptive ploys, methods of attunement or whatever label
might be deemed appropriate. Are they consciously conceived or are
they forced upon the individual by, for example, his attention being
focused on certain characteristics of his initial trials determined
by the particular model of the skill which he formulated? That is to
say, are they 'automatic' or 'effortful'? Take for example in the
above study, the variable 'amount of time for which the ball was
held'. A series of analyses demonstrated that the performance curves
for this variable were best represented (both collectively and
individually) by an exponential function with an asymptote around

0.45 secs. Thus, the closer the subject's performance to this value on his initial trials, the less possibility of his being able to achieve an improvement in 'total score' by a strategy which attempted to hold the ball for less and less time. A similar interpretation applies for the parameter 'time the ball was in flight'.

Subject Strategies

The question posed about the automatic or effortful adoption of strategies is an interesting one for this paper since such changes are indications of adaptation or attunement on the part of the person performing. Subject strategies are also receiving increasing attention in the literature since changes in strategy based upon differing task requirements can lead to differing and often spurious theoretical interpretations of the phenomenon in question. This point is well illustrated in a recent experiment of Grootveld and Tyldesley (1982) in our own laboratories and which in addition operationalises the earlier made point in Bowen's (1967) statement that 'the human operator has the capability of managing whatever resources the system affords him to meet the challenges of the situation.

Grootveld and Tyldesley (1982) are carrying out a series of experiments directed towards an understanding of the influence of movement difficulty and movement complexity on motor programming. In particular, they are concerned with the 'locus' of movement preparation i.e. where does the 'load' on preparation for future components express itself? A typical movement tapping apparatus – with multiple components – elaborated from earlier work of Fitts and his co-workers (Fitts, 1954; Fitts & Peterson, 1964) – is being used. The task involves the sequential tapping of either one, two, three or four successive targets (the 'complexity' variable – varied per trial) in one of two directions (left or right) under two conditions of 'difficulty' (20 mm or 5 mm target widths – varied per session). The dependent variables in the experiments being discussed were reaction time to the imperative signal and movement times to reach each of the targets (M_1, M_2, M_3, & M_4).

In the first experiment, subjects were instructed to carry out the movements as quickly and as accurately as possible while in the second experiment stress was placed on movement speed with no explicit mention being made of movement accuracy (although this was implicit in the two target widths provided*). In the third experiment not only was stress placed on speed of movement, but this was emphasized by an auditory deadline presented on each trial at the time that the total movement should have been completed (calculated from the same Ss mean times on experiment 2 x 80%). Thus, over this series of experiments, the possibilities for strategy variation were constrained by the imposed task requirements. Progress through

---

* Measurement of 'effective' target widths indicated that subjects did not utilise the whole of the 20 mm. target.

the series of experiments led to an overall decrease in the time
scale for carrying out the actions. Analysis of these results
enabled Grootveld and Tyldesley to suggest that the change in speed
constraint from experiment 1 to experiment 2 resulted in a change
in the 'control locus' from execution-time control (components 1
and 3 in experiment 1) to control during the reaction time and
component 1 in experiment 2. The more stringent speed instructions
of experiment 3 did not bring about any further shift in programming.
Interesting questions remain. For example, the apparent disappearance
of a long component 3 (MT_3) in experiments 2 and 3 would appear to
be an expression of the subjects' strategy in attuning to the
additional speed stress. What made the subject choose to make up
his time here and not in some other place? Did all the subjects
follow the same pattern? The authors suggest that:

> ...given the nature of the task – a relatively
> large upper limb movement involving several
> muscle groups and with average component MT's
> of about 250 msec. – it was impossible to use
> traditional measures of programming which
> restrict themselves to a consideration of the
> RT effects. Compression of the preparation of
> movements with large anatomical scope and with
> multiple degrees of freedom into a period prior
> to the initiation of the first component appears
> both unrealistic and difficult to obtain.

The sobering thought following on this experiment is the differing
interpretations of programming which would have been made had
experiments 1 and 2 been carried out by different experimenters. A
failure then to appreciate the significance of the differing
instructions given to the two groups of subjects used might have
led to considerable theoretical controversy.

CONTINUOUS MEASURES OF PERFORMANCE

    In spite of the additional insight gained from the operational
analysis outlined in the experiment on a ball throwing and catching
task (Whiting, 1967) in which a number of relevant dependent
variables were used, it is to be noted that these were in a way also
outcome measures. This is not to denigrate their value. They could
for example be used for teaching purposes (e.g., try not to hold on
to the ball so long) with the advantage, that instructions which
might lead to improvement on these parameters place no constraint
on the way in which this is to be brought about. It was possible
through these analyses to demonstrate differences in strategy on
the part of the subjects which in some instances were constrained
by the initial performance. The question is whether more fine-grained
analysis of the movements themselves would provide more meaningful
information, with respect to generalizations about skill learning

that can also incorporate individual differences. For this and other
reasons, subsequent experimental work in our laboratories moved
towards the adoption of the use of continuous measures of performance
while maintaining the operational analytic approach.

In a series of elaborate operational analyses within the
context of table-tennis skills, Tyldesley (1979) was able to
demonstrate stages in the adaptive strategies of players classed as
novice, intermediate and expert when they were required to perform
with speed and accuracy or accuracy alone. For example, it was
possible to demonstrate differences between novices and the other
two classes of player with respect to the following variables:

1. selection of the required motor program (the form of which
differed from player to player).

2. the production of this motor program in a consistent manner.

3. the spatial prediction of the initiation point for the
program.

4. the temporal prediction of the initiation point for the
program.

Intermediate and expert players on the other hand were
distinguished only by differences in consistency with respect to
the fourth variable - temporal prediction.

It was possible through this analysis to propose a new concept
operational timing to denote the ability of a player through the
consistency of his movement patterns to replicate time intervals
accurately. The adaptive value in terms of the release of attention
capacity for other aspects of the task when it is no longer
necessary to think about delineating a particular time interval
should be apparent. The nature of this concept is illustrated in
Fig. 3. which shows the results of computer graphic analysis of
typical movement patterns for the forehand drive shot in intermediate
and expert players. It is clear that for both categories of player
identical movement patterns in terms of displacement over time traced
back from ball/bat contact point can be achieved, but that this
pattern is initiated at different points in space and/or time.
(Although not shown on this figure, similar consistency can be shown
for different anatomical points, e.g., wrist, elbow, shoulder, even
when velocity is used as the parameter in place of displacement).
There are differences with respect to the parameter 'initiation time'
in the consistency shown by expert and intermediate players - the
former showing greater consistency in this respect.

By means of this analysis, it was possible to suggest that with
transition through the player levels, errors type 1 and 2 (in the
list previously given) would drop out first followed by type 3 until
the expert is faced solely with a problem of temporal prediction of
when to start a movement sequence which has been planned in its
entirety in advance.

The first two sources of error to drop out, accord well with the
model of skill acquisition proposed by Gentile (1972) who suggested
that during the early stages of skill learning, the individual learns
'a general motor pattern' which is moderately effective (this idea

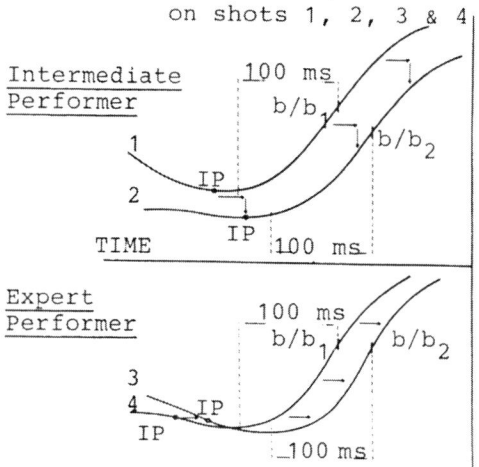

IP = initiation point of replicated
        movement patterns
b/b = time of bat/ball contact
        on shots 1, 2, 3 & 4

Fig. 3.   Diagrammatic reconstruction of the shifts necessary to
           overlay the ballistic portions of the intermediate and
           expert performers' movement patterns (Tyldesley and
           Whiting, 1975).

will be returned to later in another context) then proceeds either
to refine and retain this pattern in closed environmental conditions
(such as the present experiment) or markedly alter it to match
variable environmental conditions (diversification).

    In the analyses outlined above, consistency of spatial
displacement or velocity (in expert and intermediate players) was
shown with respect to separate anatomical data points such as wrist,
elbow or shoulder joints. While such a complex of muscle groups
might - through learning- come to operate as a 'coordinative
structure', it might also be expected that differences in the
build-up of control over a system with so many degrees of freedom
would be apparent. Thus, in putting together the required motor
program (which may differ in form for different players) the
question arises as to which parameters and anatomical points have to
be attuned in coming to the consistency of performance shown by the
expert?

    In further analyses of a similar kind, Tyldesley (1979) has
demonstrated not only differences in the dimensions of information
extracted from a visual display by novice table tennis players in
comparison to that extracted by experts within the visual modality,

but has also extensively analyzed the movement control parameters
involved. It is the latter series of analyses which throw light on
the degrees of freedom problem. With the aid of continuous fine
analysis, of high-speed film records, spatial and temporal
parameters describing the output variables (response motor patterns)
were obtained. Novice, intermediate and expert performers were
utilised under two experimental conditions - 'speed and accuracy'
or 'accuracy' alone. Not unexpectedly, the most clearcut significant
differences were those between the expert and the novice particularly
under the 'accuracy' condition where the novice appeared to vary three
of the four measured parameters (bat displacement, elbow displacement
and elbow velocity) to a far greater extent than the expert in an
effort to match his movement patterns to the demands of a relatively
non-variant environment. A further significant finding was that
velocity control in this closed situation seemed to be achieved
before displacement control of the immediate anatomical locus. The
control of the hand gave way in the expert to control of the hand
plus elbow and this control persisted throughout preliminary and
ballistic phases of the movement.

More detailed analyses of changes taking place as between
expert and novice were illuminating. Degree of control for example
became more discriminable in the elbow movements than those of the
bat. Control of elbow movements from trial to trial was a luxury
not afforded to the novice - as evidenced by the ballistic and pre-
ballistic phases of the accuracy condition. The better performers
showed no accuracy/speed main effect for their elbow movements, but
a skill level effect became distinguishable during the final 150 msec.
to contact, where the intermediate level player became less
consistent. The possibility to differentiate consistencies in movement
loci, particularly during the ballistic phase of the speed plus
accuracy condition, contrasted with the bat data and were interpreted
as characterising the spread of anatomical locus of control with
practice. Bernstein's (1967) perceptive view of motor learning as
being the reduction of the degrees of freedom of wrist, elbow,
shoulder then trunk movements was thus reflected in the present data
(Tyldesley, 1979).

Achievement of bat velocity control occurred sooner under speed
stress in all subjects, but unlike the bat displacement variability
results, velocity control showed no significant skill level effects.
Bat velocity variability was equally efficient in all subjects, and
it is likely - Tyldesley (1979) hypothesizes - that velocity was
more fundamental in adaptive control than displacement. Control
order changes from good velocity control in the novice to good
displacement plus velocity control in the expert indicates a
kinematic extension of the 'mastery' of the degrees of freedom.

The rather unexpected superiority of first-order (velocity)
control over displacement control in the novice provided supportive
evidence that control of the kinematic features progresses from
force through velocity to displacement. Bates (1947) suggested in
this respect that:

> ...to attempt a desired velocity and a desired
> displacement are in theory more complex operations
> than to attempt a desired force... our everyday
> experience is a demand for accurate displacement
> outputs i.e. practice in double integration.

In fast accurate movements, the novice was equally effective in
velocity production as the expert and it was likely that his low
outcome success rate was attributable to poor displacement control,
in particular the positioning in space of a pattern already 'written'
in force terms (Tyldesley, 1979).

Imaging

While this elaboration of the work of Tyldesley (1979)
demonstrates general trends in attunement to the task requirements
in a particular class of skills, i.e., discrete ballistic actions,
it must be asked whether they are generalizable to other categories
of skill. Unfortunately, there is a dearth of experimental work in
this respect. However, at about the same time as the work of
Tyldesley was progressing, Franks (1980) working with Wilberg in
Canada completed a series of seven related motor learning (tracking
task) experiments. His thesis that the production of movements is
based upon the interplay of a number of psychological and
physiological sub-routines and that in consequence the measurement
used to describe motor performance should be both diverse and
complete with regard to these complex processes has already been
referred to. This reflects very much the approach of Tyldesley.
As Franks comments:

> Each measure used adds to the description of
> the performance and provides a more integrated
> view of the manner in which a subject acquires
> a movement sequence.

Implicit within the work of Franks was that the subjects very
early in their performance trials built up a generalized image of
the form of the movement required (indexed by their ability to
reproduce post-experimentally freehand sketches of the stimulus
pattern) albeit without consciousness of changes in the speed of the
stimulus during parts of its course. Not only is this finding
interesting in its own right, but it has interesting relationships
to ongoing work of Whiting and den Brinker (1982). In a general way,
this work arises out of our attempts to resolve a difference of
opinion between Bernstein (1967) and Pribram (1971) with respect to
the nature of the representations to be found in and outside the
motor cortex. Pribram maintains - contrary to Bernstein's predictions
- that it is not topological properties of space which are
represented in the motor cortex, but the forces exciting muscle
receptors. This 'image of achievement' - in Pribram's (1971) terms -
comprises 'the learned anticipations of the force and changes in

force required to perform a task rather than an abstract model of
external space'. In our opinion, the conceptualisation of Pribram
need not be incongruent with that of Bernstein, if it is assumed that
images related to human overt actions can be conceived of at
different levels. We believe that what den Brinker (1979) chooses to
call the 'image of the act', and which he maintains exists at
'higher levels' than the motor cortex, is a necessary construct to
adequately account for motor learning. 'Images of the act' are a
specification of the essential form of movements - a qualitative
representation - necessary to tackle a particular motor problem.
They are schema forms in the sense referred to by Gallistel (1980):

> ...the schema for a skilled movement contains no
> elements that specify which group of muscles are
> to be active, in what order, and for how long.
> That sort of detail is left to lower centres to
> fill in when the code is activated.

Thus, the 'image of the act' specifies the form of the movement
rather than the pattern of neuromuscular activity to be used in
producing that form.

Normally, these two images ('of the act', 'of achievement') are
confounded, in that as soon as the performer has made a movement to
solve a particular motor problem he has knowledge both of the form
of the movement required and the forces to be overcome. Thus, in
most learning situations, inaccuracies in both images are likely
to be encountered. It would seem to us, that the best way for an
actor to discover the properties of one or other of the images would
be to keep the properties of the other image as stable as possible.
Thus, in the formation of an 'image of the act' we hypothesise that
the learning situation should be so structured that the field of
external forces together with the required movement parameters
(amplitude, timing and phase) is kept relatively constant while the
actor gives attention to establishing a reliable and appropriate
'image of the act'. It is not possible here to examine in detail
further predictions from the theory accompanying these ideas, these
can be followed in the article of Whiting and den Brinker (1982).
However, the outcome of pilot experiments are interesting,
particularly in relation to the previous operational analyses of
Tyldesley (1979) and Franks (1980). We have for this purpose chosen
a more concrete series of experiments which in themselves do not
focus specifically on imaging. For this purpose, we are utilizing
a commercially available mechanical ski-simulator (Fig. 4) together
with a SELSPOT movement registration system to investigate the
acquisition course of slalom ski-type movements. A paradigm has
been adopted - similar to that of Franks (1980) - which involves the
appraisal of the cyclical movement patterns involved by means of
three parameter measures:

1. the amplitude of the movement - the average absolute
deviation from a middle position.

2. an auto-correlation coefficient as a measure of timing.

Fig. 4.   Ski movement simulator apparatus.

   3. a cross-correlation coefficient as a measure of the <u>fluency</u>
or smoothness of the movement.
   Well trained subjects are able to make large and uniform
movements in different tempos (maximum 1 Hz.) very similar to those
which occur in slalom skiing. Untrained subjects find the skill very
difficult and generally only succeed in making small and irregular
movements. Such differences in movement of the platform can be
picked-up and registered by means of the Selspot system. Fig. 5 shows
the output traces of a well trained and un untrained subject with
respect to the parameters amplitude and speed of movement. In these
pilot experiments, twelve naive subjects (with respect to the
apparatus and also with respect to slalom skiing) trained for a
period of four days in the making of gross, regular movements. For
the parameter amplitude, subjects showed strong learning effects
both with respect to the pre- and post- tests on a particular day
as well as from day to day. The fall-off in gains towards the fourth
day are reflected both in the normal exponential growth curve to be
expected in this kind of learning as well as the restrictions imposed
by the apparatus design. No differences in amplitude learning were
shown between the slow and fast tempos.
   With respect to the parameter of 'timing', the most noticeable
and significant effect was the fall-off in performance between pre-
and post-tests on the first day with subsequent improvements on
each of the subsequent days.
   It would appear that at the beginning of the learning process
the subject is not able to pay equal attention to improving his

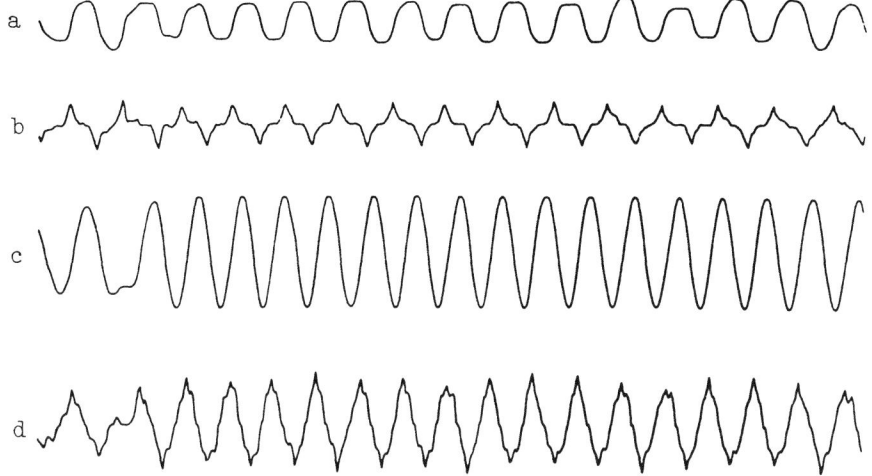

Fig. 5.   (a) Position pattern of an untrained person
           (b) Speed pattern that is derived from position pattern
               1.
           (c) Position pattern of the same person after training
           (d) Speed pattern derived from 3.

performance on all the parameters which are required of him. He
would seem to choose a strategy which in the first instance gives
more attention to the amplitude of the movement than the timing,
i.e. there is a trade-off between amplitude and timing.

    In addition to the three parameters of cyclic movements already
named, our interest in future experiments will focus on 'the
external forces to be overcome' - Pribram's (1971) 'image of
achievement' - which we will be able to manipulate by means of
similar ski simulators utilizing different tension spring systems.

CONCLUSION

    What I have tried to do by means of this rather complex
analysis is to present alternative viewpoints and methodologies in
the study of the skill acquisition process in the hope that
communalities in findings might be apparent which could lead to
meaningful generalizations. One of the great problems with some of
the analytic approaches presented is the data base which it is
necessary to acquire in order to carry out the kinds of analysis
which it has been suggested might provide some of the answers for
which we are looking. This particularly restricts the number of
subjects which can be used in any design and thus to merit caution
about the making of such generalizations. It is perhaps better

therefore to use the information presented as a starting point for asking more precise questions about the way in which the process of skill acquisition proceeds. This in fact has been our own approach in relation to the last series of experiments described and on which we have just begun.

We are also particularly attracted by the similarities in acquisition stages suggested by the research of Tyldesley & Whiting (1975) on operational timing and of Franks (1980) on the learning of tracking skills. It would seem possible to specify learning stages in this way with the additional advantage that they may not be specific to particular categories of skill.

It may be that these kinds of generalization prove to be less influenced by individual differences and thus more usable in any training system particularly as they do not restrict the way in which different individuals adopt different strategies to reach common ends.

REFERENCES

Bates, J. A. V., 1974, Characteristics of the human operator. Journal of the Institution of Electrical Engineers, 94: 298-304.

Bernstein, N., 1967, "The coordination and regulation of movement", Pergamon, London.

Bowen, H. M., 1967, The 'imp' in the system, in: "The human operator in complex systems", W. T. Singleton, R. S. Easterby & D. Whitfield, eds., Taylor & Francis, London.

Brinker, B. P. L. M. den., 1979, The influence of variations in training procedures on the learning of complex movement patterns. Unpublished paper, Department of Psychology, Interfaculty of Physical Education, The Free University, Amsterdam.

Eysenck, H. J., 1966, Personality and experimental psychology, Bull. Brit. Psych. Soc., 19: 1-28.

Fitts, P. M., 1954, The information capacity of the human motor system in controlling the amplitude of movement, Journal Exp. Psych., 47: 381-391.

Fitts, P. M., and Petersen, J. R., 1964, Information capacity of discrete motor responses. Journal Exp. Psych., 67: 103-112.

Fowler, C. A., and Turvey, M. T., 1978, Skill acquisition: an event approach with special reference to searching for the optimum of a function of several variables, in: "Information processing in motor control and learning", G. E. Stelmach, ed., Academic Press, New York.

Franks, I., 1980, Unpublished Ph.D thesis, School of Physical Education, University of Alberta, Edmonton, Canada.

Gallistel, G. R., 1980, "The organisation of action - a new synthesis", Erlbaum, Hillsdale, N.J.

Garner, K. C., 1967, Evaluation of human operator coupled dynamic
        systems, in: "The human operator in complex systems",
        W. T. Singleton, R. S. Easterby & D. C. Whitfield, eds.,
        Taylor & Francis, London.
Gentile, A. M., 1972, A working model of skill acquisition with
        application in teaching, Quest, 17: 3-22.
Gibson, J. J., 1979, "The ecological approach to visual perception",
        Houghton-Mifflin, Boston.
Glencross, D. J., 1975, The effects of changes in task conditions
        on the temporal organisation of a repetitive speed skill,
        Ergonomics, 18: 17-28.
Grootveld, C. C., and Tyldesley, D. A., 1982, The influence of
        movement difficulty and movement complexity on motor
        programming, Submitted Journal Mot. Beh.
Hayes, K. C., and Marteniuk, R. G., 1976, Dimensions of motor task
        complexity, in:"Motor Control: Issues and trends", G. E.
        Stelmach, ed., Academic Press, New York.
Hull, D. L., 1974, "Philosophy of biological sciences", Prentice-Hall,
        New Jersey.
Jones, J. C., 1967, The disigning of man-machine systems, in: "The
        human operator in complex systems", W. T. Singleton,
        R. S. Easterby, and D. C. Whitfield, eds., Taylor & Francis,
        London.
Koestler, A., 1964, "The act of creation", Hutchinson, London.
Pribram, K. H., 1971, "Languages of the brain", Prentice-Hall,
        New Jersey.
Rossum, J. H. A. v., 1980, The schema notion in motor learning
        theory: some persistent problems in research, Journal
        Hum. Move. Studies, 4: 269-279.
Tyldesley, D. A., 1979, Timing in motor skills. Unpublished Ph. D
        thesis. Department of Physical Education, University
        of Leeds, England.
Tyldesley, D. A., and Whiting, H. T. A., 1982, Sport psychology
        as a science, in: "Introduction to sport psychology",
        E. Geron, ed., Wingate, Israel.
Tyldesley, D. A., and Whiting, H. T. A., 1975, Operational timing.
        Journal Hum. Move. Studies, 1: 172-177.
Warburton, F. W., 1969, The structure of personality factors.
        Unpublished paper, Department of Education, University of
        Manchester, England.
Whiting, H. T. A., and Brinker, B. P. L. M., den, 1982, Image of the
        act, in: "Learning difficulties", J. P. Das, R. Mulcahy
        and A. E. Wall, eds., Plenum, New York.
Whiting, H. T. A., 1967, Hand-eye coordination. Unpublished Ph.D
        thesis, Department of Psychology, University of Leeds,
        England.
Whiting, H. T. A., 1982, "Skill in sport - descriptive and prescriptive
        appraisal", Proceedings of the 5th World Congress on Sport
        Psychology, Ottawa, Canada.

VISUOMOTOR COORDINATION: FROM NEURAL NETS TO SCHEMA THEORY*

Michael A. Arbib

Center for Systems Neuroscience,
Department of Computer and Information Science
University of Massachusetts
Amherst, MA 01003, U.S.A.

INTRODUCTION

In much of control theory, the system to be controlled is represented by an n-dimensional vector, representing for example the position and momentum of key components. In this paper, we look at the adaptive control of systems which cannot be well-defined in such terms. Here, the system to be controlled is the body of a human, animal, or robot in interaction with a complex world made up of diverse objects. We shall study controllers which represent this world by a family of 'schemas', and which embed their computations in layers of highly-parallel computing elements. We particularly note the flexibility of 'schema-asemblages' as representations when compared to n-vectors; and the way in which identification algorithms within each (motor) schema can provide important tools for adaptive control.

Animals perceive so that they may act adaptively in their world, and as they act they afford themselves new opportunities for perception. This action-perception cycle is at the very heart of cognition, and in this paper we use an analysis of visuomotor coordination as an entry point into the study of neural nets which subserve cognitive processes. Our presentation will involve models at three levels. At one extreme, there will be neural net models whose components and interconnections are highly correlated with the available anatomy and physiology. At the other extreme there will

---

* The research reported in this paper was supported in part by the National Institutes of Heath under grant no. NS14971 from the National Institute of Neurological and Communicative Disorders and Stroke.

be studies which fall not so much under the rubric of brain theory
as under that of artificial intelligence or of cognitive psychology.
Between these two levels there lies a third, in which one seeks to
represent processes in a way constrained to conform to 'the style of
the brain' though not necessarily to the details of neural
circuitry. For example, in the section on "Computing the Optic
Flow" we shall provide an algorithm which requires interaction
between a number of control surfaces, each of which functions
through the parallel interaction of many local processes. It will
be clear that the model has not been constrained by data on, for
example, the visual cortex; but I hope that it will also be clear
that in understanding an explicit algorithm developed in this style,
we may be better placed to design experiments which will begin to
tease apart the way in which mammalian visual systems make sense of
a changing world.

VISUOMOTOR COORDINATION IN FROG AND TOAD

        There are excellent control-theoretic studies of visuomotor
coordination, such as Robinson's (1976) studies of oculomotor
control, in which the visual input is 'lumped' into a single
variable representing the position of some target. But our concern
is much more with 'structured stimuli' -- how is it that the
richness of the retinal activity can be exploited so that the
animal's behavior is attuned to much of the subtlety of the world
around it? This section suggests that the study of frog and toad
allows us to explore issues all the way from explicit neural
circuitry to cognitive strategies for visually guided behavior.

        In 1959, Lettvin, Maturana, McCulloch and Pitts studied "What
the Frog's Eye tells the Frog's Brain". Some ten years later,
working at Stanford, Richard Didday and I sought to understand "What
the Frog's Eye tells the Frog" -- what are plausible networks which
can take the retinal signals and transduce them to yield appropriate
behavior? One of the key experiments for our work was David Ingle's
(1976) observation that when a frog was confronted with two fly-like
stimuli, either of which alone would be potent enough to release a
snapping response, the animal might well respond to one of them, but
might also respond to neither, as if there were 'competition'
between stimuli, which sometimes resulted in a 'standoff'. The
model that we developed (Didday, 1970, 1976) is shown in Fig. 1.
The 'foodness layer' is a retinotopic layer within tectum where
retinal ganglion cell activity is combined to provide a spatial map
whose intensity correlates with the presence of food-like stimuli in
the environment. The 'relative foodness layer' holds a modified
form of this map, where, as a result of interactions with other
maps, most of the peaks will be suppressed, so that normally but one
peak will be able to get through to trigger snapping in the
corresponding direction. (The locus of activity in the array

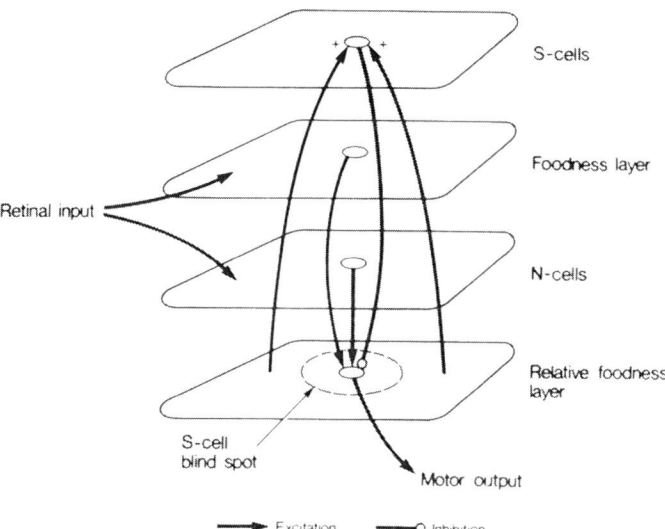

Fig. 1.   Didday model of prey-selection. Refined input yields a
          retinotopic map of prey location in the 'foodness layer'.
          This map is projected on the relative foodness layer, where
          different peaks 'compete' via S-cell mediated inhibition.
          Build up of inhibition yields diminished responsiveness to
          changes in the retinal input; N-cells signal such changes
          to break through this hysteresis.

rather than the value of a single scalar provides the control
signal. The need for different control surfaces for different
control systems may provide much of the rationale for 'the many
visual systems' (Ingle, to appear)).

    The actual 'competition' between the peaks of 'foodness' is
mediated by another retinotopic array, that of the S-cells. To the
extent that there is activity in other regions, to that extent is it
somewhat less likely that a given region will be the one that should
be snapped at. This is turned into circuitry via the S-cells, which
are excited by activity in the relative foodness layer outside a
certain blind spot, with the S-cells then providing inhibition to
the cells within that blind spot on the relative foodness layer.

Both computer and mathematical analysis show that the system will
normally converge to a pattern of relative foodness activity with a
single peak of activity, but there are cases where no peak will
survive this process of convergence, as observed experimentally.
Moreover, if activity within the network is uniform prior to input,
then the largest peak will be that to survive the competition.
However, the system does exhibit hysteresis: once a single peak has
been established, it may be hard for new activity arriving at the
foodness layer to break through. To this end, the N-cells can
respond to a sudden change of activity within the foodness layer,
and on this basis provide excitation to the corresponding locus of
the relative foodness layer, thus breaking through the S-cell
inhibition, and reducing the hysteretic effect.

   In the original version of the model, the N-cells were identified with newness cells, and the S-cells were identified with same-
ness cells, the entire circuitry being contained within the tectum.
However, experiments subsequent to those used as the basis for this
model have suggested a somewhat different interpretation. Ewert
(1976) has shown quite convincingly that, deprived of the inhibitory
influence of pretectum and thalamus, a toad will snap at moving
objects of all sizes, without showing the pattern discrimination
between small 'snappable' objects and larger objects which are to be
avoided. On this basis, the N-cells are still to be interpreted as
newness cells within the tectum, but the S-cells are to be viewed as
cells in pretectum-thalamus (Lara, Arbib & Cromarty, 1982). Of
course, this is only part of the story. Ewert and von Seelen (1974)
have built on Ewert's experiments to come up with a linear lumped
model (not spelt out in terms of detailed neural interactions) of
prey-predator discrimination, meeting Ewert's data on the rate of
response that toads exhibit to mechanical analogs of worms, to
'antiworms' (rectangles elongated orthogonal to the direction of
their movement), and to moving squares, as a function of their size.
Current modelling within my own laboratory is not only addressing
this rapprochement, but also coming up with plausible analyses
(Arbib, 1982; Lara & Arbib, 1982; Lara, Arbib & Cromarty, 1982) of
tectal microcircuitry that could underlie the facilitation effects
observed by Ingle (1976), as well as the pretectal-tectal
interactions that could underlie the habituation effects studied by
Ewert.

   In the rest of this section, I leave the neural level of
analysis to talk about a rich array of behavioral experiments which
allow us to dissect the rather rich spatial world within which the
amphibian finds itself. The experiments discussed so far have
already taken us some distance beyond the stimulus-response
paradigm: while the determination of whether a single stimulus will
be responded to as prey or predator might be analyzed within that
paradigm, observations on facilitation already begin to take us
further, and once the animal must select between a number of

stimuli, the situation becomes even more interesting. Nonetheless,
one still might say that all these experiments address the issue of
how a particular stimulus is extracted from the visual array, and
that thereafter a stereotyped response is emitted. Observations of
Ingle (1976), and subsequent studies by Collett (1979), take us well
beyond this, however. Ingle has observed that if a toad is placed
in front of a vertical grid barrier through which it can see a
moving mealworm, then the toad will sidestep to get around the
barrier to approach its prey. In another study, Ingle made a
histogram of the preferred direction of escape of a frog from a
looming dark object, and found that the histogram peaked in a
direction that was a compromise between the forward direction and
the direction immediately away from the stimulus. He then
interposed a barrier in that preferred direction of escape, and
found that on subsequent trials the animal would no longer use that
preferred direction, but would instead tend to jump to one side or
other of the barrier for its escape. We thus see that we can
approach the influence of context upon behavior with such studies
which are only one step removed from those for which we have a
moderately good understanding of neural circuitry (though grievously
impaired by the current sorry state of understanding of efferent
pathways from the tectum, and of their role in motor control). In
recent studies, Collett has placed a toad on one side of a chasm
with a mealworm on the other, and finds that the animal will jump
across a narrow chasm, will step down to, and walk across, a broad
but shallow chasm, but will turn away if the chasm is both too deep
and too broad. A recent series of experiments has analyzed the
toad's behavior in an environment in which there are both chasms and
barriers, and we are currently working with Collett to develop a
model which will be at the cognitive psychology level, rather than
the neural net level, but will be in the style of the brain to the
extent that the model will be in terms of interacting subsystems, of
which a few are already amenable to neural circuit analysis.

COMPUTING THE OPTIC FLOW

     It has become a commonplace in that branch of artificial
intelligence called computer vision (Hanson & Riseman, 1978) to
discriminate between low-level and high-level systems. Low-level
systems may carry out preprocessing to extract various features,
carry out motion and depth processing, extract boundaries within the
image, segment the image into regions which may well correspond to
surfaces of objects represented within the image, or even come up
with subtle information about the shape of the surfaces which have
been sensed. While these processes may make considerable use of the
physics of the world -- the fact that the world tends to be made up
of surfaces rather than of an aggregate array of moving points, or
properties of the way in which shadows are generated, or in which
light is reflected from variously shaped surfaces -- these low-level

systems do not make any use of knowledge of what particular objects
may be in the environment. It is the job of the high-level systems
to build upon the representations initially determined at the low
level to utilize what I shall call 'perceptual schemas' to recognize
objects within the environment (Arbib, 1981). J.J. Gibson (1955,
1966, 1977) was one of the people who most forcefully made clear to
psychologists that there was a great deal of information that could
be 'picked up' by 'low-level systems' and that, moreover, this
information could be of great use to an animal or to an organism
even without invocation of 'high-level processes' of object
recognition. For example, if, as we walk forward, we recognize that
a tree appears to be getting bigger, we can infer that the tree is
in fact getting closer. What Gibson emphasized, and others such as
Lee (1974, Lee & Lishman, 1977) have since developed, is that it
does not need object recognition to make such inferences. In
particular, the 'optic flow' -- the vector field representing the
velocity on the retina of points corresponding to particular points
out there in the environment -- is rich enough to support the
inference of where collisions may occur within the environment and,
moreover, the time until contact.

We shall detail elsewhere our current studies of how inference
from the optic flow might be used in directing the locomotion of a
robot around an obstacle-cluttered world, and the subsequent
analysis of how relevant such study may be to the cognitive
psychologist. Here, I want to emphasize a problem often glossed
over in Gibson's writings, namely that of the actual computation of
the optic flow from the changing retinal input. Our studies to date
have been 'in the style of the brain', but have not been related to
actual neural circuitry. In what follows, then, rather than asking
how neurons might pick up the optic flow on the basis of
continuously changing retinal input, we shall simply offer an
algorithm, played out over a number of interacting layers each of
which involves parallel interaction of local processes, where the
retinal input is in the form of two successive 'snapshots', and the
problem is to match up corresponding features in these two frames.
(Mathematically, then, the problem is the same as that of stereopsis
(Arbib, Boylls & Dev, 1974; Dev, 1975; Frisby, 1977; Julesz,
1971; Marr & Poggio, 1977, 1979; Sperling, 1970), where two images
taken from different places are to be matched, so that depth can
then be inferred in terms of the interocular distance; whereas in
the optic flow problem the two images are separated in time, and so
depth is expressed as time until contact, or until adjacency.
However, although there are only two eyes, there may be many
successive moments in time, and we shall see that the initial
algorithm for matching a successive pair of frames can be improved
when the cumulative effect of a whole sequence can be exploited.)

The problem is posed in Fig. 2, where we see four features
extracted from Frame 1, shown as circles, and four features from

Frame 2, represented as crosses. The <u>stimulus-matching problem</u> is
to try to match up each pair of features in the two frames that
correspond to a single feature in the external world. Fig. 2(a)
shows an assignment that seems far less likely to be correct than
that shown in Fig. 2(b). The reason that we would, lacking other
information, prefer the latter stimulus-matching is that the world
tends to be made up of surfaces, with nearby points on the same
surface being displaced similar amounts. (This use of the plausible
hypothesis that our visual world is made up of relatively few
connected regions to drive a stimulus-matching process was
enunciated, for stereopsis, by Arbib et al. (1974).) Our algorithm,
then, will make use of two consistency conditions:

> <u>Feature matching</u>: Where possible, the optic flow vector
> attached to a feature in Frame 1 will come close to bringing
> it in correspondence with a similar feature in Frame 2.
> <u>Local smoothness</u>: Since nearby features will tend to be
> projections of points on the same surface, their optic flow
> vectors should be similar.

In developing our algorithm (Prager, 1979; Prager & Arbib, in
press) 'in the style of the brain', we posit a retinotopic array of
local processors, which can make initial estimates of the local
optic flow, but will then pass messages back and forth to their
neighbors in an iterative process to converge eventually upon a
global estimate of the flow. The need for interactions if a correct
global estimate is to be obtained is shown in Fig. 3, where we see a
local receptive field for which the most plausible estimate of the
optic flow is greatly at variance with the correct global pattern.
Our algorithm is then as shown in Fig. 4. We fix two frames, and
seek to solve the matching problem for them. An initial assignment
of optic flow vectors might be made simply on the basis of nearest
match. The algorithm then proceeds through successive iterations,

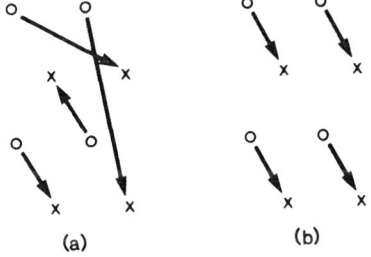

(a)   (b)

Fig. 2.   In a world made up of surfaces, nearby features are likely
to have similar optic flow. Thus the flow of (b) is far
more likely to be correct than that of (a).

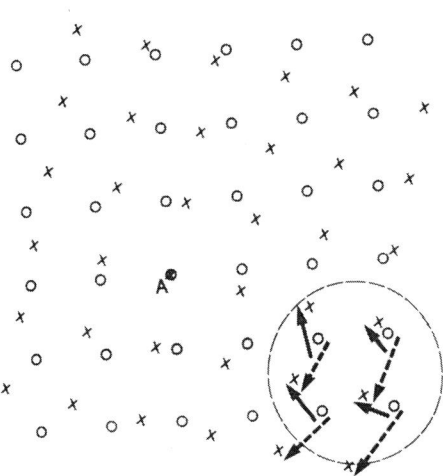

Fig. 3.   Frame 1 comprises the dots indicated by circles; Frame 2
           is obtained by rotating the array about the pivot at A to
           place the dots in the positions indicated by crosses. The
           dashed circle at lower right is the receptive field of a
           local processor. The solid arrows indicate the best local
           estimate of the optic flow, the dashed arrows show the
           actual pairing of features under rotation about A.

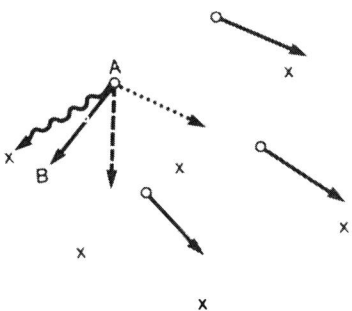

Fig. 4.   The circles indicate features in Frame 1, the crosses
           features in Frame 2, and the solid arrows the current
           estimate of the optic flow -- the head of the arrow shows
           the posited position in Frame 2 of the feature corres-
           ponding to the Frame 1 feature at the tail of the arrow.
           'Feature matching' alone would adjust A's optic flow to the
           wavy arrow pointing to the Frame 2 feature nearest to B
           (the current estimate of A's Frame 2 position); 'local
           smoothness' would yield the dotted arrow, the average of
           the optic flow of the neighbors; while our relaxation
           algorithm yields the dashed arrow as a weighted combination
           of these two estimates.

with the local estimate for the optic flow vector assigned to each
feature of Frame 1 being updated at each iteration. Consider, for
example, the Frame 1 feature A of Fig. 4, and the position B which
is the current hypothesis as to the location of the matching
stimulus in Frame 2. We see that were feature matching to be the
sole criterion, the new optic flow would be given bý the wavy arrow
which matches A to the feature in Frame 2 closest to the prior
estimate. On the other hand, if only local smoothness were taken
into account, the new optic flow vector assigned to A would be the
average of the optic flow vectors of features within a certain
neighborhood. Our algorithm updates the estimate at each iteration
by making the new estimate a linear combination of the feature
matching update and the local smoothness update, as indicated by the
dashed arrow emanating from A in Fig. 4. The algorithm works quite
well in giving a reliable estimate of optic flow within 20
iterations.

Given a sequence of frames, rather than just two, we can obtain
an increasingly accurate estimate of the optic flow, and yet use
less iterations to handle each new frame as it is introduced. For
example, if, having matched Frame n to Frame n+1 we try to match
Frame n+1 to n+2, it is reasonable to assume that -- to a first
approximation -- the optic flow advances a feature by roughly the
same amount in the two frames. If we thus use the repetition of the
previous displacement, rather than a nearest neighbor match, to
initialize the optic flow computation of the two new frames, we find
from simulations that only 4 or 5 iterations, rather than the
original 20, are required, and that the quality of the match on real
images is definitely improved.

The algorithm just described is based on two consistency
conditions, feature matching and local smoothness. It is instruc-
tive to note where these constraints break down. If one object is
moving in front of another object then points on the rear surface
will either be occluded or disoccluded during this movement,
depending on whether the front object is moving to cover or uncover
the object behind it. Thus, if we look at the current estimate of
the optic flow and find places where the flow vector does not
terminate near a feature similar to that from which it starts, then
we have a good indication of an occluding edge. On the other hand,
the local smoothness will also break down at an edge, for the two
objects on either side of the edge will in general be moving
differentially with respect to the organism. Thus, we can design
edge-finding algorithms which exploit the breakdown of consistency
conditions to find edges in two different ways, on the basis of
occlusion/disocclusion, and on the basis of optic flow discontinuity. To the extent that the estimate of edges by these two
processes is consistent, we have the cooperative determination of
the edges of surfaces within the image. What is interesting is
that, to the extent that good edge estimates become available, the

original basic algorithm can be refined, as shown in Fig. 5. (This refinement is yet to be implemented.) Instead of having 'bleeding' across edges, we can dynamically change the neighborhood of a point, so that the matching of features or the conformity with neighboring flow can be based almost entirely upon features on the same side of the currently hypothesized boundary. (But not entirely, for at any time the edges will themselves be confirmed with limited confidence, and so may be subject to later change).

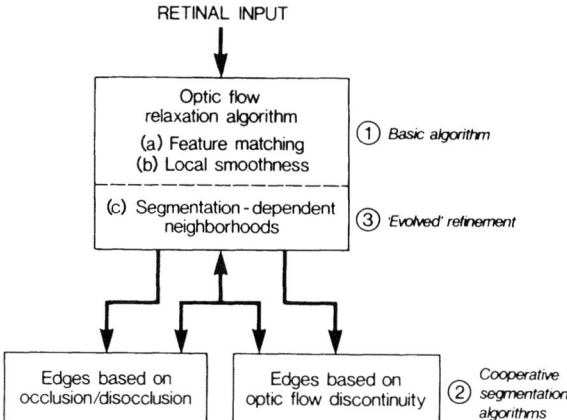

Fig. 5.   (1) Our basic optic flow relaxation algorithm uses the consistency conditions of feature matching and local smoothness.   (2) The resultant optic flow estimate permits the hypothesization of edges on cues based on both occlusion/disocclusion cues and on optic flow discontinuity. (3) The resultant edge hypotheses can be used to refine the computation of optic flow by dynamically adjusting the neighborhoods used in employing the consistency conditions.

We thus see in Fig. 5 an 'evolutionary design process'. The basic algorithm (1) provides new information which can then be exploited in the design of the cooperative segmentation algorithms (2), but once the segmentation information is available, the

original algorithm can be refined by the introduction of
segmentation-dependent neighborhoods (3). I suggest that this is
not simply an interesting engineering observation, but gives us some
very real insight into the evolution of the brain: basic systems
provide the substrate upon which 'higher level' systems may evolve;
but these higher level systems then enrich the environment of the
lower systems, and these lower level systems may then evolve to
exploit the new sources of information. While it is still useful,
to a first approximation, to talk of low-level and high-level
systems, we see that there is no longer any univocal flow of
information. We are very close to the Jacksonian (1898) notion of
levels.

INTERACTING SCHEMAS FOR PERCEPTION AND MOTOR CONTROL

     The notion of a 'schema' (with various names) as providing the
organism's perceptual representation of its environment has become a
commonplace in cognitive psychology (Arbib, 1972, 1975; Bartlett,
1932; Craik, 1943; Gregory, 1969; Mackay, 1966; Minsky, 1975).
However, I would argue that it is more fruitful to reserve the term
'schema' for the 'building block' of a perceptual representation or
motor plan, and I would thus view the current representation of the
environment as being a 'schema-assemblage'. This schema-assemblage
subsumes the slide-box metaphor of Arbib (1972), and we explore some
of its dimensions in Fig. 6 (Arbib, 1979). Consider, for example,
that whenever we see a duck there is some characteristic pattern of
neural activity in the brain which we shall refer to as 'activation
of the duck schema', and suppose that we may also speak of a 'rabbit
schema'. When we are confronted with the duck-rabbit of Fig. 6(a),
we may see it either as a duck with its bill pointing to the right,
or as a rabbit with its ears pointing to the right, but we cannot
see it as both simultaneously. This might suggest that the schemas
for duck and rabbit are neural assemblies with mutually inhibitory
interconnections as indicated in Fig. 6(b). However, we are quite
capable of perceiving a duck and a rabbit side by side within the
scene, so that it seems more appropriate to suggest, as in
Fig. 6(c), that the inhibition between the duck schema and rabbit
schema that would seem to underlie our perception of the duck-rabbit
is not so much 'wired in' as it is based on the restriction of
low-level features to activate only one of several schemas. In
other words, we postulate that to the extent that a higher level
schema is activated, to that extent are the features which
contributed to that activation made unavailable. We thus have an
efferent pathway within the visual system, and this may well tie in
with the observation that the number of fibers running from visual
cortex to lateral geniculate in mammals exceeds the number of fibers
running in the 'normal' direction (Harth, 1976; Singer, 1977).
Finally, it must be noted that we are quite able to see a scene with
several ducks in it. Thus we can no longer think of a single

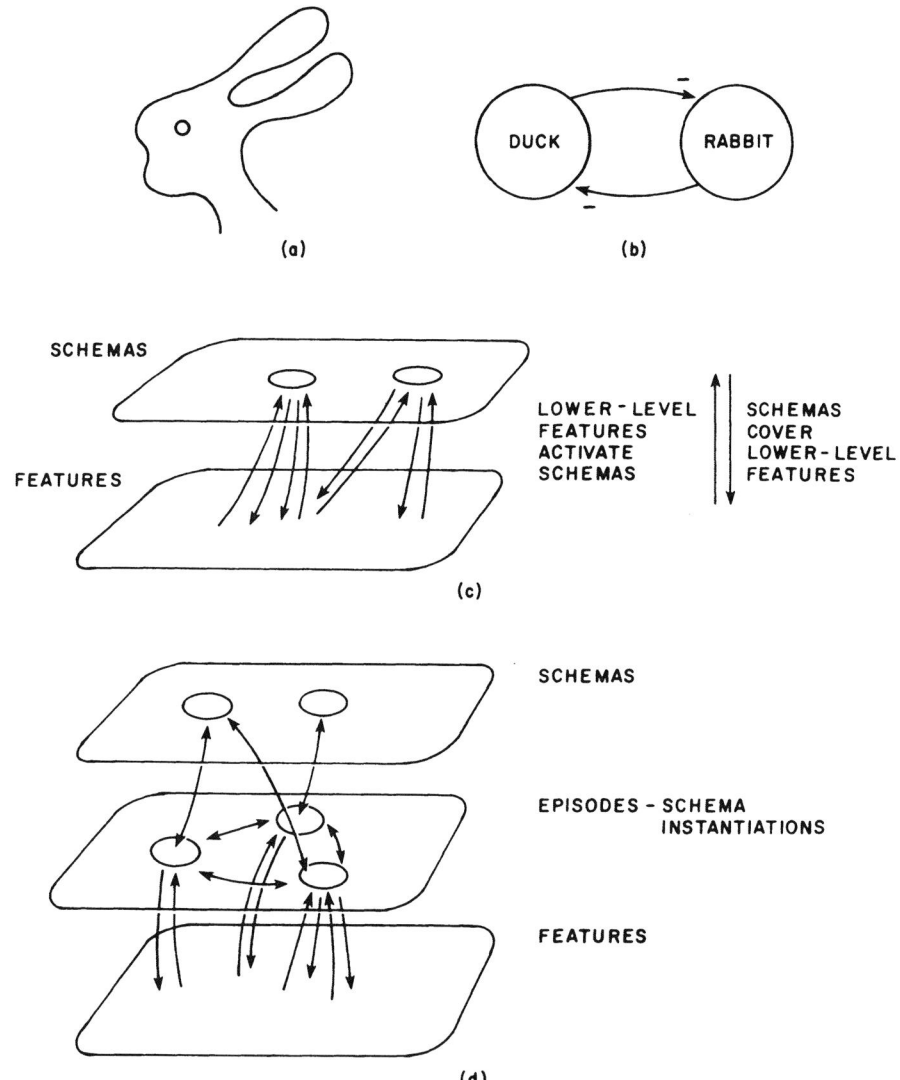

Fig. 6.   From schemas to schema-assemblages. The duck-rabbit (a)
           suggests that mutual inhibition between the schemas
           (internal representations) of duck and rabbit are mutually
           inhibitory (b). However, the fact that we can see a scene
           containing both a duck and a rabbit suggests that this
           inhibition is not 'wired in', but is rather mediated by the
           competition for low-level features (c). Finally, our
           ability to see a scene with several ducks, say, argues that
           perception does not so much activate a set of particular
           schemas as it activates a schema-assemblage consisting of
           instantiations of schemas (d).

localized schema for each familiar object in our environment, but we must rather imagine that the appropriate pattern of activity can be reproduced to an extent compatible with the number of occurrences of an object of the given type within the current visual scene as in Fig. 6(d); and we must further imagine that each of these is tuned with appropriate parameters to represent the particularities of the particular instance so represented.

Elsewhere, in arguing for a theory of schemas within an overall perspective of 'action-oriented perception' (Arbib, 1975), I have viewed a schema as a system with three components:

1. Input matching routines which test for evidence that that which the schema represents is indeed present in the environment;
2. Action routines whose parameters may be tuned by parameter fitting in the input matching routines;
3. Competition and cooperation routines which, for example, use context (activation levels and spatial relations of other schemas) to lower or raise the schema's activation level.

However, in developing this theory (Arbib, 1981), I have come to the conclusion that it is not always appropriate to imagine input matching routines and action routines as contained within the same schema. I thus now find it convenient (to some extent) to distinguish perceptual schemas and motor schemas. Through our continuing interaction with the world we build up an assemblage of perceptual schemas to represent our current knowledge about the environment. On the basis of our current goals, we then build up a 'coordinated control program' of interwoven motor schemas which guides our actions. Of course, as we begin to act, we are able to update the perceptual schema assemblage, and on this basis update our plans. As stated in the introduction, our behavior is best described by an action-perception cycle -- we act to perceive, and we perceive to act.

To briefly analyze the notion of 'motor schema', we need an important concept from modern control theory, that of the identification algorithm as shown in Fig. 7. In the familiar realm of feedback control theory, a controller compares feedback signals from the controlled system with a statement of the desired performance of the system to determine control signals which will move the controlled system into ever greater conformity with the given plan. However, the appropriate choice of control signal must depend upon having a reasonably accurate model of the controlled system -- for example, the appropriate thrust to apply must depend upon an estimate of the mass of the object that is to be moved. However, there are many cases in which the controlled system will change over time in such a way that no a priori estimate of the system's parameters can be reliably made. To that end, it is a useful practice to interpose an 'identification algorithm' which can

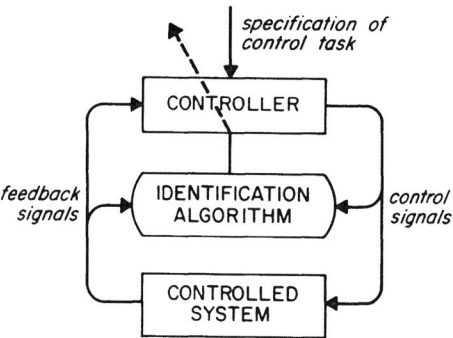

Fig. 7. An identification algorithm provides a continually updated
         parametric description of the controlled system to the
         controller. The resultant combination of controller and
         identification algorithm thus yields a control system
         adaptive to changes in its environment.

update a parametric description of the controlled system in such a
way that the observed response of the system to its control signals
comes into greater and greater conformity with that projected on the
basis of the parametric description. We see that when a controller
is equipped with an identification algorithm, and when the
controlled system is of the class whose parameters the algorithm is
designed to identify, and when, finally, the changes in parameters
of the controlled system are not too rapid, then in fact the
combination of controller and identification algorithm provides an
adaptive control system, which is able to function effectively
despite continual changes in the environment.

We owe to the Russian school founded by Bernstein the general
strategy which views the control of movement in terms of selecting
one of a relatively short list of modes of activity, and then,
within each mode specifying the few parameters required to tune the
movement. Where the Russians use the term synergy, which can be
confounded with the Sherringtonian sense of that word as a
coactivated group of muscles, we shall instead use the term 'motor
schema'. The problem of motor control is thus one of sequencing and
coordinating such motor schemas, rather than directly controlling
the vast number of degrees of freedom offered by the independent
activity of all the motor units. We have, to use the language of
Greene, to get the system 'into the right ballpark', and then to
tune activity within that ballpark -- the dual problems of activation and tuning. (We owe to Boylls (Arbib et al., 1974; Boylls,
1975, 1976) a model of how the cerebellar cortex in interaction with
the cerebellar nuclei and various brainstem motor nuclei could
provide the fine tuning of motor schemas.)

Figure 8 provides one example of what I believe to be the style of a 'coordinated control program'. Once more, we are at a level of analysis somewhere between pure artificial intelligence and an attempt at setting forth 'the style of the brain', but we are still far away from the analysis of detailed neural circuitry. Clinical studies, based on lesions in human subjects, should help us refine hypotheses such as that shown in Fig. 8 so that in fact the various 'boxes' come to better and better correspond to the function of circumscribed layers or modules or regions of the human brain. When the input-state-output specification of such a module becomes reasonably established, we are then in an excellent position to pursue detailed neural modelling, with the help of animal experiments. The program shown in Fig. 8 is for the task of reaching towards a visual target. (Some interesting data on this behavior are described by Jeannerod & Biguer, 1982.) For the present purpose, it suffices simply to note that as the hand starts to reach towards the target, it is already being rotated and the separation of the fingers adjusted in anticipation of the orientation and size of the target.

Before discussing the particular scheme shown in Fig. 8, let me first discuss the way in which the notion of coordinated control program is meant to combine features of the flow diagram of the computer scientist with the block diagram of the control theorist. In a flow diagram, each box corresponds to an activation of a single processor, whether it be an arithmetic unit adding two numbers, a retrieval from the computer store, or a test which will determine the flow of control. Thus, in the flow diagram of a conventional serial computer program, each box corresponds to a single activation of a subsystem, only one system is activated at any time, and the lines joining the various boxes correspond to transfers of activation. In Fig. 8, the dashed lines correspond to such activation transfers. On the other hand, in the block diagram of the control theorist, each box represents a physically distinct system, each such system is to be imagined active at the same time, and the lines joining the different boxes correspond to the transfer of actual data, as in the pathways conveying the control signals and the feedback signals in a conventional feedback system. Such data transfers are indicated by the solid lines in Fig. 8. In this figure, then, we have that each box corresponds to the activation of some subsystem, several subsystems may be active at the same time, but we do not imply that all systems are concurrently active. Thus, in addition to its own internal changes, the activity of a particular subsystem may serve both to pass messages -- as indicated by the solid lines -- to other activated subsystems, and also to change the activation level of other systems, as indicated by the dashed lines. In the particular diagram shown here, we have only indicated system activation, but we can just as well imagine deactivation.

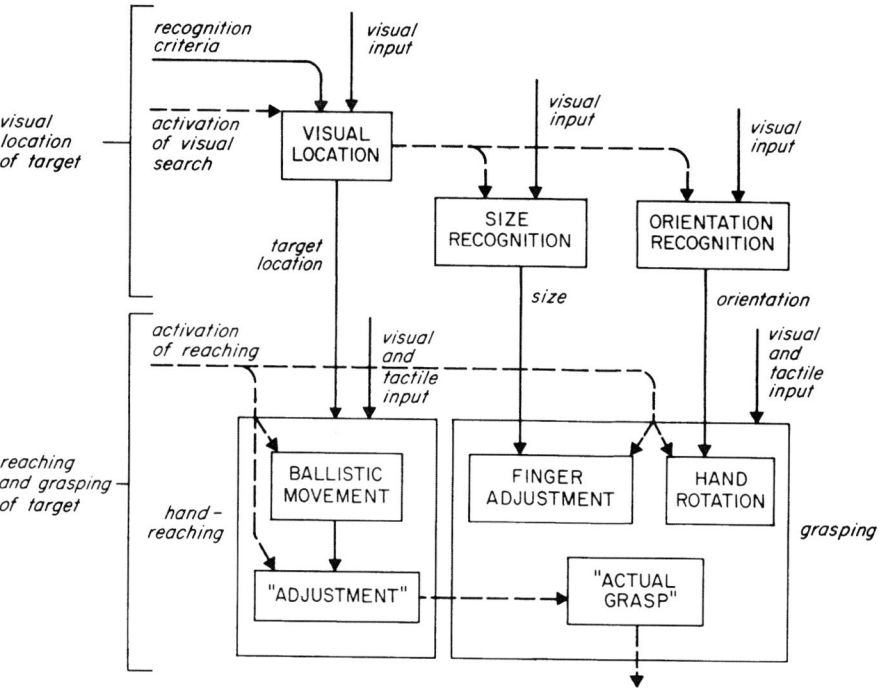

Fig. 8. A hypothetical coordinated control program inspired by the
         study of reaching towards a seen object of Jeannerod and
         Biguer (1982).

    Having understood the instructions, the subject will first
visually locate the target. This is indicated in the upper half of
the diagram by the three boxes representing perceptual schemas for
visual location, size recognition, and orientation recognition. In
the lower half of the diagram we see that there are two motor
schemas that are concurrently activated once reaching and grasping
are initiated. The hand reaching schema, upon activation, releases
a ballistic movement to the target which in the intact subject can
then be modulated at the end by visual feedback until actual contact
with the target is made. The grasping schema is activated
simultaneously with the reaching schema, and itself involves the
simultaneous activation of both finger adjustment and hand rotation.
What is particularly interesting about the hypothetical scheme shown
here is that the activation of the 'actual grasp' subschema of the
motor schema for grasping is not internally activated by completion
of finger adjustment or hand rotation, but is rather separately
activated when adjustment of the hand reaching schema yields the
appropriate tactile stimulation to the palm of the hand. While this
figure is certainly hypothetical, it does begin to give us a

language in which we can talk about the coordination and control of multiple activations of different motor schemas, and thus begin to analyze complex feats of motor coordination in terms of units (schemas) whose implementation we can explore in terms of neural circuitry.

ACKNOWLEDGEMENT. This paper, apart from minor changes, was first published in Cognition and Brain Theory, 4 (1981), 23-39. It is reproduced here by kind permission of the publisher and copyright holder, Lawrence Erlbaum Associates, Hillsdale, New Jersey. The references have been somewhat updated.

REFERENCES

Arbib, M. A. "The Metaphorical Brain: An Introduction to Cybernetics as Artificial Intelligence and Brain Theory," New York: Interscience, 1972.
Arbib, M. A., 1975, Parallelism, slides, schemas and frames, in: "Systems: Approaches, Theories, Applications," W. E. Hartnett, ed., Reidel, pp. 27-43.
Arbib, M. A., 1979, Local organizing processes and motion schemas in visual perception, in: "Machine Intelligence 9," J. E. Hayes, D. Michie and L. I. Mikulich, eds., Ellis Horwood Ltd., pp. 287-298.
Arbib, M. A., 1981, Perceptual structures and distributed motor control, in: "Motor Control," V. B. Brooks, ed., Vol. II, "Section on Neurophysiology, Handbook of Physiology," Amer. Physiological Soc., pp. 1449-1480.
Arbib, M.A., 1982, Modelling neural mechanisms of visuomotor coordination in frog and toad, in: "Competition and Cooperation in Neural Nets," S. Amari and M.A. Arbib, eds., Lecture Notes in Biomathematics 45, Springer-Verlag, pp. 342-370.
Arbib, M. A., C. C. Boylls, and P. Dev, 1974, Neural models of spatial perception and the control of movement, in: "Cybernetics and Bionics," W. D. Keidel, W. Handler and M. Spreng, eds., Oldenbourg, pp. 216-231.
Arbib, M. A. and R. Lara, 1982, A neural model of the interaction of tectal columns in prey-catching behavior. Biol. Cybern. 44: 185-196.
Bartlett, F. C., 1932, "Remembering," Cambridge Univ. Press.
Boylls, C. C., 1975, A Theory of Cerebellar Function with Applications to Locomotion. I. The Physiological Role of Climbing Fiber Inputs in Anterior Lobe Operation. Univ. of Massachusetts at Amherst, COINS Tech. Report 75C-6.
Boylls, C. C., 1976, A Theory of Cerebellar Function with Applications to Locomotion. II. The Relation of Anterior Lobe Climbing Fiber Function to Locomotor Behavior in the Cat. Univ. of Massachusetts at Amherst, COINS Tech. Report 76-1.

Collett, T. S., 1979, A toad's devious approach to its prey: a study
    of some complex uses of depth vision. J. Comp. Physiol. A. 131:
    179-189.
Craik, K. J. W., 1943, "The Nature of Explanation," Cambridge Univ.
    Press.
Dev, P., 1975, Computer simulation of a dynamic visual perception
    model. Int. J. Man-Mach. Stud. 7: 511-528.
Didday, R. L., 1970, "The Simulation and Modelling of Distributed
    Information Processing in the Frog Visual System," (Ph.D.
    Thesis) Stanford Univ.
Didday, R. L., 1976, A model of visuomotor mechanisms in the frog
    optic tectum. Math. Biosci. 30: 169-180.
Ewert, J.-P., 1976, The visual system of the toad: behavioral and
    physiological studies on a pattern recognition system, in: "The
    Amphibian Visual System: A Multidisciplinary Approach," K. V.
    Fite, ed., Academic Press, pp. 141-202.
Ewert, J.-P., and W. von Seelen, 1974, Neurobiologie und
    System-Theorie eines visuellen Muster-Erkennungsmechanismus bei
    Kroten. Kybernetik 14: 167-183.
Frisby, J. P. and J.E.W. Mayhew, 1977, Global processes in
    stereopsis. Perception 6: 195-206.
Gibson, J. J., 1955, The optical expansion-pattern in aerial
    location. Am. J. Psychol. 68: 480-484.
Gibson, J. J., 1966, "The Senses Considered as Perceptual Systems,"
    Allen and Unwin.
Gibson, J. J., 1977, The theory of affordances. in: "Perceiving,
    Acting and Knowing," R. E. Shaw and J. Bransford, eds.,
    Erlbaum.
Gregory, R. L., 1969, On how so little information controls so much
    behavior, in: "Towards a Theoretical Biology, 2: Sketches," C.
    H.Waddington, ed., Edinburgh Univ. Press.
Hanson, A. R. and E. M. Riseman (eds.), 1978, "Computer Vision
    Systems," Academic Press.
Harth, E., 1976, Visual perception: a dynamic theory. Biol.
    Cybernetics 22: 169-180.
Ingle, D., 1975, Focal attention in the frog: Behavioral and
    physiological correlates. Science 188: 1033-1035.
Ingle, D., 1976, Spatial vision in anurans. in: "The Amphibian
    Visual System: A Multidisciplinary Approach," K. V. Fite, ed.,
    Academic Press, pp. 119-141.
Ingle, D., in press, A functional approach to the many visual
    systems dilemma.
Jackson, J. H., 1898, Relations of different divisions of the
    central nervous system to one another and to parts of the body.
    Lancet, January 8 (1898).
Jeannerod, M., and B. Biguer, 1982, Visuomotor mechanisms in
    reaching within extrapersonal space, in: "Analysis of Visual
    Behavior," D. J. Ingle, M.A. Goodale and R.J.W. Mansfield,
    eds., MIT Press, pp. 387-409.

Julesz, B., 1971, "Foundations of Cyclopean Perception," Univ. of Chicago Press.

Lara, R. and M. A. Arbib, 1982, A neural model of interaction between tectum and pretectum in prey selection. Cognition and Brain Theory 5: 149-171.

Lara, R., M. A. Arbib and A. S. Cromarty, 1982, The role of the tectal column in facilitation of amphibian prey-catching behavior: a neural model. J. Neuroscience 2: 521-530.

Lee, D. N., 1974, Visual information during locomotion, in: "Perception: Essays in Honor of James J. Gibson," R. B. MacLeod and H. L. Pick, Jr., eds., Cornell Univ. Press, pp. 250-267.

Lee, D. N. and J. R. Lishman, 1977, Visual control of locomotion. Scand. J. Psychol. 18: 224-230.

Lettvin, J. Y., H. Maturana, W. S. McCulloch and W. H. Pitts, 1959, What the frog's eye tells the frog's brain. Proc. IRE 47: 1940-1951.

MacKay, D. M., 1966, Cerebral organization and the conscious control of action, in: "Brain and Conscious Experience," J. C. Eccles, ed., Springer-Verlag, pp. 422-440.

Marr, D. and T. Poggio, 1977, Cooperative computation of stereo disparity. Science 194: 283-287.

Marr, D. M. and T. Poggio, 1979, A theory of human stereopsis. Proc. Roy. Soc. Ser. B 204: 301-328.

Minsky, M. L., 1975, A framework for representing knowledge. in: "The Psychology of Computer Vision," P. H. Winston, ed., McGraw-Hill, pp. 211-277.

Prager, J. M., 1979, "Segmentation of Static and Dynamic Scenes," Ph.D. Thesis. Dept. of Computer and Information Science, Univ. of Massachusetts at Amherst.

Prager, J. M. and M. A. Arbib, in press, Computing the optic flow: The MATCH algorithm, Comp. Graphics and Image Proc.

Robinson, D. A., 1976, Adaptive gain control of vestibulo-ocular reflex by the cerebellum. J. Neurophysiol. 39: 954-969.

Singer, W., 1977, Control of thalamic transmission by corticofugal and ascending reticular pathways in the visual system. Physiol. Rev. 57: 386-420.

Sperling, G., 1970, Binocular vision: a physical and neural theory. Am. J. Psych. 83: 463-534.

RICHLY SPECIFIED INPUT TO LANGUAGE LEARNING

Lila R. Gleitman
University of Pennsylvania
Philadelphia, Pennsylvania

Eric Wanner
Harvard University Press
Cambridge, Massachusetts

Language is learned, in the course of the everyday events of the first five years of life by children bright and dull, eager or sullen, pampered or abused, exposed to Urdu or to English. This universal learning despite varying environments poses a problem to general inductive theories of language learning. This is largely because the rich input data would seem to allow the learner to form a bewildering number of generalizations, many of them absurd. Along with some others, we argue that the child has specific dispositions about how to organize and represent linguistic stimulation, and that it is these representational biases that rescue his inductions from potentially unlimited pitfalls.

Perhaps the most striking outcome of language acquisition research to date is the finding that children are good, all too good, at inductive generalization. They generalize even in the face of frequent and stable counterexamples in the data provided to them. A well-known case is induction of the weak past tense ending for English (Ervin, 1964). At two and three years of age, children are heard to utter both weak (e.g. talked) and strong (e.g. ran) past tense forms, a learning pattern that can be accounted for by assuming item by item memorization. But at about age four, "errors" suddenly make their appearance. Now approximately all the verbs take the weak ending (e.g. runned). So here is the learner systematically violating the data base: he is forming a generalization false of more than half the data he receives, for the weak ending occurs significantly less than half the time on types, and far less than this on tokens, of the common stock of English verbs. It takes many years to get rid of these morphological overregularizations. Indeed, for the rarer verbs, some of them never go away (one effect, of course, is language change).

This inclination of learners to generalize even on noisy data would appear to be a good finding, one that helps account for acquisition of a rule-governed, infinitely generative system from partial information. However, these very successes pose a problem for explaining the uniform learning process: the trouble is that there are myriad properties true 30 or 40% of the time about English words and sentences, properties that one had better not generalize about if one is to learn. For instance, it is true over 90% of the time that words preceding hood are kinship terms (e.g., motherhood, childhood, neighborhood) but it is a false step to generalize that robin is a kinship term. How to tame the inductive process so that children will make only or largely the right generalizations, for example the generalizations from old grammatical sentences to new grammatical sentences? (note 1).

A variety of answers have been suggested, but found wanting. One is that the learner could receive negative data -- corrections. As has been formally demonstrated by Gold (1967) and others, inductive learning of language-like systems is possible if the learning device receives negative, as well as positive, feedback. Unfortunately, it turns out that children are rarely corrected, rather reinforced, for ungrammatical utterances (Brown and Hanlon, 1970): if the child says "Me wuvs yer, Mom" the mother does not usually respond "ungrammatical sentence, Joey." On the contrary, mothers often positively reinforce true or socially acceptable utterances no matter their grammatical format, as in the following exchange:

(1)   2 year old: Momma isn't boy, he a girl.
       Mother: That's right.

but negatively reinforce errors of fact:

(2)   2 year old: And Walt Disney comes on Tuesday.
       Mother: No, he does not.
                                        (Brown and Hanlon, 1970, p. 49)

Woe to the learner who takes (2) as a grammatical correction, and (1) as an error of fact. Luckily, as the following interchange exemplifies, the children seem to be immune to direct corrections on their rare occurrences:

```
(3)   2 year old:   Nobody don't like me.
      Mother:       No, say "Nobody likes me."
      2 year old:   Nobody don't like me.
      Mother:       No, say "Nobody likes me."
      2 year old:   Nobody don't like me.
          (five more interchanges, all exactly the same)
      Mother: No, now listen carefully: "Nobody likes me."
      2 year old: Oh: Nobody don't likes me.
                                          (McNeill, 1966, p. 69)
```

Another popular answer to how children learn is that they rely on meaningful interpretation of the situation that accompanies heard utterances. Perhaps they would hear "The cat is on the mat" as they gazed at a cat on a mat. Unfortunately, this plausible conjecture about the context for linguistic stimulation is too imprecise and limited by itself to resolve the learning problem, for one thing because when the child is gazing at the cat on the mat he is, a fortiori, gazing at a mat under a cat, a nose of a cat, a cat and a mat on the floor, and so forth. That is, the scene in view is not what language codes; rather, it codes one of indefinitely many descriptions of a scene. So allusions to scenes are insufficient to explain how the child learns which situation is coded by which sentences. To be sure, any solution to the learning problem will have to draw "in some way" on the learner's inclinations to interpret the real world in particular, meaningful, ways (see Wexler and Culicover, 1980, and Carey, 1982 for discussion). But as we will try to show, relations between linguistic form and meaning are far from transparent; therefore, quasiformal analyses are required from the learner to mediate the linguistic form-meaning relations.

We will concentrate discussion here on a single issue within the language learning puzzle: the special way in which the child acquires the so-called closed class morphology of his native language. The particular facts about acquisition of this material suggest that the child leans heavily on the distinction between stressed and unstressed syllable, present in the sound wave. The thrust of our argument is not that the information required is present in the sound wave and hence no linguistically special apparatus is required to account for learning. Our argument is nearer to the reverse of this. The particular analyses the child seems to perform on the sound wave are hardly inevitable. No objective physicist, analyzing the same data, would have any excuse to perform just these analyses, rather than others. We argue that if the child were as open minded as the physicist in his approach to the data, induction of the language from sound waves could not be guaranteed in finite time, even less in the four or five years it (uniformly) takes real learners. We claim the learner succeeds just because he is biased to represent the speech signal in certain ways, the right ways. Most generally, our position is that the representational system, that secures motivated analyses as the data for induction, bears the major burden in explaining language learning.

EARLY ANALYSES OF THE SPEECH SIGNAL: A SEQUENCED, OPEN CLASS LANGUAGE

There is abundant evidence from studies of neonates that they perceive the continously varying sound wave of speech as a string of segments that approximate the phonetic inventories of natural lang- uages (Eimas, Siqueland, Jucsyzk, and Vigorito, 1971; Jucsyzk, in press). To be sure, there is considerable evidence that creatures ranging from chinchillas to macaques are likewise inclined toward the same discriminations (Kuhl and Miller, 1975) but this does not affect the usefulness of a segmental phonetic analysis to child language learners (though it does suggest to many, along with evidence from humans concerning categorical perception of both speech and nonspeech auditory events, that these discriminations are not specialized to the language domain). Though this discrete analysis of the continuous wave form is clearly a requirement for language learning, it appears to be insufficient as the sole basis for running the required induc- tions.   This is because the phonetic sequences vastly underdetermine the identification of words (is it "an adult" or "a nuhdult"?, a ques- tion actually posed by a three-year old to her proud mother), the word classes (is yellow a noun, verb or adjective?), and the phrase bound- aries (when you see a man eating fish, is he a human diner or an elas- mobranch diner?). The question, therefore, is whether there are units above and beyond the phonetic distinctive features, physically mani- fest in the wave form and operative in the child's induction of lang- uage structure.

There are, and we concentrate on one here: the learner attends discriminatively to an abstract distinction whose surface reflex in English is stress/nonstress, defined on syllables (note 2). This con- trast yields the distinction open class/closed class, a first parti- tioning of the morpheme-level vocabulary. Our position is that the open class, mapped onto stressed syllables, is perceptually salient to the youngest learners, who effect acquisition of sequenced, hierarch- ically organized, parse trees involving only these, as a first step (note 3). The closed class, mapped onto unstressed syllables, is ac- quired in a separate developmental step that requires the open class parse tree as the basis for its induction.

A CATEGORIAL CUT IN THE ADULT MORPHOLOGY

The distinction between two classes of morphological items was initially made by the historical linguists, who noticed that the rate of change of vocabulary is unequal, as a language evolves over time. A very large set of words, mainly the nouns, adjectives, and verbs, freely drop old members and add new members (hence, open class). A much smaller set of words and affixes, including pronouns, auxiliary verbs, prepositions and postpositions, inflectional items, specifiers, conjunctions, and complementizers, changes only slowly over historical time (hence, closed class). Potentially, you can see, the closed

class has syntactic and semantic distinctiveness. More important here
(and, anyhow, probably the only description that will hold across the
whole domain, cf. Kean, 1979), the closed class has phonological
distinctiveness: The syntactic classes last mentioned above are just
those that can appear stressless in the languages of the world
(Zwicky, 1976). In English, for instance, the relevant items are
stressless, contractable (e.g., "We'd tell'm stories frours," for "We
would tell them stories for hours), often subsyllabic, and deform
phonetically depending on their surrounding phonetic and syntactic
context. For example, to becomes ∂ after want, i.e., wann∂, but t∂
after have, which also deforms to haf, i.e., haft∂.

Evidence is accumulating that this contrast plays a number of
important roles in linguistic performance. For example, open and
closed class items are accessed differentially in lexical decision
tasks (Bradley, 1978). In such tasks, single words and nonwords
(e.g., nard) are displayed on a screen for the subject; his job is to
decide as quickly as possible whether the item shown is a word in the
language, or not, responding by pressing the appropriate key. Analysis is on the correct positive responses only (errors are easily kept
close to zero). As Bradley showed, reaction time (RT) to lexical
decision is a function of word frequency for the open class only; RT's
to the closed class show little or no such sensitivity to the frequency in the language of the items in the class. Her explanation for
the ultimate basis of this effect is that, owing to identifiable
acoustic cues to the closed class set of items, they are mentally
stored together to allow quick categorical retrieval. This would be a
very convenient tack for a parser to take, for a language like English, just because the closed class items tend to occur at surface
phrase boundaries and so provide one basis for an initial segmentation
of the utterance into its syntactically and semantically functioning
subcomponents.

A most interesting further finding from Bradley is for Broca's
aphasics (see also Bradley, Garrett, and Zurif, 1979). These individuals, as is well known, are selectively impaired for uttering and
comprehending closed class items. (The opposing dissociation is seen
in other aphasic syndromes). Nonetheless, these individuals can perform a lexical decision task, though with longer RT's, recognizing,
e.g. both dog and the as words, and gom as a nonword. But they give
frequency dependent RT's for both closed and open class. According to
Bradley, these patients have lost the "special" access to the closed
class, a fact no doubt related to their agrammatism.

A related finding is from Garrett (1975), who has analyzed naturally occurring speech errors, finding that the type of error for the
two classes is characteristically different. Open class items or
parts of them exchange positions with each other, often with intervening material between, e.g.:

(3) a: Older men choose to tend younger wives.

    b: I'm teaching an anguage lacquisition course.

Much rarer are closed class speech errors, e.g.:

(4) ...and what would I want to check...
     (intended: and what I would want to check)

but the central fact is that open class items do not exchange places
with closed class items. It thus appears that the two classes are
treated independently during speech planning. The strongest demonstration of this fact is that the closed class material even when it
is a form bound to an open class item, as the _ing_ of (5):

(5) That's just a back trucking out
     (intended: that's just a truck backing out)

usually will remain in place even though the open class item to which
it is affixed moves.

Further related effects of the differential treatment of these
two classes are observed in tests of learning and recall. For instance Epstein -- and before him, Lewis Carroll -- showed that nonsense strings are the easier to memorize and recall if closed class
items from the language are judiciously strewn among them, e.g.:

(6) 'Twas brillig, and the slithy tove... (Lewis Carroll)

(7) a: Yig mer vol hum in yag miv
     b: The yigs mer voling hum in yagest miv
                                        (Epstein, 1961)

Epstein showed that 7b, though longer, was more readily memorized than
7a (and we know that no one ever forgets 6). Finally, paired associate learning of words is easier with a closed class item between
them, that forms a phrase-like entity, e.g. 8b, than is learning of
those words with an open class item between them, e.g. 8a:

(8) a: YIG food ZEB
     b: TAH of ZUM   (Glanzer, 1962)

Presumably, it is the closed class item, _of_, that offers phrase coherence to the string. While 8a adds up to nothing linguistically
organized, 8b forms a phrasal package that invites interpretation --
maybe the Tah of Zum is your favorite oriental potentate.

So far we have mentioned various on-line effects of the closed/
open distinction in language performance. There are many other in-
dicants of the differential mental representation and functioning of

the two classes. One finding is that closed class anomalies are difficult for adults (L. Gleitman and H. Gleitman, 1970) and impossible for children younger than about age 7 to detect and comment on, while open class anomalies are readily identified and described. Examples come from a study (L. Gleitman, H. Gleitman, and Shipley, 1972) in which youngsters are asked to decide whether sentences are "good or silly" and to comment:

(9)   Experimenter: <u>Two and two are four.</u>

    a: 6-year old :   OK.
         Experimenter: Can you think of another way to say it?
         6-year old: Three and one?

    b: 7-year old: I think it sounds better <u>is</u>.

(10) Experimenter: <u>Claire and Eleanor is a sister</u>.

    a: 6-year old: Sure, they could be sisters. I <u>know</u>
               them: They <u>are</u> sisters.

    b: 7-year old: "Claire and Eleanor <u>are</u> sisters."
         Experimenter: Then how come you can say "Two and
               two is four"?
         7-year old: (annoyed) You have to say different
               sentences different ways!

Notice that the six year old fails to remark the agreement violation in the copula, a closed class item, in (9) and (10), while the seven year old repairs this. Particularly in (10a), the six year old displays full working knowledge of the copula in speech (he says "They <u>are</u> sisters") despite its opacity to him in the judgmental task.

As a final, if somewhat arcane, example of the psychological distinctiveness of these classes, the inventors of alphabetic writing had developed a full set of symbols for the phonetic contrasts by about the time of the Periclean apogee. But even so, it took another couple of hundred years more for the closed class items of Greek to be rendered systematically in writing (for a discussion, see L. Gleitman and Rozin, 1977); similarly, the closed class items are the hardest for aspiring readers to learn (Rozin and L. Gleitman, 1977). Clearly, the closed class is the harder to bring consciously to attention. It is the background "frame" that holds the prominent open class items together in the sentence (note 4).

So this categorial distinction keeps cropping up in the most various linguistic performances. But just exactly what is the distinction? Though there is currently some contention about the precise formal specification of the closed class, it is enough for the discussion here to acknowledge that it is picked out in terms of some correlated set of semantic, syntactic, and phonological properties. This is because, as we have stated, the closed class consists of those items in those form classes that can appear stressless in the languages of the world. That is, only certain lexical classes, e.g., prepositions, are assigned low stress or no stress in the sentence prosody; this in turn correlates with certain restrictions on semantic function (e.g., nobody's name is a preposition).

We now present evidence that this contrast plays a role in the discovery of linguistic structure by the child. If this is to be in an explanatory, rather than merely descriptive sense, the claim has to be that initially it is the physical property of the closed class (stresslessness) on which the child seizes, and from which he learns. In the presence of full knowledge of the language, however, the definition of "closed class" may be in terms of the syntactic/semantic distinctiveness in addition to, or even rather than, in terms of the physical properties; on this we take no stand.

THE OPEN CLASS IS LEARNED FIRST

When children first begin to talk (at about 12 months), the vocabulary items used are overwhelmingly members of the open class. Even when sequences of words begin to be strung together (usually, between 18 and 24 months), this bias is the same, with the effect that their speech sounds "telegraphic," e.g. "No eat" or "Mommy sock." By and large, any superficial appearance of closed class items is coincidental, in the sense that such morphologically complex items as brought (in the adult language, perhaps, bring + past) spoken by these young children appear not to be analyzed into their morpholological parts. Strikingly, then, somehow the learners know how to deal selectively with a part of the lexical stock; such closed class words as the and is and affixes such as ed and s are clearly the most frequent in the corpus presented to the learner's ear; yet he does not learn them during the first two years or so of life. The question is what property of the closed class -- semantic, syntactic, or phonological -- is accounting for its absence. In particular, we want an account that does not beg the question of learning. For instance, we wouldn't want to say the child examines the semantic properties of closed class words, and finds them uninteresting, for this presupposes the child knows those properties.

Clues come from the fact that youngest learners (in the period about 12 - 18 months) often omit the unstressed syllables of the open class words they do utter, e.g. "'raff" for giraffe and "e'fant" for elephant. This suggests their deficit is in analysis of unstressed syllables; the closed class items will be omitted simply as an artifact of this. Symmetrically, these very young children often falsely analyze word boundaries when the following syllable is really a separate, closed class item, e.g., "readit book" or "Havit milk." Evidently, the learners are having trouble with the unstressed material; often it is omitted, and often it is inaccurately segmented with respect to the surrounding open class material. All this fits together on the supposition that it is a property close to the phonetic realization of the closed class items that accounts for the difficulty, for learners of English.

Supporting evidence for this interpretation comes from cross-linguistic studies. Slobin (1966) reported on the speech forms of young learners of Russian. This language marks the thematic roles of predicates (the distinction between do-er and done-to, etc.) with closed class inflectional affixes ("case markers") rather than, as in English, by word order. However, the young Russians drop the inflectional affixes. It is not because Russian children do not care to distinguish between do-er and done-to. They do make this distinction, but by means of a word order strategy that has poor support in the data to which they are exposed. Essentially, they act as though they're learning English rather than Russian, in early stages. (See also Venneman, 1975, for similar effects in Old English, and Slobin, 1976, for Serbo-Croatian). We can conclude that the initial dropping of these closed class items is not caused by their "semantic unimportance."

One might argue alternatively that it is the syntactic roles of the inflecting particles that fail to engage the attention of the Russian toddlers. This plausible hypothesis will not work either, for it turns out that the youngest speakers of certain other languages (Turkish, Slobin, 1982; Japanese, Slobin, 1976 and Lust, personal communication) do utter the verb inflections in earliest speech. The difference from the Russian case is that these inflectional items, in the languages just mentioned, are a syllable long, are stressed, and do not deform in varying phonetic contexts. In short, they are pho-nologically open class. The plausible conclusion is that the contrast stressed syllable/ unstressed syllable leaps out of the sound wave at the human learner in a way analogous to the distinction between figure and ground in the child's analysis of visual space (cf, Spelke, 1982).

So far, we have concentrated only on the late appearance of the closed class in the child's speech. But there are many related acquisitional effects. For example, learning of the closed class materials appears to require rather specific input styles, while the open class morphology and functions appear under diverse input conditions in a maturationally scheduled sequence. A sample finding is from Newport, H. Gleitman, and L. Gleitman (1977). Their question was what special features of maternal speech at some point in developmental time predict accelerated rate of growth in the child during a succeeding period. The method used was correlational, and had to do with the relation between maternal speech at some $Time_1$ and rate of growth of the child during a succeeding six month interval, on various linguistic measures of both child and mother (these correlations partialled out current age and stage of the child learners, of course, to correct for spurious correlations that might result owing to base line differences among the learners at the first measurement). It turns out that the only stable correlations between maternal usage and child growth have to do with emergence of the closed class items.

In detail, it is the use of the closed class items in positions where they take stress and are not contractable that predicts the learning advantage; on the contrary, sheer frequency of use of these items predicts nothing about the learners' progress. As a major example, mothers who preponderantly favor yes/no questions have children who learn the auxiliary items fastest. There is no way, in any known syntactic or semantic description, that such question forms can be said to be the "simplest" in the adult grammar that is pre-sumably the target of learning. But the yes/no questions of English, e.g., "Will you pick up your blocks?" present the auxiliary in initial position, where it cannot be contracted to " 'Ll you pick up your blocks?" and is often stressed, owing to general properties of English sentential prosody. This perceptual prominence is what seems to aid the learner.

A fair generalization from the findings so far described is that the young learners are at first acquiring just stressed materials from stressed materials. Some findings from Bellugi (1967) accord well with such a position. Over 90% of the mother's auxiliaries spoken in medial position (e.g., in declaratives such as "I'll smack you if you won't pick up the blocks.") are contracted; but the child seems to seize upon the few uncontracted ones for his learning model. When he begins to utter auxiliaries, it is in the uncontracted form for a significant period of time: "We will go out now." This gives an effect of precision and formality to his speech that is often remarked upon, though the source of this lay impression is rarely explicitly noted. Apparently the young learner is biased toward full syllables with stress, and statistical preponderances in his data base be damned.

Another finding bolsters this same point. We have noted that initial position of auxiliaries favors their learning. This is a very robust effect, one that has been replicated by other investigators (Furrow, Nelson, and Benedict, 1979; L. Gleitman, Newport, and H. Gleitman, 1982). Yet the child does not first utter the questions with auxiliary in initial position that presumably caused him to learn the faster. On the contrary, he first utters the declaratives, in which the auxiliary occurs medially (e.g., "We will go out now"). And he marks yes/no questions by intonation only for some period of time ("We can go out now?") although such a form is virtually never mo-delled in the input corpus. Learning is dependent on the data, to be sure, but we can see from this last finding that the form of the data does not easily account for the character of what is learned. (For discussion of the apparent basis for this last effect, the child's

early bias toward "canonical sentence form," see L. Gleitman and
Wanner, 1982; and note 5).

THE CLOSED CLASS IS LEARNED SEPARATELY

Summarizing once again, the closed class materials are the harder
to acquire, and are laid down in a distinctive developmental pattern,
one that is not only late, but is more strictly environment-dependent.
One might now wonder why languages bother with the phonologically
closed class materials at all, since they pose problems for learning.
Why not say a string of stressed words in a row? We have suggested in
beginning this discussion that the closed class plays a crucial role
in adult parsing performances, helping to establish the phrase
boundaries so as to recover compositional meanings (for a parser that
crucially exploits the classificatory distinction, see Wanner and
Maratsos, 1978). The contrast may in fact be an inevitable concom-
mittant of rapid, fluent, communication among experts (Slobin, 1977).

Supportive evidence comes from studies of pidgin languages
(lingua francas) and their creolization (evolution into full natural
languages). When a pidgin is invented by linguistically heterogeneous
adults, it is impoverished in closed class resources, marking such
semantic properties as time with optional open class elements (e.g.,
baimbai, from English by and by, as an adverbial meaning future in the
English-based Papua New Guinea pidgin language, Tok Pisin; Sankoff and
Laberge, 1973) and marking the thematic roles by word order (Sankoff
and Laberge, ibid.; Bickerton, 1975). These uniform properties of
pidgins invented by adults are remarkable since often the inventors'
native tongues are highly inflected languages with very weak word
order constraints (Slobin, 1977).

Sankoff and Laberge studied the change in Tok Pisin over generations of speakers. As the language came into very general use by
heterogeneous adults who spoke it for many years, such sentence-
initial, optional, elements as baimbai moved to a position preceding
the verb, and became obligatory for marking future tense. Essentially, "Baimbai I go home" becomes "I baimbai go home" (note 6). For the
most fluent users, the form is shortened to a single syllable, i.e.,
"I bai go home." This shows that adult populations are capable of
inventing grammatical devices, such as obligatory tense marking, in
the manner universally true of human languages; that is, to honor the
generalization that tense markers belong within verb-phrases. But at
this stage in the evolution of Tok Pisin, the item baimbai or bai is
still phonologically open class, a regularly stressed word. Now the
Sankoff and Laberge evidence is that the crowning step in the creation
of the phonological closed class is taken by the next generation: babies who acquire Tok Pisin as their native language. According to
these investigators, learners in the age range 5 to 8 years -- the
usual moment of full flowering of the closed class for learners of

English, too -- now reduce baimbai and bai to /bð/, yielding such
sentences as "I bð-go home." In sum, latest stages of learning incorporate a phonological closed class, even where this is absent from
the input corpus.

Findings from second language learning research (e.g., Newport,
1982; Supalla, 1982, for American Sign Language) suggest more generally that closed class fluency emerges fully only when acquired early
in childhood. Apparently, subtle deficits can be observed for most
learners even if learning starts as early as age 8 years. (The pro-
viso here is that a few talented adults can overcome the deficits
usual in second language learning, witness Nabokov or Conrad; the
point we are making is that all young children, no matter how dull,
acquire these language properties perfectly, while the proportion of
adults who do so is small to the point of invisibility). It's pretty
obvious to informal observation that second-language learners have the
largest troubles with the "little words." As is often remarked, sometimes you can only tell that a fluent foreigner is a foreigner because
he speaks the second language "so perfectly." He doesn't slur and
deform, i.e., he fails to acquire the intricate phonological processes
that yield the closed class. This is analogous to native speakers
very early in development who, as we have discussed, hear contracted
forms primarily, but utter the uncontracted variants.

HOW IS THE CLOSED CLASS ACQUIRED?

All parties agree that, for acquiring both the open class
and closed class subcomponents of syntax, the child must be sensitive
to the order of appearance of items in the sentences he hears; he must
examine the privileges of occurrence, or relative distribution of
items in well-formed strings. Many investigators (e.g., Bloomfield,
1933; Maratsos, 1982) have assumed that language learning can run
solely on such distributional analysis in much the sense of forming
correlation matrices. For example, Maratsos asserts that what it
takes to be a verb is to take -ed at the end, will at the beginning,
and so forth. Hence he explains induction of the form-class verb in
terms of items that occur contiguous to its members. But notice that
there are a variety of distributional correlations the learner potentially could investigate that are of no value for discovering the
syntax of the language (e.g, the correlation of black with coal,
night, and ink vs the correlation of white with swan, milk, and snow).
This means that an independent explanation is required for why the
child chooses to run just the correlations investigators must assume,
to make their model learning procedures plausible. The distributional
analysis schemes seem to work just to the extent that -- in the examples these investigators cite -- they selectively exploit the
relations between closed class items (e.g., ed) and open classes
(e.g., verb), for these are the ones, among potentially millions of
choices, that reveal the syntactic structuring of the language.

We have begun to make progress toward solution of at least one problem here in terms of the acquisition claims so far made. We have granted, on evidence, that the child distinguishes between the two classes on the basis of their differing phonological properties. Since the open class, and the structures in which it participates, is the earlier discovered, we can conclude that the child analyzes the structure of the closed class against whatever structure he has so far imposed on the open class, and not the other way around.

To bring this point to ground, notice that it is not possible to infer the existence of an open class category such as verb from its distributional relationships to an unstressed syllable such as ed. There are, for instance, no English verbs, to lightheart, to lighthead, or to lightfinger, despite the fact that these words can appear with ed, as the adjectives lighthearted, lightheaded, and lightfingered. There is a distributional regularity here characteristic of verbs, but it holds only when the ed form has been assigned a morphemic value, past tense. Therefore, to learn the open class from its distributional behavior with respect to the closed class, the child would already have had to learn the morphemic value of the closed class.

We have left the child with a problem that neither Maratsos nor Bloomfield has solved: to induce the morphemic values of the closed class items. We will now try to show that, armed with tentative semantic heuristics and exploiting phonological properties of the input strings, the child can in principle bootstrap from the partial information to converge on the correct solution. This will involve a bottom-up attempt to parse the string from its physical form, combined with a top-down attempt to establish its semantically functioning lexical and phrasal categories.

So far we have granted the learner the open class/closed class distinction, at least roughly (that is, as picked out by associated phonological properties). We have also adduced some of the (voluminous) evidence that exists that the child is sensitive to the sequencing of open class elements, from the earliest stages. Perhaps the best evidence for this last claim is that the child's first two- and three-word utterances are ordered, as in the language being learned, in a way that conforms to a predicate-argument analysis; that is, for English, actor - action (e.g., Bowerman, 1973). Each of these "slots" is realized by an item that in the adult language is classified as noun, and verb, respectively. From this it is reasonable to conclude that the learner has established rough precursors to these basic open class categories. According to many recent accounts (e.g., Pinker, in press) it is the semantic associations between simple nouns and "objectness" and simple verbs and "actionness" that provides these early categorizations.

However, even more detailed information about strings than this is going to be required to solve the problem we have just raised: put particularly, to find out that <u>ed</u> in <u>lighthearted</u> is participial, but a finite verb ending in, say, <u>hotfooted</u>. The problem still exists because neither the meaning nor the morphology of <u>hotfooted</u> renders it more or less verb-like than <u>lightfingered</u> or <u>lighthearted</u>. Thus there is no semantic heuristic basis in the contrast between action and thing for establishing the open class categories of these words. And then there is no basis for establishing the closed class morphemic value either, as we have already shown. To repeat, this is because the value of <u>ed</u> can be assigned as <u>past</u> only if the learner has secure knowledge that it is bound to a verb.

It is now clear that knowing something approximate about semantic correlates of open-class lexical categories is not enough information for resolving the <u>ed</u> discovery problem. Most generally, this is because not every verb is an action and not every noun is a person, place or thing. Thus the discovery procedure cannot be reduced summarily to the class definitions of grade-school grammar courses (ask yourself on what semantic basis, for example, <u>thunder</u> is both a noun and a verb, while <u>lightning</u> is noun only). A required further analysis, as we will show, is of the global phrase structure of the sentence.

Recent evidence is to the effect that there exist detectable clues in the spoken string that approximately cue the phrase analysis. For one thing, in a language like English, the closed class items themselves tend to occur at the phrase boundaries, and thus form a first clue to discovery of the higher order phrasal units (indeed, it is the evident phrase-bounding function of these classes that motivates the analysis of lexical decision from Bradley that we cited earlier). But this cue alone is insufficient as the sole basis for constructing the phrase-organized descriptions we will require. This is shown, for example, by the adjective <u>lighthearted</u>, whose closed class morpheme <u>(-ed)</u> occurs phrase-medially. Similarly, languages such as Hebrew quite generally have infixed closed-class material, as we have discussed. Therefore, appearance of a closed class item cannot be a secure basis for demarcation of a phrase boundary for a learner who must be as prepared to learn Hebrew as English.

Luckily, therefore, it is becoming apparent from recent studies of speech perception and production (e.g., Sorenson, Cooper, and Paccia, 1978), and from studies of natural (e.g., Read and Schreiber, 1982) and artifical (e.g., Morgan and Newport, 1981) language learning that there are a variety of cooperating cues in the sound wave to help the learner group formatives into phrases. A major example is pre-pausal lengthening, associated with the last stressed syllable before phrase and clause boundaries, and before deletion sites (Klatt, 1975, Sorenson et al., ibid.). That is, stress timing in the acoustic wave provides very strong clues to phrase bracketing of English sentences. These clues are likely to be stronger and more consistent in speech to

young children, which is known to be intonationally exaggerated. If
the learner is specially prepared (unlike the objective physicist) to
note and exploit such information, he can derive a phrase bracketing
of the input string. Recent formal demonstrations suggest that phrase
labelling can be derived from the bracketings (Levy and Joshi, 1978).
Of course whether the labels in the brain are called "noun phrase" and
"verb phrase" is not the point. What is important is that differential labelling for phrase types is formally demonstrable.

     This much information in hand, we can now describe how the child
learns the facts about ed.   One traditional way in which the syntactic values of grammatical morphemes have been determined in linguistics is by means of their relative position in the phrase structure of
the sentences in which they appear. The advantage of the phrase
structure representation is that it permits global description of the
sentence, as divided into an integral sequence of phrases, hierarchically organized together. In terms of the information about stress
timing, we can grant the advancing learner this kind of open class
parse. Once he has this, he is in a position to make further discoveries about the closed class material. At the point at which we are
now engaging the learner, then, he is in possession of a partial open
class parse, but only for items that conform to the semantic heuristic. The higher-order category noun-phrase (NP) is established posi-
tionally, and because its head is a concrete noun (leprechaun, in the
example that follows). A following verb-phrase (VP) is established
owing to the child's analysis of the predicate-argument structure of
the language. On the basis of physical clues in the wave form, he has
also been able to perform the required phrase bracketing. This determines the phrasal positions of the closed class items -- now first
noticed, and presently under his investigation:

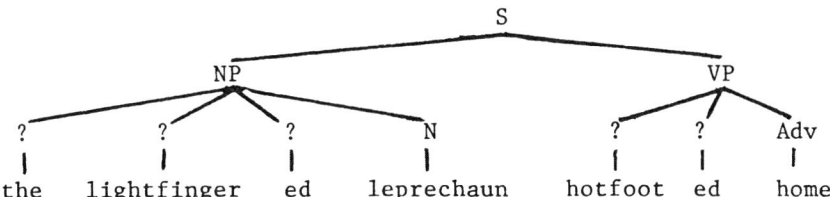

What remain to be specified are the values for lightfinger and hotfoot, plus those for the closed class elements: the (determiner), ed
(participle), and ed (finite verb ending). For present purposes, we
ignore the solution for the. If the child has the mental equivalents
of grammatical rules that allow him to construct the parse tree above,
then there can be little if any uncertainty about the appropriate syntactic categorization of lightfinger and hotfoot and the correct assignment of the morphemic value past in the second case but not the
first. The reasons are straightforward: lightfinger occurs cophras-
ally before the noun and within the noun-phrase, and hence in a position appropriate to an adjective; that is, before a noun. Hotfoot

occurs in a verb-phrase, in the position appropriate to the verb.
Since the first _ed_ is bound to an adjective, it cannot be assigned a
finite verb interpretation. In contrast, the second _ed_ occurs within
the verb-phrase and postposed to the verb. Hence _past_ is a possible
analysis of _ed_ (note 7). Assuming that a similar analysis deals with
the _the_ case, the learner can now construct the final labellings for
the parse tree:

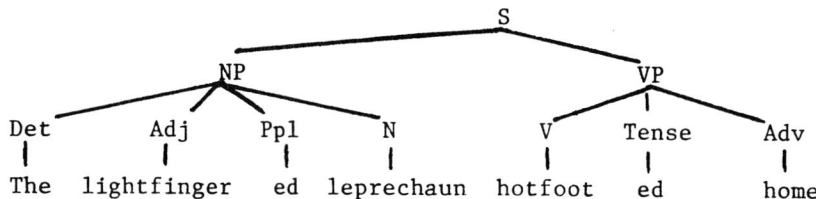

If we accept the moral of this story, then the child must learn
to parse (though tacitly and unconsciously) and he must acquire syntactic rules on which parsing depends, to determine the placement and
syntactic class values of the closed class. Neither unabetted semantic learning (that _ed_ means _past_) nor induction over surface regular-
iities (that _ed_ often follows verbs) escapes this conclusion. As we
have mentioned in connection with the thunder/lightning example, the
problem is not specific to such rare items as hotfooted, but is a
general consequence of the fact that semantic properties are only
loosely correlated with the formal lexical classes. To converge on
the real richness of the lexical and phrasal properties of any real
language, then, the child is forced to consider a deeper and more
formal analysis. Detectable clues to the correct analysis can be
found in the wave form, by an organism so constructed as to seek them
out.

Before closing, we must emphasize that deriving parse trees and
assigning morphemic values in terms of them is only the beginning of
language learning. These trees form part of the required representation on which further inductions can be performed. For example, such
principles as structure dependence (of transformations), binding,
etc., will not fall automatically out of parse trees, but are independently required to guarantee language learning. Still, that the
speech signals themselves so richly cue certain required representational formats has not been appreciated until very recently.

CONCLUDING REMARKS

We have given an argument supporting the view that language
learning can begin to be described if we assume that the child successively becomes able to analyze two subcomponents of the lexical
stock, open class and closed class items. Such a partitioning, prior
to full language knowledge, is possible if the distinction is cued in

the speech signal by its superficial phonetic-prosodic features --
stress and nonstress. Similarly, sequencing of the formatives (marked
by lexical stress on one syllable) is clearly available as a cue to
structure, for learners willing to attend to it. Moreover, higher
order phrasal categories are cued in the wave form by properties such
as prepausal lengthening, marked on the last stressed syllable of an
open class item. With these representations in hand, the learner is
in a position, finally, to analyze the unstressed materials as they
fit into the structures constructed on the earlier bases.

The larger claim behind this analysis of learning is that it is
the representational biases -- how the learner is disposed to analyze
and organize the sound stream of speech, among the myriad ways available to an open-minded inductive device, even one with the same discriminatory apparatus -- that chiefly make possible and determine the
character of what is learned. We believe that, for the complex organisms acquiring complex systems and processes (as opposed, say, to
moths' accomplishment of trailing, cf. Selfridge, this volume), it is
the representational system, far more pervasively than the general
inductive system, that must bear the major burden for learning.

Notes

1. Nothing very general about defaults (e.g., "use an inference
unless it is specifically blocked"; or "don't use an inference unless
it is inescapably instantiated") can be used to evade these issues.
This is because children turn out to be conservative generalizers for
some language properties, e.g., the subcategorization properties of
verbs (see Pinker, in press) but radical generalizers for other
properties. e.g., denominative verb creation (see Clark, 1982). For
explanation, then, we appear to require a very precise, language-
specific, set of biases in the learner as to the properties safe or
unsafe to make grand generalizations about, based on partial data.

2. Stress is complexly realized in the sound wave. In English,
roughly, stress is realized in terms of higher fundamental frequency
and longer duration of the syllable; intensity plays a much smaller
role. It is well known that these physical cues can trade off with
each other, i.e., that any of them, as well as more than one together,
will be interpreted equivalently as "stress" in the linguistic signal,
under most circumstances. The discussion of learning in this paper is
limited to the stress-accent and pitch-accent languages, that clearly
exploit this acoustic property. The extent to which it can be generalized as a significant part of the learning account for all languages
depends in part on what the acquisitional facts look like, of course,
but learning in nonstress-accent languages has hardly been investigated. But it depends also in part on whether studies in universal
phonology uncover an analysis in terms of which physical properties

underlying "stress" in English are realized and are systematically operative in all human languages. At minimum, should all else fail, it is likely that a very small set of specially discriminable cues at this level are exploited by the various human languages. In that case the child learner would have to be prepared to recognize that stress will provide a basis for analysis in some languages; while for certain others, alternative cues must be exploited. However, the claims we make above cannot be very much weakened (i.e., we must make the claim that the number of alternates to stress, if required, would be very few) without the explanatory effect of our proposal collapsing completely. We must rest content with what seems to us, provisionally, a useful way of organizing known properties of the learning sequence.

3. As we have stated, we concentrate discussion here on the closed class/open class distinction, and its reflex, stress/nonstress. Still, our analysis presupposes further claims about what the learner is disposed to notice at early stages; these will be sketched, though in much less detail, as the discussion proceeds. First, we assume that the learner is specifically inclined to notice the order in which the open class items appear, during the speech event. Second, we assume that a further prosodic feature, namely prepausal lengthening (see Klatt, 1975; Sorensen, Cooper, and Paccia, 1978) is exploited by the child as an aid to discovering phrase-boundaries. We will try to show that, armed with these kinds of discriminatory bias, the child has a first basis for constructing the precedence/dominance facts about surface structure (the parse trees) in the language to which he is exposed.

4. It is very interesting that the West Semitic scripts were syllabaries, and that the syllables were rendered in terms of their consonantal content, dropping the vowels. L. Gleitman and Rozin (1977) conjecture that this is because the vowels in, e.g., Hebrew, characteristically are infixed morphemes that represent the syntactically closed class functions (e.g., tense, number) while the consonants represent the open class roots; this is like goose/geese or lead/led in English. On the contrary, Greek, like English, usually prefixes and suffixes the closed class functions; the vowels in open class words are just part of the root, usually. If, indeed, it is easier to bring the open class to conscious attention, then it begins to be explicable why the Semites failed to incorporate the vowels orthographically in the same ways as they did the open class. We do know that there was a good deal of jeering from the Greeks about these syllabaries, that they inherited from the Semites, and that they promptly fixed them up by reinterpreting certain Phoenician consonant signs (the laryngeals, that are not in the Greek phonetic inventory) as vowel signs.

5. In this discussion, we have not cited all the evidence that currently exists in favor of the generalizations we are making. But some findings from learning in pathological environmental circum-

stances are worth mentioning. A child locked in an attic for the first 13 years of life, and isolated from language, has approximately acquired the open class but not the closed class vocabulary since she was discovered some years ago, and attempts at rehabilitation began (Curtiss, 1977). Six deaf preschool children of hearing parents, not exposed to sign language, invented gestural systems appropriate to their age levels that marked the thematic roles by word order, but which lacked the sign analogues of closed class items (Feldman, Goldin-Meadow, and L. Gleitman, 1978). These findings reinforce the notion that closed class learning is best earliest in developmental time, and that the closed class acquisition requires more specific environmental support. A related finding concerns long-term forgetting. Dorian (1978) studied elderly native speakers of Gaelic who had spoken English only, ever since early childhood. In this case, there was selective preservation of the closed class morphology, with most of the open class vocabulary forgotten. This is another demonstration of the mental dissociation of these two components of the morphological stock.

6. In these examples, we use only the one Tok Pisin word we know, baimbai, rendering the remaining material in English.

7. Possibly it will be asserted that we have been highhanded (if not lightfingered) in assuming that the learner is disposed to believe properties (adjectives) are of nouns, and times (tenses) of verbs. We acknowledge that we are assigning such meaningful interpretations of the world, as coded by language, to the child ab initio, even though the extent and usefulness of such knowledge is sharply limited by issues we mentioned in introductory remarks: interpretation of sentences by reference to scenes is a tricky business. We here grant only, following Pinker, a bias to associate whole concrete objects with the nouns and whole activities with the verbs; even this can be accomplished, presumably, only in cases of particularly dramatic or compelling circumstances. The scope and abstractness of such problems is made evident by the finding that congenitally blind children, whose exposure to the world language encodes is different from the usual, acquire meaningful language quite unexceptionally, even including the sight-related vocabulary (e.g., such words as look and green; Landau and Gleitman, forthcoming). However the issues here may work out in detail, we submit, without such a rough ability to interpret the world in terms of forms and structures not too distant from the ones used by natural languages, there simply is no account for the acquisition of language (for discussion, see Wexler and Culicover, 1980). As for evidence, it is at least relevant that the creolizing languages we have mentioned (Sankoff and Laberge, 1973; Bickerton, 1975), developed by preliterate societies, move time markers into verb-phrases. And we have mentioned the evidence that even 18 month olds distinguish, by word ordering, actions and objects from each other in their utterances.

REFERENCES

Bellugi, U. The acquisition of negation. Unpublished doctoral
    dissertation, Harvard University, 1967.

Bickerton, D. Dynamics of a creole system. New York: Cambridge
    University Press, 1975.

Bloom, L. One word at a time. The Hague: Mouton, 1973.

Bloomfield, L., Language. New York: Holt, 1933.

Bradley, D. C., Computational distinctions of vocabulary type. Un-
    published doctoral dissertation, MIT, 1978

Bradley, D. C., Garrett, M. F., and Zurif, E. G., Syntactic deficits
    in Broca's aphasia. In D. Caplan, ed., Biological studies of
    mental processes. Cambridge: MIT Press, 1979.

Brown, R. and Hanlon, C. Derivational complexity and the order of
    acquisition in child speech. In J. R. Hayes, ed., Cognition
    and the development of language, New York: Wiley, 1970.

Carey, S. Semantic development. In E. Wanner & L. R. Gleitman, eds.,
    Language acquisition: State of the art, New York: Cambridge
    University Press, 1982.

Clark, E., The young word maker. In E. Wanner & L. R. Gleitman, eds.,
    Language Acquisition: State of the art, New York: Cambridge
    University Press, 1982.

Curtiss, S. Genie: A psycholinguistic study of a modern-day "Wild
    Child. New York: Academic Press, 1977.

Dorian, N. D., The fate of morphological complexity in language
    death. Language, 54(3), 1978, 590 - 609.

Eimas, P. Siqueland, E.Jusczyk, P., and Vigorito, J. Speech per-
    ception in infants. Science 171, 1971, 303 - 306.

Ervin, S. Imitation and structural change in children's language.
    In E. Lenneberg, ed., New Directions in the study of language,
    Cambridge, Mass.: MIT Press, 1964.

Epstein, W. The influence of syntactical structure on learning.
    American Journal of Psychology, 74, 1961, 80 - 85.

Feldman, H., Goldin-Meadow, S., and Gleitman, L. Beyond Herodotus:
    The creation of language by linguistically deprived deaf

children, in A. Lock, ed., Action, Symbol, and Gesture: The
Emergence of Language, New York: Academic Press, 1978.

Furrow, D., Nelson, K., and Benedict, H. Mothers' speech to children and syntactic development: Some simple relationships.
Journal of Child Language, 6, 1979, 423 - 442.

Garrett, M. F., The analysis of sentence production. In G. H. Bower,
ed., The psychology of learning and motivation, Vol. 9, New York:
Academic Press, 1975.

Glanzer, M. Grammatical category: A rote learning and word association analysis. Journal of verbal learning and verbal behavior,
1, 1962, 31 - 41.

Gleitman, H. and Gleitman, L. R., Language use and language judgment.
In C. J. Fillmore, D. Kempler, & W. S-Y. Wang, eds., Individual
differences in language ability and language behavior, New York:
Academic Press, 1979.

Gleitman, L. R. and Gleitman, H. Phrase and paraphrase. New York:
Norton, 1970.

Gleitman, L. R., Gleitman, H., and Shipley, E. F., The emergence of
the child as grammarian, Cognition, 1, 1972, 137 - 164.

Gleitman, L. R., Newport, E.L., and Gleitman, H., The current status
of the Motherese hypothesis (in press, Journal of Child Language)

Gleitman, L. R. and Rozin, P., The structure and acquisition of reading I: Relations between orthographies and the structure of
language, in A. Reber & D. Scarborough, eds., Toward a psychology
of reading, Hillsdale, N.J.: Erlbaum, 1977.

Gleitman, L. R. and Wanner, E., Language acquisition: state of the
state of the art, in E. Wanner & L. R. Gleitman, eds., Language
acquisition: State of the art, New York: Cambridge University
Press, 1982.

Gold, E. M. Language identification in the limit. Information and
Control, 10, 1967, 447 - 474.

Jusczyk, P. W., Auditory versus phonetic coding of speech signals during infancy. Proceedings of the CNRS Conference, 1980, in press.

Kean, M. L. Agrammatism: A phonological deficit?, Cognition 7(1),
1979, 69 - 84.

Klatt, D. H. Vowel lengthening is syntactically determined in a
connected discourse, Journal of phonetics, 3, 1975, 129 - 140.

Kuhl, P. K. and Miller, J. D., Speech perception by the chinchilla, Voiced-voiceless distinction in alveolar plosive consonants. Science, 190, 1975, 69 - 72.

Landau, B. and Gleitman, L. R., Language learning and the vocabulary of perception in congenitally blind babies (forthcoming).

Levy, L. and Joshi, A., Skeletal structural descriptions. Information and Control, 39(2), 1978, 192 - 211.

McNeill, D. Developmental psycholinguistics. In F. Smith & G. A. Miller, eds., The genesis of language: a psycholinguistic approach, Cambridge, Mass.: MIT Press, 1966.

Maratsos, M., The child's construction of grammatical categories. In E. Wanner & L. R. Gleitman, eds., Language acquisition: State of the art. New York: Cambridge University Press, 1982.

Morgan, J. and Newport, E. L., The role of constituent structure in the induction of an artificial language, Journal of Verbal Learning and verbal behavior, 20, 1981, 67 - 85.

Newport, E.L. Task specificity in language learning? In E. Wanner & L. R. Gleitman, eds., Language acquisition: state of the art, New York: Cambridge University Press, 1982.

Newport, E. L., Gleitman, H. and Gleitman, L. R., Mother, I'd rather do it myself: Some effects and noneffects of maternal speech style. In C. E. Snow and C. A. Ferguson, eds., Talking to children: Language input and acquisition, Cambridge: Cambridge University Press, 1977.

Pinker, S. A theory of the acquisition of lexical-functional grammars, MIT Center for Cognitive Science Occasional Papers, 6, 1980. Also to appear in J. Bresnan, ed., The mental representation of grammatical relations. Cambridge: MIT Press.

Read, C. and Schreiber, P., Why short subjects are harder to find than long ones, in E. Wanner & L. R. Gleitman, eds., Language acquisition: The state of the art, New York: Cambridge University Press, 1982.

Rozin, P. and Gleitman, L. R., The acquisition and structure of reading II: The reading process and the acquisition of the alphabetic principle. In A. Reber & D. Scarborough, eds., Toward a psychology of reading, Hillsdale, N.J.: Erlbaum, 1977.

Sankoff, G. and Laberge, S. On the acquisition of native speakers by a language, Kivung, 6, 1973, 32 - 47.

Slobin, D. I. The acquisition of Russian as a native language. In F. Smith & C. A. Miller, eds., The genesis of language: A psycholinguistic approach, Cambriddge, Mass.: MIT Press, 1966.

Slobin, D. I., Paper read at the Conference on Syntactic Change, University of California at Santa Barbara, May 7-9,1976.

Slobin, D. I., Language change in childhood and in history. In J. Macnamara, ed., Language learning and thought, New York: Academic Press, 1977.

Slobin, D. I., Universal and particular in the acquisition of language. In E. Wanner & L. R. Gleitman, eds., Language acquisition: The state of the art, New York: Cambridge University Press, 1982.

Sorenson, J. M., Cooper, W. E., and Paccia, J. M. Speech timing of grammatical categories, Cognition, 6(2), 1978, 135 - 54.

Spelke, E. S. Perceptual knowledge of objects in infancy. In J. Mehler, M. F. Garrett & E. C. Walker, eds., Perspectives in mental representation, Hillsdale, N. J.: Erlbaum, 1982.

Supalla, T., Structure and acquisition of verbs of motion and location in American Sign Language, Unpublished Ph.D. thesis, University of California at San Diego, 1982.

Venneman, T., An explanation of drift. In C. Li, ed., Word order and word order change, Austin: University of Texas Press, 1975.

Wanner, E. and Maratsos, M., An ATN approach to comprehension. In M. Halle, J. Bresnan, and G. A. Miller, eds., Linguistic theory and psychological reality. Cambridge: MIT Press, 1978.

Zwicky, A. M. On clitics. Paper read at the Third International Phonologie-Tagung at the University of Vienna, Sept. 2, 1976.

Acknowledgments

This paper is based on a general review of language acquisition research, prepared by the present authors (1982). Insofar as our own findings and interpretations are incorporated into the present paper, we thank our collaborators, Henry Gleitman and Elissa Newport, for major contributions; of course they are not responsible for errors or detours that may appear here. We also thank B. Landau for discussions that materially affected the statement of the argument. We thank the National Foundation of the March of Dimes for a grant to L. Gleitman which helped to support the work, as well as NATO, which funded the most interesting conference for which the present version was specifically prepared. We are also grateful to Michael Arbib and to Oliver Selfridge, whose editorial comments on an earlier draft were of much aid in many aspects of the writing.

THE SENSIBLE BRAIN: ADAPTATION AS A POSITIVE AND AS A NEGATIVE FACTOR IN THE REORGANIZATION OF NEUROPSYCHOLOGICAL SYSTEMS AFTER BRAIN DAMAGE

Pierre Marie Lavorel

CNRS, INSERM Unité 94
Lyon-Bron, France

In neuropsychology, adaptation is not a mechanism or an effect which has to be considered only occasionally. Adaptation is a permanent factor of behavior and of physical development or decay. Therefore, when neurophysiologists, neuropsychologists, and neurolinguists try to model their observations into brain theory or into cognitive theory, they always incorporate dynamic vectors. But difficulties arise when they have to define or decompose such general dynamic notions as adaptation into measurable, calculagle or predictable facts. An epistemological reflexion on how those scientists tackle their problems and what they discover about the most complex control systems known will perhaps suggest some analogous or homologous approaches in artificial intelligence, in engineering or even in social sciences like economics. To focus on one paradigm I have decided to insist here on some negative consequences of adaptation in aphasic behavior. But before dealing with the restructuring of cognitive processes used for language after brain damage, it is useful to recapitulate the concepts and the approaches, as well as the experimental knowledge and beliefs which have oriented neuropsychological research in recent years. For neurolinguistic theory has to relate linguistic research to advances in neurosciences.

There are two levels at which neuroscientists have tried to describe adaptation and readaptation.

First, the organization of biological functions of the central nervous system (chemical, electric, etc) are studied at the microscopic level of neurons, membranes, synapses, or at the molar level of columns, areas, cortical hemispheres, subcortical organs and connections. The emphasis is put on the changing chemical regulation of excitation and inhibition, on the growth or decay of tissue (particularly of dendrites), on developing cortico-cortical pathways, and on afferent and efferent rhythmic signals. The master words are genetic code, homeostasis and plasticity. Processes are distributed across the system (Lashley, 1950) and correspond to initial or to acquired anatomo-physiological specialization. Reorganization after brain damage or after a period of erratic development is seen as a collection of interacting phenomena which will eventually be characterized in terms of physical laws and complex mathematical functions. Such an approach is classical and in harmony with tranditional studies of the material aspects of the physical world.

A complementary approach is favored by several schools of psychologists, ethologists and ergonomists. Here, the emphasis is put on a comparison of human and animal behavior in a physical and social environment. Adaptation and learning are seen as observed results of conditioning and of passive or active reactions of individuals. Interesting questions have been brought up about whether adaptation is a first step towards learning or towards habituation without learning. Adaptive phenomena following modifications in the environment or in the processing biological machine can thus be considered as learning again, learning more, learning differently or, on the contrary, as regressing to a reduced level of interaction with the environment. Communication, feed-back, trial and error are the main concepts used to characterize observed facts. Models first tended to be little more then statistical analyses, and then became stochastic models of dynamic processes. At its best, this approach has yielded representations of how relations between stimulating systems and stimulated systems are gradually memorized as abstract structures of growing complexity. Thus, theoretical models can bridge the gap between neobehaviorism and cognitive approaches like Piaget's.

The two complementary scientific attitudes which have just been rapidly alluded to have constituted separately or together what groundwork there is for the future edifice of cognitive science and neuropsychology. If we want to be critical, it could perhaps be argued that their contributions at the level of theory - more specifically at the level of adaptive control theory are not original. Almost every specific model suggested by classical brain scientists or by classical social scientists can become an appendix to primitive all-encompassing theories offered by cyberneticians or by information scientists. The general definition of a learning machine which Craik conceived around 1940 (Craik, 1943 : See Arbib, 1980) would probably satisfy them all as it was formulated by Arbib in 1966 (Meetham, 1969, article : "learning") :
$$M : \{I, O, S, \pi, \lambda\}$$
A learning machine is here described as a system of inputs (I), outputs (O), states (S) and two types of operators (π which matches associated inputs and states with outputs ; λ which matches associated inputs and states with new states). According to cyberneticians of the preceeding decades, if this machine has a controlling

device, and if its <u>dynamics is irreversible</u>, it is adaptive. If, besides, it can be oriented towards a <u>goal</u> and <u>progress in the complexity of its processes</u> by generalizing or categorizing its operations,
it becomes a learning machine (Arbib, 1966).

It must however be said that to-day, all those basic notions are
far from being sufficient to characterize adaptive control processes
in perception, in motor programming and in verbal activity. New experiments in biology, as well as new clinical observations, have
introduced sophisticated questions which will make the first theories appear insufficient and too general.

The following part of this paper will be devoted to an illustration of some concepts which do not contradict former models, but
bring into light factors whose interactions must be analysed in advanced control theories of intelligent systems.

LESION EFFECTS ON THE PROCESSING OF PERCEPTION AND OF WORLD REPRE-
SENTATIONS

If, in lesion studies, initial curiosity and final conclusions
are not restricted to biological changes or to environmental effects,
if cognitive or semiotic arguments are called forth, a richer understanding of processes can be gained. The nature of mental calculation and how information is transformed and transferred in the brain
is what must be the moot point of psychologists, linguists, and
ethologists, if they really want to formulate together some general
explanatory principles of natural intelligence. Biologists themselves may find that, by paying attention to information processing
models, they can regroup scattered observations into better systemic accounts of the physiological substrates of mental representations and schemas, coordination and control, adaptation, learning
and memorizing.

A major breakthrough in the interpretation of puzzling anatomical, electrophysiological and radiological facts has been helped by
the progress of research in <u>cooperative computation</u>, a notion introduced jointly by computer scientists (Lesser & coll., 1980), by phy-
siologists (Edelman & Mountcastle, 1978 ; Kaas & al., 1979), and by
neo-cyberneticians (Szentagothai & Arbib, 1974 ; Arbib, 1980). PETT
scans have shown that many areas of the brains seem to be active at
the same time during perceptual and gnosic tasks, as if top-down and
bottom-up calculation were constantly going on between primary and
associative areas (Figure 1).

Almost at the same time, microanatomical studies (Allman & al.,
1971, 1974 ; Galaburda & Sanides, 1977 ; Seltzer & Pandya, 1978 ;
Zeki, 1980) have shown that the associative areas often called tertiary following Flechsig's conceptions, were in fact fitted for the
processing of information fed by different sensory channels.

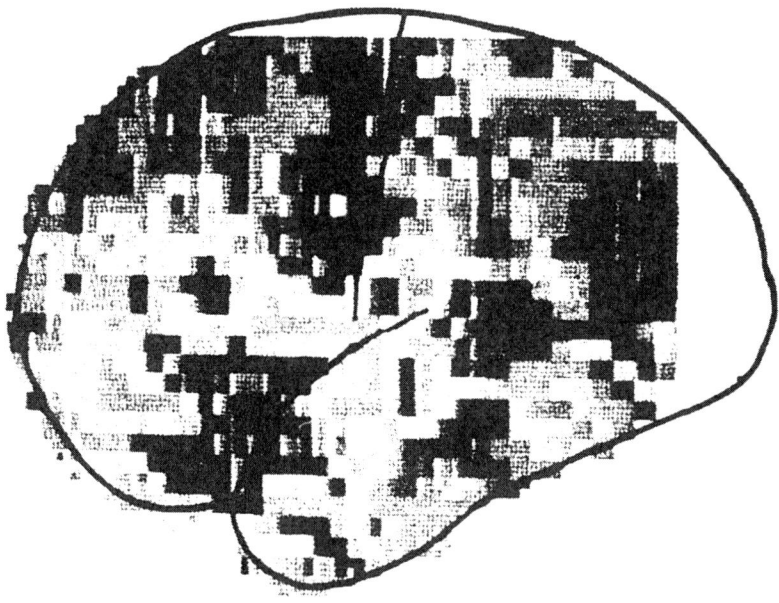

Fig. 1. PETT Scan of the left hemisphere of a subject reading sil-
        ently (N.A. Lasse, D.H. Ingvar & E. Skinhøj, Scientific
        American, 1978, 239, 4, p 57). Note that the occipital lobe,
        the temporo-parietal juncture, the tip of the temporal lobe,
        Broca's area, the prerolandic and prefrontal motor areas are
        functioning at the same time.

Such observations can match traditional knowledge in evoked potentials or in neuron activity microelectrode measurements (Lavorel,1982
Steps). Tissue of the posterior associative cortex, in the temporo-
parietal juncture for instance, was found to be rich in many neurons which respond either to auditory, or to visual, or to somato-
sensory stimuli. These studies show for instance that secondary
visual, auditory, or somato-sensory cortex, gradually becomes tuned
to the same recurring inputs, until it is specialized for the processing of one sensory modality. But at the same time it can also
interact with several sensory or motor subsystems.

    Thus, the computation of representations by the posterior he-
misphere is multimodal and cooperative, in the sense that information processing is not only distributed across somatotopic, acous-
tico-topic areas or centers, but that knowledge is the result of
harmonious interaction and well-timed propagation or inhibition of
signals processed by many specific modes. Rather than clinging to
former bottom-up processing models with three successive perceptual
and gnosic levels (primary, secondary, tertiary), and dysfunctions
closely linked to loss of centers or of connections between these
centers, it will be more fruitfull for future research to start

thinking in terms of the growth of efficiency and equilibrium in the cooperative representational computation. Convergence of top-down and bottom-up processing towards correct or incorrect representations is probably the best abstract approximation of cognitive processing that can be suggested to-day. Evidence of this form of calculation has provided for instance by eye movement studies in reading (Lavorel, 1980 : "Aspects de la performance"), or by error simulation by computer (Dev, 1975 ; Gordon, 1981 ; Lavorel 1982 : Production strategies). To-day, neuropsychologists can ask some more refined questions about the original division or duplication of computation, the coordination of individual processes, and the timing of transfers. What takes place during early development ? How does it go wrong with age or with lesions ? What is the relative importance of individual centers in cooperative computation ? Is there really a redundancy of subsystems ? How does adaptive organization and reorganization of the central nervous system modify the performance of the subject ? If and when preservation or restitution of complex behavior are observed after natural or artificial lesions, how are the monitoring and the maintenance of the system controlled ? How is the system capable of testing itself and of evaluating its states ? Is there a permanent possibility of compensation or of substitution of elementary cognitive functions in the complex representational calculus ? Or is world knowledge always reduced or degraded after posterior brain damage ?

It is well-known that men suffering partial or total lesions of Brodmann's cortical areas 17-18-19 (visual) or 41-42 (auditory), or 1, 2, 5, 7 (somato-sensory) lose part or all of these senses for ever. As a rule, no restitution of perceptual processing is ever possible for adults after the loss of primary perceptual areas. It is however interesting to note that experiments in animals have shown that it is only at birth or very soon after that the perceptual subsystems of one hemisphere lose the possibility of being partially compensated by those of the other hemisphere. Of course, rapid hyper-specialization of cells was first thought to be the key concept to account for those phenomena of adaptive cul-de-sac. Recent research shows that it is necessary to be a little more inquisitive in order to understand what underlies the negative aspect of anatomically constrained interactions between the brain and the afferent pathways of sensory information. Studies in the deafferentation of the visual cortex of young monkeys have confirmed and complemented Hubel, Wiesel & coll's studies on kittens and monkeys (Blakemore & coll, 1980). Those experiments teach us that the maintenance of the biological substrates of visual perception is genetically programmed in such a way that competition between inputs is a major force in post-lesion evolution. Biochemical development seems to be almost constant, and even the momentary loss of one mode of the processing system is nefarious. With the exception of a few favorable events which protect a lesioned area (if it is small enough) (Stein & al., 1974 ; Stein & Dawson, 1980 ; Spinelli & Jensen, 1979), it must be consid-

ered that <u>competitive effects of contralateral stimulation do not</u>
<u>help but rather harm cooperative computation</u>. In a few days, the
system becomes adapted to the loss of one modality and functions
without it.

If some processing units are still available, they may even be
converted to new tasks. This has been shown in a spectacular way by
experiments in somato-sensory deafferentation (Wall & Egger, 1971).

Not only unimodal but also multimodal calculus in superior nam-
mals seems to be drastically reduced or distorted by cortical lesions.
Such is the case for the recognition of music in right temporal
deficits, for visually-cued spatial organization in right parieto-
occipital deficits, for arithmetic calculus in left parietal deficits,
and for color identification in left parieto-occipital deficits.
Besides, studies on successful makeshift representational cognition
after macroscopic lesions in one hemisphere have indicated that there
is no duplication of processes in the posterior hemispheres. As
Bever (Cerebral asymetries in humans, 1975) and others suggested,
it could be possible that the left hemisphere tends to provide the
analytical approach to objects and phenomena, while the right one
provides a different, more holistic comprehension of patterns.

All the remarks about how subjects compute multimodal representations in the case of macroscopic posterior lesions could be simplified by saying that brain damaged patients neither recuperate com-

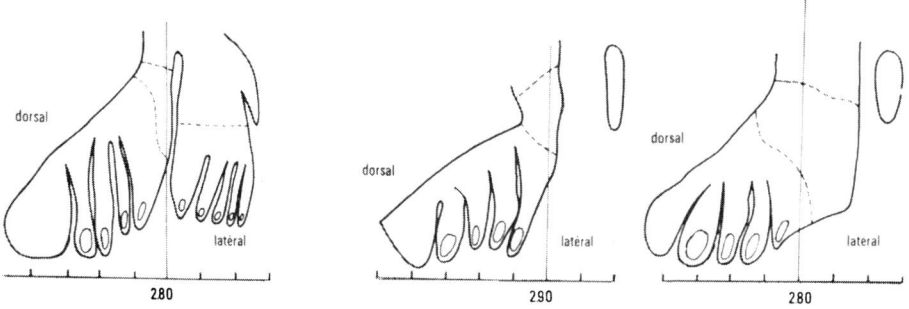

Fig. 2. (Wall & Egger, 1971). The somato-sensory representation of
       the posterior and anterior paws of rats in the thalamus.
       (a) Normal ; (b) One day after deafferentation of the paw ;
       (c) Seven weeks later.

pletely nor learn again all the gnosic and praxic processes which
have been lost. The brain only adapts its strategies to ignore or
to overcome its partial deficits. But how then is ersatz calculation
built from scratch with partial information ? When the subject's
neuropsychological system is consciously or unconsciously aware of
its shortcomings, then, active responses to failure, like lip reading in cortical deafness, can be observed. Such sustitution strategies, where previously disregarded information channels may compensate for lost ones, forces us to consider the preeminent role of the
frontal lobes in the adaptive control of action-oriented cognitive
processes.

LESION EFFECTS ON MOTOR SCHEMAS AND ON STRATEGIES FOR ACTIVE PERFOR-
MANCE

If any neurologist were asked "would you rather lose part of
your frontal lobes or part of your posterior hemispheres" ?, he
would undoubtedly admit that a frontal lesion is by all means less
to be feared than a posterior one. This evidence must not be understood in terms of the importance of centers or functions, but rather
in terms of adaptive possibilities and of the neurocybernetic
organization of the central nervous system.

Any unilateral or bilateral loss of very large prefrontal areas
is of course catastrophic, since subjects then become a-dynamic (to
use Luria's expression (Luria, 1973)). They are incapable of initiating, planning and keeping track of acts, of complex movements, and
of continuous discourse (Luria, 1976). But smaller frontal lesions,
or even relatively large ones in one hemisphere, are often followed
by some recuperation of functional efficiency and even by a spectacular reconstruction of very specific and elaborate cognitive processes.

Something may help us to understand why such deficits can be
overcome. Unlike posterior representational areas which are performing very tricky converging computation to equate the many dimensions
of single objects into one meaningful pattern for each object, the
nervous system which supports act-planning is organized as a redundant hierarchy of monitoring units, some of which compensate, regul-
ate, or even duplicate others. All this has been well described by
Greene, Bernstein, Eccles, Szentágothai & Arbib, and others (eg. in
Stelmach & Requin Eds.). (Greene, 1972 ; Bernstein, 1968 ; Eccles,
1977). Szentágothai & Arbib, 1975 ; Stelmach & Requin (Eds), 1980).
What is interesting is that physiological models parallel similar
claims in artificial intelligence (Newell, 1973 ; Sacerdoti, 1974).
The very fact that cooperative control is achieved hierarchically
and redundantly allows for different structures of coordination
between control levels, and consequently for different qualities of
functional efficiency. Acts can be more or less appropriate for a

goal, more or less correct in their execution. Indeed, all our movements, all our strategic moves could be improved upon, and always
seems inaccurate or ill-timed. Therefore, in a system which is only
approximately efficient in normal subjects, minor or major reorganization problems are expected and provided for.

Examples of the restoration of lost motor control have been re-
capitulated by Jeannerod and Hécaen, 1969 (see their extensive bibliography). It is important to distinguish at once the direct command
of the muscular system, via several sub-cortical and medullar filtering pathways, from higher control processes (plans, schemas, regulatory monitoring etc).

Just like primary perceptual decoding, direct motor command is
relatively autonomous. Except for neo-natal lesions (Dejerine &
Dejerine, 1902 ; Goldman, 1974), no inter-hemispheric or intra-he-
mispheric tranfer of motor centers has ever been witnessed (Jeannerod & Hécaen, 1979).

Although the partial destruction of primary motor cortex or of
one of the descending pathways regularly causes hemiplegia, it has
been shown by many neurophysiologists, like Denny-Brown (1966) that,
in a few cases, parallel processing at the microscopic level allows
for a gradual restitution of quasi-normal transfer and transformation
of information, even when a small quantity of tissue has been pre-
served. The restoration of transfer functions can be understood be
comparing the motor command circuits of the primitive system of the
aplysia or or the triton (Kupferman & Kandel, 1979 ; Willows, 1969)
(Fig. 3) to noise correcting networks or to multiplexing linear networks which are well-known to electronicians (Nilsson, 1965 ; Arbib,
1964). See Figures 3 and 4.

It is important to stress the fact that the reduction of fuzzing
effects or the retuning of processing after lesions depend on the
frequency of activity of the healing system. And so, therapeutic
stimulation appears to be vital in order to stimulate what subsystems are left. However, it is interesting to point out that quick
habituation to a recently-suffered deficit is not a favorable factor.
For example, ambidextrous subjects who find that hemiplegia does not
affect them as much as other patients, tend to neglect therapy and
do not heal as well (Bisiach & Luzzati, 1978).

Frontal associative processes are susceptible to complex reorganization. Weiss and coll. (1977), Sperry (1943), and Bernstein &
coll (1978) who compared mammals which benefit from cortical control
to animals without a cortex (newt species), suggested as Jackson
(1874) had claimed, that the optimization of behavior after a lesion
was mediated by several hierarchically high levels of processing and
that the higher the lesion was in hierarchical control, the more
favorable the prognosis could be for motor activity.

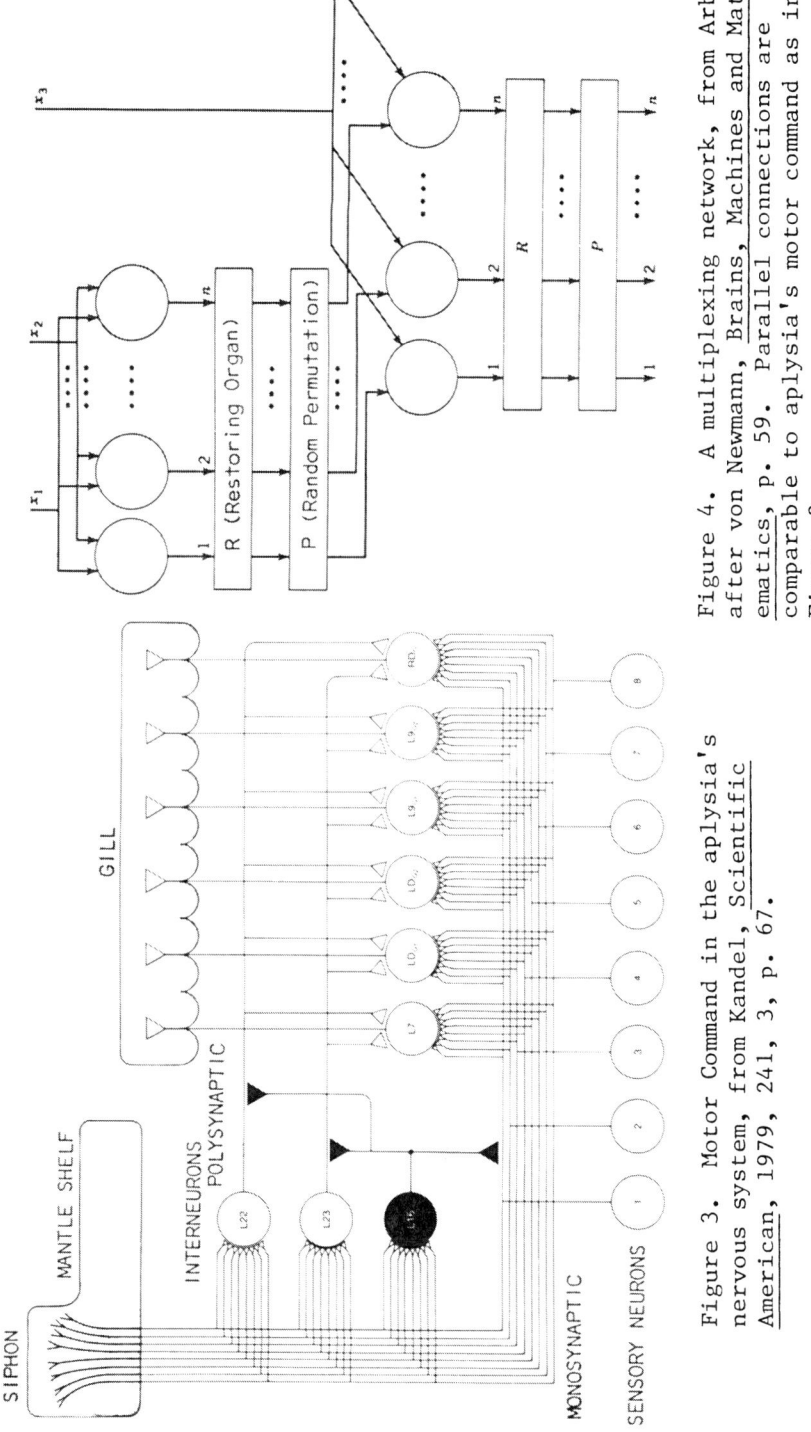

Figure 4. A multiplexing network, from Arbib after von Newmann, Brains, Machines and Mathematics, p. 59. Parallel connections are comparable to aplysia's motor command as in Figure 3.

Figure 3. Motor Command in the aplysia's nervous system, from Kandel, Scientific American, 1979, 241, 3, p. 67.

The heuristic approach of the brain in high level control makes rehabilitation or successful therapy possible for even the most abstract frontal and prefrontal activities, like arithmetic problem solving. For example, elaborate search processes are severely reduced by lesions of mediofronto-basal or postero-frontal, or prefrontal areas (Luria's problem solving complex (Luria & Tsvetkova, 1966 ; Pribram & Luria, 1973)). Yet, all neuropsychologists know that those problem solving handicaps can be considerably reduced with careful preprogramming of the subject's strategies. By contrast, acalculia and problem representation difficulties caused by posterior brain damage can never be overcome.

Many other instances could be found to show that goal-oriented movements and strategies which presuppose motivation, purpose calculus, dynamism of will, heuristic schemas, or evaluative control of the sequence of moves, are not durably marred by a single frontal lesion (Lashley, 1960 ; Messerli & al., 1976 ; MacNeilage, 1980).

Leaving aside technical aspects of synaptogenesis, of sprouting, of glial growth (Cotman, 1978 ; Changeux & Danchin, 1976 ; Danchin, 1978), and taking into account only the efficiency of performance, it is on the whole obvious that, after brain damage, motor schemas and strategies for active performance are more easily recovered than mental representations of the world. It is easier to be slightly inaccurate in movements than to do without proper mental imagery.

If anatomo-physiological constraints are also considered, the posterior hemispheres through stimulated by external inputs from a more and more familiar world tend to specialize spontaneously as a distributed system of specialized centers, themselves subdivided into parallel processor whose maintenance is ensured competitively. Such a situation, where biological and informational adaptation are basically irreversible, only benefits from adaptation if no accident disrupts the ever-growing stability of the whole.

On the contrary, the frontal lobes being already trained for planning renewed behavior for the changing events of life will cope better with internal crises and even catastrophes. After frontal lesions, reliable information still continues to flow in from the posterior hemisphere. Part of the motor system can often ensure at least a few automatic responses while the rest is gradually recuperating control at one level or at another. It is only in ageing subjects that hyperadaptation to unchanging habits seems to produce stereotyped acts which render the learning of new strategies and related nervous plasticity impossible (Obler & al., 1978).

It must be understood that these views on the negative and positive consequences of biological and of processing adaptation have

been simplified for expository purposes. Most intelligent manifest-
ations are both representational and active. Thus, before stating
that classical models of goal-oriented adaptation suffice or do not
suffice to explain progress as well as regression in the history of
an individual's performance, it is necessary to analyze a few instances of really complex performance, like natural or artificial oculomotor difficulties, or like language production and comprehension.
An interesting example of abstract cognitive processes involving
complex anterior and posterior cooperative calculation is vocal
tract and articulatory control. Word production deficits caused by
lesions are classified as anarthria and apraxia of speech. They have
recently been studied separately by Nespoulous & Puel (1981), and by
Itoh, Sasanuma & Hirose (1980). In the first case, Nespoulous and
Puel's patient (identified as "pure anarthria" to respect French no-
menclature) suffered a frontal lesion in Hexner's center and was
unable to elaborate and coordinate motor schemas for long strings
of phonemes. In the second case, Itoh and Sasanuma's patient (iden-
fied as "speech apraxia") had a deep lesion in the opercular part
of the rolando-parietal area and had lost the voluntary control of
his own body-movements (ideo-praxic deficit). What is worth noting
is that Nespoulous and Puel's patient had fully recovered speech
(as in similar cases already reported in the literature (Lecours &
Lhermitte, 1979)), while Itoh and Sasanuma's patient still had the
same apraxia after seven months of therapy.

THE LANGUAGE OF THE SHATTERED MIND

    Although language is an autonomous faculty, it cannot be stud-
ied by leaving the rest of the neuropsychological system aside. On
the one hand, representations and motor schemas or strategies for
action constrain verbal communication. On the other hand, and reci-
procally, language facilitates the semiological function used in
many forms of non-verbal communication or of symbolic behavior. Many
anthropologists (Taylor-Parker & Rita-Gibson, 1979) and even anatom-
ists like Yakovlev (1948) have argued that men could not genetically
have acquired all the semantic, syntactic and logical universals
that linguists are studying without at the same time having developed representational processes and complex operational strategies.

    An exciting evolution in neurolinguistics, which parallels si-
milar progress in the neurophysiology of motor coordination (see
Schmid and Jeannerod's 1979 model of optimization and control in
the vesticulo-ocular reflex), or of visual perception, has drawn
attention to the advantage of also studying language performance
in the light of brain cooperative-distributive control. The cognitive mechanisms for verbal comprehension and production are thus
approached through a description of the interactivity of several
processes working simultaneously. Lavorel and Arbib (Lavorel, 1980:

"Aspects"; Lavorel & Arbib, 1981)have formulated those ideas first in
a systemic methodology for the study of verbal behavior, then in a
prototheory of linguistic performance. Our remarks on the reorganization of language after brain damage are not in contradiction with
the survey presented above. On the contrary, knowledge about representational and act planning processes is necessary in order to understand success or failure in adult language recovery.

Child aphasia is an altogether different problem where physical
development (e.g. myelinization), premorbid education, social and
therapeutic stimulation play a much greater part than in adult pathology (Meecham & al., 1966).

Lesions affecting one representational modality in two hemispheres.

It is not uncommon to see bilateral parieto-occipital lesions
shattering complex visual representations (causing simultagnosia,
prosopagnosia, spatial agnosia etc... (Lecours & Lhermitte, 1979 ;
Michel & al. 1976 ; Helm, 1979)). There are also bilateral rolandic
lesions affecting sensory-motor processes (which may be at the origin of an annihilating pseudo-bulbar syndrome). Finally, there are
bilateral lesions restricted to the primary auditory tissues of the
temporal lobe (causing cortical deafness). The first two situations
are not expected to have close links with language. Yet, all clinical neuropsychologists know that these patients who are confused in
different ways often have undefined difficulties for lexical retrieval, for discourse and sentence semantics, as well as for the mental
representation of embedded sentences (Michel & Lavorel, 1983 : An
unusual case). The recovery of those abilities is very difficult if
lesions are large, fragmentary and frail if lesions are small.
Constant therapy seems to be needed, in order to prevent their rel-
apsing into negligent withdrawal from the world and from communication. More exactly, it seems that the readaptation of processes or
the new learning of erased knowledge is permanently imperilled by
poor conservation factors as well as by the lack of stimuli (destroyed input channels).

Lesions affecting one representational modality in one hemisphere

One would expect that the effects of unilateral lesions in the
dominant hemisphere should not always cause language deficits. Or,
if they do, they should at least be compensated for. However, it
must be admitted that cases of hemianopia, hemianacousia, or hemianesthesia, except if the lesion affects these unimodal representations only in parts, severely reduce speech or discourse possibilities for ever. In cases of right ear hemianacousia reported by
Michel & coll. (personal communications & Cases SS, PT, forthcoming)
language comprehension, lexical, syntactic, and phonological production were affected. Speech therapy has never been totally success-

ful in helping these patients to do away with paraphasic production, especially for unfrequent words and abstracts words. Except for short concrete words, everything works as if transformations and transfers of phonological information were regularly degraded, or distorted by noise. In fact, these aphasics have been known to substitute mimes and left hand gestures for verbal exchanges, especially when they wish to express their moods and their comments on the quality of verbal exchanges (Labourel, 1982). It could be predicted that they tend to adapt to the loss of acoustic verbal signals in the left hemisphere and that some adaptation to the right hemisphere control of left hand gestures has replaced other modelization possibilities.

Supramodal representational problems.

Many varieties of agnosia, apraxia and typical Wernicke, anomic, or conduction aphasia can be classified under this heading. In fact, it is interesting to note at once that posterior aphasias hardly ever occur without signs of either agnosia or apraxia. If the two posterior hemispheres suffer large lesions, one may even be faced with classical dementia together with aphasia. It is interesting to observe that, if lesions are small, pathology may realize experiments in the isolation or dissociation of sub-processes (graphic, phonological, semantic, etc.). In such cases, rather than a recuperation of lost processes, a new partial type of language performance is observed, with characteristic errors in naming (Lavorel, Production Strategies, 1982), in reading (Coultheart, 1980), or in repetition (Michel & Andreewsky, forthcoming). If brain damage is unilateral (in the dominant hemisphere), but affects several modalities (hemianesthesia + hemianacousia, or hemianacousia + apraxia + acalculia, or hemianopia + acoustic agnosia, etc), it has been observed that premorbid competence plays almost as decisive a role for recovery as the size and the site ot the lesion, or as the variety and quality of therapeutic stimulation (Von Stockert, 1978). On the whole, education helps such patients, for they have learned how to learn, they have kept a better long-term memory (when the lesion spares enough of the temporal lobe), and they are motivated by a better sociocultural context. Perhaps, bio-sociological or environmental evolution factors, conservative factors, compensate for poor intermodal representation factors (Séron, 1979) or, to put it differently, for the reduction of cortico-cortical exchanges in the posterior hemisphere.

Lesions affecting the schemas and plans for active speech

It is not necessary to insist on the effects of bilateral prefrontal or orbital lesions on language and on discourse. Adynamic mutism, illogical discourse, relational difficulties are expected. What is interesting is that, except when the etiology is hopeless (e.g. Pick's disease), patients can be trained as good robots and,

in spite of frequent emotional lability, well-structured discourse
therapy is successful. Memory and fairly good understanding (conservative and representational factors) make up for creativity
(evolution factor). The only problem which cannot be overcome is the
difficulty of programming long interviews, extended writing sessions,
and of keeping track of past utterances.

Unilateral frontal lesions of associative cortex in the dominant
hemisphere cause anarthria, speech apraxia, or Broca's expressive
aphasia. The first important criteria for recovery are age and living
conditions. Broca aphasics, for instance, often have multiple vascu-
lar problems, poor health, low spirits. They have already retired
or are to retire. Life is already well organized for them, almost
stereotyped sometimes. Yet, in spite of those negative evolution
factors, many of them improve in the first weeks.If they do not, it
often means that they have an extended lesion also destroying much
underlying white matter, or some of the insula and of the opercular
part of the rolandic lobe, or the anterior part of the temporal lobe.
In such cases, comprehension is reduced and aphasia is of a mixed
or global type. Hécaen and Consoli (1973) have reported that when
lesions only hit the foot of the third frontal convolution, spontaneous recovery is the rule. But Pierre Marie and Moutier (Moutier,
1980) had already provided some proof for that claim. An insight
into the spectacular recuperation of language after pure Broca's
aphasia can be gained by carrying out Wada's test (injection of sodium amytal (Wada & Rasmussen, 1960)). If such a test is carried out
soon after the onset of aphesia, the subject temporarily loses what
language output possibilities were left in him (his minor hemisphere
cannot play its ancillary role). After recovery, Wada's test still
affects Broca aphasics more than normal subjects, but not so dramatically as earlier. It seems then that natural rehabilitation and
therapy call both hemispheres into action. It is difficult to say
if the minor hemisphere is actually learning more language (It is
perhaps the case when patients are still young ; it is certainly
the case for children). Either a new distribution of processes can
be gradually organized by both hemispheres, or some biological healing of the lesioned hemisphere can take place while the other one
is helping. More than for any other type of aphasia, the therapy of
Brocas should not be organized erratically. Unfavorable habits might
be developed by introducing wrong information (error factors). For
it must be remembered that sensitiveness to stimuli and the calculation of mental representations are normal or nearly normal. Improper adaptation, just as well as insufficiently intense stimulation
may be harmful (Beyn & Sokkor-Trotskaya, 1966).

Learning how to time and organize noves in all sorts of games
which imply semiotic judgments, hierarchical analysis and transformational operations, like language, is also vital if the patient is
agrammatic (i.e. incapable of construing sentences in comprehension
or of concatenating words in production (Séron, 1979).

Studies in cognitive control for the future.

Other studies of language in hemidecorticated children, of aphasia in deaf, left-handed, bilingual, illiterate, musically-minded
subjects have been published. Languages and cultures have been shown
to determine changes in adaptation to the processing of oral and
written messages. But it seems that the most interesting approaches
will be those which can test and evaluate hemispheres or areas with
competition tasks. Dichotic, dichoptic tests, delayed auditory feedback, conflicts between visual and auditory cues will enable neuropsychologists and neurolinguists to assess what harmony or conflict
there is in the control of converging cooperative computation and
in the control of hierarchical planning and monitoring.

But pathology may also realize experiments in disrupting the
timing of cooperative computation between interacting modes.

Michel has reported the case of a right handed patient with two
lesions, one in the left occipital lobe, another which severs all
the posterior callosal connections between the two hemispheres (Michel & al. 1979, case PT). Right hemianopia and alexia without agra-
phia were diagnosed. This is not surprising for those who know Dejerine's anatomo-pathological studies on visual agnosia, or "verbal
blindness". But something more particular was found by Michel, which
taught us something new about how such patient's seeing and naming
are coordinated after brain damage.

The subject was asked to name objects presented in the order
shown here : Figure 5.

This patient sometimes answered promptly and correctly, or after
some careful thinking, he answered inappropriately, but with errors
indicating a frequent delay in the transfer of information. This slow
transfer, together with the parasitic distorsions, seem to indicate
a right visual cortex to left hemisphere transfer through the anterior commissure, instead of through the direct connection (the posterior and central part of the corpus callosus). Visual images thus
had to travel a long roundabout way to the left hemisphere language
areas. It was only when naming was prompt that transfer from right
hemisphere visual perception to right hemisphere semantic processing
could be hypothesized. The patient died before more refined tests
could be organized to differentiate left and right hemisphere naming
possibilities. In spite of this, such a case demonstrated the existence of timing constraints in cognitive processes. Coordination,
delays, as well as resonance phenomena probably play a great part in
many linguistic disturbances. They are now studied together for visual and auditory naming (Lavorel and Gigley, 1982) for syntactic
parsing (Gigley, 1982), for anarthria and apraxia (Messerli & Lavorel, to appear). Computer simulation will probably help to verify
sophisticated models of the possible mistiming or mismatching of

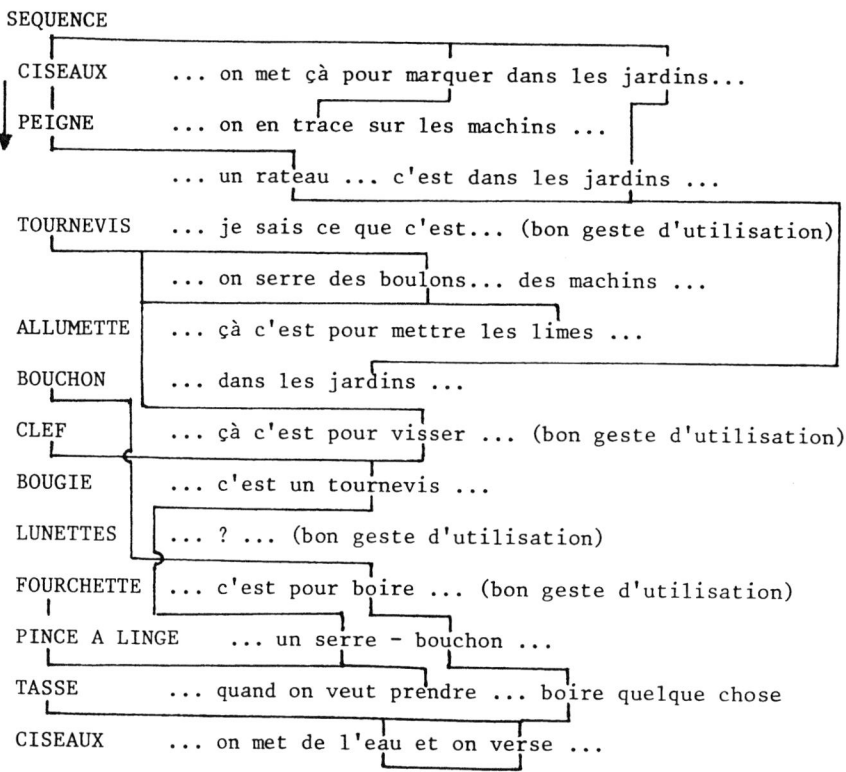

SEQUENCE

CISEAUX   ... on met çà pour marquer dans les jardins...

PEIGNE   ... on en trace sur les machins ...

               ... un rateau ... c'est dans les jardins ...

TOURNEVIS   ... je sais ce que c'est... (bon geste d'utilisation)

               ... on serre des boulons... des machins ...

ALLUMETTE   ... çà c'est pour mettre les limes ...

BOUCHON   ... dans les jardins ...

CLEF   ... çà c'est pour visser ... (bon geste d'utilisation)

BOUGIE   ... c'est un tournevis ...

LUNETTES   ... ? ... (bon geste d'utilisation)

FOURCHETTE   ... c'est pour boire ... (bon geste d'utilisation)

PINCE A LINGE   ... un serre - bouchon ...

TASSE   ... quand on veut prendre ... boire quelque chose

CISEAUX   ... on met de l'eau et on verse ...

Fig. 5. Michel's patient sees the stimuli named on the left of the
        page (scissors, comb, screwdriver, cork, key, fork, pin,
        cup). His comments are recorded on the right. Note that,
        although words are inappropriate, they are semantically re-
        lated to the stimuli (e.g. rateau = rake, for comb ; boulon
        = nut, and lime = file, for screwdriver).
        A moment later, the expected answer comes when new stimuli
        are presented (e.g. visser = to screw, tournevis = screw-
        driver, when a key is shown).
        The semantic relations between boxes have been schematized
        by links.

mental representations and of action schemas. For instance, slow transfer of noisy proprioceptive information associated with a rapidly decaying buffer memory for motor schemas would be the base for a simulation of some phono-articulatory errors in aphasia. Similarly, a simulation of agrammatism has been envisaged by programming degrading factors in the topological representation of structured objects, and by restricting at the same time the short term memory for words (or for functional morphemes (Marcus, 1980)).

Other studies on adaptive control in complex posterior aphasias should also be devoted to Wernicke aphasias which evolve towards conduction aphasias, because the patients usually recover better than others. Jouanette, Keller and Lecours (1980) have reported how, in conduction aphasia, patients can use an auditory (or visual) loop control in order to improve paraphasic speech by successive approximations. If this feedback and control mechanism is used by one subject in therapy, it shows that part of the input subsystem is functioning well enough to be used, and that some heuristic technique has been evolved to overcome the original deficit. Evolution factors allied with conservative factors can then facilitate the development and the remembering of heuristic methods which compensate for lost representational processes.

Minor hemisphere phasic problems cannot be considered within the scope of a short paper. But it should be remembered that anomia and dysprosody can occur and be long-lasting after right temporo-parieto-occipital lesions. However, in such cases, readaptation does not follow the same pattern as after dominant hemisphere lesions. Habituation is probably the greatest difficulty, for patients tend to neglect their deficits when they do not prevent them from keeping their usual occupations and hobbies (Springer & Deutsch, 1981).

A DYNAMIC SYSTEMS APPROACH TO THE COGNITIVE PROCESSES SUBSERVING LANGUAGE PERFORMANCE

In this chapter relating language to other intelligent processes, I have argue that the preservation of competence after damage the restitution of transfer and transformation, the compensation of hardware or software loss, the substitution of new processes for former ones are by no means purely adaptive phenomena. On the contrary, the installation of reduced active performance or the habituation to minimal world representations are the unfortunate consequences of adaptation. The brain seems to be too sensible a system in the sense that it adapts too quickly to an uncurable handicap in the representation of a complex environment. But the brain is also a sensible entity in that, when it is sufficiently and conveniently stimulated, it finds wise heuristic strategies in order to reorganize communicational activities.

This sentient and rational central nervous system can thus
manage its <u>dynamic evolution by a double control method</u>.

First, the environment influences the physiological specialization of cortical subsystems cooperating together, and functional
efficiency is ensured by a progressive stabilization of behavior for
categories of stimuli and of acts. But specialization, centraliza-
tion, and stabilization are constantly checked by outer changes or
by inner physiological accidents. By being partly specialized for
input processing, the system runs the risk of hyperadaptation and
of consecutive decay. Of course, by being also capable of a categorial approach to problems, the system anticipates small changes.
Major changes or accidents, on the contrary, introduce abrupt sucess-
ions of stable and unstable phases in the organization of cooperative processing. Such structural disruptions could be fatal to the
system as a whole if another level of control were not maintained
inside the system.

This second level of control which either anticipates or solves
catastrophes as mere crises is the genetically inherited power to
intelligently equate a number of factors of order and disorder in
the cognitive processes which are at work as long as the brain is
functioning. Some of those factors are : conservation factors ($\mathscr{C}$),
representational factors $\mathscr{R}$), evolution factors ($\mathscr{G}$), error factors
(ε), and stimuli themselves (favorable : S^+, or unfavorable : S^-).

Frécon and Lavorel (1980) suggested a mathematical model based
on such factors which accounts for several types of abnormal language performances. If memory (part of $\mathscr{C}$) is satisfactory and learning
$\mathscr{G} \times \mathscr{R}(S^+)$ reduced, language becomes conservative, stereotyped, based
on past knowledge (deafness : $\mathscr{R}$ low ; sclerosis : $\mathscr{G}$ low ...). If $\mathscr{C}$
is low but $\mathscr{C} \times \mathscr{R} (S^+)$ high, we find the situation corresponding to
that of gifted speakers or children with a form of language which is
overadapted to fashion and environmental stimuli (they reproduce the
idiosyncracies of other speakers). If a lesion permanently impairs
long term memory, the patient will continuously learn and forget.
Therapy must be uninterrupted. If $\mathscr{C}$ and $\mathscr{R}$ are both reduced, there
is gradual senescence. If some factors of ε are relatively high, $\mathscr{R}$
may for instance, be permanently or transitorily degraded. In speech
therapy, the systematic repetition of unfavorable information (S^-)
may mar rather than mend language, especially if $\mathscr{C}$ is low and $\mathscr{G}$ and
$\mathscr{R}$ high.

Many other situations could be justified by the interaction of
the above factors. Of course, they may remind us of Arbib's 1966
model. But, in fact, we are now dealing with a much more complex
"machine", and adaptive automata-theory no longer serves the descriptive purpose. Besides, any report on neuropsychological or neurolinguistic processing deficits would have to differentiate the
relatively <u>negative aspects of adaptation to disturbances in input</u>

representation from the positive aspects of adaptation to disturb-ances in act planning and control.

ACKNOWLEDGEMENTS

This theoretical approach to language systemics has been great-ly helped by interaction with M. Jeannerod, F. Michel and F. Vital-Durand. I also wish to express my thanks to M. Arbib and to V. Lesser of the University of Massachusetts for their useful suggestions.

REFERENCES

Ajuriaguerra, J., (Ed.), 1965, "Déafférentation expérimentale et clinique", Masson, Paris.

Alajouanine, Th. and Lhermitte, F., 1960, Les troubles des activités expressives du langage dans l'apahsie ; leurs relations avec les apraxies. Revue Neurologique, 102, 66.

Allman, J.M., and Kaas, J.H., 1971, Representation of the visual field in striate and adjoining cortex of the owl monkey. Brain Research, 35, 89-106.

Allman, J.M., and Kaas, J.H., 1974, A crescent-shaped cortical vis-ual area surrounding the middle temporal area in the owl mon-key. Brain Research, 81, 199-213.

Arbib, M.A., 1964, "Brains, Machines and Mathematics", McGraw-Hill, New-York.

Arbib, M.A., 1966, Automata theory and control theory - a rapproche-ment. Automatica, 3, 3-4, 161.

Arbib, M.A., 1972, "The metaphorical brain", Wiley, New-York.

Arbib, M.A. 1980, Perceptual structures and distributed motor con-trol. In Brooks V.B. Vol. III on motor control of the "Hand-book of Physiology". Bethesda ; Maryland : American Physiolo-gical Society.

Arbib, M.A. & Caplan D., 1979, Neurolinguistics must be computational. The Behavioral and Brain Sciences, 2.

Beauvois, M.F. & Derouesné, J., 1981, Lexical and orthographic agra-phia. Brain, 104, 21-49.

Benson, D.F., 1979, "Aphasia, alexia and agraphia". New York : Chur-chill Linvingstone.

Bernstein, N.A., 1968, "The coordination and regulation of movements. Oxford : Pergamon Press.

Bernstein, J.J., Wells M.R. & Bernstein M.R., 1978, Spinal cord re-generation. In C.W. Cotman, "Neuronal platicity", New York, Raven Press, 49-71.

Bever, T.G., 1975, Cerebral asymetries in human are due to the different-iation of two incompatible processes : holistic and analytic. N.Y. Acad. of Science.

Beyen, E.S. & Shokkor-Trotskaya, M.K., 1966, The preventive method of speech rehabilitation in aphasia. Cortex, 2, 96-108.

Bisiach, E. & Luzzati, C. 1978, Unilateral neglect of representation-al space. Cortex, 14, 129-133.

Blakemore, C., Garey, L.J., Zaineb Henderson, Swindale N.V. & Vital-Durand, F., 1980, Visual experience can promote rapid axonal reinnervation in monkey visual cortex. Journal of Physiology, 307, 25-26.

Brodmann, K., 1909,"Vergleichende Lokalisationslehre der Grosshirnende in ihren Prinzipien dargestellt auf Grund des Zellenbanes". Leipzig : Barth.

Changeux, J.P. & Danchin, A., 1976, The selective stabilisation of developing synapses, a plausible mechanism for the specification of neuronal networks. Nature, 264, 705-712.

Coltheart, M., Petterson, K. & Marshall, J.C.,"Deep dyslexia". London : Routledge & Kegan Paul.

Cotman, C.W. (Ed.) 1978, "Neuronal plasticity". New York : Raven Press.

Craig, K.J.W., 1943, "The nature of explanation". Cambridge University Press.

Danchin, A.1978,Spécification épigénétique des réseaux nerveux par stabilisation fonctionnelle des synapses en développement. In Delacour J. (Ed.) "Neurobiologie de l'apprentissage". Paris: Masson,199-209.

Déjerine, J., 1914, "Sémiologie des affections du système nerveux". Paris : Masson.

Déjerine, J. & Serieux, P., 1898, Un cas de surdité verbale pure terminée par aphasie sensorielle. Revue de Psychiatrie, 2,7.

Déjerine, J., & Pelissier, A., 1914, Contribution à l'étude de la cécité verbale pure. Encéphale, 7, 1.

Déjerine, J. & Déjerine-Klumpke, 1902, Sur l'hypertrophie compensatrice du faisceau pyramidal du côté sain dans un cas d'hémiplégie cérébrale infantile. Revue Neurol. 10, 642-646 (Comments in Jeannerod & Hécaen).

Delacour, J.,1981,"Conditionnement et biologie". Paris : Masson.

Dennis, M., 1980, Language acquisition in a single hemisphere : semantic organization. In Caplan D. (Ed.) "Biological studies of mental processes". Cambridge : MIT Press.

Dennis, M., 1980, Capacity and strategy for syntactic comprehension after left and right hemidecortication. Brain and Language, 2, 287-318.

Denny-Brown, D., 1966, "The cerebral control of movement". Liverpool : Liverpool Press.

Derouesné, J., Séron, X. & Lhermitte, F. 1975, Rééducation de patients atteints de lésions frontales. Revue Neurologique, 131, 677-689.

Dev, P., 1975, Computer simulation of a dynamic visual perception model. Man-Machine studies, 7, 511-527.

Diamond, I.T., 1979, The subdivisions of neocortex : a proposal to revise the tranditional view of sensory-motor ans association areas. Progress in psychobiology and physiological psychology, vol. 8, Acad. Press.

Eccles, J.C., 1977,"The understanding of the brain'.' New York : Mc Graw-Hill.

Economo, C., Von & Koskinas, G.N., 1925, "Die Cytoarchitektonik der Hirnrinde". Berlin : Springer, 1931.

Edelman, G.M. & Mountcastle, V.B., 1978, "The mindful brain". Cambridge, Mass : MIT Press.

Ewert, J.P., 1970, Neural mechanisms of prey-catching and avoidance behaviors in the toad. "Brain, Behavior, Evolution", 3, 36-56.

Flechsig, P., 1976, "Die Leitungsbahnen in Gehirn und Rückenmark des Menschen auf Grund Entwicklungsgschichtlicher Untersuchungen". Leipzig : Engelmann.

Frécon, L. & Lavorel, P.M., 1980, Context-sensitive selection models for speech errors. T.A. Informations, 1, 38-44. Paris : Klincksieck.

Galaburda, A.M., 1981, Histology and cytoarchitectonics of the speech areas and asymetries. In Arbib, M., Caplan, D. & Marshall, J. C. "Neural models of language processes". New York : Academic Press.

Galaburda, A.M. & Sanides, F., 1977, The human auditory cortex : A new architectonic map. Neurosciences Abstracts, 3, 67.

Gigley, H.M., 1982, Artificial Intelligence meets Brain Theory. In Trappl, R., "Cybernetics and systems". La Haye : Mouton.

Goldman,P.S., 1974, An alternative to developmental plasticity : heterology of CNS structures in infants and adults. In Stein, D.G. & coll. (Eds.) "Plasticity and recovery of function in the central nervous system". New York : Academic Press.

Gordon, B., 1981, Confrontation naming : computational model and disconnection simulation. In Arbib, M.A., Caplan, D. & Marshall J.C. (Eds.)"Neural models of language processes". New York : Academic Press.

Greene, P.H., 1972, Problems of organisation of motor systems. In Rosen, R. & Snell, F.M. (Eds.)"Progress in theoretical biology" New York : Academic Press, vol. 2, pp 303-338.

Hécaen, H. & Angelergues, 1963, "La cécité psychique". Paris : Masson.

Hécaen, H. & Consoli, S., 1973, Analyse des troubles du langage au cours des lésions de l'aire de Broca. Neuropsychologia, 11, 377-388.

Held, R., 1963, Plasticity in human sensorimotor control. Science, 142, 454-462.

Held, R., 1962, Adaptation to arrangement and visual-spatial after effects. Psychologische Beiträge, 6, 439-450.

Helm, N.A., 1979, "The gestual behavior of aphasic patients during confrontation naming". Doctoral dissertation Boston University.

Itoh, M., Sasanuma, S., Hirose, H., Yoshioka, H. & Ushijima, T.,1980, Articulatory dynamics in a patient with apraxia of speech. Brain and Language, 11, 1, 66-75.

Jackson, J.H., 1874, On the nature of the duality of the brain. Medical Press and Circular, 1, 19-63.

Jeannerod, M. & Hécaen, H., 1979,"Adaptation et restauration des fonctions nerveuses". Lyon : Simep.

Jeannerod, M. & Schmid, R. 1978, La plasticité du réflexe vestibulo-oculaire. In Delacour, J. (Ed.) "Neurobiologie de l'apprentissage". Paris, Masson, 168-182.

Joannette, Y., 1980,"Les troubles de la fonction verbale dans les lésions de l'hémisphère droit". Doctoral dissertation. Université du Québec à Montréal.

Joannette, Y., Keller, E. & Lecours, A.R. 1980, Sequences of phonemic approximations in aphasia. Brain and language, 11, 1, 30-44.

Kaas, J.H., Nelson, R.J., Sur, M., Lin, C.S. & Meizenich, M., 1979, Multiple representation of the body within "SI" of primates. A redefinition of primary somato sensory cortex. Science, 204, 521-523.

Kertesz, A., 1979,"Aphasia and associated disorders : taxonomy, localisation and recovery". New York : Grune ans Stratton.

Kinsbourne, M., 1971, The minor cerebral hemisphere as a source of aphasic speech. Archives of Neurology, 25, 302-306.

Kupferman, I., & Kandel, E.R., 1969, Neuronal control of a behavioral response mediated by the abdominal ganglion on Aplysia. Science 164, 847-850.

Labourel, D., 1982, Communication non verbale et aphasie. In Séron, X. & Laterre C. "Rééduquer le cerveau". BRuxelles : Mardaga, 93-107.

Lashley, K.S., 1950, In search of the Engram. "Symposia of the Society of Experimental Biologists in Physiological Mechanisms in Animal Behavior", 4, New York : Academic Press.

Lashley, K.S., 1960, Studies of cerebral functions in learning. In Beach, F.A. & coll. (Eds.)"The retention of motor habits after destruction of the so-called motor areas in primates". New York : McGraw Hill.

Lavorel, P.M., 1980,"Aspects de la performance linguistique". Thèse pour le Doctorat d'Etat. Université Lyon II, Paris : Champion.

Lavorel, P.M., 1980, A propos d'un cas d'aphasie de Wernicke : mise en question de l'opposition paradigme-syntagme. La Linguistique, 16, 2, 43-66.

Lavorel, P.M., 1980, Interprétation lexicaliste de l'incohérence verbale dans les aphasies postérieures. Etudes de Linguistique Appliquée, 2, 65-91 (Paris : Didier)

Lavorel, P.M., 1980, Sept formes de jargon. Troubles de la sélection dans le dictionnaire mental. Grammatica, 2. Presses de l'Université de Toulouse.

Lavorel, P.M., 1982, Production strategies : a systems approach to Wernicke's aphasia. In Arbib, M.A., Caplan, D. & Marshall, J.C. (Eds)"Neural models of language processes". New York, Academic Press.

Lavorel, P.M., 1981, Knowledge and beliefs in the human brain. "NATO Symposium : Natural and Artificial Intelligence". Château-Cornu, forthcoming.

Lavorel, P.M. & Arbib, M.A., 1981, Towards a theory of language performance. Neurolinguistics, perceptual-motor processes, and cooperative computation. Theoretical Linguistics, 1.

Lavorel, P.M., 1982, Steps towards Natural Computation. Informatica, 6, 2, 3-12. Ljubljana, Yugoslavia.

Lavorel, P.M., & Gigley, H.M., 1982, How we name or misname objects. In Trappl, R.,"Cybernetics and systems" La Haye : Mouton.

Lecours, A.R., & Lhermitte, F., 1979,"L'Aphasie". Paris : Flammarion et Presses de l'Université de Montréal.

Lesser, V., Bates, P., Brooks, R., Corkhill, D., Lefkowitz, L., Mukunda R., Pavlin, J., Reed, S. & Wileden, J., "A high-level simulation test bed for cooperative distributed problem-solving". University of Massachusetts Report, Dep. Comp. and Inf. Science.

Luria, A.R., 1973,"The working brain". Harmondsworth : Penguin.

Luria, A.R., 1976,"Basic problems of neurolinguistics". New York : Mouton.

Luria, A.R. & Tsvetkova, L.S., 1966,"Les troubles de la résolution de problèmes". Paris : Gauthier-Villars.

Macneilage, P.F., 1980, Distinctive properties of speech motor control. In Stelmach, G.E. & Requin, J. (Eds.) "Tutorials in motor behavior". North-Holland.

Marcus, M.P.,1980,"Atheory of syntactic recognition for natural language". Cambridge Mas. : MIT Press.

Mecham, M.J., Berko, M.J., Berko, F.G. & Palmer M.F., 1966,"Communication training in childhood brain damage" . Springfield I11: Thomas.

Meetham, A.R., 1969,"Encyclopedia of linguistics, information and control". Oxford Pergamon.

Messerli, T., Tissot, A. & Rodriguez, J., 1976, Recovery from aphasia : some factors of prognosis. In Lebrun, Y. & Hoops, R. "Recovery in aphasics". Amsterdam : Swets & Zeitlinger.

Miller, G.A., Galanter, E. & Pribram, K.H., 1960,"Plans and the structure of behavior". New York : Holt, Rinehart and Winston.

Monakow, C., Von, 1911, Lokalisation der Hirnfunktionen. Journal of Neurology and Psychiatry, 17, 185-200.

Michel, L.F. & Lavorel,P.M., 1981, An unusual case of simultagnosia which teaches us something of language representation in the left hemisphere. Working paper, INSERM U94, Lyon, (to appear)

Michel, F., Martin, M.M. & Peronnet, F., 1976, A propos d'un cas clinique de surdité verbale. Lyon Médical, 236, 691-698.

Michel, F., Péronnet, F. & Schott, B., 1976, A propos d'un cas de surdité de l'hémisphère gauche (hémianacousie droite). Revue d'Electroencéphalographie et de Neurophysiologie clinique, 6, 175-178.

Michel, F., Péronnet, F., Labourel, D. & Martin, M.M., 1974, Confrontation des données du test d'écoute dichotique et celles de l'enregistrement des potentiels évoqués dans divers cas d'aphasie. Revue Neurologique (Paris).129, 295-296.

Michel, F., Péronnet, F. & Schott, B., 1980, A case of cortical deafness : clinical and electrophysiological data. Brain and language, 10, 367-377.

Michel, F., Schott, B., Boucher, M. & Kopp, N., 1979, Alexie sans agraphie chez un malade ayant un hémisphère gauche déafférenté. Revue Neurologique (Paris), 135, 4, 347, 364.

Michel, F. & Andreewsky, E., Deep dysphasia, an equivalent to deep dysphasia in oral repetition. Brain and Language (fortcoming)

Marslen-Wilson, W. & Tyler, L.K., 1980, The temporal structure of spoken language understanding. Cognition, 8, 1-71.

Messerli, P. & Lavorel, P.M., 1982, "L'expression orale". Actes du colloque de la Société de Neuropsychologie de Langue Française, Genève, (to appear).

Meizenick, M.M. & Brugge, J.G., 1973, Representation of the cochlear partition on the superior temporal plane of the macaque monkey. Brain Research, 50, 275-296.

Morrel, F., 1972, Integrative properties of parastriate neurons. In Karczmar, A.G. & Eccles, J.C. "Brain and human behavior". Berlin : Springer, 259-289 (Cited and commented in Jeannerod & Hécaen).

Moutier, F., 1908, "L'aphasie de Broca". Thèse. Paris : Steinheil, (Reproduction of diagrams by Wernicke, Lichtheim, Charcot, Freud & others pp 47-59).

Nespoulous, J.L. & Puel, M., 1981, Etude neurolinguistique d'un cas d'anarthrie pure, Brain and Language, (forthcoming).

Newell, A., 1973, Production systems, models of control structure. In Chase, W.G. Ed.) "Visual information processing". New York : Academic Press.

Nicolosi, L., Harryman, E. & Kresheck, J., 1978, "Terminology of communication disorders". Baltimore : Williams-Wilkins.

Obler, L.K., Albert, M.L., Goodglass, H. & Benson, D.F., 1978, Aphasia type and aging Brain and Language, 6, 316-322.

Perenin, M.T. & Jeannerod, M., 1975, Residual vision in cortically blind hemifields. Neuropsychologia, 13, 1-7.

Prablanc, C., Jeannerod, M. & Tzavaras, A., 1975, Independent and interdependent processes in prism adaptation. In Vital-Durand & Jeannerod (Eds.) "Aspects of neural platicity". Paris : INSERM, 139-157.

Pribram, K.H. & Luria, A.R., 1973, "Behavior electrophysiology of the frontal lobes". New York : Academic Press.

Sacerdoti, E.D., 1974, Planning in a hierarchy of abstraction spaces. Artificial Intelligence, 5, 114-135.

Selzer, B. & Pandya, D.N., 1978, Afferent cortical connections and architectonics of the superior temporal sulcus and surrounding cortex in the rhesus monkey. Brain research, 149, 1-24.

Séron, X., 1979, "Aphasie et neuropsychologie". Bruxelles : Mardaga.

Sperry, R.W., 1943, Visuomotor coordination in the newt. Journal of comparative neurology, 79, 33-35.

Spinelli, D.N. & Jensen, F.E., 1979, Plasticity : the mirror of experience. Science, 203, 75-78.

Springer, S.P. & Detusch, G., 1981, "Left brain, right brain". San Francisco : Freeman & Co.

Stein, D.G. & Dawson, R.G., 1980, The dynamics of growth, organisation and adaptability in the central nervous system. In Bromo, G. & Kagan, J. (Eds.) "Constancy and change in human development". Harvard University Press.

Stein, D.G., Rosen, J.J. & Butters, N. (Eds.), 1974, "Plasticity and recovery of function in the central nervous system", New York : Academic Press.

Stelmach, G.E. & Requin, J. (Eds.), 1980, "Tutorials in motor behavior". New York : North Holland.

Stockert, T.R., Von, 1978, A standardised program for aphasia therapy. In Lebrun, Y & Hoops, R."The management of aphasia". Amsterdam : Swets & Zeitlinger.

Szentágothai, J. & Arbib, M.A., 1975, Conceptual models of neural organisation. NRP Bulletin, 1974, 307-510. Hardcover : MIT Press.

Taylor-Parker, S. & Rita Gibson, K., 1979, A development model for the evolution of language and intelligence in early hominids. The Behavioral and Brain Sciences, 2, 367-408.

Wada, J.A. & Rasmussen, T.,1960,Intracarotid injection of sodium amytal for the lateralisation of cerebral speech dominance. Experimental and clinical observations. Journal of Neurosurgery, 17, 266-282.

Wall, P.D. & Egger, M., 1971, Formation of new connexions in adult rat brains after partial deafferentation. Nature, 232, 542-545.

Walton, J.N., 1977, "Brain's diseases of the nervous system" Oxford University Press, (Revised edition of Lord Brain's)

Warren, J.M. & Akert, K., 1964, "The frontal granular cortex and behavior". New York : MacGraw-Hill.

Weiss, P., 1937, Further experimental investigation on the phenomenon of homologous response in transplated amibian limbs. Journal of Comparative Neurology, 67, 269-315.

Willows, A.O.D., 1969, Neuronal network triggering a fixed action pattern. Science, 166, 1549-1551 (Triton).

Wind, J., 1976, Phylogeny of the human vocal tract. Annals of the New York Academy of Sciences, 280, 612-630.

Wing, A.M., 1977, Perturbations of auditory feedback delay and the timing of movement. Journal of Experimental Psychology, 3-2, 175-186.

Yakovlev, P.I., 1948, Motility, behavior and the brain. Journal of Nervous and Mental Disease, 107, 4, 313-335.

Zaidel, E., 1977, Unilateral auditory language comprehension on the token tesk following cerebral commissurotomy and hemispherectomy. Neuropsychologia, 15, 1-18.

Zeki, S.M.,1980, The representation of colours in the cerebral cortex. Nature, 284, 412-418.

PIAGET AND EDUCATION

C. J. Brainerd

Department of Psychology, University of Western
Ontario, London, Ontario, Canada N6A 5C2

During the past several years, there has been a surge of interest in the potential applications of Piagetian theory to the
classroom, especially in North American early-childhood education circles. A new curriculum movement has coalesced around
the theory and a new generation of instructional programs, the
so-called cognitive curricula, has emerged (for reviews, see
Brainerd, 1978a; Hooper & DeFrain, 1980).

In one respect, the current concern with the educational implications of Piaget's work is quite remarkable. Piagetian theory
is a complex and, all too often, obscure system. Unlike, say,
operant theory, it hardly seems like the sort of model from which
concrete instructional recommendations would flow. Nevertheless,
they do, or at least many such recommedations have been put forward by students of the theory. My purpose in this paper is to
discuss some of the major ones. For convenience of exposition,
I shall distinguish between two categories of recommendations,
namely, prescriptive and proscriptive.

PRESCRIPTIVE RECOMMENDATIONS

In view of the intrinsic difficulty of the theory, it is not
surprising that even Piaget scholars are inclined to disagree about
this or that curriculum recommendation. For example, the literature contains a not inconsiderable number of instances in which
one author criticizes the curriculum of another author on grounds
of insufficient theoretical orthodoxy (for several examples, see
Brainerd, in press; Johnson & Hopper, in press). Such disagree-
ments notwithstanding, there are some general prescriptions which
most people seem to accept. It is these that I shall be concerned
with.

Sequential Introduction of Concepts

In Piagetian theory, much is made of the fact that infants and children seem to acquire certain concepts in fixed, immutable sequences (e.g., Piaget, 1960, 1970a). Whenever such a sequence is observed, three explanations suggest themselves. First, the sequence may be a trivial consequence of logical connections between the target concepts. There are many cases in which one developmental ordering of a pair of cognitive skills A and B is conceivable but the other ordering is inconceivable. If, for example, A = "can count up to five" and B = "can count up to ten," A precedes B is an imaginable sequence, but B precedes A is not. The reason is that the skills involved in A form a proper subset of the skills involved in B and, therefore, B cannot be measured without also measuring A. For this reason, such relationships are called measurement sequences (Brainerd, 1978a, 1978b). Second, an invariant sequence may result from universal regularities in the environment in which cognitive development takes place (Skinner, 1974). If one were to measure the understanding of fractions and decimals in any sample of North American elementary schoolers, fractions would be understood first. But this is simply a consequence of the fact that fractions have always been taught before decimals in standardized arithmetic curricula.

The third possibility, the one that developmental researchers have traditionally regarded as the most interesting, is that the unfolding structure of the organism builds in some concept orderings and rules out others. This, of course, is the interpretation favored by Piagetians. More specifically, invariant sequences in concept acquisition are viewed as evidence of universal underlying stages of cognitive development. Each stage is said to be characterized by a unique set of cognitive structures, and the sorts of concepts that we measure in the laboratory are said to require particular levels of structuration. Thus, if A is invariably acquired before B, the Piagetian explanation is that A belongs to an earlier stage (and to a more primitive level of structuration) than B. This explanation has not infrequently been challenged on grounds of cicularity (e.g., Brainerd, 1978b, 1981).

If different concepts require different types of cognitive structures and if such structures emerge in a stratified hierarchy of stages, the obvious conclusion is that one should seek to order the introduction of concepts in the classroom to reflect their "natural" ordering in everyday development (Sigel, 1969). Here, there are two principal sources of information on which the curriculum programmer may rely. The first and most reliable source is hard data from studies of concept development. As researchers have long been interested in the issue of sequentiality, a substantial fact base on this topic is available. The evidence is especi-

ally rich in the areas of mathematics, science, and logic (for some
reviews, see Brainerd, 1978a, 1979; Flavell, 1970, 1977). The other
source of information is to make inferences from the theory. It
will often be the case that the developmental data on target concepts are too thin to support conclusions as to their natural orderings. If so, the general principles of the theory may give
guidance as to whether some or all of the target concepts should
be regarded as belonging to different stages. Thus, a concept
that involves straightforward inferences from everyday experience
is probably concrete operational and, consequently, it should be
introduced to children before some other concept that involves
abstract inferences and is probably formal operational.

There is another feature of cognitively-oriented curricula
that is implicit in undertaking to match instructional and developmental sequences, individualized diagnosis. In an elementary or a
preschool classroom, the children will inevitably vary in their
current levels of cognitive development. Hence, achieving an
instructional-developmental match presupposes that we have some
information available on this variable. This means that, somehow,
we must undertake to measure the stages of individual children.
As the current stage will vary from child to child, it also means
that at any given point during the school year, the curriculum
that is developmentally appropriate for some children will be developmentally inappropriate for others.

The fact that cognitive curricula require preinstructional
stage diagnosis has been one of the most serious obstacles to their
implementation. To begin with, there has never been any consensus
among researchers about how one measures a Piagetian stage (cf.
Flavell & Wohlwill, 1969). The recent literature suggests that
this problem is not any nearer resolution than it was a decade
ago (see various commentators' remarks in Brainerd, 1978b). Assuming that stage diagnosis could be satisfactorily effected, there
would then be the matter of cost to contend with. By comparison
to more standardized programs, cognitive curricula comprised of
separate diagnostic and instructional components are more costly
to implement than one-step curricula comprised of instruction only.
Moreover, the fact that instruction must be fine tuned to the cognitive levels of individual children entails that pupil-teacher
ratios must be very low in such curricula, much lower than they
normally are.

What to Teach

With children in the elementary school range, Piagetian theory
is chiefly concerned with cognitive skills that are mathematical
(e.g., number, addition), logical (e.g., classes, relations), or
scientific (e.g., time, mass). By and large, these concepts are

associated with the concrete-operational stage. Some of them are
routinely taught in the mathematics and science sections of most
elementary school curricula. But many others are not. Illustra-
of concepts that are rarely taught but, according to the theory,
could be come from the logic of relations (principles of transi-
tivity, reflexivity, and symmetry), the logic of classes (principles of classification and inclusion), topological geometry (principles of closure and neighborhood), projective geometry (principles of rotation and translation), and elementary physics (principles of duration and momentum).

Perhaps the most novel recommendations about curriculum content that have been derived from the theory are those concerned
with geometry. Historically, geometry was viewed as a much more
advanced subject than arithemtic and algebra. Little of it was
taught until plane Euclidean geometry was introduced, usually during the second year of high school. But the theory says that the
concepts of both Euclidean and projective geometry belong to the
concrete-operational stage, which means that they are developmentally appropriate by roughly the second grade. Further, because the
concepts of topology are thought to emerge during the preoperational stage, topological geometry can presumably be taught during the
preschool and elementary school years.

Teaching Strategies

Some of the most controversial proposals in cognitive curricula have to do with the methodology of transmitting new information
to children. There are three instructional strategies that have
frequently been advocated, namely, self-discovery teaching, conflict teaching, and peer teaching. The advocacy of each is based
on some of Piaget's ideas about how learning occurs.

Concerning self-discovery teaching, much is made of the active
role of children in Piagetian analyses of learning. In the most
comprehensive series of learning experiments that has emanated from
Geneva, Inhelder, Sinclair, and Bovet (1974) describe the guiding
thesis of their training methodologies as follows: "in terms of
successful training procedures ... the more active the subject is,
the more successful his learning is likely to be" (p. 74). Similarly, Sinclair (1973) has observed that the most effective learning
methods are those in which "the subject himself is the mainspring
of his development, in that it is his own activity on the environment or his own active reflections that make progress" (p. 58).
Finally, Inhelder and Sinclair (1969) stated that Genevan training
methods share the feature that "in all of them we avoid imposing
definite strategies on the child ... the child is encouraged to
make his own coordinations ... the child is asked to anticipate
the likely outcome of certain transformations and then to observe
the actual outcome of the transformation" (pp. 4 & 5).

In sum, Piagetians see learning as an active, self-discovery process. This interpretation is based on two other assumptions, namely, that the best training procedures are those that mirror spontaneous processes of cognitive development and that the most important of these spontaneous processes is construction. On the former assumption, Sinclair stated that "learning is dependent on development ... in the sense that learning--that is, in situations specifically constructed so that the subject has active encounters with the environment--the same mechanisms as in development are at work to make progress" (1973, p. 58), and Inhelder et al. noted that "We started with the idea that under certain conditions an acceleration of cognitive development would be possible, but that this could only occur if the training resembled the kind of situations in which progress takes place outside an experimental set-up" (1974, p. 24). On the second assumption, Sinclair simply remarked that "active discovery is what happens in development" (1973, p. 58).

It is not surprising that curriculum designers have translated such statements into discovery-based instruction. One of the most passionate appeals appeared in an early paper by Duckworth: "the chief outcome of this theory is that children be allowed to do their own learning ... You cannot further understanding in a child simply by talking to him. Good pedagogy must involve presenting the child with situations in which he himself experiments, in the broadest sense of the term--trying things out to see what happens, manipulating symbols, posing questions and seeking his own answers ..."(1964, p. 2).

It is often objected that although self-discovery instruction may be endorsed by the theory, it is tremendously time consuming to implement in comparison to standard, tutorial teaching. Piagetians usually counter this argument by saying that the additional time is well spent because learning by self-discovery is qualitatively superior: "the child learns more through direct experiments, and ... he learns even more if this experience is discovered rather than being offered" (Kamii, 1973, p. 207).

Concerning conflict teaching, the proximal source of cognitive development in theory is change in the underlying cognitive structures. Structural change, in turn, is caused by a reciprocal mechanism of assimilation and accommodation that, as many writers have observed, resembles the principles of balance and congruity posited in classical theories of attitude change. Briefly, structural change, or accommodation, is induced when the child is confronted with types of information that exceed the assimilative powers of his or her current level of structuration.

Because successful training procedures are supposed to imitate spontaneous cognitive development, these assumptions about the na-

ture of structure change have been used to support procedures that
involve an element of conflict. The specific kind of conflict is
conceptual rather than emotional. The general idea is that instruction should take children's current beliefs into account, and attempt to pit those beliefs against new, discordant information. An
especially good synopsis of the theoretical rationale for this
technique of "conflict teaching" was given by Sigel: "A major
thrust ... is to confront the child with the illogical nature of
his point of view. The reason for this confrontation is that it
is a necessary and sufficient requirement for cognitive growth.
The shift from egocentric to sociocentric thought comes about
through confrontation with the animate and inanimate environment.
These forces impinge on the child, inducing disequilibrium. The
child strives to reconcile the discrepancies and evolves new processes by which to adapt to new situations" (1969, p. 473).

    Last, concerning peer teaching, Piaget argued in some of his
earliest works that child-to-child social interaction is the principal experiential medium in which cognitive change takes place.
In The Language and Thought of the Child, for example, he maintained
that the transition from self-stimulative, egocentric language to
socialized, communicative language hinges on peer interaction.
Piagetian educators have interpreted such arguments as favoring
small-group instruction: "cooperation among children is as important as the child's cooperation with adults. Without the opportunity to see the relativity of perspectives, the child remains prisoner
of his own naturally egocentric point of view. A clash of convic-
tions among children at similar cognitive levels can often help
the child more than the adult can to move out of his egocentricity"
(Kamii, 1973, p. 200).

    One technique for implementing small-group instruction makes
use of free periods when children are working on assignments. In
place of the usual procedure of solitary work, children are told
to work in groups of two to five. They are also encouraged to
thrash out alternative answers among themselves and to present mutually agreed answers to their teachers. What Piagetian educators
seem to have in mind is essentially a committee work model.

    Because teachers are normally adults rather than peers, wide-
spread adoption of the committee work model will obviously require
solid experimental evidence as to its effectiveness. Actually,
considerable evidence of this sort is available. Most of it comes
from a series of experiments by Murray and his associates concerned with learning conservation concepts (e.g., Murray, 1972;
Botvin & Murray, 1975). The prototype experiment employs a three-
phase design. First, a battery of pretests is administered to measure the current conservation knowledge of a group of children,
usually kindergarteners or first graders. On the basis of these
pretests, the children are classified as nonconservers and con-

servers. During the second phase, small groups are formed that
consist of two children who understand conservation and one child
who does not. The experimenter administers a new series of conservation tests to each group. The children are not allowed to
give individual answers to the test items. Instead, they must
discuss possible responses and arrive at a consensual answer. During the third phase, the pretest conservation battery is readminis-
tered to individual children, and their responses are compared to
the pretest data. It is commonly found that subjects who were
classified as nonconservers on the pretests are classified as con-
servers on the posttests.

PROSCRIPTIVE RECOMMENDATIONS

From what has been said so far, it would be natural to conclude that the differences between Piaget-based instruction and
more traditional methods lie mainly in what is taught and how
it is taught. In fact, however, the key difference lies in what
is not taught. This proscriptive aspect of Piagetian curricula de-
volves from the particular philosophy of learning that Piaget es-
poused.

This philosophy is distinctly Rousseauian, and North Americans
have traditionally interpreted it as a classical readiness doctrine
(Brainerd, 1977). The guiding tenet is that learning is controlled
by cognitive development. It is even argued that learning can be
reduced to development: "Learning is no more than a sector of
cognitive development which is facilitated by experience" (Piaget,
1970a, p. 714). As cognitive development is a stage-like process
in the theory, it follows that children's learning will be "subject
to the general constraints of the current developmental stage"
(Piaget, 1970a, p. 713) and that it will "vary very significantly
as a function of the initial cognitive levels of the children"
(Piaget, 1970a, p. 715). This leads to the controversial proposal
that children are simply incapable of learning concepts that are
beyond their current stage of cognitive development: "As for
teaching children concepts that they have not attained in their
spontaneous development, it is completely useless" (Piaget, 1970b,
p. 30). Piaget's co-workers have reiterated this proposal in more
circumspect language: "operativity is malleable only within certain limits ... children at the preoperational level do not acquire
truly operational structures" (Inhelder & Sinclair, 1969, p. 19).

The instructional principle that has been said to follow from
these views is that it is bad to attempt to speed up the spontaneous tempo of cognitive development by teaching concepts that exceed children's current stages. Such instruction is called acceleration, not "learning," and it is strictly forbidden in Piagetian

curricula. Teachers are cautioned to replace acceleration with forms of instruction that aim at thorough mastery of concepts and that are congruent with the current developmental stage. To take a concrete instance, rather than introduce Euclidean concepts to a child that is still preoperational, geometry instruction should be confined to mastery of topological concepts until the transition to concrete operations occurs. This is not to say that teachers should actively discourage such children from discoverying Euclidean concepts on their own, merely that systematic instruction in such concepts is not developmentally appropriate.

The prohibition of teaching that deals with concepts that are not stage congruent has serious ramifications for arithmetic teaching. As things now stand, well over half the elementary curriculum in most North American schools is devoted to number, computation, and other arithemtical skills. But according to Piagetian theory, such concepts are the province of the concrete-operational stage. Because seven or eight is the nominal age for the onset of concrete operations, arithmetic instruction is not stage appropriate before the second half of elementary school. Moreover, thanks to individual differences in transition age, substantial numbers of children in the fourth grade will not yet be concrete operational. This means that although arithmetic instruction may be appropriate for some children in the early elementary grades, universal introduction of arithemtic should be postponed until fourth or fifth grade. It is interesting to note the obvious inconsistency between this recommendation and the practice of teaching advanced arithmetical concepts to young children that became popular with the advent of the New Math.

CONCLUDING REMARKS

Throughout this paper, my aim has been to adumbrate Piagetian recommendations without commenting on their validity. However, good scholarship demands some passing attention to this matter in closing. Briefly, much current debate on the usefulness of Piaget-inspired curricula centers on the fact that either the underlying theoretical rationales for many proposals have not been subjected to empirical study or the data are consistently disconfirmatory. Unfortunately, there is no room here for a detailed discussion of contradictory data; instead, one illustration will have to suffice.

The illustration concerns the readiness assumption of Piaget's philosophy of learning, according to which children are unable to learn concepts that exceed their current stage of cognitive development. Many investigators have noted that two simple predictions appear to follow from this assumption. First, if we perform a learning experiment in which children who are classified as occupying Stage $\underline{k}$ are taught concepts from some later Stage $\underline{k} + \underline{i}$,

learning effects should be poor (small, nongeneral, nondurable) or
nonexistent. Second, if we perform a learning experiment in which
concepts from some Stage k are taught to subjects whose current
stages vary from some Stage $k - i$ to Stage k, there should be a
monotonic relationship between learning and stage classification
such that the size of learning effects increases as subjects'
stage classifications approach k.

Massive evidence against both these predictions--and, therefore, against the readiness assumption--is available in the literature on learning concrete-operational concepts (for reviews, see
Brainerd, 1977, 1978c; Brainerd & Allen, 1971). Concerning the
first prediction, robust learning effects have been found for concepts such as conservation both with children who showed no evidence
of the concepts on pretests and with children who were far below
the age norm for concrete operations (preschoolers). Concerning
the second prediction, size of learning effects has not been found
to covary with pretraining stage classification for concrete-
operational concepts.

All this is not to say that Piagetian programs are utterly
worthless or ill conceived. I merely wish to add a note of caution to the tide of enthusiasm that seems to accompany any curriculum movement. The fact is that the experts disagree about the
relative merits of Piagetian curricula and about their cost ef-
fectivenss. Consequently, interested readers will have to decide
for themselves, something that obviously is in keeping with the
self-discovery approach. My recommendation is to begin with recent literature reviews in a monograph by Hooper and DeFrain
(1980), a paper by Johnson and Hooper (in press), a chapter by
Lawton and Hooper (1978), and Chapter 7 in Brainerd (1978a). Access to most of the pertinent technical literature can be gained
from the bibliographies in these sources.

REFERENCES

Botvin, G. J., & Murray, F. B. The efficacy of peer modeling and so-
    cial conflict in the acquisition of conservation. Child De-
    velopment, 1975, 46, 796-799.
Brainerd, C. J. Cognitive development and concept learning: An in-
    terpretative review. Psychological Bulletin, 1977, 84, 919-
    939.
Brainerd, C. J. Piaget's theory of intelligence. Englewood Cliffs,
    N.J.: Prentice-Hall, 1978. (a)
Brainerd, C. J. The stage question in cognitive-developmental
    theory. The Behavioral and Brain Sciences, 1978, 1, 173-
    213. (b)
Brainerd, C. J. Learning research and Piagetian theory. In L. S.
    Siegel & C. J. Brainerd (Eds.), Alternatives to Piaget:

   Critical essays on the theory. New York: Academic Press,
   1978. (c)
Brainerd, C. J. _The origins of the number concept._ New York:
   Praeger, 1979.
Brainerd, C. J. Stages II. _Developmental Review_, 1981, 1, 63-81.
Brainerd, C. J. Modifiability of cognitive development. In S.
   Meadows (Ed.), _Issues in childhood cognitive development._
   London: Methuen, in press.
Brainerd, C. J., & Allen, T. W. Experimental inductions of the con-
   servation of "first-order" quantitative invariants. _Psycho-
   logical Bulletin_, 1971, _75_, 128-144.
Duckworth, E. Piaget rediscovered. In R. E. Ripple & V. N.
   Rockcastle (Eds.), _Piaget rediscovered._ Ithaca, N. Y.:
   Cornell University Press, 1964.
Flavell, J. H. Concept development. In P. H. Mussen (Ed.),
   Carmichael's manual of child psychology. New York: Wiley,
   1970.
Flavell, J. H. _Cognitive development._ Englewood Cliffs, N. J.:
   Prentice-Hall, 1977.
Flavell, J. H., & Wohlwill, J. F. Formal and functional aspects of
   cognitive development. In D. Elkind & J. H. Flavell (Eds.),
   Studies in cognitive development. New York: Oxford Universi-
   ty Press, 1969.
Hooper, F. H., & DeFrain, J. The search for a distinctly Piagetian
   contribution to education. _Genetic Psychology Monographs_,
   1980, _101_, 151-181.
Inhelder, B., & Sinclair, H. Learning cognitive structures. In P.
   H. Mussen, J. Langer, & M. Covington (Eds.), _Trends and issues
   in developmental psychology._ New York: Holt, Rinehart, &
   Winston, 1969.
Inhelder, B., Sinclair, H., & Bovet, M. _Learning and the develop-
   ment of cognition._ Cambridge, Mass.: Harvard University Press,
   1974.
Johnson, J. E., & Hooper, F. H. Piagetian structuralism and learn-
   ing: Reflections on two decades of educational application.
   Contemporary Educational Psychology, 1982, in press.
Kamii, C. Pedagogical principles derived from Piaget's theory:
   Relevance for educational practice. In M. Schwebel & J.
   Raph (Eds.), _Piaget in the classroom._ New York: Basic Books,
   1973.
Lawton, J. T., & Hooper, F. H. Piagetian theory and early childhood
   education: A critical analysis. In L. S. Siegel & C. J.
   Brainerd (Eds.), _Alternatives to Piaget: Critical essays on
   the theory._ New York: Academic Press, 1978.
Murray, F. B. Acquisition of conservation through social interaction.
   Developmental Psychology, 1972, _6_, 1-6.
Piaget, J. The general problems of the psychobiological development
   of the child. In J. M. Tanner & B. Inhelder (Eds.), _Discussions
   on child development._ (Vol. 4). London: Tavistock, 1960.
Piaget, J. Piaget's theory. In P. H. Mussen (Ed.), _Carmichael's_

manual of child psychology. New York: Wiley, 1970. (a)

Piaget, J. A conversation with Jean Piaget. Psychology Today, 1970, 3(12), 25-32. (b)

Sigel, I. E. The Piagetian system and the world of education. In D. Elkind & J. H. Flavell (Eds.), Studies in cognitive development. New York: Oxford University Press, 1969.

Sinclair, H. Recent Piagetian research in learning studies. In M. Schwebel & J. Raph (Eds.), Piaget in the classroom. New York: Basic Books, 1973.

Skinner, B. F. About behaviorism. New York: Knopf, 1974.

IMPLICATIONS AND APPLICATIONS

OF PIAGET'S SENSORIMOTOR CONCEPTS

John Churcher

Department of Psychology
University of Manchester
Manchester M13 9PL   U.K.

ADAPTATION, ASSIMILATION AND ACCOMMODATION

For Piaget, the only invariants are functional ones: the same function is served by a variety of structures in different places at different times. In biology, the function of circulation, for example, is served by different but in some sense analogous structures in different organisms, or in the same organism at different moments of its development. And within this conception of biology, it is only the functional identity between morphologically diverse structures that gives you any principle of functional classification of organs. The two most general functional invariants are adaptation and organization. Piaget defines adaptation as a "progressive equilibrium between two component processes, assimilation and accommodation" (Piaget, 1953 (1936), p.6). These two processes constitute the relationship between an organism (or a scheme or a structure) and its environment. The organism is regarded as a closed cycle of state transformations:

$$a \rightarrow b, \ b \rightarrow c, \ c \rightarrow \ldots \rightarrow a \ \ldots$$

To each state, there corresponds (in some sense of corresponds) a certain state or element of the environment whose occurrence or presence is necessary for the transformation to the next state of organism, thus:

$$a+x \rightarrow b, \ b+y \rightarrow c, \ c+z \rightarrow \ldots \rightarrow a, \ \ldots$$

State a combines in some way with x to give b, b combines with y to give c, and so on (where x, y, z, $\ldots$ are the elements in the

environment, corresponding to $\underline{a}$, $\underline{b}$, $\underline{c}$, ..., the successive states
of the organism). Assimilation is simply whatever is denoted by
those plus signs; the continual and repeated incorporation of the
environment into the cycle of state transformations. And what
Piaget calls a scheme is just the cycle itself, considered as a
finite, abstract entity rather than as the indefinitely long
sequence of repeated transformations which, in a sense, it
generates; it's an abstract object, like a grammar.

But pure assimilation can't occur, or at least it can't last,
because the environment is always changing. What happens if
element $\underline{x}$ of the environment fails to occur and is replaced by
$\underline{x}'$? Either the cycle grinds to a halt (death in the case of an
organism, or the action just stops in the case of a scheme), or
some other way to complete it must be found. And if some other
way is found, then $\underline{a} + \underline{x}'$ will result in some other state $\underline{b}'$,
which like $\underline{b}$ is capable of combining with $\underline{y}$ to form $\underline{c}$. The
transformation or substitution of $\underline{b}$ into $\underline{b}'$ is what Piaget calls
accommodation.

So the scheme only exists by constantly and repeatedly
assimilating elements of the environment; it can assimilate in a
constantly changing environment only by repeatedly accommodating
to it; and in accommodating, the scheme is transformed. Obvious
examples of assimilation are the biochemical processes involved in
digestion and metabolism, which continually reproduce an organism
capable of digesting and metabolizing. But Piaget intends the
concept to have a much more general application.

SENSORIMOTOR SCHEMES AND RECIPROCAL ASSIMILATION

The inclusion of a new particular under some concept, i.e. a
judgement, is an example of assimilation at the level of
operational thought; whereas sensorimotor assimilation is a
function of sensorimotor schemes, i.e. cycles of muscular
activation and of physical movements of the body, with sensory
feedback (for example, grasping an object or sucking). Such
sensorimotor schemes, which first appear in the infant as the
rhythmical-cyclic functioning of a reflex organization, are forced
to accommodate by material properties of the objects they
encounter. As I shall argue, they accommodate to much more than
that, and that's the interesting point, but they are at least
forced to accommodate to the material properties of the object
they encounter. An obvious example is that when the hand grasps a
stick or someone else's finger, it necessarily takes up a certain
posture (with all that that involves in terms of a temporary
equilibrium of motor-kinesthetic processes, and so on) that is
different from that involved in grasping an orange, a piece of
blanket, someone else's nose, or even empty air (i.e. the hand
itself). And when grasping persists in such a circumstance, that

is to say, when adaptation does occur and the cycle does not break down, then the accommodation is evident in the morphology of the movement itself.

I shall not try to give a complete summary of Piaget's theory of sensorimotor development; rather, what I want to do is to pick out what I think are certain crucial applications of the concept of sensorimotor assimilation which are relevant to what we're discussing here, particularly the concept of reciprocal assimilation which for Piaget is the means of coordination between different sensorimotor schemes. Consider, for example, the coordination between the schemes of moving the hand and the schemes of looking and seeing. Note that, for Piaget, looking is not a passive process in contrast to grasping; it's just as active.* In Piaget's account, you start with two independent sensorimotor structures: an organized scheme of the hand, for which the eye and everything else in the universe is some external, unknown object; and an organized scheme of the visual system, for which the hand and all its motions are unknown, external. From this situation of mutual independence at a sensorimotor level (though in fact they have been preceded by a coordination at a biological level, as we shall discuss below) a process of coordination takes place in development which results in a new composite scheme, not of grasping at something feelable or looking at something visible, but of grasping at something seen or of looking at something grasped. How does that coordination occur? Piaget is explicitly dismissing any associationist account:

> "...we place in opposition to the passive concept of association the active concept of assimilation. That which is fundamental and without which no relationship between sight and hand movements could be established is that the hand's activity constitutes schemes which tend to conserve and reproduce themselves (opening and closing, grasping bodies and holding them, etc.). Through the very fact of this tendency toward conservation such activity incorporates in itself every reality capable of supporting it. This explains why the hand grasps that which it encounters, etc. Now comes the moment when the child looks at his hand which is moving. On the one hand he is led, by visual interest,

---

*Unlike grasping, the adaptation involved in looking is not as manifest in the morphology of the behavior. Nevertheless, strictly speaking, in both cases the adaptation is only partially observable: you can watch the movements of eyes or hands; you can't see what goes on in the retina or the joints.

to make this spectacle last - that is to say, not to
take his eyes off his hand; on the other hand, he is
led, by kinesthetic and motor interest, to make this
manual activity last. It is then that the coordination
of the two schemes operates, not by association, but by
reciprocal assimilation. The child discovers that in
moving his hand in a certain way (more slowly, etc.) he
conserves this interesting image for his sight. Just as
he assimilates to his glance the movement of his hands,
so also he assimilates to his manual activity the
corresponding visual image. He moves with his hands the
image he contemplates just as he looks with his eyes at
the image he produces. Whereas until now only tactile
objects served as aliments for the manual schemes,
visual images now become material for exercises of the
hands. It is in this sense that they may be called
'assimilated' to the sensorimotor activity of the arms
and hands." Piaget, 1936 (1953), pp.107-108

Try to think phenomenologically about this. Piaget is saying that
in moving the hand in one way rather than another, the infant can
control an image for the visual system, i.e. prolong and reproduce
the conditions for a certain assimilatory functioning of the
visual system, even though the movement is controlled by the
manual system. From this moment onwards there is a new structure,
which eventually becomes the composite scheme of grasping
something seen or looking at something grasped.

The first thing to be said about reciprocal assimilation is
that it provides a mechanism of transformation between
sensorimotor stages in Piaget's theory. Stages should be
conceived as the starting-points and end-points of
transformations; in this respect the concept of a stage is
secondary, and the primary concepts are those which refer to
transformations. The stage is only interesting in this context
because it defines that moment of temporary and relative
equilibrium at the beginning or at the end of a transformation -
where it is coming from, or where it is going to.

SCHEMES AS OBJECTS OF ASSIMILATION; MATERIAL REALITY AS SOCIAL

The second thing about reciprocal assimilation (and I haven't
seen this stated clearly anywhere by Piaget or anyone else) is
that what gets assimilated is not just an inert, physical object.
In the reciprocal assimilation of eye and hand, the looking scheme
assimilates the hand in movement; but given the abstract form of
the assimilatory scheme, this is tantamount to assimilating the
abstract entity manifested in that movement, i.e. the manual
scheme itself. (In an analogous sense, learning to understand
speech is tantamount to 'acquiring' a grammar). Thus reciprocal

assimilation means, literally, the assimilation of scheme A by scheme B and vice versa.

Now although this point about the schematic nature of the assimilated object comes out most clearly in the case of reciprocal assimilation, I think it has profound implications for a more general interpretation of Piaget's sensorimotor concepts. If the objects of assimilation were themselves always schemes, then assimilation would be as much a social relation as a physical one. Piaget always argued, though it is often overlooked, that from the onset of concrete operations at about 7 or 8 years the coordination between individuals, the social coordination of action, is as important as the intra-individual coordination. (For examples, consider the coordination between your two hands, and that between you and me in building a bridge or carrying a piece of furniture). He repeatedly stressed that there is no difference in principle between these two sources of coordination, and in practice both are necessary for the development of operational thought. (Piaget, 1951, pp. 165 et seq.)

But if the object of assimilation were always itself a scheme, there could not be any non-social objects even for an 'egocentric' subject. In fact, the world of the infant does not consist of an array of objects given by nature; it consists of a materially produced and socialised world, which is just as socialised in the case of external things as is that special, privileged object, your own body. It is a world of things that are presented to the child, shown to it, put in its hands or in front of its eyes; the child is picked up, carried around, brought to face things. In this sense, the objects of assimilation are always schemes, whether or not they all 'belong' to the same individual. Reciprocal assimilation occurs between schemes in different individuals as well as within an individual, and the ways in which this happens are part of our social practice, and all objects of sensorimotor knowledge are caught up in it. Thus there is no natural, non-social relationship between an infant and an object; the infant lives in a world in which things are as essentially social as they are material.

GLEITMAN: Are you saying there are no natural objects in the world that the child would perceive as objects?

CHURCHER: I am making a theoretical point which I think goes against the prevailing zeitgeist. Sinha has tried to develop the concept of canonicality in the object-concept: he has shown that in an object-permanence task it matters whether a cup used as an occluding object is presented the normal or the wrong way up. (Freeman, Lloyd and Sinha, 1980) The cup is not just an object with physical properties; it is embedded in a social practice, and the child can only see it as such. You can't partition the

child's cognition into its relationship with the social world and
its relationship with the physical world.

MINSKY: It seems you're throwing out this baby with its
bathwater. You've made an advance in suggesting that the
different parts of the mind are partly separate. My real
objection to the discussion of memory was that, implicit in this
idea of memory retrieval, was the idea that there's only one
memory and that anything put in it should be automatically
retrievable; whereas I feel on theoretical grounds that this idea
(that the hand has a mind, and the vision has a mind, and these
aren't ego minds, but they do different things and have to
communicate) is very sound. Now, it seems to me, in the
enthusiasm of that you're destroying your own point and heading
into another pit.

CHURCHER: Why?

MINSKY: Because I think that there must surely be physical
minds and social minds, and by making this canonical idea you're
going to get into just as serious troubles as the ones you've
criticized. I think that children probably have an innate and
well-built piece of machinery for seeing natural objects in
certain ways that are not social, and that these have to interact
with the social things. So that indeed there's a problem of
seeing a cup upside down, and the problem is going to be the
interaction of these two ways.

CHURCHER: I appreciate there's an issue here; can we leave it
for now?

SENSORIMOTOR COGNITION AFTER THE SENSORIMOTOR PERIOD

It's not often recognized that Piaget's concept of
sensorimotor cognition applies to adults as well as infants. You
don't leave your sensorimotor cognition behind as you grow up; you
couldn't survive without it, because you need it to get in and out
of this room. Rather, it persists in a different psychological
context. Piaget gives a detailed example: driving a car, he uses
a cloth to wipe the steering-wheel, then pushes it between the
seats to get rid of it; later he is searching for something to
prop open the windshield:

> I look around me but nothing is in evidence. While
> looking at the windshield I have the impression that the
> object could be put, not at the bottom of the windshield
> (one pushed it at the bottom to open it), but by wedging
> itin the angle formed by the right edge of the
> windshield and the vertical upright of the body of the
> car. I have the vague feeling of an analogy between the

solution to be found and a problem already solved
before. The solution then becomes clarified. My
tendency to put an object in the corner of the
windshield meets a sort of motor memory of having just a
few minutes before placed something into a crevice. I
try to remember what it was, but no definite
representation comes to mind. Then suddenly, without
having time to imagine anything, I understand the
solution and find myself already in the act of searching
with my hand for the hidden handkerchief. Therefore the
latter scheme directed my search and directed me toward
the lateral corner of the windshield when my last idea
was a different one." (Piaget 1953 (1936) p. 345 fn.)

Here there is an interaction between a high-level, reflective
representation and the actual problem-solving which occurs by
sensorimotor reciprocal assimilation. It is sometimes assumed
that different levels of functioning (what you do with your hands,
as well as what you do with the English language) can all be due
to various kinds of symbol-manipulation. I can't provide a cast-
iron reason why that assumption is wrong in general, but I think
the burden of the argument should be on anyone who wanted to
assume it. When your car goes wrong and you develop "cognitive
tunnel vision", and persist in doing the same thing over and over
again fruitlessly (e.g. pressing the carbureter), from a Piagetian
viewpoint one should not think of that as a high-level process
that has become restricted in scope; rather, the restriction
reflects the temporary dominance of sensorimotor functioning.
Then, at a higher level you become aware of yourself repeating the
action, and this reflective process inaugurates an interaction
between the two qualitatively different cognitive domains, of
which only one may involve symbolic processes.

SENSORIMOTOR KNOWLEDGE OF 4-D SPACE

I'd like to give an example from something I'm starting to
work on, where I think taking Piaget's sensorimotor concepts
seriously may do some good. Allan Muir, of the Mathematics
Department in the City University (London), and I have started to
investigate the development in adults of sensorimotor knowledge of
objects in four-dimensional Euclidean space, under active
manipulation with real-time visual feedback. A number of
investigators have observed the two-dimensional projections of
objects moving in four-space (MacKay, 1955; Noll, 1967; Sperling,
1976; Johannsson, 1980; Davis and Hersh, 1981). Davis and Hersh
describe their experience of rotating a hypercube as follows:

"The user sits at a control panel in front of a TV
screen. Three knobs permit him to rotate a four-
dimensional figure on any pair of axes in four-space.

As he does so, he sees on the screen the different
three-dimensional figures which would meet our three-
dimensional space as the four-dimensional figure rotates
through it...

"I tried turning the hypercube around, moving it away,
bringing it up close, turning it around another way.
Suddenly I could <u>feel</u> it! The hypercube had leapt into
palpable reality, as I learned how to manipulate it,
feeling in my fingertips the power to change what I saw
and change it back again. The active control at the
computer console created a union of kinesthetics and
visual thinking which brought the hypercube up to the
level of intuitive understanding...

"The existence of this possibility opens up new
prospects for research on mathematical intuition.
Instead of working with children or with ethnographic or
historical material, as we must do to study the genesis
of elementary geometric intuition (the school of
Piaget), one could work with adults ..." (Davis & Hersh,
1981, pp. 403-404)

Our own experience of manipulating the hypercube does not yet
corroborate that reported by Davis and Hersh,* but if we can
confirm their results we should be able to reinvestigate in 4-
space some aspects of what the infant, according to Piaget, goes
through in sensorimotor development in 3-space, in particular the
reciprocal assimilation between vision and prehension. We are
making the representation of the motor process less arbitrary by
building a single 'virtual hand' in 4-space, such that to each
pair of positions of the operator's two real hands there
corresponds a position of the virtual hand; the 10 degrees of
freedom required (4 displacements and 6 rotations) are split
symmetrically between the two manipulanda, which have 5 each. If
visuo-manual coordination, object invariance, etc., develop anew
in such a world, then the dimensionality of spatial intuition, as
Poincaré guessed (Poincaré, 1905), cannot be the psychological
given that Kant believed it to be. And one can create worlds
stranger than this, e.g. non-Euclidean ones.

---

* To date we have only had limited experience of a hypercube, and of a few other rigid 'wire' objects in four-space,
with and without stereo viewing of the 3-D projection. We
use the quaternion representation of the group of rotations,
which requires 6 separate controls for rotations, not 3 as
used by Davis & Hersh.

GLEITMAN: Is sensorimotor action a <u>necessary</u> way to learn about the world? What would Piaget say about a paralyzed child, for example? Would its conceptions of objects be inadequate? Or is it a weaker claim than that?

CHURCHER: I think there is a mistake in understanding being made by many people, a mistake that Piaget specifically warned against, which is that of collapsing the psychological and the biological. For Piaget, psychological assimilation is an extension of biological assimilation onto a different level. The reason why the sensorimotor period is there, according to Piaget, is because it's the only way you can get from biology to logic. You can't do it in one step; you have to go in two. The only way you get from digestion to judgement, from assimilating a piece of food to assimilating a new particular under a concept, is through the intermediate step of sensorimotor assimilation of an object.

You can show that an infant has a supramodal space by experiments on facial imitation (Meltzoff, 1982); you can show that it has precocious reaching for visible objects (Bower,1974). But what such findings mean depends crucially on whether they reflect a biological property of the organism (which has none of the open-ended and, I think, in Boden's sense, creative possibilities), or whether you are showing something at a sensorimotor level. Piaget was clearly aware that vision and prehension, for example, show innate reflex coordination (Piaget, 1957, p. 74).

BODEN: There are some studies of a Thalidomide child who was above average intelligence and perfectly normal on all the tests of spatial concepts and so forth. This is a child without any limbs at all, who could only just bat objects with its trunk; but still the concepts come.

MINSKY: Papert had a 17-year-old who was terribly handicapped in flailing around and had never controlled anything; and he was remarkably good at constructing those turtle scenes and making trains and figuring out which way to orient things. And then what he did was to become rather a good programmer. He used to just sit there and imagine rather long programs and then come in the next day and produce them rapidly. This was a bright 17-year-old who was thought to be very retarded. So there are such anecdotes.

CHURCHER: Yes, there are. But no-one could survive to the age of 17 if they hadn't got a fantastic amount of sensorimotor structure already, even if they hadn't got limbs.

SUBJECT, BODY AND PROSTHESIS

My interpretation of assimilation as always having a schematic object, and our investigation of 4-D manipulation, have been stimulated by the work of Andre Bullinger in Geneva and Jean Pailhous in Marseilles. In a recent paper, Bullinger (1982) has developed Piaget's sensorimotor theory starting from a clarification of the distinction between the subject and the subject's body. Not only during early sensorimotor coordination in infancy, but throughout life, the body is 'cognitively transparent' only when the subject is not confronted by new tasks. A new task brings out new, objective properties of the body - physical and informational properties which were always latent within it as a complex, organized, biological object, but which never had to be internalized until the moment when the new task or situation made them evident. Learning to use a pencil throws up new material (physical & informational) properties of the hand that were not known or knowable through any previous experience, and until you internalize these you cannot use a pencil as an extension of your body.

This idea has consequences for what we understand by "innate". Bullinger's best example is that of the retina itself, which may be neurologically wired up to the superior colliculus and visual cortex at birth as a result of embryological development, but which has to be cognitively internalized before it can be used. The default assumption in most work on eye-movements, whether in children or adults, is that where you point your eyes is where you are preferentially sampling information from; but this will only be true when the task you are engaged on does not present new problems in terms of the objective properties of your eyes. What an infant may be doing, in looking to and fro between two objects, is putting into relation not just those objects but two spatial locations on the retina, i.e. coordinating by reciprocal assimilation the acts of fovealisation and peripheralization of images.

From this perspective, there is a functional equivalence between parts of your body, artificial sensory prostheses, and tools: a blind person's stick, an aeroplane (for the pilot), a mechanical digger (for its operator), the 'sonic guide' that a few blind babies have now worn, the tactile stimulator attached to the skin and connected to a video camera on the head (Bach-y-Rita, 1972). But such artefacts also have in common the fact that although the users' internalization of them may change and develop, they themselves do not. A stick, for example, does not adapt when you use it as a probe, it doesn't change its informational material properties (even though new situations may arise which reveal hitherto unused properties). Nor does the camera on your head change its way of transferring information to the stimulator on your skin.

LIVING WITH AN ADAPTIVE PROSTHESIS

But what will happen when the prosthesis is adaptive? Supposing you have a microprocessor between the camera and the stimulator which is adapting in some way to the conditions under which it is being used, at the same time as you are using it and, as it were, internalizing it. Or suppose you have a remote manipulator, of the kind used for handling materials in inaccessible environments, and instead of merely reproducing the operator's hand movements, the system modifies itself as some function of the way it is used. Then, if the prosthesis is complex anyway, you have an interesting problem, for which a good analogy is the relationship between the rider and the horse: what is the distinction between communication with such a system and control of it?

That brings me on to Pask's paper. Twenty two years ago, at the seminar at which Selfridge presented a well-known theological paper (Selfridge, 1959), Pask discussed a chemical computer which grew thread-like metal electrodes existing in a dynamic equilibrium between deposition and re-solution of ions (Pask, 1959). He used this object to illustrate a general principle concerning the relationship between a human being and a complex system: if someone is to attribute thinking (and specifically concept formation) to a machine, i.e. to treat the machine as having cognitive processes similar to his or her own, he or she must adopt the stance of a participant observer, interacting with the system and not merely observing it:

> "...it is possible to attribute concept formation to something outside of myself, if, and only if, there is a field of activity common to myself and the system concerned.... ...the rider might say the horse "thinks" because he participates with it in solving the problems that are set by a common environment, namely the topography of the place in which the horse is ridden." (Pask, 1959 p.881)

But this interaction, directed to some end, creates a new object, the combined system of observer and machine, which is all the observer can describe:

> "...it would be fruitless to ask whether the trainer, by continual training, had imposed his way of thinking upon the animal's decision process or whether due to continual proximity the man had horse-like or dog-like thoughts in his head. It seems impossible to usefully separate the two components of the interacting system

which have become functionally indistinguishable."
(Pask, 1959 p.891)

Pask goes on to make it a condition on any interesting machine that it

"force the observer to interact with it, in the sense that interaction yields benefits. It must be an assemblage for which the reference frame is badly specified and we are seeking a physical condition on the assemblage which makes a well specified reference frame difficult or impossible to construct" (Pask, 1959 p.892)

A sufficient condition for the reference frame being badly specified is that there not be a fixed mapping between structural and functional units.

"Thus we are led to consider an assemblage which is less of a machine, and more of a plexus of elements." (Pask, 1959 p.894)

It still remains to be seen whether Pask's intuitions concerning hardware (along with those of a generation of enthusiasts for self-organizing systems) are technically realisable. Certainly, the fashion for highly-parallel systems is now enjoying a re-emergence after a twenty year eclipse. But even at the level of simulation I would suggest that cellular automata might be a fruitful alternative.

PIAGET, A.I. AND CELLULAR AUTOMATA

This brings me to the implications for artificial intelligence and simulation of Piaget's notion of assimilation. In a way, Pask's model was, knowingly or unknowingly, an attempt to do something very similar to what Piaget might have done if he'd been born thirty years later and were trying to produce an AI model.

Firstly, suppose we interpret Piaget's formal model of assimilation as a cellular automaton; what would be the conditions for adaptation? To make this clear, imagine a two-dimensional matrix whose elements consist of instructions which are either L ("turn left") or R ("turn right"). Suppose you are following a path through this, and it's a closed path, let's say, and you've got four elements in the cycle: L,L,L,L. There you have a closed state transformation system. Supposing God or a cosmic ray alters one or more of the elements in the matrix, then Piaget's question concerning adaptation becomes: what are the conditions for the re-closing of the loop by another means? (It is embedded in a large matrix with random elements L or R).

Secondly, supposing we have adaptive cellular automata, and two of them meet, we might have a model for the process of reciprocal assimilation.

Thirdly, if in a real machine, e.g. a robot with hands and eyes, such automata were made to function as indices of the instantaneous physical state of the machine, and if reciprocal assimilation between the automata occurred, it might be possible to produce robots that developed their own hand-eye coordination rather than having to have it pre-programmed.

CONCLUDING QUESTIONS

I'm going to finish by asking some questions:

1. What are the primitives to be? One aspect of this problem is whether the primitives can be developmental or not. Widespread in current AI and psychology, there is an epistemological assumption concerning the order of logical priority between transformations and states. It is that when you have worked out the states of the system at times T1 and T2, only then you will be in a position to understand the transformation between state 1 and state 2, and that in this sense the development of a system is more complex than a time slice through it. I think this assumption should be questioned. We might equally well say that the notion of transformation is primitive, and we can only understand what a state of a system is in terms of the starting point or end point of a transformation. That's just as logical an idea as the former one. Piaget, however, rejects both of these in favor of the dialectical proposition: there can be no genesis without structure, no structure without genesis (see Piaget, 1968 (1964)).

2. A second aspect of the problem about primitives is whether they are spatial or not. Piaget, Pask and Poincaré all give the same answer to the question: "How do we recognize invariance?" We identify invariance, they say, with group structure (in the mathematical sense). For Poincaré, the group presented no psychological problem, because he regarded the re-identification of states over time as a priori and thus the distinction in general between changes of state and changes of place, i.e. between non-spatial and spatial transformations, is given by the group of displacements. (The intuition of any particular geometry, however, was for Poincaré ultimately a matter of 'convention'; and Poincaré was among the first clearly to discuss the possibility of developing non-standard spatial intuitions and specifically of 4-space).

For Piaget, the re-identification of particular states presupposes an assimilatory structure, so the group is not cognitively given but constructed, on the basis of the 'practical' groups implicit in the spatial structure of action.

In terms of AI the question is the one somebody asked Marr at a Royal Society meeting a few years ago: "What is the distinction between a spatial and a non-spatial algorithm?". Marr, as far as I could tell, did not recognize that as a sensible question. Is it? If so, what is the answer?

3. Finally, why are rigor and formalizability regarded as equivalent? No-one asks for a formalizable theory of glaciation, but there is arguably a fairly rigorous one. Piaget insisted on this distinction, knowing that his own notion of the 'grouping' (a species of degenerate group), while central to his theory was hard to formalize.

"The central idea of this work is that formalization is not a state, but a process, and that consequently it depends on structures which are worked out stage by stage" (Piaget, 1971, pp. xii-xiii, my translation).

MINSKY: A distinction that people feel is important is whether there is a small handful of axioms or a huge knowledge base. That is, something is not considered formal if it has a thousand axioms, because you can't do much with it. I don't think there's much more to it than that, is there?

CHURCHER: What about the proof of the four-color problem?

MINSKY: That only take a few axioms, whereas glaciers takes a lot, unless you believe in exclusion principles. You see, my complaint is that Piaget, Pask and Poincaré are all pre-computational, which is why they agree on groups. Because until them there wasn't anything but groups. But now this great structure of ideas about computational complexity and ways of distinguishing between different kinds of algorithms has appeared, and you're admiring the past. And I think the time to admire the past is in another 25 years when the new ideas have run out, rather than fighting them off now.

CHURCHER: Then is the question: "What is the difference between a spatial and a non-spatial algorithm?" meaningful?

MINSKY: Probably that's very meaningful because spatial algorithms have something to do with two- or three-dimensional symmetry groups.

CHURCHER: That seems to be at odds with what you were saying before.

MINSKY: It is? I'm saying spatial algorithms can exploit the symmetries of space, which are very simple , so you can do a lot with that sort of thing. However, you can get carried away, and groups won't help you tell a dog from a cat. And David Marr's algorithms unfortunately, although he understood the retina slightly better than his predecessors, did not advance pattern recognition because he didn't develop non-spatial algorithms with vision. He explored very deeply what could be done with two-dimensional symmetric calculations. To me it was a disappointment, because in 1970 we could tell dogs from cats slightly better than in 1980 in our laboratory.

REFERENCES

Bach-y-Rita, P., 1972, "Sensory Substitution", Academic Press, New York.
Bower, T.G.R., 1974, "Development in Infancy", W.H. Freeman and Company, San Francisco.
Bullinger, A., 1981, Cognitive Elaboration of Sensorimotor Behavior, in: "Infancy and Epistemology," G. Butterworth, ed., Harvester Press, Brighton.
Davis, P. and Hersh, R., 1981, "The Mathematical Experience", Birkhauser, Boston.
Freeman, N.H., Lloyd, S., and Sinha, C.G., 1980, Infant search tasks reveal early concepts of containment and canonical usage of objects, Cognition, 8:243.
Johansson, G., 1980, personal communication.
MacKay, D.M., 1955, High speed electronic analogue computing techniques, J. Inst. Electr. Eng., 102:609.
Meltzoff, A., 1981, Imitation, intermodal coordination and representation in early infancy, in: "Infancy and Epistemology", G. Butterworth, ed., Harvester Press, Brighton.
Noll, A.M., 1967, A computer technique for displaying n-dimensional hyperobjects, Communications of the A.C.M., 10:469.
Pask, G., 1959, Physical analogues to the growth of a concept, in "Mechanisation of Thought Precesses", (N.P.L. Symposium No. 10), H.M.S.O., London.
Piaget, J., 1951, "The Psychology of Intelligence", Routledge and Kegan Paul Ltd., London.
Piaget, J., 1953, "The Origins of Intelligence",,Routledge and Kegan Paul Ltd., London.
Piaget, J., 1957, "Logique et Equilibre", Presses Universitaires de France, Paris.

Piaget, J., 1968, "Six Psychological Studies", Harvester Press,
        Brighton.
Piaget, J., 1971, "Essai de Logique Operatoire", Dunod, Paris.
Poincaré, H., 1905, "Science and Method", Dover Publications,
        New York.
Selfridge, O.G., 1959, Pandemonium: a Paradigm for learning, in:
        Mechanisation of Thought Processes", (N.P.L. Symposium
        No. 10), H.M.S.O., London.
Sperling, G., 1976, Movement perception in computer-driven visual
        displays, Beh. Res. Meth. Inst., 8:144.

FAILURE IS NOT THE SPUR

Margaret A. Boden

University of Sussex
Brighton
England

The concept of "ill-defined system" collapses into triviality
if it is used to refer to any system that has not yet been well
defined. One might take it rather to mean one that can never be
understood in a well-defined way. This interpretation, however,
invites troublesome disputes over what is to count as "well-defined",
and also prejudges the question of whether human knowledge will
ever be adequate to the system concerned. For instance, Schrodinger's
wave-equations are mathematically well-defined, but they concern
quantum phenomena which many would regard as a paradigm case of ill-
definedness; and though the Copenhagen School believed this ill-
definedness to be grounded at the ontological level, Einstein cited
his conviction that "God does not play at dice" in interpreting
quantum indeterminacy as a merely epistemological matter.

So let us rather say that an ill-defined system is one with
respect to which certain prima facie relevant types of theoretical
description are inappropriate, because they treat the system as
being more well-defined in a specific respect than it actually is.
This prompts us to specify the ways in which certain currently
available theoretical approaches are inadequate to characterize the
system, while leaving open the question whether any satisfactory
theoretical description of it can in principle be found.

Minds (especially human minds) are ill-defined in a number of
ways. That is, there are several sorts of theoretical description
that one might expect to apply to mental phenomena but which are
in fact inappropriate, because each wrongly assumes that minds are
well-defined in some specific way in which they are not. As I have
argued at length elsewhere (Boden, 1972) there are at least five
aspects of mental life with respect to which this is true. (It is

305

sometimes claimed that the insights of Merleau-Ponty, Wittgenstein, and Godel show that minds are ill-defined in other ways too; I have discussed these arguments in (Boden, 1977, ch. xiv).)

   First, minds are intentional systems, whose actions are mediated by inner representations; so they cannot be described by the natural sciences, whose terms do not make any distinction between the "subject" and the "object" of thought. Second, because of what Perry called "the independent variability of purpose and belief" and others have called "the hermeneutic circle" (Perry, 1921; Taylor, 1971) there can be no behavioral definition of their goals, intentions, or beliefs. Third, they are symbolic systems within which complex structural transformations take place, transformations that cannot be defined in the (quantitative rather than qualitative) information-processing terms of classical cybernetics -- i.e. the cybernetics of feedback and adaptive networks, prior to the incorporation of notions of symbolic knowledge structures, etc., gleaned from artificial intelligence (AI). Fourth, they are systems with a rich generative potential, which cannot be conceptualized in terms of general laws linking dependent and independent variables. And last, they use many purely conventional symbols, so that statistical averaging over the stimulus input may fail to capture crucial differences: compare the effects of a telegram saying "Our son is dead" and one saying "Your son is dead", where only a single letter distinguishes the two messages.

   All these characteristics, each of which identifies a sense in which minds are ill-defined systems, apply also to complex AI programs. Since the latter are, in one important sense of the term, eminently well-defined -- for they are rigorously specified by the instructions comprising the program -- it should be clear that, as I noted above, "ill-definedness" is not an absolute term: it is always relative to some type of definition or explanation which one might prima facie expect to be relevant to the system in question.

   A sixth way in which minds are ill-defined systems, which is especially important in relation to theories of adaptive control, is that they do not function merely so as to minimize and correct failures. They are not controlled simply by the degree of match-mismatch between the current state and a specific goal-state. That is, failure is not the prime trigger of cognitive change, and adaptive control cannot be explained in terms only of differential response to distinct classes of failure.

   There are two reasons for doubting the centrality of failure in development. First, even where behavior is of a sort to which the concept of failure can sensibly be applied, failure is neither necessary nor sufficient for adaptive change. Adaptation without the goad of failure is shown, for example, by children drawing maps, who spontaneously improve their spatial representations although

they are successfully solving the problem set (Karmiloff-Smith,
1979). To be sure, their increased computational efficiency enables
them to solve problems later which they could not have solved before,
but it was not forced on them by any earlier mistake. Failure without adaptation occurs when it is recognized and yet ignored, treated
as an inexplicable nuisance rather than as a spur to development.
For instance, studies of children's understanding of balance-
problems suggest that events initially ignored as anomalies are
only later taken seriously as counterexamples enabling refinement
of the child's current theory (Inhelder & Karmiloff-Smith, 1975).

Second, a point which will turn out to be intimately related
to the previous one: theories focussed on failure implicitly assume
that the mind is well-defined in a way in which it is not. Failure
can be the main factor in adaptation only if organisms always aim
at some specific goal. For a failure is always a failure to do
something specific, in that the concept of "failure" invites the
question "failure to do what?" Insofar as behavior is not goal-
directed, then, the mind is an ill-defined system requiring
explanation in other terms.

In fact, creatures do not always aim at pre-defined goals, but
often appear to delight in activity for its own sake. Or rather,
they commonly aim at goals (such as economy, clarity, elegance, and
interestingness) which are high level meta-goals that control the
adaptive exploration of their own cognitive processes. Because
people commonly think of "goal-directedness" in terms of relatively
specific, well-defined goals, to conceive of adaptation in terms of
response to failure is to risk losing sight of the exploratory
aspects of thought and action. Learning, development, and creativity
are not mere responses to failure, which is neither necessary nor
sufficient for adaptation. They are controlled by more general
considerations than match-mismatch with a specific goal-state, and
they are grounded in some relatively autonomous creative urge (n.b.
this concept is not "ill-defined," as I am using the term, but vague).

How can we conceptualize such an urge (the evolutionary advantage of which is obvious)? Like the "track and trail" strategies
of lowly organisms (Selfridge, in press), it must both lead the
creature to engage spontaneously in novel behavior, and enable it
to take advantage of the results when this exploration throws up
something useful. This of course implies that the creature has
available some form of evaluation function in terms of which it can
recognize something "useful," or at least "interesting." "Track and
trail" may describe some aspects of the exploratory activity of the
higher animals (for instance, the locomotion of predators who have
not yet scented game). But it cannot be used as a paradigm for all
adaptive control, because (as posited above) the mind is a richly-
structured system that cannot be described by classical cybernetics.
If creative exploration is not to degenerate (sic) into mere chaotic

novelty, the generation of new forms, as well as their consequent evaluation, must take place within certain structural constraints. In general, to understand a creative phenomenon would be to have a theory of the various transformations, at more or less basic levels, by which the relevant structural potential can be selectively explored.

For instance, mathematical, scientific, and artistic creativity involve the deliberate exploration and disciplined transformation, or relaxation, of structural constraints. Non-Euclidean geometry originated in the (deliberate) dropping of Euclid's last axiom. Kekule's discovery of the benzene ring involved the (unconscious) transformation of one topological structure into another; it is significant that Kekule dreamt not of a little girl's hoop, but of a snake biting its tail -- in other words, of a closed curve that one would have expected to be an open curve. A prime root of Einstein's creative achievement was his query whether the concept of simultaneity can be analysed and the resultant "parts" variously combined to form distinct conceptual structures. And the development of tonal into atonal music, in broadly the way in which this happened, can with hindsight be seen as intelligible, and even inevitable (Rosen, 1978). In all of these cases, of course, the initial transformation (which may or may not have been consciously effected) was followed by some sort of evaluative assessment, whether by mathematical proof, experimental method, or artistic discipline. Everyday adaptation presumably involves similar transformational processes, with varying opportunities for conscious initiation and/or control, and varying criteria of "interestingness."

In the biological domain, a theory of morphological creativity would explain how it is possible for a gill-slit to be transformed into a thyroid gland, or a normal blastula into a deformed embryo or non-viable monster; also, it would explain why certain fabulous beasts could only have been imagined, not created (Boden, 1981). In biology as in psychology, we need some account of processes that can explore the space defined by background creative constraints, and of processes that can transform these constraints themselves.

Some psychologists have stressed the role of exploratory play in the development of cognitive skills, positing autonomous motives such as "competence" or "curiosity," but they have said little or nothing about mental structures (White, 1959). Piaget, by contrast, realized that the life sciences need some concept of autonomous adaptive creativity, characterized in structural terms. In his account of "equilibration" he tried to illuminate the way in which new, more differentiated, structures arise out of simpler ones, whether in psychological, embryological, or evolutionary development. He recognized the profound theoretical problem of how it is possible for harmonious structural novelties to develop, along with novel integrative mechanisms whereby the overall regulation of the system is maintained. And he tried to give an account of spontaneous, as opposed to reactive, structural development.

However, as I have argued elsewhere (Boden, 1982), his concept of equilibration was so vaguely expressed that it provided no clear questions, still less clear answers. Attempting to explain psychological adaptation, he made vague reference to "positive and negative disturbances," "regulations," and "regulations of regulations." These cybernetically inspired concepts cannot express qualitatively distinct mental structures and processes. Also, Piaget overestimated the role of failure in development. He spoke of "reproductive, or functional assimilation" as the natural, spontaneous, propensity to exercise one's new skills. But he assumed that this exercise leads to adaptation by way of gradual corrective processes of "accommodation," processes initiated by increasingly demanding assessments of failure.

One might expect computational concepts to be helpful in clarifying Piaget's remarks about cognitive exploration, because they articulate complexities and transformations within symbolic structures (and so provide intentional, or hermeneutic, explanations rather than physical ones). Indeed, much of what Piaget had to say about equilibration can be better stated in these terms (Boden, 1982). However, current "learning" programs are mostly concerned with the fine tuning of already structurally adapted computational systems, rather than with their structural adaptation itself. Some of them, too, overemphasize the role of failure (e.g. Winston, 1975) (although others (e.g. Samuel, 1970) use a hill-climbing strategy controlled by some notion of "getting better"). Almost nothing has been done to model systems where the structuring principles themselves change over time in an integrated fashion. This is a key notion in understanding development and creativity, and this was what primarily concerned Piaget.

For example, Winston's program can recognize only a few properties of the input, these being all and only the relevant ones, each of which was initially defined by the programmer (Winston, 1975). Given these predefined properties, the program can learn from counter-examples as well as from examples, but only if they are presented in an epistemologically suitable (highly constrained) order. A more "Piagetian" self-modifying program is Sussman's HACKER, which can diagnose five classes of mistake and adapt differentially to them, generalizing its adaptive insights so that they can be applied to many problems of the same structural form (Sussman, 1975). It can even modify successful procedures, for example by removing redundant steps, and by replacing repeated code by subroutines. The structure of HACKER's problem-solving does become more complex and differentiated, and better adapted to the specific constraints of the problem-situation. Its creative potential is however very limited, for it is capable of exploring only a small number of transformational paths.

Humans can try out many new ways of thinking to see what they will find. They need not have any problem in mind, to which they hope the exploration may be relevant; even if they do, they may be very unclear about how this could be so. Admittedly, where a newly acquired structure is concerned, people often explore its generative potential without making any attempt to transform the structure itself. For instance, children practice grammatical permutations of words when left alone in their cribs (Weir, 1962). And, as we have seen, children sometimes ignore a failure as an irrelevant anomaly instead of treating it as a spur to adaptation. The experimenters suggested that they need time for "consolidation" of their new theories -- but what is consolidation, and why is it necessary?

I am reminded here of Descartes' fourth rule, "Recapitulate!". At first sight this seems banal in the extreme, qualifying perhaps as mental hygiene but hardly as 25% of "The Right Method of Conducting the Reason." However, it is a fact that recapitulation of an argument -- for example, going over and over a geometrical proof -- may lead one to "see directly" relations which earlier one could only infer by remembering a series of steps. In Descartes' terms, deduction gives way to intuition. And rereading a proof, paper, or program enables one not only to eliminate "howlers," but to find economies, generalizations, and improvements in clarity. Recapitulation, that is, seems to be a method of achieving consolidation.

In general, during the period of consolidation one does things that enable one to represent and improve the structure of the cognitive structure itself. That is, one engages in meta-activities, and/or one follows high-level meta-goals, of various kinds (cf. Rissland, 1978). So one eliminates redundant steps; one constructs higher-level representations that economically summarize a number of already available sub-structures; one explores the sorts of transformation allowed by the unfamiliar structure; one classifies the states that can be generated within it; and one compares this structure with others in various ways.

Until one thus understands the general potential of a structure, one may not be motivated to change it, nor able fruitfully to pay attention to counterexamples to it. Kuhn's (1962) account of the activity of normal science, which continues despite theoretical anomalies, seems to fit this description. So does the exploration of any new artistic style before it is superceded by another. Once consolidation has been achieved, other meta-processes may come into play by which relatively radical changes can be effected. For example, dropping a very basic constraint (such as Euclid's last axiom, or the "stringlike" nature of molecules) may lead to a coherent structure with generative properties very different from its predecessor. Again, combining sub-structures or procedures in different combinations, and with different orders of priority, may be a general method by which the mind can spontaneously generate new structures out of old. The technique of "brainstorming" is based on this principle.

If consolidation is a mapping of the generative geography of one's current structures, a theory of adaptation should explain how one realizes that the terrain has now been reasonably well-mapped, so that more adventurous explorations may be appropriate. Clearly, one's judgments about the extent of unexplored territory must influence the evaluation of what is "interesting." This self-tuning (whereby what is of interest today may be boring tomorrow) is analogous to the successive strengthening of evaluation criteria in "track and trail" adaptation. But in the human case the criterion is non-metric and multi-dimensional: one may have explored some aspects of a structure to one's satisfaction -- indeed, satiation -- but not others.

An adaptive system must also be able to judge the "interest" of the results of its (more or less radical) explorations, and of the exploratory paths it decides to follow. Without this control, which determines what the exploring mind will find worth pursuing, exploration would degrade into mere chaotic thrashing about. Literary criticism, criticism of music or the visual arts, critical history of ideas, and scientific discussion all aim to express our intuitions in this regard. A psychological theory of creativity should try to make these insights even more explicit. This problem is not seriously addressed by theories of "adaptation-levels", "discrepancy principles," and the like (e.g. Helson, 1959), which equate degree of interest with degree of novelty (novelty being measured with respect to the subject's current schemas, or competence). Adaptation is not a matter of nobbling the new, but of pursuing the promising.

A study of creativity which has addressed this question is D. B. Lenat's "automatic mathematician" (Lenat, 1977). This program uses several hundred heuristics (not just a few transformational rules) to explore the space defined by a hundred primitive concepts. "Exploration" here means asking about certain facets of a given (primitive or constructed) concept. For instance: is it named; is it a generalization or a special case of some other concept; what examples fit the definition of the concept; which operations can operate on it, and which can result in it; are there any similar concepts; and what are some potential theorems involving the concept? One of the facets is "interestingness": Lenat attempts to control the exploration by guiding it into areas likely to be more adaptive than others. For instance, he provides it with the general heuristic that if the union of two sets has a simply expressible property not possessed by either of them, then it is probably worth exploring. Lenat claims to have identified several very general heuristics, but also stresses the need for large numbers of domain-specific, knowledge-based heuristics (some of which are specializations of the more general ones).

Granted that the heuristics were thought up by Lenat rather than by the program, it is significant (and surprising to many people) that this sort of fruitful exploratory thinking can be formally represented at all. However, the degree of creativity evinced by the program is difficult to assess. Critics (Hanna & Ritchie, 1981) have remarked that Lenat does not list all the concepts regarded by the program as interesting: perhaps a high proportion were mathematically trivial. It is not clear from the published accounts whether some crucial "discoveries" were made possible only by the use of unacceptably ad hoc heuristics, nor is it easy to draw the line between an acceptably specialized expert heuristic and a disingenuous programming trick. Certainly, many of the heuristics are highly domain-specific, relevant only to set-theory. But it is a prime theoretical claim of Lenat's (and of many other workers in AI) that intelligence depends heavily on expert knowledge, as opposed to very general skills. To the extent that this is so, there cannot be a truly general theory of adaptation.

Perhaps similar considerations concerning creative exploration might illuminate various biological phenomena which, on a neo-Darwinist account of evolution, are very puzzling. These include the facts that the fraction of DNA that does not code for the synthesis of specific proteins increases phylogenetically; that species have evolved remarkably quickly, and that the more complex species have if anything evolved at a greater rate than their predecessors; and that the speed at which a species evolves morphologically seems quite unrelated to the rate at which its individual proteins evolve (so frogs have protein-synthesizing mechanisms of comparable complexity to those of man). Such facts are not explicable in terms of "Random-Generate-and-Test," the mutational strategy favoured by neo-Darwinism. This is because (as was discovered by the early workers in automatic programming), the combinatorics of such a process are horrendous (cf. Arbib, 1969). Switching to a higher-level biological language (cf. "consolidation"), might be effected by random processes of gene duplication and recombination; but this merely reduces the exponent without preventing an exponential explosion.

Instead, some strategy of "Plausible-Generate-and-Test" is needed, whereby mutations of a type likely to be adaptive become increasingly probable. The initial heuristics must evolve by random mutation (since there is no suggestion of teleology here), but these survive by natural selection and can eventually enable a form of biological bootstrapping by modifying each other. This is possible because they are embodied as DNA and their "target" for interpretation is itself DNA. That is, they are heuristics recommending certain "copying errors" and preventing others. The sort of transformational processes they influence are gene substitution, insertion, deletion, translocation, inversion, recombination, segregation, and transposition.

In a recent, speculative, paper (Lenat, 1980), Lenat likens these transformational processes to Production Rules, saying the IF... part of the heuristic might be specified by proximity on the DNA molecule, whereas the THEN... part could direct gene rearrangement, duplication, placement of mutators and intervening sequences, and so on. For instance, one heuristic might be that gene recombinations should involve neighbour-genes rather than genes at opposite ends of the DNA string: in a creature where genes for morphologically related structures happened to lie next to each other, this heuristic would encourage mutations of both genes together, which would tend toward a structurally integrated evolution.

Whether we are concerned with set-theory or genetic evolution, to explain creative development we need to posit specialist as well as general heuristics. Adaptation requires one (individual or species) to learn a large number of special tricks in terms of which to generate things likely to be interesting, and can be aided by special principles with which to evaluate the interest of anything that turns up. (Natural selection is a very general way of assessing interest post hoc). Insofar as this is so, the extent to which one can hope for a general theory of creativity is limited. But any such tricks and principles function against a background of creative constraints, in whose terms adaptive control is basically intelligible.

Finally, what of unpredictability, in virtue of which also the mind is an ill-defined system? Unpredictability is due in part to the fact mentioned previously, that the mind has a very rich generative potential. We should not expect to find psychological laws reliably predicting the generation of this symbolic structure rather than that one. However, unpredictability is grounded not only in idiosyncracy but also in contingency -- in the richness of the world, and the fact that it goes its own way independently of our designs. A structural-transformational theory of adaptive control need not deny a creative role to contingencies, provided that they can be integrated into the mental structure concerned by way of the criteria of "interestingness" already functioning within the mind.

For instance, a drummer suffering from Tourette's syndrome is able to make his involuntary tics the seed of exciting musical improvisations. Presumably, he notices (classifies as interesting) a novel rhythmic or tonal aspect of the noise produced by his hands during the tic, which he then explores in musically intelligible ways. If the whole process were random, the result would only on chance occasions be judged "exciting" (much as it would be a rare monkey that could type Hamlet). A structural theory can even allow

that contingency is sometimes _essential_ to creative intelligence.
For example, because of the cognitive structures already active in
his mind, Fleming was able to take advantage of the accidental
appearance of the penicillium mould -- but he could not have originated it himself. A designer-God might even put a random-generator
into creatures' brains, to produce (hardly to "generate") ideas by
chance that might be useful to them during their insightful explorations.

A theory of creativity therefore has to be, in part, a theory
of adaptive opportunism. Its core, however, must concern exploratory processes that can range over the space defined by background
structural constraints, and that can even transform those constraints
themselves. These processes are not controlled by pre-defined
specific goals, though they may achieve high-level goals such as
improved economy, elegance, and clarity. In short, failure is not
the spur, and opportunism is not enough.

REFERENCES

Arbib, M., 1969, Self-Producing Automata -- Some implications for
    Theoretical Biology, _in_ "Towards a Theoretical Biology, Vol.
    2," C. H. Waddington, ed., Edinburgh University Press,
    Edinburgh.
Boden, M. A., 1972, "Purposive Explanation in Psychology," Harvard
    University Press, Massachusetts.
Boden, M. A., 1977, "Artificial Intelligence and Natural Man," chap.
    xiv., Basic Books, New York.
Boden, M. A., 1981, "Minds and Mechanisms: Philosophical Psychology
    and Computational Models, _in_ "The Case for a Cognitive Biology,"
    chap. 4, Cornell University Press, Ithaca, New York.
Boden, M. A., 1982, Is Equilibration Important?," _Brit. J. Psychol._,
    73: 165-173.
Hanna, F. K., and Ritchie, G. D., 1981, "AM: A Case Study in A. I.
    Methodology," Dept Computer Science Memo, University Kent at
    Canterbury.
Helson, H. 1959, Adaptation-Level Theory, _in_ "Psychology, A Study of
    a Science, Vol I: Sensory, Perceptual, and Physiological
    Formulations, S. Koch," ed., McGraw-Hill, New York.
Inhelder, B., and Karmiloff-Smith, A., 1975, If You Want to Get Ahead,
    Get a Theory, _Cognition_, 3:195-212.
Karmiloff-Smith, A., 1979, Micro- and Macro-Developmental Changes in
    Language Acquisition and Other Representational Systems,"
    Cognitive Science, 3:81-118.
Kuhn, T. S., "The Structure of Scientific Revolutions," University
    Chicago Press, Chicago.
Lenat, D. B., 1977, Automated Theory Formation in Mathematics, _Proc._
    Fifth Int. Joint Conf. Art. Int., Cambridge, Mass., 833-842.

Lenat, D. B., 1980,"The Heuristics of Nature: The Plausible Mutation
    of DNA," Stanford University Computer Science Dept., Report
    HPP-80-27.
Perry, R. B., 1921, The Independent Variability of Purpose and
    Belief, J. Philos., 18:169-180.
Rissland, E., 1978, Understanding Understanding Mathematics,
    Cognitive Science, 2:361-383.
Rosen, C., 1978, "Schoenberg," Fontana, London.
Samuel, A. L., 1970, Some Studies in Machine Learning Using the
    Game of Checkers, II:- Recent Progress, in "Human and
    Artificial Intelligence," F. J. Crosson, ed., Appleton-
    Century-Crofts, New York, pp. 81-116.
Selfridge, O. G., in press, Track and Trail in Adaptation, MIT Press,
    Cambridge, Massachusetts.
Sussman, G. J., 1975, "A Computer Model of Skill Acquisition,"
    American Elsevier, New York.
Taylor, C., 1971, Interpretation and the Sciences of Man, Rev.
    Metaphysics, 25:3-51.
Weir, R., 1962, "Language in the Crib," Mouton, The Hague.
White, R. W., 1959, Motivation Reconsidered: The Concept of Com-
    petence, Psychol. Rev., 66:297-333.
Winston, P. H., 1975, Learning Structural Descriptions from Examples,
    in "The Psychology of Computer Vision," P. H. Winston, ed.,
    MIT Press, Cambridge, Massachusetts.

GENETIC ALGORITHMS AND ADAPTATION

John H. Holland

Department of Computer and Communication Sciences
The University of Michigan
Ann Arbor, Michigan 48109

ABSTRACT

Genetics provides us with a canonical example of a complex search through a space of ill-defined possibilities. The basic problem is one of manipulating representations -- the chromosomes -- so as to search out and generate useful organization -- the functional properties of the organism.

Even simple models of adaptation, based on (simplified) versions of reproduction, crossover and mutation, search the space of chromosomes in a way much more subtle than a "random search with preservation of the best." In fact, the usual notion of evolution in terms of pools of alleles falls far short of describing what happens. Rather, the system acts as if it were continually testing a wide variety of combinations of alleles for use as components in the construction of new chromosomes. (In terms familiar to geneticists, the process is searching out coadapted sets of alleles. The alleles belonging to a given coadapted set may be distributed over the chromosome, and a given allele may belong to many distinct coadapted sets.) The overall effect is one of steadily biasing the generation of chromosomes toward incorporation of combinations (components) that have proved useful in similar contexts. It can be proved that this adaptive process, though dealing with a population (sample) of size M, usefully tests and exploits information about far in excess of M^3 (M cubed) distinct combinations of alleles. For populations of any considerable size this number M^3 is astronomically larger than the total number of alleles in the population. The corresponding speed-up in the search rate, a property called implicit parallelism, increases the adaptive potential tremendously. Moreover the

implicit parallelism makes the process all but immune to some of the
difficulties -- particularly, high-dimensionality, discontinuity and
false peaks -- that attend complex ill-defined problems.

The laws of the models we have studied constitute a set of
axioms that must at least be satisfied by any more sophisticated
model involving more complicated versions of the genetic operators;
as a consequence the basic properties of these models -- the theorems -- must hold in more sophisticated models that come closer to
biological reality. In particular, implicit parallelism will be a
property of these more realistic models.

It is possible to give genetic processes an algorithmic formulation that makes them available as control procedures in a wide
variety of situations. By using an appropriate production (rule-
based) language, it is even possible to construct sophisticated
models of cognition wherein the genetic algorithm, applied to the
productions, provides the system with the means of learning from
experience. Such models are currently being tested. Even the early
models show surprising capacities for "adaptation under sensory guidance." Among the more important properties they exhibit are:
(1) the ability to modify and develop decision and action sequences
when payoff or feedback about performance occurs only after long
sequences of context-dependent action; (2) the ability to generate
a model for the environment based on the system's experience, a model
usable for lookahead and prediction.

INTRODUCTION

In evolutionary genetics the basic problem is one of manipulating representations -- the chromosomes -- so as to discover useful
organizations -- the functional adaptations of the organism. Even
simple models of adaptation, based on simplified versions of the
basic genetic operators (such as reproduction, crossover and mutation), search out possibilities much more subtly than a "random
search with preservation of the best." The concern of the first
part of this paper is to explore these subtleties and show how they
come about. The latter part of the paper will show that, with the
help of an algorithmic formulation, these procedures can be lifted
from genetics and applied to a wide variety of problems involving
control and decision.

The usual way of describing evolution mathematically is in terms
of changing frequencies of alleles within a "pool of alleles" (the
set of variants of a given gene). This mode of description falls
far short of describing what goes on in even simple algorithmic
models of the genetic process. To gain some insight, it is necessary to attend to the shifting combinations of alleles. As we shall
see shortly, the genetic process actually evaluates and exploits

combinations of alleles as well as individual alleles. This is important because the effects of alleles are <u>not</u> usually additive; with chromosomes, as with most complex entities, the whole is much more than the sum of its parts. At first sight keeping track of these combinations is an overwhelming task; a single chromosome with k genes contains 2^k distinct combinations (various pairs, triples, etc.) of its constituent alleles. How can we attend to this vast array? More basically, how can the genetic process possibly access and use information about this vast array?

UNDERSTANDING GENETIC ALGORITHMS

To penetrate this mystery, we must first set up a simple model of the genetic process. For convenience, let us assume that the chromosomes of interest have k genes, where k is fixed, with n possible variants for each gene. (This simple model, by assuming a fixed length for chromosomes, ignores much that is currently of interest in biochemical genetics, such as intrachromosomal duplication, and the translocation of introns and exons. However, our interest here is in the efficiency of adaptation given this very limited repertoire. Even this limited process is remarkably efficient, and subtle, as we will see. I will make some comments about extensions in the last section.) With this limitation, the set of all possible "chromosomes" (genotypes) is the set of all strings of length k that can be formed from n "letters." Call this set $\underline{C}$.

In brief, and very roughly, a genetic algorithm can be looked upon as a sampling procedure that draws samples from the set $\underline{C}$; each sample drawn has a value, the fitness of the corresponding genotype. From this point of view the population of individuals at any time t, call it B(t), is a <u>set</u> of samples drawn from $\underline{C}$. The genetic algorithm observes the fitnesses of the individuals in B(t) and uses this information to generate and test a new set of individuals, B(t+1). As we will soon see in detail, the genetic algorithm uses the familiar "reproduction according to fitness" in combination with crossing over (and other genetic operators) to generate the new individuals. This process progressively biases the sampling procedure toward the use of <u>combinations</u> of alleles associated with above-average fitness. Surprisingly, in a population of size M, the algorithm effectively exploits some multiple of M^3 combinations in exploring $\underline{C}$. (We will soon see how this happens.) For populations of more than a few individuals this number, M^3, is vastly greater than the total number of alleles in the population. The corresponding speed-up in the rate of searching $\underline{C}$, a property called <u>implicit parallelism</u>, makes possible very high rates of adaptation. Moreover, because a genetic algorithm uses a distributed database (the population) to generate new samples, it is all but immune to some of the difficulties -- false peaks, discontinuities, high-dimensionality, etc. -- that commonly attend complex problems.

Our task now is to give some substance, and intuition, to this outline. Using the model just outlined, we can reach an understanding of some of the advantages and limitations of genetic algorithms via three short steps. First, in order to describe the non-uniform sampling procedure generated by a genetic algorithm, a special class of subsets of C is defined. Then, in the second step, an explicit sampling procedure emphasizing the sampling of combinations is used to examine the role of these subsets in the non-uniform sampling procedure. The final step is to show how the genetic algorithm accomplishes implicitly and rapidly what is an intolerable computational burden for the explicit procedure.

To begin, the subsets of interest, called schemata, can be characterized as follows. We first fix values at a selected set of positions in the k-position strings and then collect all strings which share these fixed values. For example, for strings based on a 2-letter alphabet {0,1}, we might require a 0 at position 2 and a 1 at position 5 and then collect all strings in C satisfying this condition. By using a "don't care" symbol, *, for the positions not fixed, we can specify schemata quite compactly. Thus, *0**1**...** spells out the condition just stated; 1**...** specifies the set of all strings that start with a 1; *11...11 specifies a subset of exactly two elements, namely {011...11, 111...11}; etc. The set of schemata is the set of all collections that can be defined in this way.

(Schemata can also be characterized in a way familiar to mathematicians: if we look upon the k-position strings as vectors in a k-dimensional space (each component having one of n values 0,1,..., n-1), then the schemata are the hyperplanes of the k-dimensional space. Schemata name particular subsets of the set C of k-position strings. These subsets are of interest because they correspond to particular combinations of letters and because they are easily and compactly defined by strings on an alphabet {0,1,...,n-1,*} with n+1 letters.)

We are now ready for the second step. To provide a better understanding of the way in which schemata can aid a search, we will consider an algorithm that manipulates schemata explicitly. Though this algorithm is an aid to understanding, it is impractical from the computational point of view because of the enormous amounts of time and storage it would require. The genetic algorithm, to be described in step three, accomplishes the same actions concisely and rapidly via an implicit manipulation. The explicit version involves the following steps:

1) Set t=0 and generate, at random, a set B(t) of M strings.
2) Observe the value v(C), the "fitness", of each string C in B(t). (From a more formal point of view, steps (1) and (2) amount to sampling the random variable v, using a sample

of size M taken from C.)

3) Let $M(s,t))$ be the number of strings in $B(t)$ belonging to the schema s (i.e., the strings are instances of s). If $M(s,t) > 0$ for s, calculate the average value $\hat{v}(s,t)$ of the strings in $B(t)$ belonging to that schema. Calculate, also, the average value $\hat{v}(t)$ of the set of M samples. (There will be somewhere between 2^k and $M*2^k$ schemata with one or more instances in $B(t)$. More formally, $\hat{v}(s,t)$ is the marginal sample average of v over the subset s.)

4) Select a new set $B(t+1)$ of M strings so that the number of instances of each schema s in the new set is equal to

$$M(s,t+1) = [\hat{v}(s,t)/\hat{v}(t)]*M(s,t)$$

for as many schemata as possible. (Informally, this recursion says that schemata observed to be above-average, $\hat{v}(s,t) > \hat{v}(t)$, receive more samples on the next time-step. Similarly, below-average schemata receive fewer samples. At first sight it may seem impossible to meet this requirement in any meaningful way because there are so many schemata, but see below.)

5) Set t to t+1 and return to step (2).

It is difficult to satisfy the requirement of step (4) because the schemata (hyperplanes) intersect each other over and over again; in fact there are so many intersections that each classifier belongs to 2^k distinct schemata. Thus, any sample allocated to one schema is as well a sample of $(2^k)-1$ other schemata. However a little thought and some calculation show that it is possible to distribute M new samples so that all schemata with more than a few elements receive the requisite number of samples. (Note that this means that schemata with more than a few *'s in their defining strings can be sampled according to the dictates of step (4).) To actually carry out the distribution explicitly, allocating samples schema by schema so that step (4) is satisfied, would of course require an enormous amount of computation.

Setting aside the difficulties of implementation, we find that the algorithm uses very plausible inferences in seeking "fit" strings. Most importantly, it samples with increasing intensity schemata that contain strings of above-average strength. The net effect of increasing the proportion of samples allocated to above-average schemata is to move the overall average $\hat{v}(t)$ upward. Because the average $\hat{v}(t)$ increases with time, this sampling rule is a global "force" driving the search into subsets observed to contain valuable strings. Moreover, because the algorithm works from a database of M points distributed over C, it is not easily caught on "false peaks" (local optima). (Standard optimization procedures work well only with single peak functions, relying on a uniform random search for "starting points" when there are multiple peaks.) Overall, this algorithm is much more globally oriented than standard optimization procedures, searching through a great many schemata for regularities and inter-actions that can be exploited. This point has been established, for the algorithm described next, by extensive experimental comparisons between that algorithm and standard procedures (Bethke [1980], De Jong [1980]).

From an intuitive point of view, good schemata (schemata con-taining strings of above-average fitness) can be thought of as use-ful "building blocks" for constructing new strings. For example, if the schemata 1*0**...** and ***001**...** are both good then it seems reasonable to investigate strings constructed with these building blocks, viz. strings belonging to the schema 1*0001**...**. The power of this kind of algorithm lies in its rapid accumulation of large numbers of better-than-average building blocks -- building blocks that exploit regularities and interactions in the sample space C. By carefully choosing TM samples over T iterations, the algorithm accumulates information about somewhere between 2^k and $TM*2^k$ poten-tial building blocks. (See Figures 1 and 2.)

Our object now is to see how we can obtain the effects of this direct algorithm without paying the tremendous computational cost. To enter upon this, the third step of the explanation, we must first describe the genetic algorithm and then explain its implicit manipu-lation of schemata.

First the specification:

1) Set t=0 and generate, at random, a set B(t) of M strings.
2) Observe the value v(C) of each string C in B(t).
3) Compute the average strength $\hat{v}$ of the M strings in the database B(t) and assign a normalized value $v(C)/\hat{v}$ to each string C in B(t).
4) Assign each string in B(t) a probability proportional to its normalized value and then select n, n<<M, pairs of strings from B(t) using this probability distribution.
5) Apply genetic operators to each pair, forming 2n new strings. The most important of the genetic operators is crossover: A position along the string is selected at ran-dom and then, in the pair being operated upon, the segments to the left of this position are exchanged. This simple operation has subtle effects when used in combination with the "emphasis" provided by step (3), as we will see shortly. The other operators such as mutation and inversion have lesser roles in this use of the algorithm, mainly providing "insurance" against overemphasis of a given kind of schema. (See Holland [1975], Chapter 6, secs. 2, 3, and 4, for details.)
6) Select 2n strings from B(t) and replace them with the 2n new strings resulting from step (4). (There are some

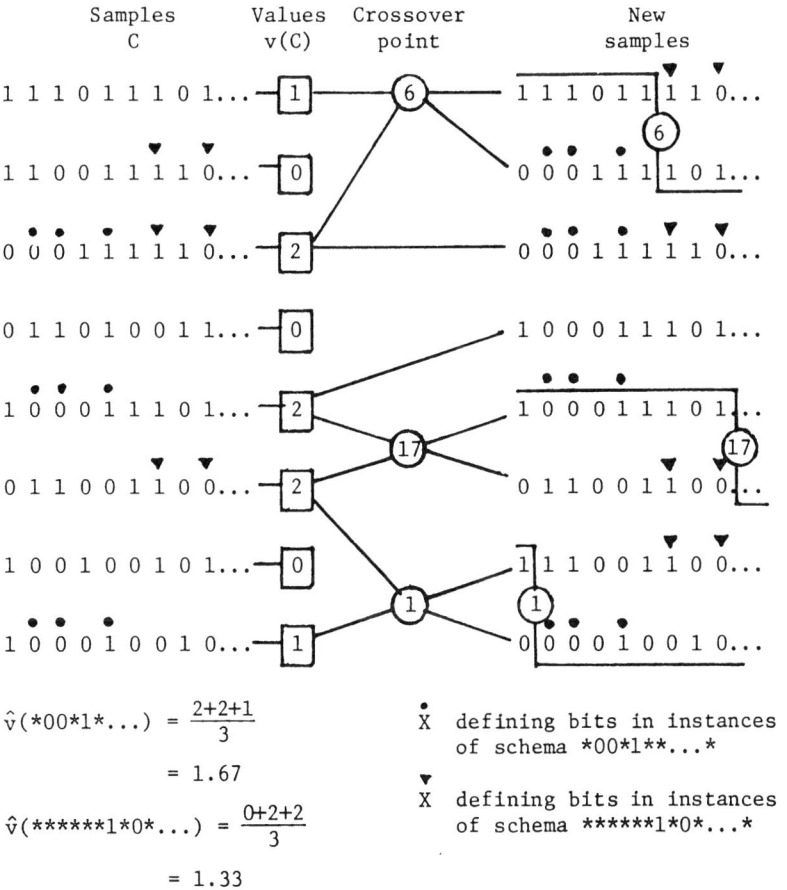

Fig. 1. Example of the genetic algorithm's effect on schemata.

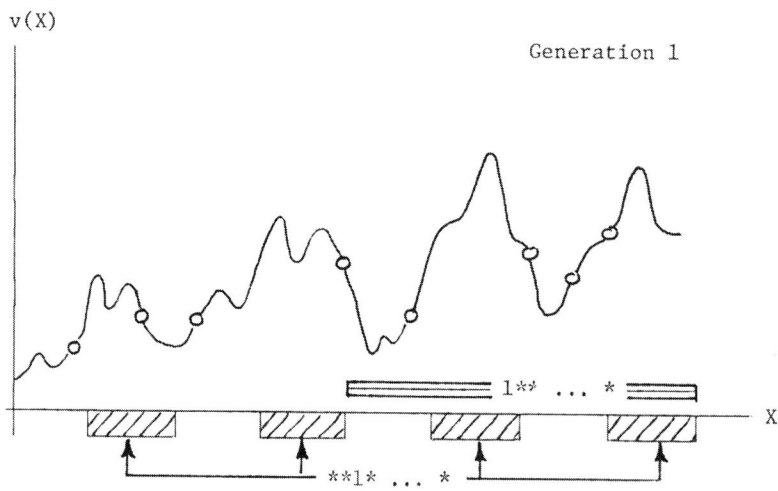

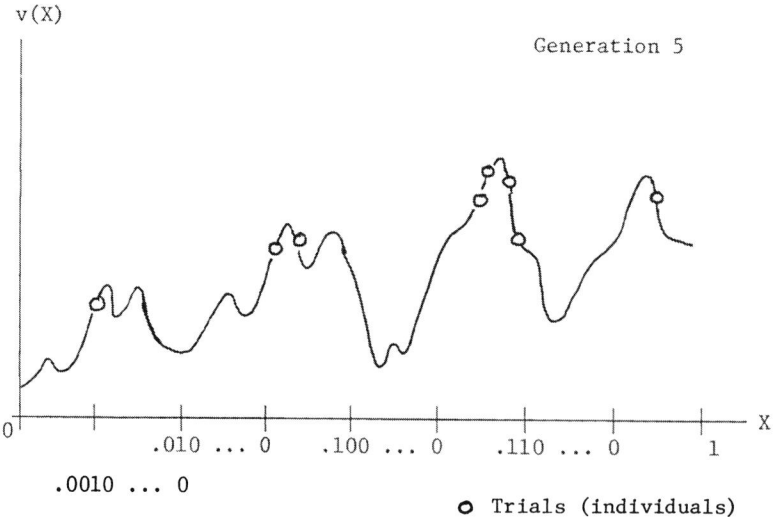

Fig. 2.   Example of function optimization by genetic algorithm.

technical issues involved in the selection of the strings
to be replaced. These issues primarily concern limitations
on the portion of the database allocated to strings of a
given type. In effect each string belongs to a "niche" in
the database and its spread is to be limited to the size
(carrying capacity) of that niche. (See Bethke [1980] and
De Jong [1980] for details.)
7) Set t to t+1 and return to step (2).

Unlike the earlier direct algorithm the genetic algorithm never
deals directly with schemata -- it only manipulates the strings in
B(t). To explore the action of the algorithm relative to schemata
it is helpful to divide the algorithm's action into two phases:
phase 1 consists of steps (2)-(4); phase 2 consists of steps (5)-(6).

Consider first what would happen if phase 1 were iterated without the execution of phase 2 (but with the replacement of strings in
B(t)). In particular, let phase 1 be iterated M/2n times (assuming
for convenience that M is a multiple of 2n). It is not difficult to
show that the expected number of instances of a schema s at the end
of this iteration is just $\hat{v}(s)$ times the number of instances at the
outset (see Holland [1976b]). This is true of every schema with
instances in B, and this is just what we required of the direct algorithm in step (4).

What, then, is accomplished by phase 2? The problem is that
phase 1 introduces no new strings into B, it merely introduces additional copies of strings already there. Phase 1 provides emphasis,
but no new trials. The genetic operators, applied in phase 2, obviously modify the strings in B. It is a fundamental property of
genetic algorithms (Theorem 6.2.3, Holland [1975]) that the emphasis
provided by phase 1 is little disturbed by phase 2. That is, after
phase 2, schemata with instances in B will largely have the number
of instances provided by phase 1 but they will be new instances.
Thus, the genetic algorithm as a whole generates new samples of
schemata already present, increasing or decreasing the sampling rate
according to the multiplier $\hat{v}(s,t)/\hat{v}(t)$, as desired. From the point
of view of sampling theory, these new samples increase confidence in
the estimates $\hat{v}(s)$ for each above-average schema s in B. Some calculation (Holland [1975], Chapter 4) shows that considerably more than
M^3 schemata are so-treated every M/2n time-steps. Moreover, without
disrupting this procedure, samples are generated for schemata not
previously tried. All of this comes about through simple, and fast,
manipulations of 2n strings per step. This implicit manipulation of
a great many schemata via operations on relatively few strings is
called implicit parallelism.

This property of implicit parallelism fits well, I think, with
some of Margaret Boden's [this volume] key points about the peripheral role of failure in arriving at complex adaptations. The large

number of schemata being tested implicitly offers a wide range of
possibilities for (partial) success and improvement. Even "activity
for its own sake" becomes justified when each specific instance sampled provides additional information (confirmation) for some large
proportion of 2^k schemata. The conflict between exploitation and
exploration is much easier to bear when individual trials (and simple variations) provide such a large return. (The discussion in the
next section adds emphasis to this point.) It is also clear that
the algorithms just discussed are much more driven by success than
failure -- it is the above-average ("successful") schemata that serve
as building blocks for future structure. (Again, the discussion in
the next section adds emphasis to this point.)

    The foregoing argument does suggest caveats relative to Lenat's
[1980] speculations concerning genetics. Lenat suggests that neo-
Darwinism has serious difficulty in accounting for the rapid evolution of species (the more complex the species, the more rapid the
evolution), the independence of morphological evolution from protein
evolution, and the large amount of "silent" DNA. (He does not lay
much emphasis on polymorphism and heterozygosity, but these are also
frequently cited.) If one concentrates on mutation as the main
source of variation (in the biological 'generate-and-test' procedure),
then these difficulties are indeed serious. (Several participants
of the Wistar Symposium -- Moorhead and Kaplan [1967] -- make this
argument both forcefully and rigorously.) However the effects of
crossing-over ("crossover") in the presence of epistasis have been
little analyzed in classical mathematical genetics (despite an
increasing agreement, based in part on biochemical studies, that
epistasis is pervasive). Even a brief analysis (see Holland [1976a])
shows that time estimates based on mutation alone are badly awry when
crossover is taken into account. Once the analysis is carried out in
terms of "building blocks" (schemata), Simon's [1981] informal "watch-
maker" arguments can be verified in detail and estimates for the time
of emergence of complex, self-reproducing systems come in line with
the geologic time-spans available. (The arguments developed by Eigen,
nicely summarized in Eigen and Winkler [1981], mesh well with this
analysis in terms of schemata.) Fragmented genes, introns and exons
(see, for example, Lewin [1981]) add greatly to crossover's already
great power for accomplishing significant variations based on extant
building blocks. It is possible that Lenat's mechanisms accomplish
the goals he sets for them, and they may even have some biological
counterparts. However, in my opinion, it is best to find out first
what can be accomplished with well-established mechanisms -- one
should not multiply hypotheses without good reason.

ADAPTIVE CONTROL

    The power and flexibility of genetic algorithms suggests their
use for other searches through vast, combinatorially-complex spaces.

The broad range of problems involving decision and control in complex environments is a particularly attractive target -- solution procedures for this domain have consequences ranging all the way from cognitive psychology to business. Most problems of this kind are so complex that it is impossible, at any given time, to specify decision procedures that cover all contingencies. Rather the system must adapt as experience accumulates. Genetic algorithms offer an adaptive procedure that is (1) fast (because of the implicit parallelism), (2) relatively immune to misdirection (because of the distributed database), and (3) capable of sophisticated generalization (because of the role of schemata). However, there are several obstacles to bringing genetic algorithms to bear on this target. Somehow the algorithm must be provided with data structures and procedural structures that are amenable to its operations (akin to the knowledge structures familiar from extensive studies in artificial intelligence; see, for example, Buchanan and Mitchell [1978], Buchanan [this volume] or Fahlman [1979]). This section describes one way of overcoming these obstacles.

To use the particular genetic algorithms described above for searching the space of decision procedures, we must find suitable string representations for the decision procedures. One approach is to define the procedures via a set of decision rules (productions) where the form of the rules has been standardized to the point that they can consistently be represented by strings of a fixed length.

We can produce a standardized string representation by orienting the performance system (the set of decision rules) to the processing of messages of a standard length. The messages being processed by the performance system at any given time can be collected together on a message list, a kind of blackboard that specifies the state of the performance system at that time. As is usual, each rule consists of two parts: (1) a set of conditions and (2) an action to be taken when the rule's conditions are satisfied. The result is a kind of production system (see Davis and King [1974] for an excellent review of standard production systems), but one with significant differences. We can think of the messages on the message list as being broadcast, in "to whom it may concern" fashion, to all rules. Each condition specifies the kind or class of message that it will accept. (Technically, the condition specifies a subset of the set of all possible messages; if a message on the message list belongs to this subset, then the condition is said to be satisfied.) When a rule's conditions are satisfied, it takes action by emitting a message. The message emitted will appear on the message list on the next timestep. In the same vein, information from the environment is translated, by an interface, to a set of messages added to the message list, and messages control the system's outputs (effectors). (See Figures 3 and 4.)

Because the only effect of the simultaneous execution of rules

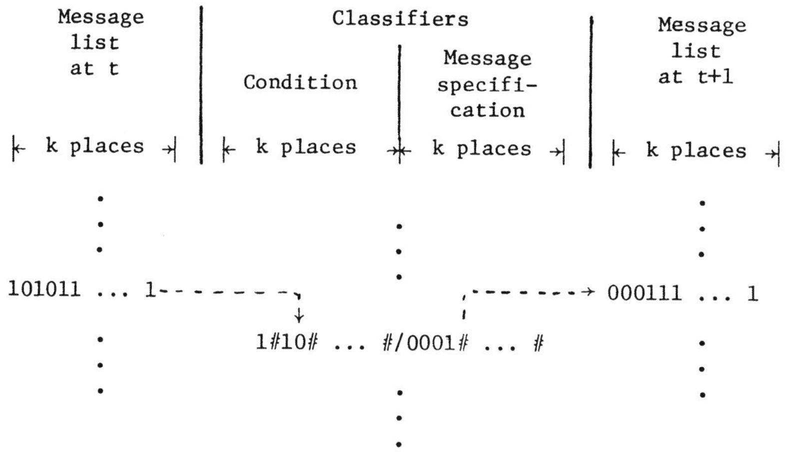

Message list at t	Classifiers		Message list at t+1
	Condition	Message specifi- cation	
⊢ k places ⊣	⊢ k places ⊣	⊢ k places ⊣	⊢ k places ⊣

```
                  .                          .
                  .                          .
                  .             .            .
                  .             .
101011 ... 1------------,                ,--------→ 000111 ... 1
                        ↓                '
                  .    1#10# ... #/0001# ... #
                  .             .
                  .             .
                                .
                                .
```

\# in condition ⇒ "don't care"

\# in message specification ⇒ corresponding bit in output
message has same value as bit at that position in message
satisfying condition ⇒ "send on"

M(C) = measure of generality of condition
     = k - (no. of #'s)

[A classifier may have more than one condition.]

Fig. 3. Action of a typical classifier.

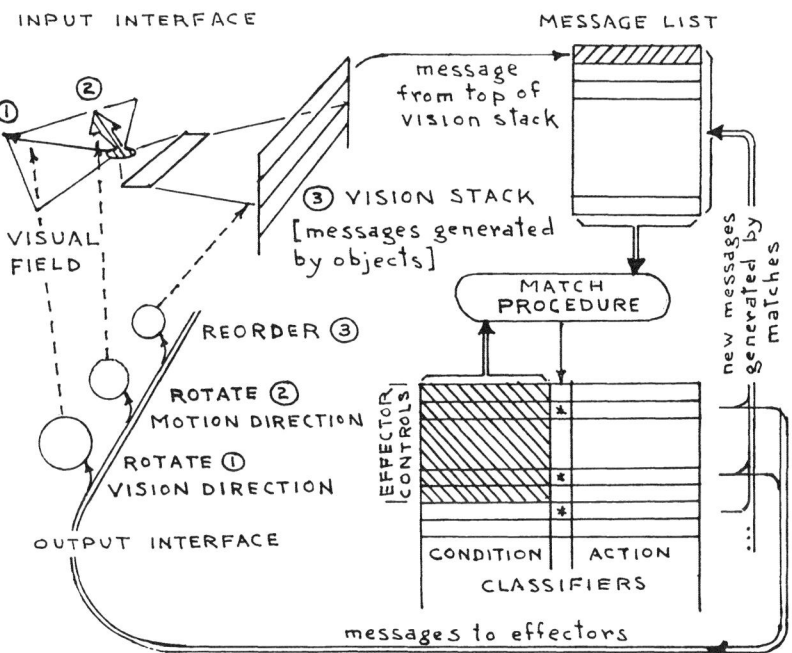

Fig. 4. Schematic for classifier-based cognitive system

is the addition of messages to the message list, there is no possibility for internal conflicts. The resulting conflict-free concurrency frees such production systems from the constraining (and often
unnatural) conflict-resolution techniques usually required (see
McDermott and Forgy [1978]). Equally important, control sequences
do not depend upon a high-level interpreter and the order of execution is independent of the ordering of the rules -- the effect of a
message is determined syntactically (the meaning of tags and labels
is implicit). These two differences, combined with the simple syntax
and fixed length of conditions, actions and messages, yield a production system well-suited to a variety of learning procedures.

There is one additional point that should be emphasized when one
considers the expression of procedures and computations in such a performance system. Whenever it is desirable, messages can be directed
to a specific destination (rule) in the system. This can be accomplished simply by using a part of the message as a "tag" (cf. address)
that is only accepted by a condition of the intended recipient rule.
(Davis' [1976] remarks about tagging, and the resulting enforced
sequence, have little force here because of the concurrency and
position-independence of execution.) It is also important to note
that the message sent by a rule may be dependent upon the messages
it accepts -- in effect the rule becomes a message processor, with
its output conditioned on the information it receives. Performance
systems of this kind can be defined formally (see Holland [1980]) --
we call them classifier systems -- and it can be proved that they
are computationally complete. That is, any algorithm specifiable in
a general-purpose computer language (such as C or LISP) can be exe-
cuted by a properly chosen set of rules in a classifier system.

There is only room here to suggest the form that learning or
adaptation takes when classifier systems are used as the substrate.
We use two kinds of algorithm: a bucket brigade algorithm and a
genetic algorithm.

The bucket brigade algorithm assigns weights to the rules; the
weight assigned to a given rule is tied, by the algorithm, to that
rule's cumulative value as a part of the system's mechanism for
generating action sequences. In effect, the weight measures the
rule's helpfulness in the past in those contexts in which the rule
has been activated.

At each time-step all rules with satisfied conditions undergo
a competition for activation; the larger the weight assigned to a
rule the more likely it is to be one of the winners of that competition. Thus the winning (activated) rules will be those that score
highest on a combination of relevance (conditions satisfied by messages currently on the message list) and past success (weight).
Formally, the bidding procedure is defined as follows. Each rule,
C, that has its conditions satisfied (by messages on the message

list), makes a <u>bid</u>

$$U(C,t) = c*M(C)*S(C,t),$$

where $S(C,t)$ is the strength of C at time t, $M(C)$ measures the specificity of the conditions (it ranges between 0, for a condition that accepts any message, to an upper limit, k, for a condition that accepts only a single, specific message), and c is a constant considerably less than 1 (e.g., c = 1/8 or 1/16). (Informally, again: $M(C)$ measures relevance -- a condition that accepts only a small subset of the set of possible messages enters the competition only in very restricted contexts. $S(C,t)$ will only be large if past successes have been large -- see below.) The <u>winning</u> (high) bidders have their strengths reduced by the amount of their bid,

$$S(C,t+1) = S(C,t) - U(C,t).$$

The classifiers $\{C'\}$ that sent the messages matched by a winner have their strengths <u>increased</u> by the amount of the bid (it is shared among them in the simplest version),

$$S(C',t+1) = S(C',t) + a*U(C,t),$$

where a = 1/(no. of senders in $\{C'\}$). This amounts to a kind of economy made up of "middle-men", where a given middle-man survives only if he makes a net average profit on his transactions (bids received > or = bids paid out, averaged over the times when he is a winning bidder). The net effect of the algorithm is to tie a rule's strength to the frequency with which it participates in action <u>sequences</u> leading to payoff (reward, reinforcement, utility).

The <u>genetic algorithm</u> is used to generate new rules. The weights assigned by the bucket brigade algorithm are used as "fitnesses" and hence supply the values v for the strings that represent the rules. In the manner described earlier, the genetic algorithm favors the construction of new rules from "building blocks" (schemata) that appear as components in the definition of rules that have already proved useful to the system. It is important to recognize that these building blocks may involve tags and other portions of messages that determine rule interaction and control sequencing. Thus, the genetic algorithm can encourage useful subroutines and hierarchical, concurrent organization. (For example much of Fahlman's [1979] NETL can be transcribed into a classifier system, on a "classifier per node" basis, making it suitable as grist for the learning mill.) Further theoretical work makes it clear that newly generated rules can be introduced without seriously disturbing capabilities already well-established. Well-established (successful) rules will always score high in the competition when they are relevant; hence they will win whenever they are relevant. (This quality, <u>gracefulness</u>, is vital for any system which is to generate and test a variety of rules or hypotheses which, as alternative possibilities, may "contradict" each other.) New rules get their chance when no successful rule is relevant to the current situation. There is also a strong indication from the theoretical work (though this must be demonstrated in the simulations) that the system will <u>automatically</u> organize itself into a default hierarchy. As a result, the actions taken at any time should depend upon the specificity of the information available to the system (as measured by the specificity of the conditions defined for the current set of productions).

Several years ago, we completed a preliminary series of simulations based on a simplified version of this organization (reported in Holland and Reitman [1978]). The environments in this simulation were mazes involving up to a dozen independent choices. Each choice point was characterized by a unique bit string (the input message). The system employed 100 single-condition productions. The object was to test the system's ability to uncover and use regularities in the information received as the system moved about in the maze. (E.g., in the input bit string, a 1 in position 2 coupled with a 0 in position 4 might consistently signal that a "left turn" should be made.) The results made it clear that we could obtain (1) learning an order of magnitude faster than with weight-changing techniques alone, and (2) transfer of learning from maze to maze.

We are currently (1982) finishing a "test-bed" simulation that permits (1) up to 1000 2-condition productions, any 32 of which can be active on a given time-step, (2) an environment consisting of up to 256 objects (each with an arbitrary set of properties) moving over a 65,000 by 65,000 grid divided into 256 regions (each with an arbitrary set of "textural" properties), and (3) a time-step of about 0.1 second (allowing the system to operate in "real time"). With this test-bed we will explore the abilities of a variety of cognitive systems organized along the lines outlined. We also expect to learn a good deal about systems, particularly production systems, having many control procedures active simultaneously.

ACKNOWLEDGEMENTS

The research reported here was supported in part by the National Science Foundation through Grants MCS 78-26016 and IST 80-18043.

REFERENCES

Bethke, A. D. [1980]. "Genetic Algorithms as Function Optimizers."
     University of Michigan Ph.D. Dissertation.
Boden, M. A. [this volume]. Failure is not the spur.
Buchanan, B. G. and Mitchell, T. M. [1978]. Model-directed learning
     of production rules, <u>in</u>: "Pattern-Directed Inference Systems,"

D. A. Waterman and F. Hayes-Roth, eds., Academic Press, New York.

Buchanan, B. G. [this volume].

Davis, R. and King, J. [1976]. An overview of production systems, in: "Machine Intelligence 8," E. W. Elcock and D. Michie, eds., Wiley, New York.

De Jong, K. A. [1980]. Adaptive system design -- a genetic approach, IEEE Trans. Systems, Man, and Cybernetics, 10:9.

Eigen, M. and Winkler, R. [1981]. "Laws of the Game," Knopf, New York.

Fahlman, S. E. [1979]. "NETL: A System for Representing and Using Real-World Knowledge," MIT Press, Cambridge.

Holland, J. H. [1975]. "Adaptation in Natural and Artificial Systems," University of Michigan Press, Ann Arbor.

_____ [1976a]. Studies of the spontaneous emergence of self-replicating systems using cellular automata and formal grammars, in: "Automata, Languages and Development," A. Lindenmayer and G. Rozenberg, eds., North Holland, Amsterdam.

_____ [1976b]. Adaptation, in: "Progress in Theoretical Biology, 4," R. Rosen and F. M. Snell, eds., Academic Press, New York.

_____ [1980]. Adaptive algorithms for discovering and using general patterns in growing knowledge bases, Int. J. Policy Analysis and Information Systems, 4:3.

Holland, J. H. and Reitman, J. S. [1978]. Cognitive systems based on adaptive algorithms, in: "Pattern-Directed Inference Systems," D. A. Waterman and F. Hayes-Roth, eds., Academic Press, New York.

Lenat, D. B. [1980]. The Heuristics of Nature: The Plausible Mutation of DNA. Stanford University Computer Science Department Report HPP-80-27.

Lewin, R. [1981]. Biggest challenge since the double helix, Science 212, April 3.

McDermott, J. and Forgy, C. [1978]. Production system conflict resolution strategies, in: "Pattern-Directed Inference Systems," D. A. Waterman and F. Hayes-Roth, eds., Academic Press, New York.

Moorhead, P. S. and Kaplan, M. M. [1967]. "Mathematical Challenges in the Neo-Darwinian Interpretation of Evolution," Wistar Institute Press, Philadelphia.

Simon, H. A. [1981]. "The Sciences of the Artificial," MIT Press, Cambridge.

CONTRIBUTORS

Michael A. Arbib
Computer and Information Science
University of Massachusetts
Amherst, MA 01003, USA

Sheldon Baron
Bolt Beranek and Newman, Inc.
10 Moulton Street
Cambridge, MA 02138, USA

Margaret A. Boden
School of Social Sciences
The University of Sussex
Falmer, BN1 9GN Brighton, ENGLAND

Charles J. Brainerd
University of Western Ontario
London, Ontario N6A 5C2 CANADA

Bruce G. Buchanan
Department of Computer Science
Stanford University
Stanford, CA 94305, USA

John Churcher
Department of Psychology
University of Manchester
Manchester M13 9PL, ENGLAND

Thomas Dietterich
Department of Computer Science
Stanford University
Stanford, CA 94305, USA

Lila Gleitman
Department of Psychology
University of Pennsylvania
Philadelphia, PA 19104, USA

John H. Holland
Department of Computer and
  Communication Science
University of Michigan
Ann Arbor, MI 48109, USA

Pierre Lavorel
19 Rue CDT Faurax
69006 Lyon, FRANCE

Marvin L. Minsky
A.I. Laboratory
M.I.T.
545 Technology Square
Cambridge, MA 02138, USA

Neville Moray
Department of Industrial
    Engineering
University of Toronto
Toronto, M5S 1A4, CANADA

Edwina L. Rissland
Department of Computer and
    Information Science
University of Massachusetts
Amherst, MA 01003, USA

Penelope Rowlatt
Her Majesty's Treasury
Parliament St.
London SW1 ENGLAND

Oliver G. Selfridge
45 Percy Road
Lexington, MA 02173, USA

Henry Shaffer
Department of Psychology
University of Exeter
Exeter EX4 4QG, ENGLAND

H.T.A. Whiting
Vakgroep Psychologie
Vrije Universiteit
1081 HV Amsterdam, THE NETHERLANDS

W.M. Wonham
Department of Electrical Engineering
University of Toronto
Toronto M5S 1A4, CANADA

F. Eugene Yates
The Crump Institute for
 Medical Engineering
UCLA
Los Angeles, CA 90024, USA

Richard M. Young
MRC Applied Psychology Unit
15 Chaucer Road
Cambridge CB2 2EF, ENGLAND

AUTHOR INDEX

SUBJECT INDEX

Supervisor, 78
Symbolic servo-mechanism, 116
Synergy, 220
System, 97
  open system, 97
  dissipative, 97
  complex, 97

TEIRESIAS, 133, 136
Thalamus, 210
"The Advice Taker", 117
Therapy, 264
Thermodynamic engine, 103, 104
Thermodynamic variables, 2
Time until adjacency, 212
Timing, 254, 255, 265-267
Toad, 208
Tok Pisin, 237
Tracking, 21, 75
Trailing, 21, 24, 242
Transmission zero, 85
Transport coefficients, 108
Tuning, 220
Tuning of motor schemas, 220
Twiddling, 22
Typing errors, 179
Typing skill, 178

Ultra-stable systems, 14, 115
Uncertainty, 28
Uncertainty principle, 14
Ungrammatical utterances, 228
Unobservable, 82
"Us" and "them", 5

"Virtual hand", 296
Visual tracking, 67

WM, see World model
World model (module in
        learning systems),
        128
Worms, 210

Zipfian distribution, 105